PROOF

Herman Melville's copy of his contract with Harper and Brothers for *The Whale*, published in the United States as *Moby-Dick*. From the Melville Collection, Houghton Library, Harvard University.

"The Whale"

Agreement.

Between

Harper and Brothers

and

Herman Melville

Sept 12th 1851.

To be signed by
Harper & Brothers &
returned to
H. Melville
14 days of—

Copy right = Title page filed
Oct 15th 1851. Deposited work
Nov 19th 1851.

Agreement made between Harper and
Brothers of the city of New York publishers, of
the one part and Herman Melville of Pittsfield
Massachusetts of the other part witnesseth
That the said Harper and Brothers have agreed
to publish and
sell and keep for sale a certain work entitled
"The Whale" whereof the said Herman Melville
is the author upon the following terms —
First the copyright of the said work is to
be the sole property of the said Herman Melville
(subject to this contract) and shall be entered
and stand in his name as author and proprietor.
Second, the said Harper and Brothers are to be
the sole publishers of the said work in the limited
States of America during the continuance of
this agreement. Third. In consideration
of the sole right to publish said work hereby
granted to them the said Harper and Brothers
hereby agree to publish said work from the
stereotype plates now in the possession of
R. Craighead at their own cost and expense
(paying said Craighead for the cost of said
plates) and to pay to said Herman Melville
one half of the net profits accruing from the
publication and sale of said work; Provided
that at any time after the cost of the stereotype
plates shall have been liquidated the said
payment shall if the said Herman Melville
demand it be commuted for a sum
certain per copy for all copies sold. Fourth.
Harper and Brothers agree to make semi annual
settlements with said Herman Melville on
the first days of February and August in
each year, so long as this agreement remains
in force and the balance due said Herman

Melville shall be paid by the notes of the said Harper and Brothers at three month from these dates, or in cash interest off

Fifth. This agreement shall continue for seven years from the day of publication by said Harper & Brothers: at the expiration of which time the said Herman Melville shall have the right to the possession and complete ownership of the stereotype plates of the said work on paying to the said Harper and Brothers one half of their original cost deducting a fair valuation for the wear and tear they may have sustained in their use or injury from other causes: Upon which payment which may be made at anytime after the expiration of the said seven years the said stereotype plates shall belong to the said Herman Melville as his sole property.

Sixth. The said Harper and Brothers are to have the right to dispose of all copies of said work remaining on hand at the expiration of this agreement, they accounting upon the sale of said copies as herein provided.

Seventh. It is distinctly understood that this agreement refers solely to the publication of said work in the United States of America — In witness whereof the parties hereto have hereunto subscribed their names this twelfth day of September one thousand eight hundred and fifty one —

Harper & Broths

Herman Melville
per Allan Melville his atty

Harper & Broth.

Herman Melville
per Allan Melville to Richd &c

Mem:— Proof sheets of "The Whale" were forwarded to Richard
Bentley London under cover to Mr Davis Secretary
of Legation London in the government despatches
by the Asia which sailed Sept 10th

PROOF

THE YEARBOOK OF

AMERICAN

BIBLIOGRAPHICAL

AND TEXTUAL

STUDIES

Edited by Joseph Katz

Volume I, 1971

UNIVERSITY OF SOUTH CAROLINA PRESS · *Columbia · S·C·*

EDITORIAL ASSISTANTS
Artem Lozynsky
Sandra I. Anderson

Contributions offered for publication must be accompanied by a self-addressed return envelope and unaffixed return postage. Contributors should follow *Proof* style for quotations, dates, and footnotes. Publication decisions are made by the Advisory Panel to *Proof* within a short time, usually a month. Opinions expressed in *Proof* are those of its contributing authors and do not necessarily represent the beliefs of its editorial staff or Advisory Panel. *Proof* is a member of the MLA Abstract System. *Proof* is in the Master List of the MLA International Bibliography.

Address all orders to the Annual Subscription Department, University of South Carolina Press, Columbia, SC 29208.

Address all other correspondence to Joseph Katz, Editor, *Proof*, Department of English, University of South Carolina, Columbia, SC 29208.

**FIRST IMPRESSION
1971**

International Standard Book Number: 0–87249–700–3
Library of Congress Catalog Card Number: LC 70–158622

Suggested Library of Congress classification furnished by McKissick Memorial Library of the University of South Carolina: PS3. P

CONTENTS

Collator, allow the accumulation of massive data. There is a danger that pointless information may overwhelm significant facts—but only if bibliographers forget that raw data are just working notes. A descriptive bibliography is a piece of historical scholarship, not a compendium of everything available. The capability of recovering bits of information is valuable only if the material is digested, organized, and presented as part of a well-proportioned and coherent demonstration.

ceive the most attention. But he also was a master of the short story. This bibliography lists all textually significant forms of Faulkner's short fiction — published and unpublished — including the locations of all known manuscripts of them. It is annotated to give information on such matters as dating and the relationships between different versions of the same work.

LIST OF ILLUSTRATIONS

PROOF

CONTRACT:

Moby-Dick, by Herman Melville

HARRISON HAYFORD

ON 12 SEPTEMBER 1851 HARPER AND BROTHERS AGREED TO PUBLISH 'a certain work entitled *"The Whale"'* — the book they published as *Moby-Dick* on 14 November of that year. There are three copies of that contract extant, as there are of those for Melville's *Omoo* (1847), *Mardi* (1849), *Redburn* (1850), *White-Jacket* (1850), *Pierre* (1852), and *Typee,* which they took over in 1849. Two were publisher's copies, and one was the author's copy. Melville's copies of his contracts are among his other business papers in the Melville Collection of the Houghton Library, the publisher's originals are in the files of Harper and Row, and its second copies are in the Harper Contract Book I now in the Morgan Library.[1]

From Raymond W. Weaver on, Melville's biographers have mined both his annotated copies of the Harper contracts and additional contracts in the light of statements rendered him by publishers to

---

[1] I have intentionally excluded the contract for the *Typee* reissue from this exploratory study.

1

get information about the publication and sales of his books.[2] The focus, however, has usually been on the accounts, with the contracts subjected to less thorough scrutiny.[3] For this reason, interesting facts and promising lines of inquiry about Melville and publishing in his time have so far gone unnoticed. They emerge when Melville's six surviving contracts with Harper and Brothers are compared; their further pursuit, now obviously required, would involve comparing them additionally with other contracts of the period.

The basic problem is determining the extent to which Melville's Harper contracts may have been standard agreements, since they are not on printed forms but are all engrossed in a scrivener's hand. These six contracts generally are similar, with repetition in most of the topics, a number of their provisions, and a certain amount of the phraseology. But though some phrases, and even whole items, are repeated verbatim from one contract to another, the topics are not always taken up in the same order, stated in the same words, or comprised of the same items. That is, even when the substance of the contractual provisions remains substantially alike, there is variation in wording and order of presentation. Why this is so is not now clear. It is possible that there was no standard Harper contract at the time; it is more likely that there were standard provisions but that the scrivener worked either from memory or from a contract selected at random from the files; it is most likely, however, that Melville's contracts were a blend of standard provisions, variously drawn, and specific provisions included as the occasion required.

The following provisions are substantially the same in all of his Harper contracts: (1) the copyright shall belong to Melville; (2) the Harpers shall be sole publisher in the United States; (3) the Harpers shall render semiannual accounts, on the first of February and August; (4) the contract shall run seven years; (5) after the expiration of the contract, Melville may buy the plates at one-half cost, less depreciation, with the Harpers retaining the right to sell any remaining copies of the book; and (6) the agreement refers solely to publication in the United States.

There are, however, differences among the contracts. Some of them are relatively minor as they affect *Moby-Dick*.

[2] *Herman Melville: Mariner and Mystic* (New York: George H. Doran, 1921).
[3] See especially G. Thomas Tanselle, 'The Sales of Melville's Books', *Harvard Library Bulletin*, XVIII (April 1969), 195–215.

(1) For all the books except *Pierre*, Melville was to receive one-half net profits, after the cost of stereotyping was paid; for *Pierre* he was to get twenty cents a copy, with Harper and Brothers paying for the plates (1190 copies were equated to the plate cost, based on a book of 360 pages, with the equation to vary in proportion to the actual length of the book). For *Omoo* and *Mardi*, no per-copy price was stipulated; for *Redburn* and *White-Jacket*, the price was to be agreed upon before publication; for *The Whale*, again, no per-copy price was stipulated.

(2) For *Omoo* no medium of payment to Melville was stipulated; from *Mardi* on, payment was to be made in notes at three months; for *The Whale*, the phrase 'or cash less interest' is added to modify the note payment.

(3) For *Omoo*, no advance was stipulated; for *Mardi*, $500 on 1 December; for *Redburn*, $300; for *White-Jacket*, $500; for *The Whale* and *Pierre*, no advance.

(4) For *Omoo* and *Mardi*, contracts were signed by Melville himself; for the others—including *The Whale*—his lawyer-brother Allan Melville signed.

(5) For *Omoo* and *Mardi*, 125 review copies were to be charged to joint account; for *Redburn* and *White-Jacket*, the contracts specify that 25 of these were to be turned over to Melville; for *The Whale* and *Pierre*, there is no provision at all for review copies.

If these changing provisions do not reflect some general shift in Harper and Brothers policy, they seem to suggest a hardening of attitude by the publisher toward Melville at the time of *Moby-Dick*—accompanied by a loosening of Melville's attitude at the same time. There is, for example, some speculative possibility in the disappearance of the clause providing Melville with review copies of his own. It may be simply that because Melville was no longer in New York when *Moby-Dick* was to be published he thought there was little value in distributing those copies; but it may also be that by this time he had lost interest in promoting his own books. Either explanation may lead to sharper focus on Melville's situation as a professional writer.

Not at all minor, and certainly of great immediate interest, is a category of provisions which reveal a major fact about the publication of *Moby-Dick*. In the four earlier contracts Harper and Brothers agreed to publish 'a manuscript'; here they agree to publish 'a work'. When the publisher took over *Typee*, which already had been published by Wiley and Putnam, they also specified publication of a 'work' in their

PLATE 1

𝔐𝔢𝔪𝔬𝔯𝔞𝔫𝔡𝔲𝔪 of an AGREEMENT, made this *thirteenth*

day of *August* 18 *57*, between *Herman Melville*
Pittsfield, Berkshire County, Massachusetts
Esq. of New York in the United States of America

on the one Part, and RICHARD BENTLEY, of New Burlington Street, Publisher, on the other Part.

It is agreed that the said RICHARD BENTLEY shall Publish at his own Expense and Risk, *an original work written by the said Herman Melville, descriptive of an American Whaling Voyage with its accompanying Adventures, more particularly described in a letter of the said Herman Melville to the said Richard Bentley*

and, after deducting from the produce of the Sale thereof, the Charges for Printing, Paper, Advertisements, Embellishments, if any, and other Incidental Expenses, including the Allowance of Ten per Cent. on the gross amount of the Sale, for Commission and risk of Bad Debts, the Profits remaining of every Edition that shall be Printed of the Work, are to be divided into two equal Parts, one Moiety to be paid to the said *Herman Melville*

and the other Moiety to belong to the said RICHARD BENTLEY.

The Books Sold to be accounted for at the Trade Sale Price, reckoning 25 Copies as 24, unless it be thought advisable to dispose of any Copies, or of the Remainder, at a lower Price, which is left to the Judgment and Discretion of the said RICHARD BENTLEY.

In Witness whereof, the said Parties have hereunto set their hands this day.

It is moreover agreed by & between the aforesaid parties, that the said Richard Bentley shall pay to the said Herman Melville the sum of One Hundred and Fifty Pounds, in his two promissory notes, for £75 each at the respective dates of three and six months from the day of his receiving the whole of the Copy of the aforesaid work in a fit state for the press, which sum it is understood is to be debited to the account of the said Herman Melville as an advance on account of his share of profit on the Sale of the aforesaid work according to the terms hereinbefore stated. It is further agreed that in the event of his share of profit not reaching the aforesaid amount of One Hundred & Fifty Pounds, he is not to be held liable to refund the said amount nor any part thereof to the said Richard Bentley. It is understood moreover that the above named work is to be published in England previous to its appearance in the United States at Greater London

Witness to signature of Herman Melville
Samuel H. Savage   *Herman Melville*
J.E. Brevoort   *Richard Bentley*

PLATE 2

contract with Melville.[4] The significance of that slight change in wording appears in the item corresponding to the one in all other contracts in which the Harpers agreed 'to stereotype, publish, and sell' the book. In the case of *Moby-Dick* they agree 'to publish said work from the stereotype plates in the possession of R. Craighead . . . paying said Craighead for the cost of said plates'. The 'work' already had been composed and plated when Melville signed *The Whale* with Harper and Brothers.

In a brief conjectural note to their Norton Critical Edition of *Moby-Dick* (1966), Hayford and Parker first pointed out that the novel therefore was not from the beginning a Harper and Brothers venture.[5] Instead of waiting to contract with his regular publishers when his manuscript was completed, or virtually completed, Melville evidently arranged for Craighead to set and plate it before he had finished writing, during the summer of 1851. In June he had written Hawthorne that he soon was going to New York 'to bury myself in a third-story room, and work & slave on my "Whale" while it is driving thro' the press.' Later that month, on 29 June, Hawthorne heard from him from Pittsfield that the book 'was only half thro' the press', and that 'wearied with the long delays of the printers', and disgusted with the heat of the city, he had come back to the country to finish it. On 20 July Melville wrote Bentley, his English publisher, that he was 'now passing thro' the press, the closing sheets of my new work', and would be able to forward it to him in two or three weeks, or a little longer. In a 7 August letter, Evert Duyckinck reported that he had urged Melville to let Redfield publish the new book, but that apparently the Harpers were to have it. Not until 12 September did Allan Melville sign the agreement with them.

There is another important fact revealed by the absence of a clause in the contract for *Moby-Dick* that had been present in the earlier contracts and that reappeared in the one for *Pierre*. In that clause Harper and Brothers agreed each time to furnish Melville a corrected proof copy of the work and to defer publication of their edition up to four months. The function of this proof was not specified, but clearly in each case it was intended as a copy Melville could send to London as the basis for an English edition. Evidently no such clause was needed in the *Moby-Dick* contract. Before it was signed, Melville

---

[4]The *Pierre* contract also uses the word 'work'. What significance this may have is not now apparent. Perhaps it simply was an echo of the *Moby-Dick* contract.

[5]Pp. 473–75.

already had received the requisite proofs from Craighead, made numerous alterations in them, and sent them off to London. On the back of his copy of the contract, in another hand, there is a note supporting this conclusion: 'Mem: — Proof sheets of "The Whale" were forwarded to Richard Bentley London under cover to Mr Davis secretary of Legation London in the government dispatches by the Asia which sailed Sept 10th.'

So Craighead, not the Harpers, did the setting and plating from which the proofs were pulled as printer's copy for the English edition and from which the American edition was manufactured. But the change of title from *The Whale* to *Moby-Dick* is evidence that after Harper and Brothers took over the plates neither Melville nor they considered them unalterable. It is likely, then, that there are as yet unidentified characteristics of the American edition that can be traced to this history. It is also likely that it helps to explain two significant differences between the American and English editions: first, that the 'Extracts' appear as preliminaries in New York but as the conclusion of the third volume in London; second, that the 'Epilogue' is present in New York but is absent in London. The probable explanation is that both sections were relatively late additions to the book, the 'Extracts' coming first — in time for inclusion in the English edition — and the 'Epilogue' coming afterwards — too late for Bentley to publish it.

Melville's copies of the contracts for *The Whale* (*Moby-Dick*) are reproduced here for the first time, by permission of the Houghton Library, Harvard University.[6]

[6] The Harper and Brothers contract is reproduced as the frontispiece to this volume of *Proof* (see pp. iii–vi). The Editor and I join in grateful acknowledgment of the extraordinary cooperation of Mr. William H. Bond and Miss Carolyn Jakeman at the Houghton Library and Miss Coté at the Fogg Art Museum in producing the illustrations for this article.

ANALYTICAL BIBLIOGRAPHY AND LITERARY HISTORY:
The Writing and Printing of *Wieland*

JOSEPH KATZ

WIELAND IS A SORRY SHOWPIECE. AT THE SAME TIME LITERARY HISTO-rians nominate it the first published novel by the first American pro-fessional writer, they deplore its badness as a work of art. Every student of American literature is taught to recognize the defects in Charles Brockden Brown's novel as the weak foundation on which later writers had to build. Alexander Cowie has summarized:

The structure of the whole narrative is poor. The Conway-Maxwell sub-plot bears no sensible relation to the rest of the story. The au-thor's plan to allow the reader to follow the action from the successive points of view of Clara, Pleyel, Wieland, and Carwin goes astray partly because Carwin's narrative gets out of hand. Yet even the narrations of the other characters are exceedingly involved and disproportion-ate. Careless use of punctuation, tense, reference, and even of the names of the characters creates a condition that at times borders on chaos. Motivation is needlessly flimsy. Incoherence is so general that

Brown's lavish use of coincidence seems almost a blessing: at least it brings a flash of clearness.[1]

Literary historians always conclude that *Wieland*'s failings point to Brown's deficient sense of authorial responsibility. We are told that he plunged into fiction, beginning many books within a few years but doing little to polish any of them either in manuscript or in proof. 'Brown never revised; he never reread his works; slovenliness was inevitable', charged Fred Lewis Pattee. So Larzer Ziff's comprehensive indictment thirty-six years later might have been predicted. In Ziff's opinion, 'Brown was a hasty, careless writer and rather than go back and revise his novel so as to fit his change in direction into the work consistently, he accepted his exposition and wrote a number of *deus ex machina* explanations for it in the denouement: killing off Pleyel's wife, allowing Carwin to slink away, and producing one Maxwell to take the blame for what the original Carwin appears to have been created for.'[2] The logic of blame—assigning to the novelist the fault for the flaws in his novel—is pellucid.

But while the syllogism is valid logically, the assumptions on which it is based are untrue. No one can deny that *Wieland* is defective; what is needed is an understanding that the development of professionalization in the Federal period encouraged the publication of unfinished masterpieces. Before the literary historian can recognize this, however, he must be aware of matters that he traditionally has relegated to the bibliographer.

[1] *The Rise of the American Novel* (New York: American Book Company, 1948), p. 73.
I am grateful to my colleague William S. Kable for reading and commenting on this paper. My gratitude is no less to my friend Hyman W. Kritzer, Director of Kent State University Libraries, for the use of the Charles Brockden Brown materials in his care. I am additionally grateful to the Departments of English of Kent State University and the University of South Carolina for time and other assistance at different stages of this work.
[2] Pattee, Introduction to *Wieland* (New York: Harcourt, Brace and Company, 1926), p. xlii; Ziff, 'A Reading of *Wieland*', *PMLA*, LXXVII (March 1962), 53.
Other representative statements are in William Dunlap, *The Life of Charles Brockden Brown* (Philadelphia: James P. Parke, 1815), I, 258–59; Henry S. Pancoast, *An Introduction to American Literature* (New York: Henry S. Holt & Co., 1898), p. 111; Walter Fuller Taylor, *A History of American Literature* (New York: American Book Company, 1936), p. 70; and Cowie, *The Rise of the American Novel*, p. 73.

9

Charles Brockden Brown did not set out to be a sloven. He began his career in novel writing with a commitment to serious authorship. The evidence is the record of the completion of *Sky Walk*, his first novel, in his journal around the beginning of 1798. 'It was at first written in an hasty and inaccurate way', he said. 'Before I can submit it to a printer, or even satisfactorily rehearse it to a friend, it must be wholly transcribed. I am afraid, as much time will be required by it, as was necessary to the original composition.'[3] One assumes he took the time to revise, because he did not speak to his friends about *Sky Walk* until three months later. The journal shows that Brown worried over his first novel, concerned not only about how it would be received but also about how it would stand in relation to his succeeding productions. Painfully weighing these considerations, he judged *Sky Walk* a smaller achievement than *Caleb Williams* but a more substantial one than those of contemporary American romancers. He confided to his journal that it 'is preserved from a total extinction only by the reflection that this performance is the first. That every attempt will be better than the last, and that considered in the light of a prelude or first link, it may merit that praise to which it may possess no claim, considered as a last best creation.'[4] Writing novels was important to him because he looked forward to a distinguished career as a novel writer. This was the burden of his advertisement for the book in the *Weekly Magazine* that March. But the public had little opportunity to test his sincerity, because *Sky Walk* was never published in full. When its publisher died in a yellow fever epidemic, the novel was tied up by his executors and it eventually disappeared.[5]

Brown began writing *Wieland* soon after completing *Sky Walk*. The problem is how to account for what seems to be far different attitudes towards art in the two novels. A solution begins with biography. Little is known about how Brown supported himself up to the time he entered his first major period of literary activity, but it is known that his occupation galled him and that he would rather have been a man of letters. As soon as he thought he could earn a livelihood from his

[3]Brown's journal is lost, but this entry is preserved in Dunlap, *The Life*, I, 107–8.

[4]Ibid.

[5]The advertisement appeared in the *Weekly Magazine*, I (17 March 1798), 202; reprinted in Harry R. Warfel, ed., *The Rhapsodist and Other Uncollected Writings* (New York: Scholars' Facsimiles & Reprints, 1943), p. 135. An 'Extract' from *Sky Walk* was published in the *Weekly Magazine*, I (24 March 1798), 228–31, and parts of the book seem to have been adapted into *Ormond* and *Edgar Huntley*. The complete novel, however, is lost.

pen, he gave up his other work and devoted himself to the new career. The turning point was the year 1798: *Alcuin*, a pamphlet on the situation of women, was the first step; *Sky Walk* was the second; and *Wieland*, the third, marks his commitment to professionalization. Money had been promised for the first two; there was every reason to expect more from the third.

In July 1798, when Brown arrived in New York with part of a manuscript of *Wieland*, the émigré bookseller Hocquet Caritat was eager for new novels with which he could feed the reading appetite he was helping to whet. 'Closely associated with Caritat, Brown must have acquired the illusion that there was a commercial future for the author of novels as well as for the distributor, and Caritat must have shared the illusion — for he published and advertised at his own expense Brown's *Wieland* and *Ormond*.'[6] Whether or not the arrangement anticipated in details the relationship that eventually would develop between authors and publishers, in this case it required a heavy contribution from Brown. His cost was the need to function primarily as producer rather than as artist. He had been able to spend time reworking *Sky Walk* to his satisfaction before showing it to anyone because it was not a source of bread. *Wieland* was. Brown decided to become a professional writer even before a first draft of it was complete; thus the key to *Wieland* is that it had to be written against the press. With *Alcuin* and *Sky Walk* both in process of publication, Brown's good friend Elihu Hubbard Smith was able to sell Caritat the new novel on the basis of opening chapters and little more than enthusiasm for the rest. Brown needed money; the promise of *Wieland* was negotiable; Caritat paid $50 on it; Brown was trapped.

The history of *Wieland*'s composition and printing is outlined in the diaries of Brown's intimates, Smith and William Dunlap.[7] On 29 March 1798 Dunlap recorded the birth of the novel: 'Smith show'd me a letter from C B Brown in which he describes himself as assiduously writing novels & in love.' When Dunlap visited Brown in Philadelphia on 12 April, however, *Wieland* was no more than substantially under way. He noted Brown reading from it that day, but not the next day when he called again. Brown broke from Philadelphia for

[6]William Charvat, *The Profession of Authorship in America, 1800–1870* (Columbus: The Ohio State University Press, 1968), p. 27.

[7]Smith's diaries for 1794–98 survive unpublished at the Yale University Library. Dunlap's have been published. The *Diary of William Dunlap*, 3 vols. (New York: The New York Historical Society, 1930), covers the period of *Wieland*.

New York a few months later, but when he went to Dunlap's house on 3 July his friend saw more of 'his 2d novel but not compleated.' Dunlap 'read in Wieland' after the parade on the Fourth, and after supper on the fifth Brown resumed reading it to him 'as far as he has gone.' Smith also gives evidence of the partial state of *Wieland*. Out of the city until 8 July, he read eighty-four manuscript pages on the tenth, finishing the novel 'as far as [Brown] has carried it' on the eleventh. In the meantime Brown was writing new material: Dunlap read a 'continuation' on 22 July.

Nevertheless, when Thomas and James Swords—who had printed *Alcuin*—began setting type on *Wieland* on 23 July 1798, they were working from an incomplete manuscript of an uncompleted novel. The manuscript was incomplete because Dunlap had taken the continuation with him when he left New York on 21 July, not returning with it until the evening of 24 July; the novel was uncompleted because, as Smith and Dunlap both record, Brown was writing ahead in the month that followed the start of printing. Despite this, printing went on at top speed. On 25 July, when Dunlap took tea with Brown and Smith, he found them correcting the first proof sheet. In the four preceding days, Brown had written more manuscript: both Smith and Dunlap read 'part of the remainder' of *Wieland* that evening. Brown also talked with Smith about a 'suitable catastrophe' for the novel that day; Dunlap did not participate in the discussion, but when he finished his reading the next day he joined the friends in talking over 'proposed alterations'. Still the printer was working: Smith notes that more proof was corrected on 30 July and 2 August. But still the novel was not complete: Brown showed his friends new copy on 5 August. Smith called it 'Brown's conclusion to Wieland', but he probably was too sanguine. Dunlap undoubtedly saw the same material, and he recognized it as 'additions'. After Smith saw more proof on 8 August and 13 August, he knew that the new manuscript material showed him on 24 August was 'additions'.

From these sketchy notes one can at least surmise the progress of *Wieland* through three landmarks in the plot. By 25 July Brown probably had not taken it past chapter 16, the point at which discussion of a 'catastrophe' would have been most appropriate. Chapter 26, the penultimate chapter—in which Wieland kills himself and Clara renounces the world, thereby providing a breathless anticlimax to the published novel—almost certainly was produced during the first week of August. The last chapter, 27, had to have been written after

7 August. On 5 September Dunlap, who had been visiting his family in Perth Amboy since then, received a letter in which Brown announced, 'This afternoon I revised the last sheet of *Wieland*. It will form an handsome volume of 300 pages. Some ten or twelve have been added since you last saw it.'

But the Smith and Dunlap diaries are only one record of the novel's development. The other is in the physical makeup of the book itself. With even a rudimentary knowledge of analytical bibliography the literary historian can use these complementary records to understand more clearly why *Wieland* is defective. The first edition collates [A]² B–I K–U X–Z Aa–Cc⁶, with every folio 3ʳ in a gathering signed to the paradigm B2. The text was imposed twelvemo in one forme which was printed work-and-turn to produce duplicate half sheets. It is likely that the imposition scheme used was one laid out by Joseph Moxon and repeated in succeeding printer's manuals (see plate 1). (In *The History and Art of Printing*, p. 413, Philip Luckombe calls the result a 'common half sheet of twelves.' The implication of normativeness is reinforced by Theodore Low De Vinne in *Modern Book Composition* [New York, 1904], pp. 363, 364, where it is termed 'the old method'.) With this forme, one side of a demy sheet was printed first. Then the sheet was turned on the long cross between pages 12 and 11, and the same forme was used to perfect the other side of the sheet. The perfected sheet then was cut twice: once along the long cross, and a second time along the short cross between pages 3 and 5. In that way the printer used twelve pages of type to produce two complete duplicate gatherings. At the time of folding, the binder inserted the four-page inset into the eight wraparound pages in each gathering.

An examination of the watermarks in *Wieland* supports the indications of this procedure in the signing. *BAL* 1496 reports *Wieland* on 'Wove paper watermarked 1798 <1793?>; 1795; 1796.' That is only a partial record of the watermarks to be seen in the several copies examined for this paper. In them the watermarks actually are 1795; B1795; 1796; B1796; 1798; B1798. (What sometimes appeared to be '1793' turned out to be '1798' on closer scrutiny.) Not every gathering has watermarked leaves, and those that do may have either one or two leaves watermarked. When watermarks do appear they always are on leaves 1 or 6, 3 or 4, always parallel to the edge of the leaf as in plate 2. This position suggests that the original sheet was watermarked as indicated in plate 3. Because many gatherings have a mixture of watermarked leaves and countermarked leaves in no apparent

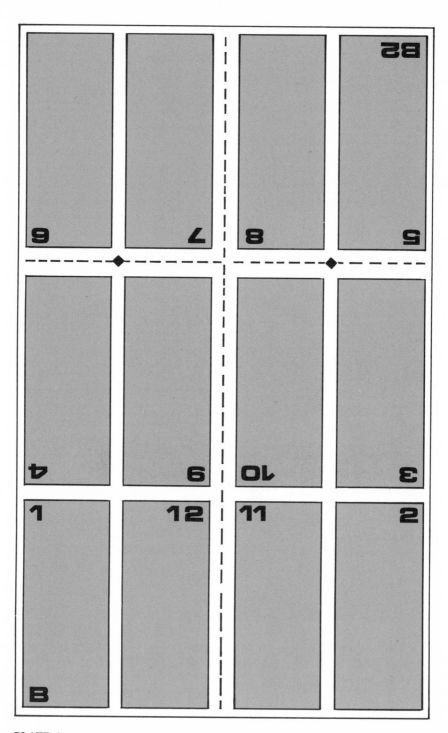

PLATE 1

sequence, the offcut must have been separated from the printed sheet prior to folding. That means no gathering can be considered to have an inset and a wraparound printed from the same sheet: chance dictated the mixture of insets and wraparounds in any copy of the book.[8]

This analysis makes possible a more precise reconstruction of *Wieland*'s pell-mell progress towards publication. During the period it still was customary for a proof sheet to be pulled from the forme of a gathering imposed as it was ultimately intended to be printed. The proof sheets of *Wieland* probably were unperfected full sheets of each gathering: twelve pages arranged as in plate 1, complete with running titles and folios, printed on only one side of the sheet, the other side blank. Brown's friends indicate that he saw only one proof sheet at a time, one after another, because their diaries note that on any particular day he 'corrected a proof'—never 'proofs'. These circumstances have great implications.

For one thing, they mean that Brown was forced to see the developing *Wieland* from a printer's—not an author's—point of view. As an author he divided his novel into structural units of chapters. But once printing began he was shown it only in structural units of gatherings, arbitrary bits of twelve pages at a time—physical, rather than novelistic, units of structure. The first proof, the one he corrected on 25 July, contained all of chapter 1 but only the first page of chapter 2; the second proof had the seven remaining pages of chapter 2 but only the first five of the seven pages in chapter 3; and so on, according to the coincidence of pages with gatherings in the proof sheets. Since the printer must have had most of the extant manuscript after 23 July, and retained it until at least 5 September, and since the rush of time probably did not permit Brown to copy for himself new material before he sent it to the printer, seriatim composition and proof correction by the forme meant that he never had access to the entire book at any time after printing began. One clue to his having only memory to rely on for early details in the novel is the confusion in the names of Major Stuart's wife for which he has been criticized: before her marriage she is 'Louisa Conway' (p. 30), and after it she is 'Lady Jane Conway' (p. 157). Under the circumstances, the wonder is not that he blundered but that he blundered so little.

[8] A report of the watermark distribution in copies examined appears in Appendix II.

PLATE 2

B1795

1795

PLATE 3

These circumstances imposed even a more severe restriction on the writer. Printing house custom was that when the compositor received corrected proof he would make the indicated corrections in type, then release the revised forme to the pressman—who would immediately machine the sheets needed to make up the edition. When the pressman was finished, the compositor would distribute the type in that forme so it would be ready for further setting. In this cycle there simply is no place for an author's afterthoughts. William Charvat's remarks about the succeeding period in literary history reflect this situation: 'A persistent shortage of type ran up costs because, since frequently a whole book could not stand in type at once, books had to be entirely recast for successive editions. As late as 1832 H. C. Carey wrote J. P. Kennedy that

to send you one form [of proofs of *Swallow Barn*] per day, it is necessary that we should always have six forms in type, and that quantity is about twice as much as an ordinary fount of type will set up. The printers have, most stupidly, so great a variety of [styles] in the type now used that although one of them may have two thousand weight of one size in the office, it will be of three or four different founts, differing from each other so much that they cannot be used together.[9]

Although Kennedy was in one city and his publisher and printer in another, Brown, Caritat, and Swords were all in New York. Consequently the printer of *Wieland* could work faster than the printer of *Swallow Barn* without holding so much imposed type ahead—and he did, doing twenty-seven full gatherings and one short preliminary gathering in thirty-six working days. But the Swords's shop was small—'two printing presses & 6 or 8 hands, with more work to execute than they can perform', according to a contemporary, John Pintard—and it must have been subject to similar shortages.[10] So Brown was further restricted as he wrote. He could not revise earlier sections to fit later turnings as the novel developed under his hand; nor could he even make substantial revisions in current proof without the risk of upsetting the several succeeding gatherings already set in type. Critics who accuse him of irresponsibility because *Wieland* shows the results of these restrictions are just not offering an informed judgment.

To the contrary, there is evidence that Brown made use of whatever

[9]Charvat, *The Profession of Authorship in America*, pp. 45–46.
[10]Quoted in Austin Baxter Keep, *History of the New York Society Library* (New York: Trustees of the New York Society Library, 1908), pp. 239–41.

opportunity he had to revise the proof before him. The Swordses took pride in their craftsmanship and in their association with the world of letters. Thomas Swords was a member of the New York Society Library and printed its 1792 catalog. On its title page the Swords's imprint advertised their office as 'where printing in general is executed with Neatness, Accuracy and Dispatch, and on reasonable Terms.' Their vaunt is supported by John Pintard's comment that Thomas and James Swords 'are the neatest & most correct printers on the continent.'[11] *Wieland* shows how its printers troubled to adhere strictly to accepted rules of good bookmaking. For example, they took pains to avoid widows. To prevent a page from beginning with an incomplete line of type, they shortened the preceding page by a line that they would transfer to the next one. And again according to the rules, they would back up the now shortened type page with a page with the same number of lines. These two rules are the reason that eight groups of pages have only thirty-five, rather than the usual thirty-six, lines of type: pages 25, 26; 36, 37; 38, 39; 201, 202; 231, 232; 271, 272; 293, 294; 295, 296. But the rules of good composition and presswork do not explain shorts on pages 39, 40; 91; 113, 114; 275, 276; 297. Some of these even violate the foregoing rules. One explanation could be that these pages indicate compositorial doublings corrected without compensating by shifting lines from forward pages. In any decent shop of the time, however, this was an offense for which a compositor could be fined. The Swords's pride in craft makes it more likely that these pages indicate regions of the proof in which Brown substantially revised in such a way as to result in less material than was originally set.[12]

In practical terms, correction and revision of current proof were the only ways in which Brown could adapt earlier composition to the novel's later development. The restrictions under which he was forced to operate are impressive. He could not consult either early or immediately succeeding material: the printer had that. He could not see current material in authorial terms: proof was sent him in the way the book made up into type, one gathering at a time. He could not revise earlier portions of the text: it had already been fixed by printing. Speaking practically, all he could do was adapt new material to fit what had come before. This restriction on his creativity further

[11] Ibid. The title page is reproduced in Keep, p. 240.
[12] A combined table of coincidence in gathering, chapter, and page, and number of lines to each page in the first edition is in Appendix I.

when he uttered it. It was of no moment, he said, that we could not explain by what motives he that made the signal was led hither. How imperfectly acquainted were we with the condition and designs of the beings that surrounded us? The city was near at hand, and thousands might there exist whose powers and purposes might easily explain whatever was mysterious in this transaction. As to the closet dialogue, he was obliged to adopt one of two suppositions, and affirm either that it was fashioned in my own fancy, or that it actually took place between two persons in the closet.

Such was Carwin's mode of explaining these appearances. It is such, perhaps, as would commend itself as most plausible to the most sagacious minds, but it was insufficient to impart conviction to us. As to the treason that was meditated against me, it was doubtless just to conclude that it was either real or imaginary; but that it was real was intimated by the mysterious warning in the summer-house, the secret of which I had hitherto locked up in my own breast.

A month passed away in this kind of intercourse. As to Carwin, our ignorance was in no degree enlightened respecting his genuine character and views. Appearances were uniform. No man possessed a larger store of knowledge, or a greater degree of skill in the communication of it to others; Hence he was regarded as an inestimable addition to our society. Considering the distance of my brother's house from the city, he was frequently prevailed upon to pass the night where he spent the evening. Two days seldom elapsed without a visit from him; hence he was regarded as a kind of inmate of the house. He entered and departed without ceremony. When he arrived he received an

PLATE 4

unaffected welcome, and when he chose to retire, no importunities were used to induce him to remain.

The temple was the principal scene of our social enjoyments; yet the felicity that we tasted when assembled in this asylum, was but the gleam of a former sun-shine. Carwin never parted with his gravity. The inscrutableness of his character, and the uncertainty whether his fellowship tended to good or to evil, were seldom absent from our minds. This circumstance powerfully contributed to sadden us.

My heart was the seat of growing disquietudes. This change in one who had formerly been characterized by all the exuberances of soul, could not fail to be remarked by my friends. My brother was always a pattern of solemnity. My sister was clay, moulded by the circumstances in which she happened to be placed. There was but one whose deportment remains to be described as being of importance to our happiness. Had Pleyel likewise dismissed his vivacity?

He was as whimsical and jestful as ever, but he was not happy. The truth, in this respect, was of too much importance to me not to make me a vigilant observer. His mirth was easily perceived to be the fruit of exertion. When his thoughts wandered from the company, an air of dissatisfaction and impatience stole across his features. Even the punctuality and frequency of his visits were somewhat lessened. It may be supposed that my own uneasiness was heightened by these tokens; but, strange as it may seem, I found, in the present state of my mind, no relief but in the persuasion that Pleyel was unhappy.

PLATE 5

tightened, of course, as the novel drew closer to the end and as printing neared completion. These circumstances—not haste, carelessness, or unwillingness to revise—account for the major structural defect in *Wieland,* the Conway-Maxwell subplot.

Recently, Robert E. Hemenway discovered an early plan of *Wieland* in the Brown family commonplace books.[13] In it Brown detailed the plot of two 'acts' in his novel, taking it through the protagonist's escape from prison. The plan shows what he thought *Wieland* would be before printing began: such an important feature of the book as the elder Wieland's combustion is missing, characters are sketched in different stages of development, and even their names are shown in process of change from early tries to those by which they eventually are known. But in spite of these profound differences, book and plan coincide on the major developments through chapter 5— through the family's history, the marriage of Theodore and Catherine, the first two biloquistic deceptions, and, of course, through the story of Louisa. After that point coincidence diminishes and the plan becomes less an outline than a series of notes which are most useful in suggesting how the novel might have looked. The subplot, for example, is recorded last of all in a series of jottings, sketch-notes which show Brown changing his mind while he was making them:[14]

<Marcrieve> birth, education. Acquaintance of Conway. In love with a beautiful woman but Conway he introduces to her. Louisa seduced by <Conway> Ludloe. & prevailed upon to aid him in persuading M. to concur with C. scheme.

<M> Carwin made unintentionally instrumental in terrifying Mrs. C. Efforts of this kind ineffectuall prevailed upon fully to adopt the scheme of destroying Mrs. C. by means of faith. This done. Likewise her daughter. Residing at a distance.

Discovers the perfidy of Louisa. Colvill accused by <Conway> Ludloe of Murdering Mrs. C. Circumstantial evidence strong. Before trial escapes prison. by changing clothes with Louisa. Comes to Am.

Inducements. Affluence. Marriage with Louiza he is poor. Relief of distress.

[13] Hemenway transcribes the outline on pp. 75–78 of his 1966 Kent State University Ph.D. dissertation, 'The Novels of Charles Brockden Brown: A Critical Study', and reproduces it in the dissertation's appendix. The original is in the Brown family's Commonplace Book No. 14, which is cataloged as 'Book of Selections Copied from Papers, etc.' at the Pennsylvania Historical Society, Am. 03399.

[14] Angle brackets (or chevrons) surround canceled material.

Critical ingenuity may some day fully unravel the tangled relationship between this scheme and that in the novel. The point now is that it suggests that the subplot originally was intended to reinforce the theme of destruction 'by means of faith' in the major plot. But as *Wieland* developed into something more than a simple gothic romance, this element was subordinated. As Clara's turbulence at the beginning of chapter 6 may reflect Brown's own tentativeness, the novel changes direction with the introduction of Carwin. At this point, however, it was too late to remove the leads into the original subplot, young Louisa and her father. They were introduced in the beginning of chapter 4, and that had been printed no later than the first week of August. By now it was some time after. As the novel continued to diverge from the plan along its own lines, Louisa receded into the background further and further until she is all but forgotten by the middle of the novel. When Brown recollected her it was too late. He may have thought he could solve his problem by killing her off during the course of Wieland's massacre. That was one death not in the plan so it must have been an unanticipated way out of an unexpected difficulty. But Brown could not do as Wieland had done — eradicate her so 'that not a *lineament remained!*' And her father's history could not be eradicated at all. It had been given too much prominence. So Brown's need was to justify emphasis retroactively, by connecting it in some way to the major events. The justification required by an episode that no longer had a place in *Wieland* ruined the novel.

The trouble is that, aside from these incursions of the subplot, *Wieland* is coherent from its beginning to the end of the penultimate chapter. Clara's story is framed completely by chapters 1 and 26: her tale is in explanation of her despair, and when chapter 26 is concluded she is back in the present, her despair fully explained. Because the frame gains its structural function from her unhappy emotional state, the novel loses its unity when she is remotivated in chapter 27. The frame is broken.

But Brown had no other choice. He had been trapped by a situation that would become increasingly common in the early history of American literature. William Dunlap understood that situation:

It is very evident that this unsystematic mode of composition must give a motley appearance to works so written. The parts must occasionally be disproportioned to each other, and incidents imagined which excite great expectations in the reader, and involve the story in mystery, which the author trusting to after thought for the explanation or the sequel, and not finding, when the printer called for the remaining *copy,* any adequate solution of difficulty or termination of adventure, the event either does not answer the expectation raised, or the reader is put off with the intimation of a continuation at a further time.[15]

Perhaps it was Dunlap's lack of sympathy that led readers of those words in his biography of Brown to forget them. After all, Dunlap had not shared Brown's problems. He was not a professional writer, but a theatrical manager whose writings seem to have come after even his miniature portraits as a way of supplementing his major source of income. Brown had no such financial bases. Once he decided to earn his living by writing novels, he had no choice except to produce them at a steady pace, always in debt to the publisher and always behind the printer.

That was the cost of being a professional writer early in the history of American literature. It does not excuse a novel's flaws, but it does put them into perspective: they were the fault of the situation as much as they were of the writer. Brown learned, evidently to his bitterness later, what those who succeeded him had to relearn: without a patron, with no other means of support, a writer who became a professional had to sell his words immediately. Ironically, the process of professionalization meant writing against the machine that made it possible, and that wrought the artistic ruin of its first landmark in this country. Analytical bibliography can help the literary historian understand that point.

---

[15]Dunlap, *The Life,* I, 259.

Appendix I

Combined Analytical Table

The following table reports the makeup of *Wieland* (1798) after the unsigned preliminary gathering [A]².

SIGNATURE	CHAPTER	PAGE	LINES
B	I	1	20
		2	36
		3	36
		4	36
B2		5	36
		6	36
		7	36
		8	36
		9	36
		10	36
		11	25
	II	12	32
C		13	36
		14	36
		15	36
		16	36
C2		17	36
		18	36
		19	13[16]
	III	20	31
		21	36
		22	36
		23	36
		24	36
D		25	35
		26	35
		27	9
	IV	28	31
D2		29	36
		30	36
		31	36
		32	36
		33	36
		34	36

[16] Lines 1–7 are in body type; line 7 is followed by leading; lines 8–13 are a footnote.

SIGNATURE	CHAPTER	PAGE	LINES
		35	36
		36	35
E		37	35
		38	35
		39	35
		40	35
E2		41	7
	V	42	31
		43	36
		44	36
		45	36
		46	36
		47	36
		48	36
F		49	36
		50	36
		51	36
		52	36
F2		53	36
		54	36
		55	36
		56	21
	VI	57	30
		58	36
		59	36
		60	36
G		61	36
		62	36
		63	36
		64	36
G2		65	36
		66	36
		67	36
		68	36
		69	36
		70	36
		71	9
	VII	72	31
H		73	36
		74	36

SIGNATURE	CHAPTER	PAGE	LINES
		75	36
		76	36
H2		77	36
		78	36
		79	36
		80	36
		81	36
		82	36
		83	6
	VIII	84	31
I		85	36
		86	36
		87	36
		88	36
I2		89	36
		90	36
		91	35
		92	9
	IX	93	31
		94	36
		95	36
		96	36
K		97	36
		98	36
		99	36
		100	36
K2		101	36
		102	36
		103	36
		104	36
		105	36
		106	36
		107	36
		108	36
L		109	36
		110	36
		111	11
	X	112	31
L2		113	35
		114	35

SIGNATURE	CHAPTER	PAGE	LINES
		115	36
		116	36
		117	36
		118	36
		119	36
		120	36
M		121	36
		122	24
	XI	123	31
		124	36
M2		125	36
		126	36
		127	36
		128	36
		129	36
		130	36
		131	36
		132	36
N		133	36
		134	36
		135	36
		136	13
N2	XII	137	29
		138	36
		139	36
		140	36
		141	36
		142	36
		143	36
		144	36
O		145	16
	XIII	146	29
		147	36
		148	36
O2		149	36
		150	36
		151	36
		152	36
		153	36
		154	21

SIGNATURE	CHAPTER	PAGE	LINES
	XIV	155	30
		156	36
P		157	36
		158	36
		159	36
		160	36
P2		161	36
		162	36
		163	36
		164	36
		165	36
		166	24
	XV	167	29[17]
		168	36
Q		169	36
		170	36
		171	36
		172	36
Q2		173	36
		174	36
		175	34
	XVI	176	29
		177	36
		178	36
		179	36
		180	36
R		181	36
		182	36
		183	36
		184	26
R2	XVII	185	29
		186	36
		187	36
		188	36
		189	36
		190	36
		191	36
		192	27

[17] Leading above and below line 12.

SIGNATURE	CHAPTER	PAGE	LINES
S	XVIII	193	29
		194	36
		195	36
		196	36
S2		197	36
		198	10
	XIX	199	30
		200	36
		201	35
		202	35
		203	36
		204	36
T		205	36
		206	36
		207	36
		208	36
T2		209	36
		210	36
		211	14
	XX	212	29
		213	36
		214	36
		215	36
		216	36
U		217	36
		218	35[18]
		219	36
		220	36
U2		221	27
	XXI	222	29
		223	36
		224	36
		225	36
		226	36
		227	36
		228	36
X		229	36

[18] Lines 1–33 are in body type; line 33 is followed by leading; lines 34–35 are a footnote.

SIGNATURE	CHAPTER	PAGE	LINES
		230	36
		231	35
		232	35
X2		233	18
	XXII	234	30
		235	36
		236	36
		237	36
		238	36
		239	36
		240	36
Y		241	38[19]
		242	37[20]
		243	36
		244	36
Y2		245	36
		246	36
		247	36
		248	35[21]
		249	9
	XXIII	250	29
		251	36
		252	36
Z		253	36
		254	36
		255	36
		256	36
Z2		257	36
		258	36
		259	36
		260	36
		261	31
	XXIV	262	29

[19] Lines 1–23 are in body type; line 23 is followed by leading; lines 24–38 begin a footnote that is carried over to p. 241. See note 20.

[20] Lines 1–27 are in body type; line 27 is followed by leading; lines 28–37 conclude the footnote begun on p. 241. See note 19.

[21] Lines 1–33 are in body type; line 33 is followed by leading; lines 34–35 are a footnote.

31

SIGNATURE	CHAPTER	PAGE	LINES
		263	36
		264	36
Aa		265	36
		266	36
		267	36
		268	34
Aa2	XXV	269	29
		270	36
		271	35
		272	35
		273	36
		274	36
		275	35
		276	35
Bb		277	36
		278	24
	XXVI	279	29
		280	36
Bb2		281	36
		282	36
		283	36
		284	36
	XXVII	285	28[22]
		286	36
		287	36
		288	36
Cc		289	36
		290	36
		291	36
		292	36
Cc2		293	35
		294	35
		295	35
		296	35
		297	35
		298	6

[22] Line 1 is a headnote; it is followed by leading; lines 2–28 are in body type.

APPENDIX II

Distribution of Watermarks

The following table records watermarks on leaves after the unsigned preliminary gathering [A]² in the copies of *Wieland* (1798) examined for this study. Copies: (1) ViU Barrett; (2) OKentC copy 1; (3) OKentC copy 2; (4) InU Lilly; (5) PU; (6) OKentC copy 3; (7) ICN; (8) NjP copy 1; (9) PBL copy 1; (10) PBL copy 2.

COPY	1	2	3	4	5	6	7	8	9	10
LEAF										
B^1/B^4		1795	?	1795	B1795	1795	1796		1795	1795
$B2^1/B2^2$				B1795			1796?	1795	1795	1795
C^1/C^4	1795	1795	1795	1795	?		1796	1795	1795	1795
$C2^1/C2^2$	1795				1795	1795	1796	1795	1795	1795
D^1/D^4	1795	1795	1795	1795	1795		1796	1795	1795	
$D2^1/D2^2$	1795	B1795		1795	1795		1796?			1795
E^1/E^4				1795	B1795		1796?	1795	1795?	1795
$E2^1/E2^2$	B1795	1795	1795	1795	1795	1795	B1796	B1795?		1795
F^1/F^4	1795	1795	1796	1795	B1795	1795	B1796	1795	1795	
$F2^1/F2^2$	1795			1795	1795		1795	B1795	1795	B179?
G^1/G^4	1795				1795	1795		1795		1795?
$G2^1/G2^2$	1795	1795	1795		B1795		1796?	B1795	1795	1795
H^1/H^4	1796	1795	1795	1795	1795		B1796	1796	1795	1796
$H2^1/H2^2$	1796	1795		1795?	1795	1795	1796	1796		1796
I^1/I^4		1796	1796	1795	1796	1795	1796	1795		1796?
$I2^1/I2^2$		1796	1796		B1796		1795	B1795	1795	B1795?
K^1/K^4	1796	1795		1796	1796	1795	1796	B1795	1796	B1795
$K2^1/K2^2$	1796		1795	1796	B1796			1795		1796
L^1/L^4	1796	B1796		1796	1796		1796	1796	1795	1796
$L2^1/L2^2$	1796	1796	1795	B1796	1796	1795	1796	1796		B1796
M^1/M^4	B1796			B1796	1796		1796	1796	1795	1796
$M2^1/M2^2$	1796	1795	1795	1796	1796	1795	B1796	B1796		B1796

33

COPY LEAF	1	2	3	4	5	6	7	8	9	10
N^1/N^4	B1796	1795		B1796	1796	1795	B1796	1796	1796	B1796
$N2^1/N2^2$	1796		1796	1796	1796		1796	1796	B1796	1796
O^1/O^4	1796	1795			1796		1796	1796	1796	B1796
$O2^1/O2^2$	B1796		1795	1796	1796	1795	B1796	B1796	B1796	1796
P^1/P^4	1796	1796	1796	1796	B1796	1795	1796	1796	1796	1796
$P2^1/P2^2$	1796	1796	1795	1796	1796	1795	1796	B1796	1795	1796
Q^1/Q^4	B1796	1796	1795	1796	1796	B1795	1796	1796	1795	1796
$Q2^1/Q2^2$	1796	1796	B1795	1796	1796	1795	1796	B1796	B1795	1796
R^1/R^4	1796	B1796		B1796	B1796	1795	1796	1796	1795	B1796
$R2^1/R2^2$	B1796	1796	1796	B1796	1796	1795	1796	B1796	1795	1796
S^1/S^4	1796	B1796			B1796		1796	1796		1796
$S2^1/S2^2$	1796	1796	1795	B1795	1796	1795	1796	B1796	1795	1796
T^1/T^4	1795		1795	B1795	1795	1795	1795	1795		1795
$T2^1/T2^2$	1795						1795		1795	1795?
U^1/U^4	1795	1795	1795	B1795				B1795		179?
$U2^1/U2^2$		B1795		B1795	1795	1795	1795	1795		
X^1/X^4	1795	B1798?		1795	B1796		1795	1795	1795	1795?
$X2^1/X2^2$	1795	1798?	1795		1795		1795	1795		B1795
Y^1/Y^4	1795	1795	1796	1796			1795	1795		
$Y2^1/Y2^2$	1795		?	1795	B1795		1795?	1795	1796	B1795
Z^1/Z^4			1795	1795	1795	1795	1795?	1795		
$Z2^1/Z2^2$	1795	1795	1795	1795	1795		1795?	B1795	1795	
Aa^1/Aa^4		B1795		1796		1795	1796	B1796		1796
$Aa2^1/Aa2^2$	B1795	B1796	1795	1796		1795	1796	1796	1795	B1796
Bb^1/Bb^4	B1796	1796	1796	1796	1796	1796	1796	1796	1796	B1796
$Bb2^1/Bb2^2$	1796	1796	B1796	1795	B1796	1796	1796	1796	1796	1796
Cc^1/Cc^4	1795	1795	1796		B1795		B1796	B1795	1795	
$Cc2^1/Cc2^2$	1795	1795			1795	1795	1795	1795		B1795

PARK BENJAMIN:
LITERARY AGENT, *ET CETERA*

LILLIAN B. GILKES

F ROM PERHAPS NO OTHER SINGLE FIGURE ON THE A MERICAN LITERARY scene can we learn so much about early developments in book and magazine publishing, the formation of a wildly competitive literary market, and the use of publishers' advertising as from Park Benjamin. Over a period of twenty-odd years he conceived and intermittently carried on what probably was the first commercial literary agency ever conducted in this country. In addition, he was involved with the creation, publication, and distribution of literature in almost every conceivable way. Author, publisher, pirate, lecturer, agent — Park Benjamin was in his time a one-man literary industry.

An offshoot of his journalistic activities during the period of his editorship of the *New World*, Benjamin's literary agency gives one entry into both his significance and the world of writing during his lifetime. It spanned the decades of the 1840s and 1850s, but the agency was not placed on a fee basis until some years after his withdrawal from the *New World* in 1844. Up to that time, compensation for the successful placement of authors' material was in the form of

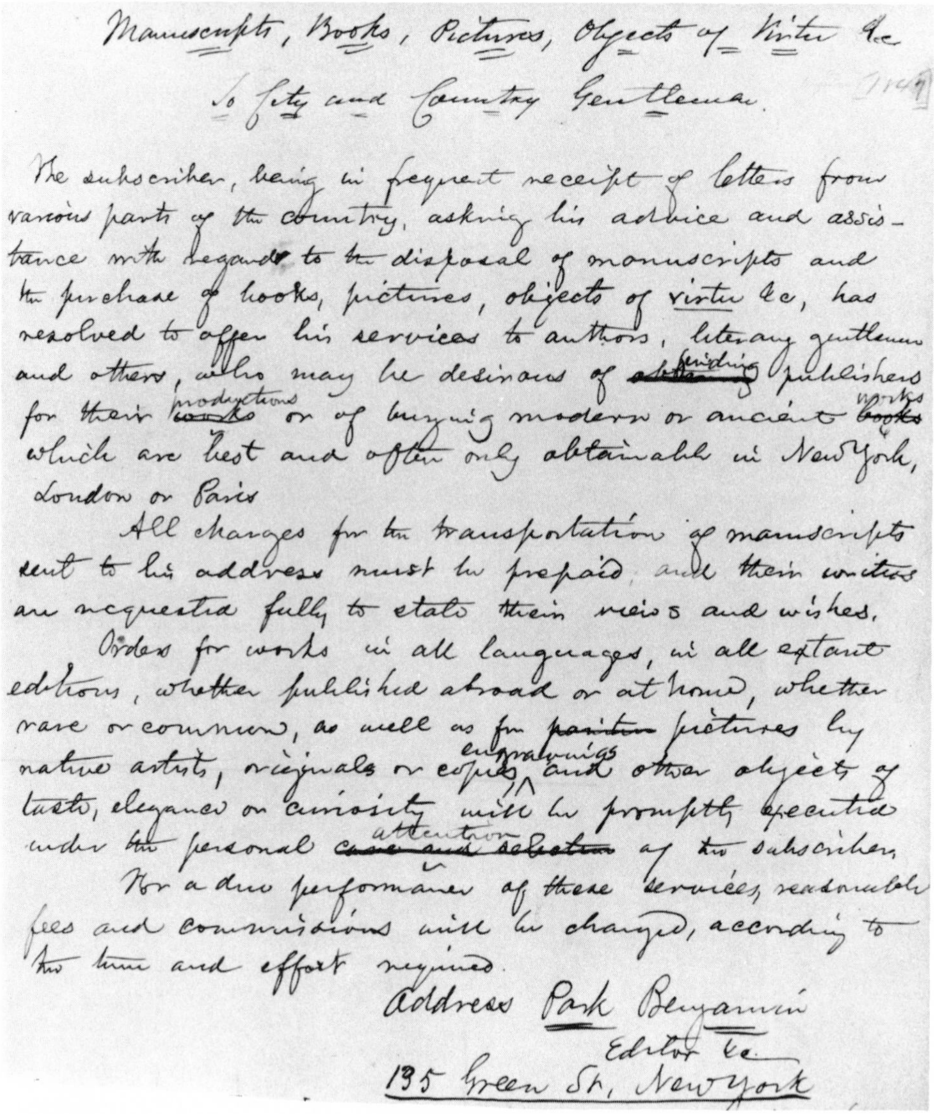

Manuscripts, Books, Pictures, Objects of Virtu &c

To City and Country Gentlemen.

The subscriber, being in frequent receipt of letters from various parts of the country, asking his advice and assistance with regards to the disposal of manuscripts and the purchase of books, pictures, objects of virtu &c, has resolved to offer his services to authors, literary gentlemen and others, who may be desirous of ~~selling~~ *avoiding* publishers for their ~~works~~ *productions* or of buying modern or ancient ~~books~~ *works* which are best and often only obtainable in New York, London or Paris

All charges for the transportation of manuscripts sent to his address must be prepaid, and their writers are requested fully to state their views and wishes.

Orders for works in all languages, in all extant editions, whether published abroad or at home, whether rare or common, as well as for ~~painting~~ pictures by native artists, originals or ~~copies~~ *engravings* and other objects of taste, elegance or curiosity will be promptly executed under the personal ~~care and selection~~ *attention* of the subscriber.

For a due performance of these services, reasonable fees and commissions will be charged, according to the time and effort required.

Address Park Benjamin
Editor &c
135 Green St, New York

PLATE 1

goodwill from both author and publisher, especially if the author's name was a valuable drawing card; in the more tangible form of reviewer's copies of new books which, if they were in multivolume sets, usually were expensive; and in the no less important form of friendly exchange of notices and free advertising among competing magazines, newspapers, and publishing houses.

A few other people also were acting as agents in like manner here and there. For with no unified system of transportation then existing between the seaboard urban centers where the publishing industry was concentrated, communications were slow and subject to the uncertainties of weather and bad roads. Ocean and river transport took even longer. So authors living in the cities of the South, the New England states, or the western frontier were glad to have a representative act for them in handling the sale of their works in other areas. William Gilmore Simms, over a period of some twenty-five years, was indebted to the friendship of James Lawson, a New York insurance agent, ex-newspaper man, and an author himself, for such services which were performed without charge.[1] The dilettante Samuel Ward, who derived a sense of importance from association with intellectuals and men of genius, acted at one time in a similar capacity for Longfellow[2] —who did not always follow his counsels. As one of the editors of *Putnam's Monthly*, George W. Curtis replied to an appeal from the widowed Mrs. Henry Cleveland: 'Putnam declines translations altogether. But if ever your friend will send me some little love story complete in one number of not more than six or eight pages, I think I can get it into Harper—if it is good;—and get, perhaps, five dollars a page (printed) for it.'[3]

So matters stood, until necessity compelled Park Benjamin to charge for his services. Likewise, until the minor roils of competition burst into open warfare with the publication of whole novels in cheap paperback editions by the 'mammoth' weeklies—of which Benjamin's *New World* was the principal—all was on a gentlemanly basis of mutual self-help.

Benjamin himself was an astonishing combination of versatile talents: a strong poetic gift yoked to a shrewd business judgment and exceptional organizing capabilities. At the time of his removal from Boston to New York in 1837, he had already gained wide recognition

[1]See Simms's letters to Lawson in Mary C. Simms Oliphant, ed., *The Letters of William Gilmore Simms*, 5 vols. (Columbia: University of South Carolina Press, 1952–56). Also see Thomas L. McHaney, 'An Early 19th Century Literary Agent: James Lawson of New York', *Papers of the Bibliographical Society of America*, LXIV (Second Quarter 1970), 177–92.

[2]Andrew Hilen, ed., *The Letters of Henry Wadsworth Longfellow*, 2 vols. (Cambridge: The Belknap Press of Harvard University Press, 1966).

[3]George W. Curtis to Sarah Perkins Cleveland, 29 June 1856, in the Berg Collection, New York Public Library.

as a poet—at the age of twenty-six—and his natural endowments might, with better luck, have placed him in the front rank of American romanticists, marked for remembrance along with his friend Longfellow and his Harvard classmate Holmes. But the loss of his entire fortune, an inheritance from his father's mercantile enterprises, in the panic of 1837 forced him to seek a livelihood in the business world of publishing and newspaper editing. 'I should have preferred a life of literary leisure,' he once remarked to a friend, 'but I have learned to labor, and it is no affliction to me.'[4] He was laboring now, he said, 'to redeem the time.'

Benjamin's chief importance today is as a transitional figure. But for a just evaluation of the nature and extent of his many-sided contributions to a young American literature struggling to be born, with particular reference to his literary agency which interlocked with all the others, we must review in outline the background of his early activities in Boston, and the publishing situation in general throughout the country.

I

Benjamin had been one of the original editors of the *New-England Magazine*,[5] in which he published eighteen of Hawthorne's early sketches and tales which had been rejected by S. G. Goodrich ('Peter Parley') for the *Token*. But before becoming sole owner and publisher of the *Magazine*, he had engineered a merger with the *American Monthly Review*, a journal published at Harvard and edited by his old professor of Hebrew, Sidney Willard. While probably assisting Willard editorially, he contributed to the *Review* important critiques on the poetry of Bryant and the elder Richard Henry Dana, a re-evaluation

[4]Benjamin to Lafayette S. Foster, 22 January 1846, in the Park Benjamin Collection, Columbia University Libraries. Special thanks are due the Trustees of the Libraries for the use of their materials in this essay; and to Mr. Kenneth A. Lohf, Librarian of Special Collections, for xeroxes and photographs. I am also grateful to the late Henry Rogers Benjamin, and especially to Gladys Benjamin Goddard, grandson and granddaughter of Park Benjamin.

Henry Rogers Benjamin and William Evarts Benjamin, Park Benjamin's sons, fortunately had preserved a considerable portion of Benjamin's business correspondence in the library.

[5]Obituaries in the New York *Times* and New York *Tribune*, 14 September 1864. For a more detailed account of Benjamin's earliest connection with the *New-England Magazine* see my 'Hawthorne, Park Benjamin, and S. G. Goodrich: A Three-Cornered Imbroglio', *The Nathaniel Hawthorne Journal*, I (1971), 83–112.

of the aesthetic principles of Longinus, and an appreciative analysis of the critical philosophy of A. W. von Schlegel. These articles have been pointed to—but not identified—by William Charvat, who called the Bryant essay 'perhaps the period's only good analysis of the function of the lyric. . . . As a statement of the ground upon which "common sense" criticism and mystical poetry can meet, it is the most important critical document of the period.'[6]

On becoming Boston editor in 1836 of the *American Monthly Magazine*, then conducted from New York by Charles Fenno Hoffman, Benjamin merged with it his *New-England Magazine*, which had come to the end of the road as an independent organ.[7] This merger, like the earlier union with the *American Monthly Review*, was one more link in Benjamin's cherished scheme of establishing a literary journal which would be truly representative of a national viewpoint. It was a hope also shared by Hoffman; and it seemed close to realization when Robert Montgomery Bird joined them as Philadelphia editor. Bird, who needed more money than the $500 a year offered him,[8] shortly afterwards withdrew and was succeeded by R. M. Walsh, editor of the Philadelphia *American Quarterly Review*, which Benjamin had tried unsuccessfully to resuscitate from the rigor mortis induced by the reactionary misrule of its poetry editor, Dr. James McHenry. In the *Quarterly*'s last year of life Walsh got rid of McHenry, and Benjamin persuaded him to run a series of articles dealing appreciatively with the English romanticists, himself contributing important pieces on Shelley[9] and the English sonnets.

But as Hoffman reminded Dr. Bird, the greatest obstacle to the creation of a national magazine was, first of all, the sectionalism 'which more or less pervades every part of our country';[10] and, secondly,

---

[6]William Charvat, *The Origins of American Critical Thought: 1810–1830* (New York: A. S. Barnes, 1961), pp. 197–98. For Benjamin's articles see *American Monthly Review*, I (January 1832) 20–23; I (April 1832), 296–304; III (July 1833), 1–14; IV (December 1833), 463–80.

[7]See Benjamin's valedictory remarks 'To the Readers and Correspondents of the New-England Magazine', IX (December 1835).

[8]Curtis Dahl, *Robert Montgomery Bird* (New York: Twayne Publishers, 1963). Bird's engagement was announced by Benjamin in the Boston *Morning Courier* and *Evening Transcript* of 2 March 1837.

[9]*American Quarterly Review*, XIX (June 1836), 257–87. These writings are discussed but not identified in Julia Power, 'Shelley in America', (University of Nebraska) *University Studies*, XL (1940), 72–86.

[10]Hoffman to Bird, 2 and 9 February, 18 March, 11 August 1837, in the University of Pennsylvania Library.

the unfavorable position in which American magazines were placed in competition with the British quarterlies by their low rate of payment. In the new prospectus Benjamin prepared for the combined journals, the editors took note of the fact that the most popular of the British magazines then circulating in the United States—the *Quarterly*, the *Edinburgh Review*, and Campbell's *New Monthly*—had 5,000 to 6,000 subscribers each, while native publications had to scrape along on a third of that figure. 'With the exception of those whom Fortune has placed beyond the necessity of exertion,' Benjamin had said in his last number of the *New-England Magazine,*

there are no authors by profession. The efforts of American writers are, for the most part, made in hours of leisure, set aside from the time devoted to their regular business. When a poor man has attempted to live by authorship, he has been compelled to seek a resource from poverty as an instructor, or a lecturer, or in some other mindwearing employment. . . . It [the *Magazine*] has presented, from month to month . . . the best papers from writers who were generously content with a very inadequate remuneration [one dollar a page]. Authors of celebrity, whose books are sure of popular reward, are vainly solicited to waste their efforts in the pages of a monthly magazine. Could the American publishers afford, like the English, to pay handsomely for articles, we should soon see our journals assuming a different character, and vieing successfully with the best transatlantic productions. As the case stands, it is unfair to make comparisons.

With the one exception of the *North American Review,* which had always enjoyed the solid backing of New England Whiggery with a circulation of 4,000, none of the *American Monthly*'s contemporaries were in a very robust condition financially. The *American Quarterly* had just succumbed, after seven years under conservative management. The *Southern Literary Messenger,* which had to be subsidized from time to time out of its publisher's own pocket, managed to hang on until the advent of the Civil War only because, except for Poe's brief term as editor, the publisher himself did all the work of printing and getting out the magazine. The *Knickerbocker* lived through three decades with an aura of false prosperity emanating from its jaunty editor's reputation as a *bon vivant* and foppish dresser. The friends of Lewis Gaylord Clark—Irving, Cooper, and Bryant among them— got together to consider ways of keeping Clark out of bankruptcy. Being above bamboozling, the 'big three' were promptly paid, but, according to Lawrance Thompson,[11] Clark retained most of the magazine's profits and paid his authors only when they threatened to quit him. In fact Longfellow, the *Knickerbocker*'s largest contributor, who 'had not the heart to press him', was kept waiting three years for payments always tearfully promised, but never paid in full.

Examples of editorial impecuniosity could be multiplied endlessly, but only two more of rather particular interest bear repeating in this discussion: Evert A. Duyckinck's *Literary World,* and J. G. Cogswell's *New York Review.* The *World* during most of its six years of life (1847–53) was the top-ranking journal in the field, but a complete failure as a commercial enterprise. Cogswell put his readers on notice, in 1841, that the *New York Review* was doomed unless it could command better support.[12] It folded after two more issues. And Cogswell departed for Europe to buy books for the library John Jacob Astor had presented to the city of New York, becoming its first director.

Cogswell had taken over the *New York Review* from its founders, Caleb S. Henry, a professor of religious philosophy at New York University, and the Reverend Francis L. Hawks, rector of St. Thomas's and later an Episcopal bishop. Soon after his arrival in the city, Benjamin met Henry, who offered him a partnership in the *Review* as reader and business manager.[13] The twenty-one-year-old Evert Duyckinck made his literary debut in this magazine with a group of articles on 'Old English Literature': the second number in the series, devoted to the religious poet George Herbert, drew from Benjamin the complaint that he found it impossible to read Duyckinck's small, cramped handwriting.[14] But though he remained an occasional contributor, and was himself an ardent Episcopalian, Benjamin probably found the position of third partner in a journal wholly committed to the religious viewpoint too limited in scope for his journalistic ambitions. He seems to have remained in his post for only two issues, leaving to devote more time to the fading *American*

[11]Lawrance Thompson, 'Longfellow Sells *The Spanish Student*', *American Literature,* VI (May 1934), 141–49.

[12]*New York Review,* VIII (April 1841), 541–42.

[13]Benjamin to Charles Sumner, 9 September 1837, in the Sumner Papers at the Houghton Library, Harvard University; a copy is in the Park Benjamin Collection. See also Greeley's publication of the *New York Review*'s prospectus in the *New-Yorker,* 31 December 1837, p. 655.

[14]Benjamin to E. A. Duyckinck, ca. July–August 1837, in the Duyckinck Collection, New York Public Library. This is Benjamin's first communication to Duyckinck.

Monthly, and to take a salaried position as literary editor of Horace Greeley's *New-Yorker.*

Benjamin kept the *American Monthly* alive one year longer than Hoffman had been able to do, but in the aftermath of the 1837 economic collapse which shook the nation on its foundations, not even his resourceful energies could save it. The educated reading public was simply not yet large enough to support a magazine of high literary quality in competition with the *North American Review* and the British quarterlies. The rise of the newspapers was already at hand, and meanwhile the taste for popular entertainment was satisfied by the annuals and 'penny dreadfuls'. Only such a publication as George Pope Morris's and Nathaniel Parker Willis's *New York Mirror*—which was not a magazine but a newspaper—with its gossipy, pseudo-literary veneer, its sentimental pap and spurious, snobbish claim of being 'the organ of the upper ten-thousand', could hold its own over the years as a money-maker. Such broadly based magazines as *Graham's* and *Godey's,* aimed at the nonliterary middle-class public and each with a circulation upwards of 20,000, would play a conspicuous part in raising standards by attracting to their columns, with substantial payments guaranteed, the foremost writers of the day. But it was not until the advent of *Harper's New Monthly Magazine* in 1850, with an initial circulation of 7,500 which in the next ten years rose to 200,000, would there be a popularly supported 'quality' magazine. The *New Monthly* owed its unprecedented success to the fact that it was aimed at the plain people rather than 'at philosophers and poets', as was Duyckinck's *Literary World* and its predecessor *Arcturus* (which relied heavily on foreign reprints).[15]

So Park Benjamin, with his acute sense for the prevailing currents of literary commerce, joined presently with Rufus Wilmot Griswold, that quirky, slippery fraud who had a finger in so many literary and journalistic pies, to launch what he termed a 'Brobdignag' popular weekly, *Brother Jonathan,* and a 'Lilliput' penny daily, the *Evening Tattler.*

[15]Perry Miller, *The Raven and the Whale* (New York: Harcourt, Brace, 1956), pp. 314–15, contains the most comprehensive discussion of magazine policies and backstage feuding. See also F. L. Mott, *A History of American Magazines: 1740–1850* (New York: Appleton, 1930) and *1850–1865* (Cambridge: Harvard University Press, 1938). Brantz Mayer's *Commerce, Literature, and Art: A Discourse Delivered at the Dedication of the Baltimore Athenæum, October 23, 1848* (Baltimore: J. Murphy, 1848) is an interesting presentation of mercantile support for literature and art by a close friend of Benjamin's.

Benjamin had left Greeley after two months, was begged back, and might have continued in association with a man he both respected and liked had he been able to overcome Greeley's 'singular, constitutional, and incurable inability to conduct business.'[16] Although the proprietor of the *New-Yorker* toiled in his shop from early morning till past midnight, wearing himself down to a vegetarian ghost—it was hopeless. Greeley lamented to a former assistant, O. A. Bowe, that he couldn't 'get rid of the Yorker', there were no takers—'O that it was at the bottom of the sea!'[17] Benjamin once came to the rescue with a loan of $575,[18] which presumably was repaid, but could never persuade his employer to abandon the fatal system of accepting subscriptions on credit which was costing the paper about $1,200 a year. Greeley moreover objected to paid articles in newspaper columns, a prejudice he retained until 1841 when he founded the *Tribune*, with T. J. McElrath as business manager.[19] Unfortunate in his aspirations as a poet, Greeley probably resented Benjamin's poking fun at his muse: 'Thunder and lightning, Horace, you don't call *that* poetry!' 'Not if you say so, Park,' acidly rejoined the wilted songbird.[20] Benjamin's improvements in the paper's appearance with wider margins and line spacing, his reorganization of the front page separating literary matter from news and business reporting, etc., may have been a further source of friction. Greeley confided to Bowe, 'I am sick of Park (sub rosa)';[21] and later gossiped to Griswold that Epes Sargent,

[16]James Parton, *Life of Horace Greeley* (New York: Mason Brothers, 1855), pp. 170–71. In Merle M. Hoover's biography, *Park Benjamin: Poet and Editor* (New York: Columbia University Press, 1948), Benjamin is misrepresented as a novice serving an apprenticeship under Greeley. The exact opposite was the case. Although he never acknowledged any indebtedness to Benjamin, to whom he seemed to have taken a dislike, Greeley learned from him much about the practical side of newspaper editing. Mr. Hoover was unaware of the extent of Benjamin's previous editorial experience.

[17]Greeley to Bowe, ca. 14 December 1839, in the Greeley Papers at the New York Public Library.

[18]Benjamin to Lafayette S. Foster, 29 August [1839], in the Park Benjamin Collection.

[19]Glyndon E. Van Deusen, *Horace Greeley: Nineteenth-Century Crusader* (Philadelphia: University of Pennsylvania Press, 1953), p. 52.

[20]Van Deusen, *Horace Greeley*, pp. 429 f.

[21]Greeley to Bowe, 8 September 1839 and 21 January 1940, in the Greeley Papers. Greeley to Griswold, 20 February 1841, in the Boston Public Library. See also W. M. Griswold, ed., *Passages from Correspondence and Other Papers of Rufus Wilmot Griswold* (Cambridge, Mass., 1898), p. 58; and Willis to Sargent, 29 December 1840, in the Massachusetts Historical Society.

Benjamin's old friend and classmate assisting him on the *New World*, had been 'poked out' of that paper. And again to Bowe, that Griswold was 'driven out.' This was probably Griswold's version of the case. But Griswold never had any financial investment in the *New World*, and according to a hostile letter of N. P. Willis to Epes Sargent (29 December 1840), it seems quite evident that Sargent also did not.

In response to the growing demand for up-to-the-minute news, the *Tattler* filled the need for a noonday publication. As stated in its announcement, the morning papers were all put to press before the arrival of the daily mails, and the evening editions at too late an hour to make the current news of value to the man of business. So successful was the *Tattler* that five days after the first issue, its weekly compendium the *Brother Jonathan* made its appearance in a blaze of advertising superlatives – 13 July 1839 – selling for six cents. Benjamin was determined to make the paper both readable and popular. Its editorials were timely and well written; its résumé of business news came not only from all parts of the country, but also from Europe by the latest boats. But its literary material was the main feature, some of it scissored but the rest from what was then a surprising number of original sources – testimony to Benjamin's wide acquaintance with authors.

Benjamin kept his name off the masthead, probably playing safe until assured of success before cutting loose from the *New-Yorker*. But word of his association with the new venture soon leaked out, and he neither confirmed nor denied it. Meanwhile, he and Griswold were not getting along with their publisher, James Gregg Wilson. So one October morning they walked out of Wilson's office and around the corner into the printing shop of Jonas Winchester, Greeley's former partner in the *New-Yorker*, and formed a new team with Winchester as owner-publisher of the *Evening Signal* and the *New World*. This development caused an incredulous stir along Ann Street, then 'publishers' row', which traveled as far as the University of Vermont where young Henry Jarvis Raymond, who eighteen years later was to become the founder of the *New York Times*, was a student. Raymond, then an admirer of Benjamin, wrote Griswold, a native of Vermont whom he had known as editor of the Vergennes *Vermonter:* 'What the deuce . . . put it into the heads of you and Benjamin to cast your own bantling, the youngest . . . the smartest of your children, upon the parish, and actually to commence so deadly a warfare upon it, I am at a loss to imagine.' Raymond had been afraid that any new paper, however well conducted, could not possibly 'strike the public so ex-

Office of the New World,

New York, 1841.

Dear Sir: We beg leave to place before you a prospectus of the New World, or rather a brief synopsis of its leading features, character and design, and to ask for it your particular attention, believing that you cannot fail to approve, cordially, the manner in which this Journal is conducted, and to extend to it your influence and support.

THE NEW WORLD.

EDITED BY PARK BENJAMIN.

This is a Journal of popular Literature, Science, Arts and News, and is supplied with original and selected articles by the first living writers of Great Britain and America. It was established in October, 1839, and so great has been its success, that, in less than two years, the circulation has attained to very nearly TWENTY-FIVE THOUSAND COPIES PER WEEK—a number larger than that of any other publication in this country or Europe. We have always given the latest and most popular works of the best authors IN ADVANCE OF ANY OTHER PRINT, by purchasing the proof-sheets at great expense; and we have made such arrangements abroad as to secure the receipt of early copies of all new works, so as to put it out of the power of any other publication to compete with us in laying them before the public. These arrangements have involved the expenditure of many thousands of dollars; and although the NEW WORLD is now considered as the best and most comprehensive newspaper in the United States, yet in the freshness, variety, and sterling character of its contents, it cannot hereafter be equalled by any other sheet.

In addition to what we have already done, we have engaged an artist of eminent talents to devote his whole time to embellishments for the NEW WORLD, which will hereafter, as it has done since the commencement of the present volume, give two or more exquisite ENGRAVINGS ON WOOD in each number, thus adding greatly to the value of our paper to every class of the community. These ENGRAVINGS will be chosen from the most pleasing subjects, or designed to illustrate the works which are published in its columns, and will themselves be worth more than the price of subscription.

The Department of INTELLIGENCE receives the most particular attention. We have an excellent correspondent resident in London, and we take especial care to make a weekly summary of all domestic news of interest. Moreover, we are always anxious to print all new discoveries and advances in science and art. No class of readers is neglected by us. For the seriously inclined, we publish original and selected discourses by eminent divines: for the farmer, accounts of agricultural improvements: for the gay lady, we give records of the latest fashions: to the lovers of music, a new, beautiful, and costly piece is presented occasionally: even children are not overlooked, and many an article is presented for their especial entertainment.

The NEW WORLD studiously avoids all party politics; and is conducted on principles of the strictest morality. No profane or improper jest, no vulgar allusion, no irreligious sentiment is allowed to soil its pages. Reverence of God and respect to man govern it always. The rule of the Editor is never to publish a line which he would hesitate to read aloud in the hearing of virtuous and intelligent females. Thus the NEW WORLD is made an unexceptionable Family Newspaper, and it is earnestly recommended to the regard of every friend of a pure literature, as well as of correct morals and the public good.

The splendid story of Military Life entitled "CHARLES O'MALLEY, THE IRISH DRAGOON," giving a vivid description of the Peninsular War under Wellington, during the occupation of Spain and Portugal by the French, is published in the NEW WORLD, and is without question the most humorous, graphic and popular story of the day, and which no one can read except with intense interest and delight.

The Third Volume of the QUARTO form of the NEW WORLD commenced on the third of July last, when it was much enlarged, and four columns given on each page, instead of three, making sixty-four columns of choice reading, without any increase in the price. New Volumes will always begin on the 1st of July and 1st of January, making two in each year, of 416 pages each, to which a handsome title-page and a copious index are given.

Terms of Subscription.—THREE DOLLARS for one year, or FIVE DOLLARS for two years—payable invariably in advance. All new subscribers will receive, gratis, the first volume of Charles O'Malley and two extra numbers of the second volume—which brings the story up to the commencement of the New Enlarged Volume of the New World on the 1st July. The bookstore price of the first volume of Charles O'Malley alone is three dollars—for which sum that popular work and the New World for one year are given! ANY PERSON WHO WILL PROCURE FIVE NEW SUBSCRIBERS, AND REMIT THEREFOR $15 IN CURRENT FUNDS FREE OF POSTAGE, SHALL RECEIVE A FREE COPY FOR ONE YEAR.

The Third Volume was commenced with a surplus edition which was considered amply sufficient to supply back numbers to all new subscribers during the six months, yet so rapidly are they called for that we do not expect to be able to furnish them but a month or two longer. Those, therefore, who are intending to subscribe, and wish all the numbers from the commencement of BARNABY RUDGE, by 'BOZ,' or the present volume, and CHARLES O'MALLEY, are requested to write without delay.

☞ Notes on all the solvent Banks of the State of New-York, the New-England States, New-Jersey, Pennsylvania, (except Erie,) Virginia, (except Wheeling,) Maryland, North and South Carolina, and all other States whose notes are less than five per cent. discount in this city, will be received at par in payment for subscriptions at $3 for one or $5 for two years. On all other Bank notes of the Union or Canada, the excess of discount over five per cent. will be deducted.

☞ All Postmasters are authorized to frank remittances to publishers in payment of subscriptions; and all letters must be either free or postpaid, or they will not be taken from the post-office. Specimen numbers sent to all who make the request free of expense.

We are desirous of increasing the number of our Subscribers in your place, and respectfully solicit your influence. If you can aid us in obtaining them, it would be esteemed a great favor. We feel convinced that our paper has only to be seen and known to insure the subscription of every lady and gentleman of taste, and of every lover of popular literature. By procuring for us five subscribers, you will be entitled to a free copy for one year, and we hope you will be induced to make an exertion for us to this extent. Address

J. Winchester,

PUBLISHER, 30 ANN STREET.

PLATE 2

actly to a T' as had the *Brother Jonathan*. And to supersede it, 'to turn the current of favor . . . into your own way, I thought was an attempt, which, for any other men than you two, would have been hopeless. But one might as well try to stop the devil himself, as either of you. . . . I honestly think "the New World" the handsomest, and the best paper of the kind I ever saw. Long may it wear the crown!'[22]

Longfellow thought so too, and ordered a subscription sent to his friend George W. Greene in Italy, where he was United States consul at Rome.[23] Clark, of the *Knickerbocker*, judged the second *New World* 'Leviathan' (4 March 1841), a special number measuring 33 by 50 inches filled with pictures, poems, stories, and reproductions of foreign works, 'remarkable for the beauty of its material, the neatness of its execution, the number and quality of its pictorial illustrations, and the immense amount and variety of its contents.'[24] It was indeed the constant boast of its chief editor, Park Benjamin, that the *New World* owed its 'handsome appearance' to the best quality of paper obtainable, the finest engravings, and its most up-to-date Napier press — a steam press which could print 3,000 sheets per hour.

A modern critic, William Charvat, has dismissed the *New World* as 'a crude, wretchedly printed mammoth newspaper',[25] a judgment evidently based on the paper's appearance in its last year of life (1844–45) when Winchester, who had overextended himself with his purchase of the rival *Brother Jonathan*, was using cheap paper and filling its columns with advertisements of quack medicines. Charvat seems not to have examined any of the earlier issues from the years when Benjamin had control. Benjamin quit the paper in March of 1844 because of disagreements arising from Winchester's letting it run down, but was called back at the end of the year in a vain attempt to rescue it and its new publisher, J. W. Judd, from bankruptcy. John Lothrop Motley, Benjamin's brother-in-law, remarked in a letter of 17 December 1844, that 'the paper depreciated most decidedly after you left it, and is already much improved.'[26]

[22]Raymond to Griswold, 31 October 1839, in the Raymond Papers, New York Public Library; and in Griswold, *Correspondence*, p. 21.

[23]2 January 1840; in Hilen, *Letters of Longfellow*, II, 202.

[24]*Knickerbocker*, XVII (March 1841), 270.

[25]*Literary Publishing in America: 1790–1850* (Philadelphia: University of Pennsylvania Press, 1959), p. 71.

[26]In the Park Benjamin Collection. For details of Benjamin's differences with Winchester, and Winchester's bankruptcy, see Benjamin's extensive correspondence with Brantz Mayer — especially his letter of 10 October and Mayer's reply of 15 October 1845, in the Maryland Historical Society.

In a farewell to the *New-Yorker* on 19 October 1839, Benjamin publicly acknowledged his role in the *Tattler–Brother Jonathan* enterprise:

It may not be unknown to many of the readers of this journal, that the subscriber has, during three months past, participated in the charge of a Lilliput daily sheet, called "The Evening Tattler," as well as of a Brobdignag weekly paper, issued under the English-derived title of "Brother Jonathan." With the last issue of the latter publication, his colleague and himself withdrew from a disagreeable connection, and, in conjunction with a publisher of discrimination and good sense, established "The Evening Signal," and its weekly compend, "The New World." A single week's experience in the conduct of these journals has convinced me that I cannot do equal justice to them and the New-Yorker. . . .

Then, after extolling at some length the character, industry, and integrity of Mr. Greeley, he counseled those who might look with favor upon his new undertaking not to desert the *New-Yorker,* but to take, 'as its companion, the New World.' However Greeley might grumble at his competitor's use of his Washington and Albany news, he was in return allowed the use of the *New World*'s superior type.[27] Benjamin's personal liking for and admiration of his former employer's newspaper vision remained constant, and when Moses Y. Beach of the New York *Sun* launched his campaign of coercion and bribery to crush the newly organized *Tribune,* Benjamin vigorously defended Greeley and his paper in the columns of the *Signal.* When the *Signal* was discontinued in the spring of 1841, having outlived its usefulness in relation to the *New World,* its subscription list was transferred to the *Tribune.*

The itinerant Griswold remained only about six weeks with the new outfit, departed for Boston, and returned to New York in the spring of 1840 as Greeley's new assistant on the *New-Yorker.* Wilson, who remained at the helm of the *Jonathan* and the *Evening Tattler,* answered a statement in another paper that Griswold had been one of the proprietors of the *Brother Jonathan* with a counter editorial: 'Mr. Griswold neither projected the Tattler nor the Brother Jonathan, nor devised any part of the plan upon which either has been conducted. Both of these papers were projected by one of the present proprie-

[27]H. J. Raymond to R. W. Griswold, 7 February 1841, in the Raymond Papers.

tors, and no part of the plan for conducting either was devised by Mr. Griswold, or by any person with whom he has been connected since the dissolution of his connection with them.'[28] This disclaimer was matched by another directed at Park Benjamin, denying that Benjamin was ever editor of the *Jonathan* or the *Tattler*, 'his connection having been short, and merely as a contributor.' The styling and general makeup of both papers, nevertheless, suggests that Benjamin's was undoubtedly the guiding hand. The nature of Griswold's participation, and what lay behind it, is still a mystery.

The 1840s was a time when newspaper editing was on an intensely personal basis, and every successful paper reflected in positive ink the colorful personality of its editor. Editors commonly engaged in fisticuffs, horsewhippings, even gun duelling, and the public at large delighted in such gladiatorial combat. Park Benjamin, lamed from poliomyelitis contracted in his infancy, necessarily clubbed his enemies with his pen—and clobber them he did. His first editorial in the *Signal* informed the public that Mr. Wilson was a disreputable character, and furthermore, that he was quite illiterate. Wilson's rejoinder resulted in a libel suit brought against the *Tattler* by Epes Sargent of the *New World* and the *Mirror*.[29] Readers loved it. They loved, too, Benjamin's boast that the *New World* was 'the largest, cheapest, and handsomest newspaper in the world'; it mattered not at all that the *Brother Jonathan*, its most formidable competitor, continued with the same boast originated by him. They particularly loved the oversized folios, the huge 'Leviathan' editions of both papers. Americans always have equated sheer size with virtue, distinction, and wealth; exaggeration remains to this day a facet of the national character.

The success of the *New World* was instantaneous and stunning— 'the wonder of the age.' On the first day of issue an edition of 10,000 copies was quickly exhausted, followed by another printing of 5,000. By April 1840, Benjamin claimed for it a general circulation of 25,000. And when the second Leviathan number appeared the next year, 'We print 35,000 copies', he gleefully informed Griswold. These figures are particularly impressive when compared with those of the

[28]Quoted from William Cullen Bryant II, 'The Brother Jonathan and Its Extra Novels: A Study of the Mammoth Literary Weeklies' (Columbia University M.A. thesis, June 1940), p. 7, n. 2. This thesis is by far the most able and valuable study of the mammoths.

[29]Ibid.

dailies, topped by the *Herald*'s 15,000 and 20,000 for the *Sun*.[30] Although used for advertising purposes, they are probably fairly reliable, for in addition to its New York City circulation the *New World* went all over the country, and had a large Canadian sale as well. Whatever the actual figure, Benjamin's biographer, Merle M. Hoover seems justified in crediting the paper with the largest circulation of any of the weeklies anywhere in the United States.

But the *Brother Jonathan* was not far behind, with 32,000 when N. P. Willis joined its staff in 1840.[31] 'The great beasts murder me', Greeley complained to Griswold on 20 February 1841.[32] 'Did you ever see more unmitigated humbugs?' Greeley, nevertheless, snatched a leaf from Benjamin's book when, given charge of the *Log Cabin*, a paper issued from Albany under Whig party auspices for use in the presidential campaign of 1840, he got out a 'Mammoth Extra Pictorial' containing woodcuts, songs, and political ballyhoo. It is interesting to note that James Parton, writing in 1855, lists among reasons for the failure of the *New-Yorker* its 'too intellectual and purist approach', and also the fact that it seldom praised and never puffed itself.[33] Benjamin had learned early the lesson that Greeley learned late, that Duyckinck would never learn, that was to become the rock Lowell and Poe both were shipwrecked on, and that in their day applied equally well to newspapers as to magazines: readers prized entertainment before instruction.

II

It yet remains to call attention to an earlier phase of Benjamin's experience which directly influenced his *New World* Library publications, Books for the People, and was a motivating factor as well in his literary agency service to authors, whether established or unknown: his early interest in book publishing. During his first years in Boston he became friendly with both members of the firm of Carter, Hendee, and this friendship led to their embarking jointly on a grandiose scheme of issuing a 'Library' of representative volumes chosen from the works of modern authors, both English and American. Park, then a young man of fortune, was the financial backer, and was to have editorial charge of the series which would not be limited to reprints

[30] Frederic Hudson, *Journalism in the United States* (New York: Harper, 1873), pp. 525–26. Hudson thought the mammoth figures were exaggerated.

[31] Bryant, 'The Brother Jonathan', p. 9.

[32] In the Griswold Papers, and in Griswold, *Correspondence*, p. 58.

[33] Parton, *Life of Horace Greeley*, pp. 170 f.

PLATE 3

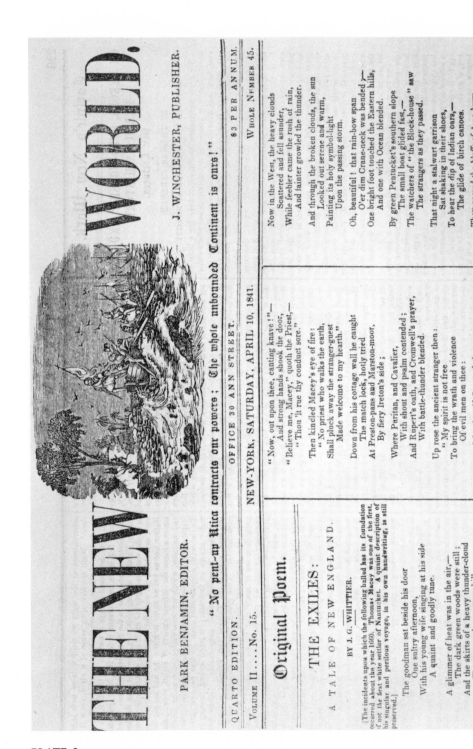

THE NEW WORLD.

PARK BENJAMIN, EDITOR.

J. WINCHESTER, PUBLISHER.

"No pent-up Utica contracts our powers; The whole unbounded Continent is ours!"

QUARTO EDITION.　　OFFICE 30 ANN STREET.　　$3 PER ANNUM.

VOLUME II...No. 15.　　NEW-YORK, SATURDAY, APRIL 10, 1841.　　WHOLE NUMBER 45.

Original Poem.

THE EXILES:

A TALE OF NEW ENGLAND.

BY J. G. WHITTIER.

[The incidents upon which the following ballad has its foundation occurred about the year 1660. Thomas Macey was one of the first, if not the first white settler of Nantucket. A quaint description of his singular and perilous voyage, in his own handwriting, is still preserved.]

The goodman sat beside his door
　　One sultry afternoon,
With his young wife singing at his side
　　A quaint and goodly tune.

A glimmer of heat was in the air,—
　　The dark green woods were still;
And the skirts of a heavy thunder-cloud
　　Hung over the western hill.

Black, thick, and vast, arose that cloud
　　Above the wilderness,
As some dark world from upper air
　　Were stooping over this.

"Now, out upon thee, canting knave!"—
　　And strong hands shook the door,
"Believe me, Macey," quoth the Priest,—
　　"Thou 'lt rue thy conduct sore."

Then kindled Macey's eye of fire:
　　"No priest who walks the earth,
Shall pluck away the stranger-guest
　　Made welcome to my hearth."

Down from his cottage wall he caught
　　The match lock, hotly tried
At Preston-pans and Marston-moor,
　　By fiery Ireton's side;

Where Puritan, and Cavalier,
　　With shout and psalm contended;
And Rupert's oath, and Cromwell's prayer,
　　With battle-thunder blended.

Up rose the ancient stranger then:
　　"My spirit is not free
To bring the wrath and violence
　　Of evil men on thee:

"And for thyself, I pray forbear,—
　　Bethink thee of thy Lord,
Who healed again the smitten ear,
　　And sheathed his follower's sword.

"I go, as to the slaughter led:

Now in the West, the heavy clouds
　　Scattered and fell asunder,
While feebler came the rush of rain,
　　And fainter growled the thunder.

And through the broken clouds, the sun
　　Looked out serene and warm,
Painting its holy symbol-light
　　Upon the passing storm.

Oh, beautiful! that rain-bow span
　　O'er dim Crane-neck was bended—
One bright foot touched the Eastern hills,
　　And one with Ocean blended.

By green Pentucket's southern slope
　　The small boat glided fast,—
The watchers of "the Block-house" saw
　　The strangers as they passed.

That night a stalwart garrison
　　Sat shaking in their shoes,—
To hear the dip of Indian oars,
　　The glide of birch canoes.

They passed the bluffs of Amesbury,
　　And saw the sunshine glow
Upon the Powwow's winding stream,
　　And on the hills of Po.

The fisher-wives of Salisbury,
　　[The men were all away,]

and translations but would include original works as well. Confidently anticipating 'the public favor', it was intended (he said in the general preface to Volume I) that these books should be valuable not only for the pure and good literature they would contain, 'but as favorable proofs of the taste, correctness, and beauty with which books may be published in this country.' The volumes then issuing from American publishing houses were, with few exceptions, wretched specimens of typography and binding. The improvement of format in periodical and book publishing was something always close to Benjamin's heart and on which he continually harped. 'They [the binders] shall not, if I can help it, mutilate this book', he admonished a later publishing associate, George Dearborn. 'I am aware that there will be some additional expense for altering the spacing of the lines: but, as the number of pages will be less—and I can indulge in superfluous paper—I am able to give more to the printing.'[34]

As intellectual interest circa 1830 had turned passionately toward the German romanticists, the choice to begin the series fell not unnaturally on Carlyle's *Life of Schiller*. Knowing little of the German language, though familiar with all of its great authors in translation, Benjamin wisely confided the editorship of the volume to Professor Charles Follen of Harvard, whose off-campus lectures on German literature had been very popular. Follen added his own editorial preface in which he carefully corrected the errors which had crept into the London edition, with its translation of English back into German. This had interesting results for Carlyle himself. Emerson had sent Carlyle, at his own request, 'if the thing is fit for making a present of', two copies of this first American edition of his book. A comparison leaves no doubt that Carlyle had Benjamin's text before him when he revised and reissued his *Life of Schiller* in 1845. Although the preface to the second edition opens with a blast against literary pirates, he corrected his original errors using Follen's preface and also employed Follen's translations.[35]

Holding fast to his belief that American authors should receive proper compensation for their work, Benjamin announced that the series as a whole would keep to that 'great objective'; he stated his conviction that 'the popular rage for temporary publications is declining . . . and with the improvement of taste, a demand for good literature is rising.' Authorship would 'soon become a distinct profes-

---

[34] 30 September 1836, in the Boston Public Library.
[35] Hoover, *Park Benjamin*, p. 40.

sion in this country as it is in Europe . . . an author is a laborer as worthy as any other of his hire. Let him demand it, then'—instead of merely enriching his bookseller, let him get something for himself. Events would prove him wrong on the first count, right on the second. 'If the subscriber', he said now, 'could be, however remotely and humbly, the cause of exalting, by one volume, the literature of the age, he would feel amply rewarded.'

The *Schiller* was favorably noticed in Boston and New York. Lewis Clark, who had gained control of the young *Knickerbocker* since the retirement of C. F. Hoffman as editor, wrote in the April 1834 number: 'The American literati are not less indebted to Mr. Benjamin for his spirited purpose of furnishing them with a series of works of the highest literary character, than for his happy selection of Schiller's biography as the commencing volume . . . and the beautiful form in which he has dressed it. . . . we hail this volume with pleasure, not alone for its individual excellence, but also that it omens happily of what we are in future to expect.'

No royalties were paid to Carlyle, but an allowance of some sort apparently was made to Follen. But the 'happy omen', like the idealism of the youthful editor-publisher, proved a mirage. Later in the *New World,* looking back, Benjamin sadly reflected on the outcome of his early venture which had in view 'not private emolument' but 'the benefit of authors'. Despite large sums spent on the plan conceived 'in former days of prosperity—to publish a library of original works, giving authors an ampler share in the profits', there were no profits. 'I wish that such excellent recommendations [as yours] would make people take the [*New-England*] Magazine', he wrote Lafayette Foster in 1835. 'Literature can never succeed till people do less business in this country. Perhaps you are not aware of the fact, but not one book out of a hundred . . . succeeds on account of its own merits.'[36]

He might more truly have said, 'until *more* business is done.' For as Stephen Longfellow told his son, the educated public possessed of the means to buy books, and of leisure to enjoy them, was not yet large enough to support a class of professional authors and keep the publishers in business.

III

The New York publishing house of George Dearborn & Co., publishers of the *American Monthly Magazine,* was for above half a decade

[36] In the Park Benjamin Collection.

a leading firm and one of the most active in the city on the Hudson, second perhaps only to the Harpers and the Appletons – a fact which might well recommend it for future scholarly investigation. Among their noteworthy publications were editions of Dryden's and Byron's works, the last-named containing also the letters and journals, and Thomas Moore's *Life of Lord Byron.* During the period of Benjamin's association as consultant and a partner in the firm, they issued a one-volume edition of Lamb's essays; a play by James Sheridan Knowles, *The Daughter;* a tragedy, *Ion,* by the English author and biographer of Charles Lamb, Thomas Noon Talfourd, then enjoying great vogue on both sides of the Atlantic; and *The New-York Book* of poems by Knickerbocker authors, a companion piece to the *Boston Book.* All of these were noticed, and of course praised, by Benjamin in the *American Monthly,* save for the *New-York Book* which was reviewed there at greater length by C. F. Hoffman.[37] Benjamin reported to his Harvard friend Charles Sumner (29 September 1837) that Lamb's essays had sold more than 2,000 copies to date, Talfourd 4,000.[38]

The publishing industry at that time was organized entirely on a local and regional basis, distribution in other areas being sometimes handled by individuals who acted as publishers' agents; more frequently, other publishing houses agreed to take a specified number of copies at the wholesaler's discount, the name of the distributing house to be added to the title page on the stipulation that the latter would not 'print on the copyright holder'. In other words, the publisher-distributor promised not to reprint the work in competition with the original publisher – a pledge not always observed.

On 15 November 1837 Park Benjamin wrote the Philadelphia publisher, Carey & Hart, that he had long desired George Dearborn & Co. to publish an edition of de Tocqueville's *Democracy in America.*[39] But 'in these times of depression in the book trade' it would be inadvisable even if the whole edition were instantly disposed of, were the usual credit of six months extended and the usual discount rate allowed. 'Printers and paper-makers, as you know, must have money.' Benjamin proposed to assume the undertaking privately, 'in response to repeated and urgent solicitations' made to him, if a portion of the

[37] *American Monthly Magazine,* VII (April 1836), 419; VIII (July 1836), 99; IX (January 1837), 87–89; (April 1837), 395–401; (May 1837), 314–18; X (January 1838), 95–104.

[38] In the Sumner Papers, Houghton Library, A copy of the letter is in the Park Benjamin Collection.

[39] In the Miscellaneous Papers, New York Public Library.

risk could be removed 'by a few of the first bookselling houses engaging to take a certain number of copies on the following terms:

15 per cent discount from the trade price for a note of 4 months. The elegant translation of Mr. [John] Keese occupies in the English edition two octavo volumes — price entire $7. I propose that it should be issued in one handsome volume royal octavo at $2 the single copy — $1.50 to the trade. They shall be charged to you at $1.25, provided you will give your note to my order for 100 or more @ 4 mos. and agree to take as many more as may be demanded by your customers on the same terms. No copies will be disposed of by Dearborn & Co. in the usual way of trade, as the undertaking is individual with me. Your acceptance of this proposition will be a strong inducement to publication.

In the same letter, he begged leave to correct an impression apparently held in regard to notices in the *American Monthly* of Philadelphia books. 'It has been my custom, when I did not receive a work from the publishers, to solicit a notice from some friend who had read it. As your Philadelphia works are rarely sent to me', notices obtained in this way were usually published without being read by the editor. 'It will always afford me much greater pleasure to praise than to criticize your own works or those of Carey, Lea and Blanchard. If your books are sent to the Monthly Magazine and New York Review they will be fairly and fully noticed.'

The outcome of these negotiations is not known, but it seems probable that the de Tocqueville was never published by Benjamin. For the Dearborn connection was to become in the next year a financial morass. In 1836 the firm's storage warehouse was destroyed by fire, and with it the August number of the *American Monthly*. Benjamin survived the brunt of these losses, but worse was to come. Unknown to him, the firm was already in a shaky financial condition when he entered into partnership with the debonair Mr. Dearborn, thereby making himself liable for the firm's debts. Later, writing again to Carey & Hart he said, referring to an earlier communication, 'Since that period, as I believe you are aware, I lost the whole of my property in consequence of the frauds and failures of Mr. George Dearborn.'[40] Benjamin himself narrowly escaped bankruptcy, saved only by the assistance of his old friend and boyhood guardian James Savage, of Boston, and a younger brother who loaned him large sums.

[40] 14 January 1839, in the University of Pennsylvania library.

IV

Dependent now for support upon his literary labors, 'I am desirous of rendering them in all honorable ways', he wrote. For *The Gift,* an annual published by Carey & Hart and edited by Miss Leslie, he offered a poetical sketch of fifty lines for $20, and a prose tale of twenty to thirty-five pages for $50 — 'either or both, as she pleases.' These prices compare with those received by Longfellow and Simms, though after the popular success of *Voices of the Night* Longfellow upped his price to $25 for a poem. Benjamin enjoyed writing for children; recalling his editorship of *Youth's Keepsake,* he proposed a short poem and a prose sketch at half the sums named for *The Violet,* another Carey & Hart publication. As to the old vexed question of copies of new works, he would be happy to announce titles in the *New-Yorker* and upon receipt of the books notice them 'fully and satisfactorily. My co-adjutor, Mr. Greeley, seemed to imagine that you withheld your most valuable books from that journal. I think however that the fault is with your agents here' in not forwarding the books promptly.

The success of Benjamin's newspaper ventures set him on the road to prosperity, at least for the time being. He had begun reprinting in the *Tattler* and *Brother Jonathan* parts of Dickens's *Nicholas Nickleby* and Samuel Warren's *Ten Thousand A Year,* an innovation at once so popular that he quickly resumed publication of these works in the *New World.* The universal custom of taking from other newspapers and periodicals the productions of native authors probably had its origin in the scarcity of good material; and, although such reprints usually were not paid for, no turpitude was associated with the practice, provided due acknowledgement was made to the original source. On the contrary, most authors accepted it as a sign of popularity, and often themselves took the initiative in resubmitting a poem or a story to numerous other outlets. Obviously, it was but one step from this to foreign reprintings. But Benjamin had begun his early serialization of whole novels, and when the question became entangled with that of international copyright, it was a different story. Then arose a horrendous hue and cry. Some persons, Benjamin among them, believed the visit of Charles Dickens to this country was motivated solely by the purpose of gaining for British authors, in alliance with their American brothers, what Parliament itself had refused them — property rights to their works in perpetuity.[41] Another group of American

---

[41] Thomas Noon Talfourd, English barrister, author, and M. P., introduced such a bill which failed of passage immediately, but which was enacted with restrictive amendments in 1842.

authors which included Bryant, Cooper, Poe, Hoffman, and Duyckinck and his inseparable incubus, Cornelius Mathews, felt themselves at a disadvantage in competition with foreign importations circulating widely in the mammoth press and costing nothing. This was the most common argument from the authors' side. Publishers, with the single exception of Wiley & Putnam, were solidly united against such a copyright measure. The opening gun on behalf of protection was let off at the Dickens dinner in New York when the 'unsinkable' Mathews interrupted to grab the floor and hold it, boring his captive audience for fifty-five minutes with his 'oracular jargon', and Mr. Dickens himself suffered some embarrassment.[42]

While the advocates of international copyright undoubtedly had the best of it on moral grounds, many other considerations were likewise involved. To judge the situation in publishing then by what has happened since is to distort the whole picture. We must keep in mind such extraneous developments as population growth, a phenomenal increase in national wealth, and the transition over the past 100 years from scarcity to a surplus economy in the various cultural branches as in industry itself. Publishers then were reluctant to invest in an author unless they could control the property they had helped to create and were assured a return. Henry C. Carey, leader of the opposition, was convinced that copyright would constitute not only an infringement of the right of Americans to read and enjoy English and European works by excessively raising production costs and retail prices, but also would create a serious obstacle to higher education and the intellectual development of the people. His *Letters on International Copyright* (1853) brought together some of the most effective arguments against the theories of the reformers. H. Hastings Weld, who followed Benjamin as editor on the *Brother Jonathan,* and who later assumed charge of the *Morning Dispatch,* maintained that the law would wreck the American publishing business in order to give to English authors wealth and protection they did not deserve; at the same time, it would set up a literary class in America consisting mainly of writers of little ability. This last charge contained much truth, for in a young country barely out of its swaddling clothes every other son or daughter of Yankee Doodle was filled with the idea that he could write a book as good as the next one; it took only ink and paper, and some hours stolen from sleep when the chores were done. 'The abundance of printed matter which is scattered broad cast over the land',

[42]Miller, *The Raven and the Whale,* p. 96.

Weld said, 'begets a taste for reading, which is altogether for the benefit of authors. Shut off the supply, and you will soon dry up the demand, and destroy the taste.'[43] Similarly, Park Benjamin editorialized in the *New World*. 'Men need not now be told', he wrote, 'that the enactment of laws is not always the surest means of effecting great objects':

If an American author can, without loss to himself, double or quadruple the number of his readers, he certainly must consider it a great point gained. This may be done by abolishing the law of copyright. Competition would oblige a publisher to sell his work at a moderate price, and to look for his remuneration to extensive sales. . . .

A free system would be quite as advantageous to English authors, as an international copyright. An exclusive right to publish their works in the United States would enhance the price, and diminish the sales, and consequently lessen the value of the copyright.[44]

And a writer in the *Democratic Review* (1843) who sounds remarkably like Benjamin flatly declared, 'The international copyright so eagerly clamored for is all a humbug.' He continued:

The fact is, that our publishers are just beginning to open their eyes to the truth that their real interest is not to raise their prices to the *maximum* that a book will tolerably stand, but to bring them down to the *minimum* which will yield a very small surplus on each volume above the mechanical cost of decent typography. . . . We shall no longer have the public limited to a little aristocracy of readers of one or two thousand. The average man will not have to wait his turn at the library, or borrow from his more fortunate friends the popular books of the day. They will be furnished cheaply enough for all to buy.[45]

While it is certainly true that development of the mammoth papers was made possible by the absence of an international copyright law, it is not true that their contents were wholly pirated. Both the *New*

[43] *Brother Jonathan* Quarto, I (19 February 1842), 212–14; Bryant, 'The Brother Jonathan', p. 33.

[44] *New World* Folio, V (20 August 1842), 126–27.

[45] Quoted from Bryant, 'The Brother Jonathan', p. 37. Horace Greeley's testimony to a committee of the House of Commons on the subject of international copyright (1851) is of interest. Hudson, *Journalism in the United States*, notes that 'Greeley at that time seems to have shifted over to Park Benjamin's view on copyright.'

World and the *Brother Jonathan,* its closest rival, were publishing material in quantity by native authors as often as original matter could be obtained, as well as the reprints from other sources. Benjamin could point with pride to the presence in his columns of such names as Longfellow, Whittier, Holmes, Epes Sargent, R. M. Bird, A. B. Street, and Simms; the dismal but immensely prestigious poet, J. G. Percival; the ubiquitous 'sweet singer of Hartford', Mrs. Sigourney; of plays and poems by J. S. Knowles and John Howard Payne, author of 'Home, Sweet Home'; and a few early specimens from an unknown printer signing himself 'W.W.'—Walter Whitman. Whitman had worked as a printer on the *New World* sometime in 1841, and he states in his Manuscript Notebook (No. 4) that he edited the rival *Tattler* in the summer of 1842.[46] He contributed to the *New World* a sentimental poem, 'The Punishment of Pride'; a juvenile story, 'The Child's Champion', which also seems to have had first publication there; and one other poem, 'Each Has His Grief', reprinted from the *Long Island Democrat,* where it was titled 'We All Shall Rest At Last'.[47] Other early verse by Whitman appeared in the *Brother Jonathan,* as did an article defending Dickens in the row over international copyright, 'Boz and Democracy'.[48] His most important contribution to the *New World* was his only novel, *Franklin Evans, or The Inebriate,* which appeared on 23 November 1842 as No. 34 in the series of *New World* 'Extras' — separate volumes issued in paperback and comprising Benjamin's most cherished undertaking, his Library of Books for the People. Some sixty-five titles, of which ten are of identifiably American authorship, were issued in this format between April 1842 and January 1844. In addition to novels, the series included biography, poetry, drama, a study of language-learning methods, and works on science, history, travel, and Arctic exploration. Whitman's novel was advertised in the *New World,* and probably also in other friendly papers, as '"A Tale of the Times. By a Popular American Author,"' to sell at 12½ cents single; ten copies for $1, or $8 per hundred. Let the orders be early.' A second advertisement appeared on 13 August 1843 with a different

[46]See Emory Holloway, ed., *The Uncollected Poetry and Prose of Walt Whitman* (New York: Peter Smith, 1932). Bryant, 'The Brother Jonathan', says Whitman may have worked on the *Tattler* as a printer, but he can find no evidence that the poet ever edited the paper.

[47]*New World,* III (18 December 1841), 394; (21 November 1841), 321–22; (20 November 1841), 1. Holloway is certain that although 'Written for the New World' is printed above 'The Punishment of Pride', the poem was written, if not published, as early as Whitman's teaching days.

[48]*Brother Jonathan,* 26 February 1842.

subtitle for the book: *Franklin Evans; or the Merchant's Clerk: A Tale of the Times.* This must have been for a later publication of the novel.

It was Benjamin's custom to solicit advertisements of featured *New World* editions among friendly editors like Weld of the *Morning Dispatch,* Clark of the *Knickerbocker,* and Roberts of the *Boston Notion;* he in turn reciprocated with pleasant notices of their publications. Although his fearless and often savage 'cutting up' of certain authors made him enemies, as did the abuse he aimed at the *Brother Jonathan* in their guerrilla warfare (to use the adjectival idiom of the time), he yet managed to keep on good terms with a surprising number of his editorial confreres. Such evidences of goodwill, so requisite to the system as it then operated, and his own scrupulous adherence to the rules of the game in his publishing relations are forcefully conveyed by his business correspondence. To Carey & Hart he wrote that he should consider it only fair compensation for books sent him to announce or advertise them in the *New World.* 'If you will send me some leaves or proof sheets of any new books in press I shall be happy to publish them . . . provided I can do so in advance of any other journal.'[49] And to George Roberts, editor-owner of the *Boston Notion* and prospective buyer of *The Evergreen*—an overflow repository of the *New World* now superseded by the 'Extras'—he said, 'As you print in your magazine pretty much the same matter as we publish, I have thought that you might take our list, unite it with yours and make a first-rate thing of it. . . . This arrangement would enable us to sustain each other's interest without infringing upon our own.'[50] Roberts promptly accepted the offer.

Benjamin's business acumen was particularly evident in making every edge cut. Nothing, however seemingly insignificant, which might possibly be turned to advantage, escaped him. We have an example of this attention to detail in his offer to release to Lea and Blanchard woodcuts used in a portion of *Barnaby Rudge,* then running serially in the *New World,* at a price of $3 each—'about half the cost.'[51] His cuts, he noted, were of superior workmanship to those in use by the Philadelphia firm which also was serializing Dickens's novel. He proposed further that

if you will supply us with copy of Barnaby Rudge so that we can publish it on the same day with yourselves—say on Saturday—I will have

[49] 11 January 1840, in the University of Chicago library.
[50] 13 April 1841, in the Park Benjamin Collection.
[51] 26 August 1841, in the Park Benjamin Collection.

the cuts engraved and sent on to you in full season. To do this, you will judge of the time, when the part should be forwarded to us. Thus you will save the whole cost of the engravings. If you will consider a moment, gentlemen, this arrangement must be advantageous, since we certainly cannot interfere with you more than the Tribune which publishes each part of Barnaby for a cent and sells it directly it reaches the city.

And next, asking pardon for a blunt question:

If you pay for Master Humphrey's Clock in advance, why do you suffer us all to publish it before you? Is it the delay in getting wood-cuts? If it be, I think the plan I propose will facilitate matters; send me the parts immediately on receiving them from the London [word left out], and I will have the cuts made in two days and sent to you — and I will pledge you my honor that the part shall not appear in the New World until the Saturday, when you advise us that your copy shall reach the city, — *provided that it shall not be previously received from England.* But whether it come from England or not, the cuts shall be yours; because it will be an advantage to us to publish with cuts on the same day that others publish without.

The extract of a new work *just published* by you was received and I cannot avail myself of your kindness. If you will forward occasionally extracts from *works in press,* I shall be happy to avail myself of them and do the book as much good as possible by notices.

Should you feel inclined to close with this offer concerning Barnaby Rudge, I would add that we should be glad, as a further return for this kindness on your part to publish your advertisements of any length in the New World.

However intense local rivalries might wax at times, it thus appears that the system in the main was one of mutual give-and-take. Benjamin's offer apparently was accepted, and the result on his part was a masterstroke, giving him the edge, temporarily, over his nearest competitors.

Benjamin's relations with Carey & Hart were especially cordial and close. This house continued lending him advance sheets of *The Loiterings of Arthur O'Leary,* a novel by Charles Lever then enjoying a fabulous popularity, and one other, *Tom Burke,* thus enabling him to get the jump on the *Brother Jonathan.*[52] On 7 April 1842 Benjamin wrote Carey & Hart that he had purchased and put to press Camp-

[52] Benjamin to Carey & Hart, 17 March 1843, in the University of Pennsylvania library.

bell's *The Pilgrim of Glencoe, and Other Poems* and Wordsworth's newest volume, intending to issue both 'in a neat and elegant style', facsimiles of the London editions.[53] They would each retail for $1. He wished to know how many copies Carey & Hart would take at 70 cents, paying him in a note to run three months, for the exclusive rights to the Philadelphia market. 'I hope you will not think it worth while to publish on my edition—and I shall be glad to put your names to the books'. He also inquired how many copies of the Campbell, ready in about ten days, they would take outright. The Wordsworth would come a month later. Then on the same day he addressed a similar inquiry to the Boston publisher, James Munroe, offering him the New England market and adding that he would publish directly through Wiley & Putnam or Appleton in New York. He had, he said, 'the exclusive copies received in this country.' We can not ascertain what the response was to these proposals, for ensuing events did not fulfill Benjamin's expectations. There is no evidence that he published Wordsworth's 'newest volume' in 1842; the Library of Congress, however, reports other editions of Wordsworth's poems issued in 1841–44.[54] It may be that when Benjamin learned of the 1841 editions, the plan was dropped. Nothing whatever has come to light concerning the Campbell, and it seems likely that neither was ever issued.

The copies purchased in London may have been sheets or advance proofs obtained through George Palmer Putnam, who had taken up residence there representing his firm, and who also acted as Benjamin's and Winchester's agent. While sending back newsletters to the paper, Putnam presumably concluded arrangements with English houses for publication of their works in America by the *New World* Publishing Co. Putnam and Benjamin were friends of long standing, Benjamin having been a boarder in the home of Putnam's 'Aunt Curtis' at 44 Bleecker Street, on first coming to New York. As a young publisher in that city, Putnam actively espoused the cause of international copyright. His son states that his father always 'declined to consider any suggestions for publishing the works of contemporary

[53] Benjamin to Carey & Hart, 7 April 1842; to James Munroe & Co., 17 March 1843, in the Boston Public Library.

[54] The recorded editions are as follows: New York: Leavitt & Allen, 1841, Preface by Henry Reed; New York: Geo. A. Leavitt, 1841, Preface by Henry Reed; Philadelphia: Hooker & Agnew, 1842; Philadelphia: J. Locken, 1844. John S. Van E. Kohn gave me generous help in an unsuccessful attempt to trace these books.

authors excepting under arrangements with those authors.'[55] With respect to foreign authors this can hardly have been true in every instance, although a letter from Benjamin dated 10 April 1841 indicates that Putnam did enter into negotiations with the London publishers for the *New World,* whenever possible, probably on an exchange basis since he was there to sell them American works. According to Luke M. White, 'some of the more conscientious publishers tried the scheme of making token payments to English authors and issuing their works in "authorized" editions.'[56]

By 1842 the publishing business had been transformed, in White's words, 'from a quiet, gentlemanly pursuit to a ruthless, cut-throat scramble after quick profits.' The mammoths of course had a prominent part in bringing about this change, though they were not the only sinners. An episode in the history of Carey & Hart casts interesting light on the buccaneering role of that eminently respectable firm. Having made arrangements with the English house of Longman & Co., they brought out in 1823 an American edition of *Quentin Durward.* 'We have the Game completely in our hands this time', they wrote their London agent. Within twenty-eight hours after arrival of Longman's copy, they had 1,500 copies struck off and ready to go. 'In two days we shall publish it here and in New York and the Pirates may print it as soon as they please. The opposition Edition will be out in forty-eight hours after they have one of our copies but we shall have . . . entire possession of the market in this country for a short time.' In 1836 the Philadelphia firm scored another triumph with Bulwer's *Rienzi,* having paid 'a handsome sum' to an English publisher for advance copy of this popular work. But the same sailing packet also brought copy to Harpers, and a wild race ensued. The Carey & Hart copy was rushed to Philadelphia, the sheets distributed among a dozen printers. The presses ran all night. At nine o'clock the next morning, the hardly dry sheets were delivered to the binders, who had cases already made. That same afternoon Abraham Hart hired every seat in the mail coach to New York. He sat in one, with 500 copies of *Rienzi* piled around him. The book went on sale next day in the New York bookstores, beating Harpers by one day.[57]

The sporting element in all of this no doubt appealed to the sensa-

[55] George Haven Putnam, *George Palmer Putnam: A Memoir* (New York & London: G. P. Putnam's Sons, 1912), pp. 31–34.
[56] Luke M. White, *Henry William Herbert and the American Publishing Scene: 1831–1858* (Newark: Cartaret Book Club, 1943), p. 14.
[57] Ibid., pp. 11–12.

tion-loving public as much as the dollars. Rival publishers hired fast boats to go out and meet the incoming vessels carrying the sought-after copy, which was then rushed through the presses and hawked on the streets by newsboys, often within a period of eighteen to twenty-four hours after reaching the city. From his carriage Park Benjamin would harangue the newsboys, coaching them on what to say: 'Arrival of the *Britannia!* Here's Dickens' *American Notes,* only a shilling!' Or, 'Bulwer's *Zanoni,* twenty-five cents!' To inspire the newsboys to greater zeal Benjamin served them hot coffee, provided them with warm gloves, and encouraged them to band together in a club which resembled an early version of a newsboys' union. When his play, *The Fiscal Agent,* was produced at the Park Theatre, he marched them through Ann Street down Broadway to the sound of fife and drum, carrying placards and crying, 'Hurrah for the Park Theatre!' Banners and streamers were hung from the *New World* office windows whenever a rival was scooped, bearing the legend, 'Io Triumphe! We have met the enemy and they are ours!' The *Brother Jonathan,* not to be outdone, staged an annual newsboys' parade at holiday time, and treated the boys to an elaborate Christmas dinner with toasts and all the trimmings.[58]

It was the age of P. T. Barnum, and such promotional antics designed to appeal to the masses were highly effective. On 19 March 1842, the editors of the *Brother Jonathan* announced plans for publishing a complete series of novels in Extra form, beginning with *Zanoni.* It would be the first appearance in four years of any work by the immensely popular Bulwer, and also the first of the Extras. But as matters turned out the *Brother Jonathan*'s announcement was premature, for their copy was delayed in crossing by bad weather. The Harpers meanwhile had obtained advance sheets of the English edition, and supposing their copy exclusive had released printings of early chapters to the *New World* for advertising purposes. To quote W. C. Bryant II, 'It was a stunning blow to the *Brother Jonathan* when their arch enemy was able to preface the first four chapters of the novel with the gleeful caption, "Glorious Victory!", accompanied by the taunt:

The NEW WORLD HAS PURCHASED AT GREAT EXPENSE and ALONE RECEIVED from England . . . proof sheets of a new

---

[58] Hoover, *Park Benjamin*, p. 141; Bryant, 'The Brother Jonathan', pp. 45–46. Bryant finds that, considering their hasty manufacture, these Extra publications are 'marvels of typography'.

novel. . . . Our stupid contemporary, the Brother Jonathan has for some weeks past been causing to be advertised throughout the country that it would "on or about the first of April," begin publishing certain "extras," the first of which should contain "Zanoni." If it should, it will be indebted to the New World — by stealing from which it has obtained pretty much all that was decent in its columns these two years past.'[59]

In a counterblast the *Brother Jonathan* termed this boast 'characteristic mendacity', assured its readers that the *New World* was merely the beneficiary of a custom observed by all book publishers who gave advance sheets to newspapers to publicize their forthcoming editions, and reaffirmed its intention of publishing *Zanoni* complete. With patent hypocrisy, Benjamin was charged with 'buying' the newsboys. His *Fiscal Agent* was labeled a mishmash of stale jokes and 'old stock', his poetry held up to ridicule, and his character and reputation in general splattered with mud. By the next steamer each of the rivals received copy for the book, the later chapters of the *New World*'s copy acquired through Putnam at what Benjamin termed 'great expense'. An article in the paper claimed that Harpers had first sold the serial rights to the *New World* and then decided to publish the book after the first few chapters had appeared there.[60] Both Extras appeared on the same day, 4 April. Bryant has remarked that one would have needed a stopwatch to determine who won the race, for they could not have been more than a few hours apart.

Accurate figures are not now available, but Bryant figured that the combined circulation of the *Zanoni* Extras must have approached 100,000. The *Brother Jonathan* claimed that its first issue went through four editions, over 33,000 copies, in less than two months; 12,000 copies were sold by the *New World* in less than three days. Harpers then entered the field with a standard two-volume edition selling at twenty-five cents the volume.

'We are doing great things with our books for the People', Benjamin boasted to an unnamed correspondent. 'Harper and Brothers have just set themselves in array against us, but I think we shall come off conquerors.'[61] The brothers retaliated, however, by reneging on

[59] *New World* Quarto, IV (19 March 1842), 192; 'Newspaper Quackery', *Brother Jonathan* Quarto, I, 353–54.

[60] 'Book Publishers and the New World Press', *New World* Quarto, VI (22 April 1843), 476.

[61] 14 November 1842, in the Henry E. Huntington Library. See Eugene Exman, *The Brothers Harper* (New York: Harper & Row, 1965), pp. 124–25. Benjamin's poems remained uncollected until 1948.

what appears to have been an oral agreement to publish their competitor's collected poems. This action was a bitter blow to Benjamin, and insofar as he is remembered at all today, it must be counted among the reasons he is known only as a quarrelsome editor and literary pirate who waged war against the publishing establishment.

The Harpers held almost a monopoly of the popular book business in New York. Their Family Library, begun in 1830, was followed the next year by the Library of Select Novels—two- and three-volume works in simple cloth bindings which sold for fifty cents a volume. The novels, their most popular item, grew to a total of 615 titles, mostly foreign works. The Family Library had about 150 titles of nonfiction, but 'new works did not find their way into the popular library editions until they had enjoyed a comfortable run at fat prices.' A few other publishers had experimented cautiously with cheap books: Curry & Co., C. S. Francis, and Israel Post, all of New York. They followed the weekly serialization plan adopted in 1835 for Carey's Library of Choice Literature, which was soon discontinued on account of high postal rates.

Benjamin's relations with the brothers, up to this time, had been extremely cordial. Beginning with the *New-England Magazine* he continually praised their books, and in an editorial in the *New World*— 13 February 1841—he came to their defense after an ill-informed, sectarian attack by a Boston reviewer in the Unitarian *Christian Examiner.* 'In New York and at the West and South', he said,

the reputation of this firm is deservedly high. No business firm in this city is in better credit; and no publishers are ranked with them— they stand alone. They never publish an unsuccessful work; the reason of this is, all their undertakings are based on a sound judgement. . . . We hope that this plan of presenting short memoirs, well prepared by competent hands, of the most distinguished writers of the language, with specimens of their productions, will be persevered in; it is excellent, and cannot fail to meet the warm approval of all impartial critics. If the Harpers will harken to our words, they will go on publishing cheap books that the poor may read as well as the rich; and they will add many volumes to the Family and District School Libraries of just such books as they have lately issued.

Such a panegyric must have thawed even the hearts of the four gentlemen of Cliff Street. But *Zanoni,* selling for 12½ cents, abruptly changed all that; and contrary to the impression given by Eugene Exman in his history of the firm, the brothers entered upon their new course not as pathfinders, but rather as followers of the beaten path. 'The journals talk of this plan [Bulwer's *Pelham* for twenty-five cents] as if it were new', Benjamin wrote.[62] 'Twenty-five cent editions are at least as old as [Samuel] Parker's Waverly novels, advertised for years past', and noticed by the very journals who now proclaim the discovery.

This plan, as they pleasantly observe, may "use up" the mammoths. . . . We promise duly to advertise the moment we are in a fair way of "being done for."

We are sorry the publishers do not like what we have done, but the milk is spilled. . . . The community, however, owes us a debt of gratitude for reducing the prices of works of light literature to the means of the poorest classes. We have begun a great literary revolution, which will result in enlarging the understandings of the masses. It is truly democratic — utterly subversive of that intellectual aristocracy which has hitherto controlled the energies of the nation. . . . But what will it lead to? . . . The public will undoubtedly inquire — Why, if you can give us novels so cheaply, do you not lower the price of historical, biographical, and scientific books? . . . Moreover, it may occur to some impertinent individuals to inquire — Why, gentlemen, have you put off selling cheaply until the present juncture? . . . How does it happen that you did not hit upon this generous plan prior to the efforts of the "mammoth sheets" — efforts which have had such brilliant success?

Benjamin has with justice been called 'the father of cheap publication in the United States.'[63] For he was certainly the prime mover and shaker in that 'beginning of a new era, the commencement of an entire revolution in the book publishing business' he had earlier foretold.[64] It should be understood, however, that it was the combined influence of the mammoth press as a whole which shook the publishing world with an impact unequaled before or since. Yet the mammoths passed quickly from the scene, the zenith of their achievement lasting only about two years. In the summer of 1843, due to the agitation of the friends of international copyright, postal regulations were altered, subjecting the mammoths to the higher rates for periodicals. Benjamin's argument that the *New World* was a newspaper, not a magazine, was disallowed; and that winter, when Parliament acted

[62] *New World* Folio, V (13 August 1842), 111.
[63] Hudson, *Journalism in the United States*, p. 589.
[64] *New World* Quarto, IV (9 April 1842), 242.

to protect British authors against foreign reprints, the paper was shut out of Canada. But while these developments contributed minimally to the early demise of the mammoths, the truth is that by 1844–45 they had outlived their usefulness. The 'revolution' begun by them was continued when the publishing establishment woke up to the fact that there were profits to be reaped by increasing their sales volume while cutting retail prices and production costs. A mushrooming of paperback editions all over the country was the consequence of this awakening. Despite periodic setbacks, the movement has never ceased.

V

It is hardly surprising, considering his past record, to find Benjamin's views on the subject of American authors at odds with the opinion expressed by Carey & Hart to W. G. Simms, in 1841. 'We do not see much hope in the future for the American writer in light literature—as a matter of profit it might well be abandoned.'[65] Soon after parting company with Jonas Winchester, Benjamin wrote the Philadelphia publishers, 'I learn from Mr. Kirkland that he has accepted your offer to publish a volume of Mrs. Kirkland's (Mary Clavers) Tales. I advised him to do so conscientiously—although from a previous proposition made by us he considered us entitled to the right.'[66] The new firm of Benjamin & Young had bought the plates.

Caroline Kirkland—who used the pen name of Mary Clavers— 'that unread and under-rated pioneer realist', one modern critic calls her, was the author of several successful novels, 'an original and talented professional' who ought not to be 'lumped with the horde of women scribblers.'[67] She had been a valuable contributor to the Carey & Hart annual, The Gift, but abandoned her writing career to become headmistress of a girl's school, because, as she said, 'my mantua-maker makes a much better living by her skill at the needle than I could do by the pen.' She politely declined to write for the stingy pay offered by Carey & Hart. But anxious to lure her back, Abraham Hart, in competition with Benjamin, apparently increased

[65]White, Henry William Herbert, p. 13.

[66]21 May 1844, in the Park Benjamin Collection. At the top the letter is marked 'Confidential'.

[67]James B. Stronks, 'Author Rejects Publisher', Bulletin of the New York Public Library, LXIV (October 1960), 548–50. See also Kirkland to Carey & Hart, 19 May 1844, in the Kirkland Letters, New York Public Library.

his offer to republish two of her works, *A New Home: Who'll Follow?* and *Forest Life.* Benjamin felt that she would do better with a well-established house 'such as yours', than with a young firm like his own. 'I have always been of the opinion', he added, 'that a cheap (say 50 cts) edition of each of Mrs. Kirkland's works would have a very large sale. They have been almost suppressed by the high prices at which they are published $1 and $1.25.'

To his friend in Baltimore, Brantz Mayer, whose book *Mexico As It Was and Is* had been a Winchester–*New World* publication, Benjamin had given similar advice — which was not followed.[68] Jonas Winchester mishandled the book by overpricing it, and it did not sell. Benjamin had urged publication 'in numbers' — paperback installments — selling at twenty-five cents each. In this way, he felt, the book would have made money. For it was next to impossible 'for so *cheap* a publisher as Winchester' — 'cheap' in the sense of poor quality — to sell any considerable number of books for $2. 'I knew this and he should have had the honesty to say as much when I so strenuously insisted on its appearing in numbers.' But Mayer had been 'taken' by Winchester: 'the result has been exactly what I foretold.' Now he urged Mayer to a settlement with Winchester. '*If you could manage to get the plates out of his hands* (since one half the property in them is already yours) *and place them with a responsible publisher so that a new edition in numbers could appear in the autumn, something might yet result.* Get the plates . . . and I could manage the rest for you.' But Mayer, a poor businessman, dallied until book and plates both were impounded by Winchester's creditors.

Benjamin began his literary agency very likely with a double purpose in mind: it could be made (1) a feeder for the *New World* and its satellite publications, and (2) a pipeline of goodwill among authors, book publishers, and magazine editors in his wide-ranging enterprises. It has never been sufficiently understood that Benjamin's was the guiding brain of the Winchester–*New World* conglomerate.

It seems quite evident that no charge was made for his placement services at this early stage. He had to accept a good deal of the dross along with the gold, but the literary mart has always been an institution of such flexible extremes that there is room for all kinds, especially the dross. And Benjamin was a kindly man whose hand was often in his pocket to assist brother poets and fellow scriveners in

[68] 23 June 1844, in the Mayer Papers, Maryland Historical Society.

need. Fully half of his clientele was unknown, indigent, and of the female 'horde'—like the unnamed lady 'of fine talents' for whom he appealed to the editor of the *Album* (another of the annuals): 'She is poor, and if you will send me an order for *three dollars* . . . it will be doing an act of kindness.'[69] He added that other prose contributions could be obtained from her at very reasonable rates. 'A new contributor of rare promise' was referred to George Rex Graham, the prosperous owner-publisher of *Graham's Magazine*.[70] With her the writer had no acquaintance, but had 'formed a high estimate of her powers' in correspondence. She would write for a moderate sum. He enclosed 'an admirable story and two poems—if you will send her $20 she will be gratified, as she is like the most of us unfortunate votaries of the muse, poor.'

Much of Benjamin's agency correspondence was with Graham, or his subordinates. 'Of the pieces I sent you', he said in a letter of 2 September 1842, 'all are paid for except $10 to Mrs. [Frances] Osgood, and $20 to [Alfred B.] Street for a poem, and I will refer those authors to you.'[71] To Griswold, who followed Poe as editor of *Graham's*, he wrote asking payment of '$2 or $3' to Mrs. Shea for a book review. 'I promised to send it to you recommending it for place among your critical notices in the magazine.[72] The poetry enclosed was by Mrs. Eliza Pratt, 'for which I think she asks nothing.' He had also promised to put in a word for Miss Jane Lomax, 'whose papers you may have noticed in the Southern Literary Messenger, and who wishes to write for Mr. Graham.' His next communication to Griswold introduced 'a translator, Mr. Hudson, whom I commend to your especial regards.'[73] Hudson's translations of Balzac and other French authors were considered 'excellent' by Benjamin, himself a master of the French language. Earlier in July of 1842 he had written Graham submitting manuscripts from Mrs. Wells, with the usual commendation.[74] If Graham liked the pieces well enough to make her an offer, she would be pleased to hear from him at the address given.

To D. Appleton & Co. he sent a novel, *Eveline Neville*, that he

---

[69] 15 June 1843, in the Park Benjamin Collection.
[70] 24 March 1842, in the Simon Gratz Collection, Pennsylvania Historical Society.
[71] In the Simon Gratz Collection.
[72] 27 June 1842, in the Simon Gratz Collection.
[73] 11 July 1842, in the Park Benjamin Collection.
[74] 1 July 1842, in the Simon Gratz Collection.

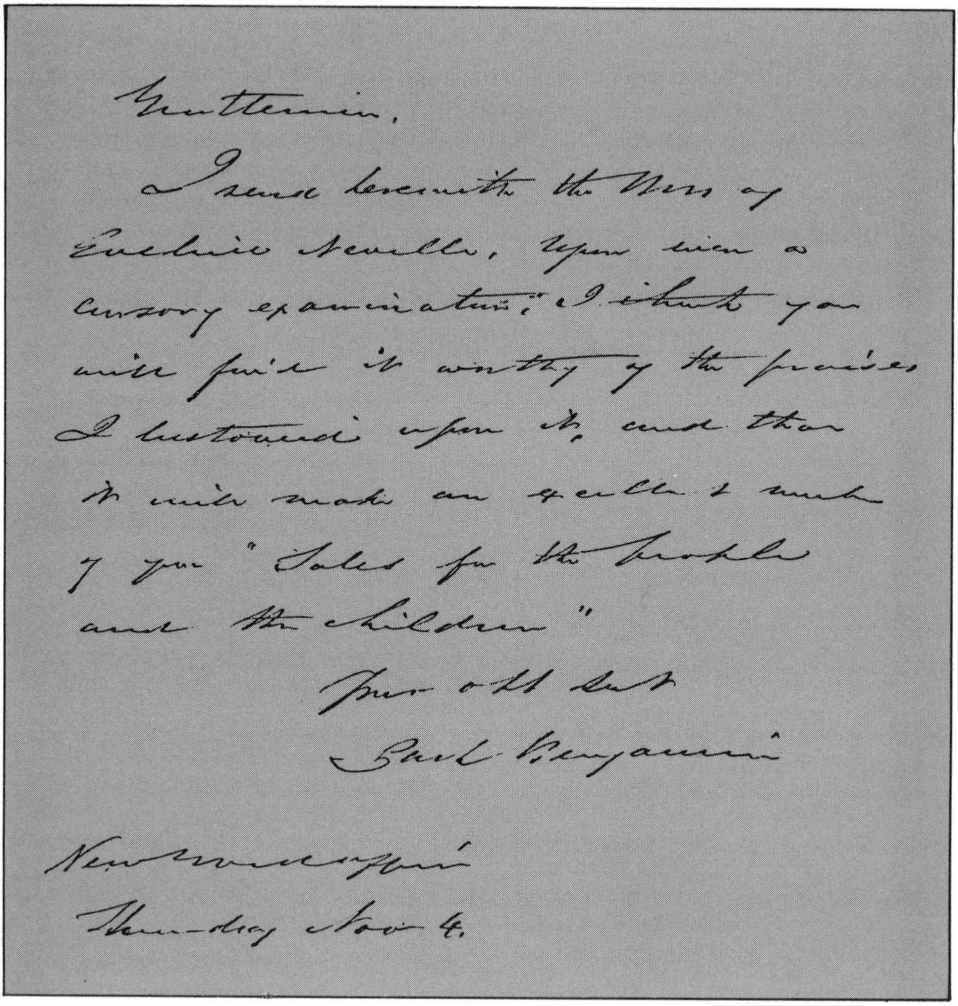
Gentlemen,

I send herewith the Mss of Eveline Neville. Upon even a cursory examination, I think you will find it worthy of the praises I bestowed upon it, and that it will make an excellent number of your "Tales for the people and the children"

Your obt Servt

Park Benjamin

New World Office

Thursday Nov 4.

PLATE 4

thought would make 'an excellent number for your "Tales for the people and the children".'[75] A manuscript which may have been the

[75] 4 November [1841], in the Park Benjamin Collection. The letter is on a sheet carrying a prospectus of the *New World* dated 1841. Lyle Wright, *American Fiction: 1774–1850*, attributes *Eveline Neville; or, 'A Spirit, Yet a Woman Too'* to Mrs. Martha Featon Hunter, carrying over Johnson's identification. Burgess, Stringer & Co., of New York, published the book in 1845.

work of Simms was returned to James Lawson, 'with many thanks for your courtesy in complying with my request so readily.'[76] Benjamin had handed this to the editor of *The Artist*, 'but as he does not think the story adapted exactly to a *Ladies* Magazine, and will not even *promise* to pay, I return it.' Carey & Hart's advertisement of anatomical plates for an American edition of a work by Dr. Jones Quain and Erasmus Wilson, of London, appeared in the *New World* 'this week' (5 November 1842).[77] The charge for a one-column insertion was $25, half-column $15, and subsequent insertions the same. Three 'excellent' offerings by Mrs. Seba Smith went to Carey & Hart in March of 1841: 'a story for The Gift and a story and a poem for your Child's annual.[78] Benjamin asked $35 or $40 for Mrs. Smith (he later referred to the Seba Smiths, husband and wife, as 'those coroners!') — 'her name is very popular.' New works seldom came to him from Carey & Hart. But he noticed them, and now suggested an advertisement in the *New World*. He had been running their ad in *The Signal* without charge.

The most illustrious and among the earliest of Benjamin's agency clients was Henry W. Longfellow, who was also a personal friend. Exactly when and how they met is not clear, but it seems very likely that Benjamin, then editor-owner of the *New-England Magazine*, was one of the people Longfellow called on in March of 1835 when he spent some days in Boston on his way to Europe. For the *New-England Magazine* had earlier taken the lead in introducing the three young poets, Holmes, Whittier, and Longfellow, to the American public.[79] Between July 1831 (when its first issue appeared) and February 1833, six numbers of 'The Schoolmaster', which together compose the first version of the essays later rewritten and incorporated in *Outre-Mer*, had appeared in the *Magazine*. Some eleven poems also had first printing there, including the first of Longfellow's many translations; and a printed prose piece, 'Torquemada', never was published elsewhere. Acceptances of the 1831–32 pieces must have been made by young Edwin Buckingham, who died at sea early in the next

[76] 6 September 1842, in the Park Benjamin Collection.

[77] To Carey & Hart, 2 November [1842], in the Ford Collection, New York Public Library. A copy is in the Park Benjamin Collection. 5 November 1842, in the Autograph Collection, Vol. VI, Pennsylvania Historical Society.

[78] 7 March 1841, in the Pennsylvania Historical Society.

[79] See Carroll A. Wilson, *Thirteen American Author Collections of the Nineteenth Century*, ed. Jean C. S. Wilson and David A. Randall (New York: Charles Scribner's Sons, 1950), pp. 182–84.

year, but those of 1833 probably went through Park Benjamin, then assisting the elder Buckingham in carrying on the *Magazine.*

Fulfilling a promise given Benjamin to send something from abroad,[80] or to write something on his return, Longfellow dispatched a poem, 'Hailing a Portuguese Man-of-War', which appeared in the December number — the last issue before the *New-England Magazine* ceased publication independently. They were not in touch again for some while afterwards. 'He seems to be much my friend, and I like him,' Longfellow wrote in his journal, 'all save his confounded positive way about everything.'[81] Benjamin never belonged to the celebrated 'Five of Aces Club' — later increased to six when Dr. Howe joined them — which did not begin its weekly bull sessions until after he had left Boston. But he knew them all, more-or-less intimately: his Harvard roommate George Hillard, whose name he gave to one of his sons; Hillard's law partner Charles Sumner, a class behind Benjamin in college and law school; C. C. Felton, the jovial professor of Greek; Longfellow; Howe; and Henry Cleveland, a frail, scholarly young man, translator of Sallust, who contributed a two-part article on 'The Origin and Progress of Music' to Volume IX of the *New-England Magazine* (July 1835). Whenever Benjamin journeyed to Boston, which he occasionally did for speaking engagements or other business, there were merry supper parties in his rooms at the Albion Hotel.[82]

Some sixteen letters that Benjamin wrote to Longfellow were preserved, evidently by the poet himself, taped in a bundle and marked with his hand; they are all deposited with the Longfellow Manuscripts at the Houghton Library. Letter No. 2 (27 November 1839) speaks of a favorable reply from Benjamin's friend Frederick A. P. Barnard, then a professor at the University of Alabama (later president of Columbia University), to whom Benjamin had written asking Barnard's help in securing for Longfellow's younger brother Sam a professorship there which had been offered to Longfellow himself. Prospects for young Samuel Longfellow looked bright for a while, but nothing materialized. In the same letter he says that W. W.

[80] To Longfellow, 2 February 1837, in the Longfellow Manuscripts, Houghton Library, Harvard University. This poem is not in Wilson.

[81] Samuel Longfellow, *Life and Letters of Henry Wadsworth Longfellow* (Boston: Houghton, Mifflin, 1893), I, 343. The entry is dated 3 January 1840. Although the name is blanked out, the reference clearly is to Benjamin.

[82] Summer to 'Dear Hal' [Henry Cleveland], [Spring 1842?], in the Berg Collection, New York Public Library.

Snowden, editor of the *Ladies' Companion*, begs him to persuade Longfellow to send occasional poems to that magazine. 'You will smile at my being the medium of this petition, after the conversation we had two years ago.' But having repeatedly criticized the *Companion* as 'a magazine for milliners', Benjamin now was anxious to do Snowden this favor. The magazine had improved of late; Longfellow might venture to publish there in 'respectable company', which included Fitz-Greene Halleck. And Snowden offered $15 for a poem, a nice little sum to have at your command every month in New York. Longfellow evidently thought so too, writing Epes Sargent to whom he was then offering 'The Wreck of the Hesperus' for the *Mirror*—one of the papers that Sargent was connected with—'If you don't like it, send it to Mr. Snowden who has just made me a liberal offer.'[83] Sargent gave the ballad to Benjamin, whose joy was great. 'Your ballad . . . is grand', he said, in a rush of majestic hyperbole:

Enclosed are $25 (the sum you mentioned) for it, *paid by the proprietors of the New World* in which glorious paper it will resplendently corruscate on Saturday next. "The Mirror," quotha! the Mirror cant pay for its printing. "The Ladies Companion!" Unworthy of *such* a poem . . . . But only to think of Harry Longfellow's magnificent Ballad keeping company with Stanzas by Miss Snooks and Lines on an Infant by Sarah Smirk and "To Julia Ann by Mortimer Montague." No! of all American journals the New World is alone worthy to contain "The Wreck of the Hesperus." . . . Your good and beautiful letter about Allston's poems appears in the Signal of today. You will also see it in the next New World. Do you wish to do a kindness to a brother poet? Richard H. Dana is in town and about to commence a course of literary lectures at the Stuyvesant Institute. Write me something in praise of his fine lyricisms, his reputation in New England and the great treat New Yorkers are to have from his lectures.[84]

But a squall was blowing up. Once more appeasing Snowden, Benjamin sold him 'Excelsior' for $15. George Hillard, through whom it came, had neglected to inform Benjamin that Longfellow asked $25. Sam Ward, the self-appointed guardian of Longfellow's interests, both literary and financial, now disclosed that O'Sullivan of the *Democratic Review* had offered him $20 for the poem. Ward had seen Benjamin only once, but took a violent dislike to him after

[83] See Hilen, *Letters of Longfellow*, II, 204–5.
[84] 7 January 1840.

some unfavorable remarks appeared in the *New-Yorker* concerning Ward's delivery and publication of his anniversary address commemorating the Battle of Long Island; in the writer's view, Ward was neither an orator nor a historian.[85] Benjamin had an equally low opinion of his essay on 'Modern French Romance' in the *New York Review* (April 1839), which he judged superficial, unworthy of the journal in which it appeared, and an example of ' "the fuddled style," each sentence seems to have taken a drop too much.' 'I need not say, that I disagree with Benjamin about the Art. on Romance', Longfellow replied, but he too thought Ward might have gone deeper into the subject of literature considered as an art. Much concerned over the business of 'Excelsior' Benjamin apologized to Longfellow, regretting his mistake; he admitted he had 'gratified' Snowden by letting him have the poem, although he had wanted it badly for the *New World*.[86] Would Longfellow send him his last two pieces? He should have $20 each for short poems—'and, putting them with this—provided they were such as you would sell for $15—we shall "strike a fair average." ' In future, he thought he could get $20 for all others —'at least what will amount to that sum each—supposing an occasional one goes for $15 and another for $25.'

Longfellow sent Benjamin an inscribed copy of *Voices of the Night* as a Christmas present, though 'quite mortified', he told Ward, 'at the fate of Excelsior. I would rather have paid the price of it, than have it go into that milk-pan, the Ladies' Companion.'[87] Snowden had said he would publish the poem immediately, but instead, he kept it nearly three months. Longfellow, disgusted, meanwhile let it appear in *Voices;* whereupon Snowden, enraged, demanded either the substitution of another piece or his money back. 'He had no manner of right to make such a demand,' Benjamin told Longfellow, 'because I told him or his editor expressly that you intended . . . to publish a volume in which "Excelsior" would be included.'[88] Knowing the character of the man, he advised Longfellow by no means to substitute another poem, but to allow himself to refund the money and have no further communication with Snowden. 'He will make a mess about it in his devilish magazine—or the newspapers and we shall both stand a chance of being copiously abused.' Which was

[85] *New-Yorker,* VII (6 April 1839), 33; (13 April 1839), 61.

[86] 2 November 1841.

[87] Longfellow to Ward, 24 October 1841, in Hilen, *Letters of Longfellow,* II, 336.

[88] 14 November 1841.

exactly what happened. Snowden had an arrangement with Benjamin whereby the latter was to furnish him a short poem and a prose piece, every month, for $20—or $30 if a notice of the *Companion* in Benjamin's own papers, or elsewhere, was included in the deal. Benjamin had been imprudent enough to write that it would be 'money well spent'; and to suggest besides, 'What say you to a first-rate notice in the Boston Evening Post?' So then the amiable Snowden took this correspondence to the *Brother Jonathan;* and they, Wilson & Co., still burning over the business of *Zanoni,* gleefully pounced upon the opportunity to do Benjamin an ill turn. In an article ironically captioned 'Impartial Criticism',[89] they published Benjamin's letters—but not their own—word-for-word, editorializing to make him out a liar and a blackmailer. According to the article, he had not lived up to his part of the agreement, but 'extorted' money for two months, after which 'Mr. Snowden stopped the supplies'. When this bilge was loosed into the runnels of Manhattan, the editor of the Boston *Post* issued a prompt and somewhat supererogatory denial that he had ever authorized Mr. Benjamin to write such a notice.

It was further insinuated that Benjamin's literary agency was a scheme to enrich himself, that he retained 'a commission' on sale of authors' works! Benjamin stated, in rebuttal, that he was paid by Snowden not to publish, but to write. And what was wrong with that? Was not the writer entitled to his pay, as much as any laborer?

This is all that is known of Benjamin's reaction to the public chastisement administered by the *Brother Jonathan* in connection with this incident. But one suspects that, given his ability to dispense abuse, he could also take it. He was probably more amused than intimidated, as was the case in Boston, long before, when the threats and squirmings of S. G. Goodrich—who did not like Benjamin's treatment of his ridiculous poems—failed to upset him. At any rate, he survived the 'stink'. He even survived the recognizable caricature of himself as 'Piddleton Bloater' (note the matching initials) addressing the newsboys' clubs, in a work of fiction purporting to be a novel—*The Career of Puffer Hopkins*—by that humorless humorist, Cornelius Mathews.[90]

Meanwhile, Longfellow's review of Wolfgang Menzel's *German*

[89] *Brother Jonathan*, 13 August 1842.

[90] H. K. Browne's ('Phiz') illustrations in the *Arcturus* edition of *Puffer Hopkins* includes one of 'Piddleton Bloater' holding up a mammoth sheet for the inspection of the newsboys. The likeness to Benjamin is evident in a comparison with his photograph. (The illustration is reproduced in Mott, *A History of American Magazines,* I, facing 360.)

Literature had appeared in three parts in the *New World*.[91] The article had originally been written for the *New York Review*, but Cogswell found that it clashed in substance with an article of his own and sent it to Park Benjamin. An abridged version appeared some time later in Cogswell's journal. Longfellow reported to Sam Ward — 17 September 1841 — that he had 'no sooner sealed and sent my last', enclosing a new poem, 'Endymion', 'than who should come in but Park Benjamin himself.' He expressed 'great grief' at what had been done, 'and to console him, I promised to write you, and cry "Stop that poem!"' Ward reluctantly complied, and 'Endymion' came out in the *New World* on 25 September.[92] But when Ward presently mixed up Longfellow's instructions concerning two other poems, 'God's Acre' and 'To the River Charles', saying he was sending the latter to O'Sullivan, Longfellow replied, 'I beg you to do no such thing. As Benjamin had the promise, he must have the poem. Moreover, he has made me a generous offer, and I think it ought to be met as generously, with the best pieces I have. He should certainly take precedence of O'Sullivan in this matter.' And in the next communication he remarked, 'Benjamin has probably been in some perplexity, between my negociations with him and yours.'[93] But matters became still more confused when Benjamin abruptly rejected 'The Goblet of Life' and 'To the River Charles', for two reasons, he said: 'we have entered into costly arrangements for a correspondence in England. The second is that I do not like the poems as well as many others you have written.'[94] 'The Goblet' accordingly went to G. R. Graham; 'The River Charles' somehow ended up in the *Ladies' Companion* and was also reprinted a week later in the *New World;* and O'Sullivan got 'God's Acre'. Confronted with this turnabout, one can only agree with Ward's remark that 'Park is a queer lark'.[95]

Benjamin had queried Graham in October, 'Would you like to have an occasional poem from Professor Longfellow? I think I could

[91] *New World* Folio, I (20 June, 27 June, and 4 July 1849).
[92] *New World* Folio, III (25 September 1841), 193.
[93] Hilen, *Letters of Longfellow*, II, 349–52, 14 and 17 November 1841. In Wilson, *Thirteen Author Collections*, the editors have wrongly attributed Ward's replies to these communications to Longfellow himself. Ward wrote the letters of 6, 10, and 11 November in the Longfellow Manuscripts.
[94] 4 December 1841, in Samuel Longfellow, *Life and Letters*, I, 408–9.
[95] *Graham's Magazine*, XXI (January 1842), 5; *New World*, IV (8 January 1842); *Ladies' Companion*, IV (1 January 1842); *Democratic Review*, IX (December 1841), 597. For Ward's remark see his letter of 22 November 1841, in the Houghton Library.

get him to write for you at \$20 — he asks \$25.'[96] Graham of course
was delighted, and Longfellow equally so with Benjamin's arrangements for a series of prose articles at \$50 each. The first of these
was a short piece on Heine. Longfellow thereafter became a regular
contributor to *Graham's Magazine*. But the most outstanding item received by Graham was the three-act play, *The Spanish Student*, on
which Longfellow staked large hopes of a lucrative financial return
that included stage production, and which was finally sold to Graham
after nine months of bickering and delay. When informed of Longfellow's plans for the play, Benjamin responded enthusiastically on
1 February 1842, 'Send me the first act as soon as you please'; and
he announced in the same letter 'an eternal settlement with the illustrious Snowden.'[97] He had bluntly told Snowden that Longfellow's name must be at once removed from his list of contributors,
and 'in his own beautifully expressive phraseology', that '"the name
had better be removed quietly."' It is impossible to believe, after
the hugger-mugger over 'Excelsior', that Benjamin could have given
'To the River Charles' to the publisher of the *Ladies' Companion*, but
the mystery of how Snowden got the poem remains unexplained.

It might have been better had Longfellow left the arrangements
for *The Spanish Student* in Benjamin's hands, instead of trying to deal
directly with Graham; as it was, his hesitations and misgivings gave
offense to the publisher and negotiations bogged down. The play
finally appeared in three installments in *Graham's*, in the September,
October, and November issues of 1842; it was first published complete in the *New World*, 5 November 1842.

VI

After his departure from the *New World* Benjamin engaged in
publishing in New York and Baltimore, first as a partner in the new
firm of Benjamin & Young, then with Farmer & Daggers, and lastly
with Taylor, Wilde & Co. From Baltimore he wrote A. L. Hart, 'I am
requested by Taylor, Wilde & Co. with which house I am connected
to . . . say that the edition of O'Donoghue sold for 12½ cents was not
printed by us, but by Collyer of New York, of whom Mr. Taylor had
generally engaged to take a certain No. of copies with his name and

[96] Benjamin to Graham, 19 October 1841, in the Boston Public Library.
Benjamin to Longfellow, 11 and 25 December 1841, and 7 January 1842;
in the Longfellow Manuscripts.
[97] *American Literature*, VI (May 1934), 141–49.

that of the house here in imprint.'[98] Taylor had not known, at the time, that Hart was going to publish the book. 'Our desire is to sell your books, not prevent the sale — and we should be glad if we could make any arrangements, by which, having them at a fair discount from wholesale price by the quantity, we could sell them to our agents generally.' Benjamin assured Hart that books sent to be reviewed by him and addressed to him personally as editor would be advertised and pushed. Taylor, Wilde & Co. 'would like to take a large quantity of books', receiving them in advance of others to supply the South and West, 'through the whole of which we are preparing to circulate advertising sheets by the hundreds of thousands.' And he repeated in closing, 'It is far from our wish, in establishing a printing and publishing concern, to interfere with other houses and especially your own.'

Benjamin had relinquished his financial interest in the *New World* for practically nothing in order to obtain a release from Winchester's creditors. In the sale of the firm's assets he and his partners were able to purchase the presses and entire stock of the *New World* Publishing Co. below cost. Yet these later ventures, for whatever reasons, were not successful. The *Western Continent,* the paper which he had gone to Baltimore to establish and edit, was launched with insufficient capital against his advice. Benjamin returned at the end of six months, dispirited and out-of-pocket, to face once more the grind and turmoil that was the lot of the newspaper editor in New York's Grub Street of the late 1840s. Although he lacked for neither ideas nor energy, good fortune eluded him. The precise answer to why Benjamin's talents brought him no lasting gain is not easily determined: possibly it was because he was finally unwilling to make the adjustments and compromises the times demanded, or perhaps it was because the competition was too tough, too cannibalistic, for a man with no other capital than his brains. 'I do not like this editing of the Metropolis', he confided to Alfred Street.[99] 'I receive, to be sure, a fair salary, but the associations about the place are disagreeable, and the proprietor suffers all kinds of twattlers to disgrace its columns.'

The *Literary World,* established with the backing of Wiley & Putnam, was in early infancy when Benjamin returned from Baltimore. In a long letter to Duyckinck[100] he expressed his pleasure in the young journal, with but one criticism: too much space was being given

[98] 19 November 1845, in the Park Benjamin Collection.
[99] 26 October 1849, in the Park Benjamin Collection.
[100] 18 March 1847, in the Duyckinck Collection.

to notices of foreign books. 'Do you not think that we are quite too colonial in our criticism?' And ought not a journal of such high character as the *Literary World* be more distinctly original? Would it not be better to omit extracts from newspapers, however good? These questions, for which he asked pardon, came from 'the real interest I take in your success.' Well aware of the difficulty of finding enough original matter of the various kinds needed, he nevertheless hoped to see Duyckinck strike a bolder posture by doing without selections, 'except such as are indispensable to a full, faithful record of what is passing everywhere in the world of art and letters.'

Such advice was probably lost on a man of Duyckinck's essentially timid disposition, but the call for something very like the modern *Publishers' Weekly* may have sounded less audacious. If the publishers know their own interest, Benjamin continued, they would advertise liberally. 'Now that the trade sales are about to take place, would it not be well for Mr. Wiley, at some meeting of the booksellers, to "move" that the Literary World be chosen as the organ of the trade, the repository of announcements, etc.? The Commercial Advertiser was once so chosen.'

The remainder of the letter, some two pages, was devoted to another proposal for 'a series of papers, written in a kindly and fostering spirit, on the living American writers — after the idea, not the manner, of Horne's Spirit of the Times.' Benjamin had often thought of getting to work on such a series himself, and he now offered his services to that end. Living in the country as he was then doing, he could afford to write for 'no extravagant sum' — less than was rightfully due the time and labor involved. Research must be extensive and thorough, every work of each author discussed should get a careful reading. He should commence with J. P. Kennedy, 'whom I know well — a noble, fine fellow, who is not appreciated at half his value.' And each paper should be a condensed memoir, both personal and literary, but a criticism as well, avoiding either eulogy or detraction. 'Such a series would excite an interest in the Literary World among the numerous friends of the authors, and yield a more abundant return in increase of circulation than the ablest reviews. You are the better judge, however, of the kind of articles calculated to elevate and enlarge the influence of your journal.' But Duyckinck, with his dislike of controversy, apparently did not warm up to the idea of publishing a series of papers devoted to living authors, fearful perhaps of igniting flare-ups and setting egos in opposition to one another.

After a second attempt at revival of the *New World* with Ross Wilk-

THE Subscriber continues his LITERARY AGENCY. Its object is to assist Authors. Manuscripts are received, and critically read. An opinion is then expressed as to their merits, and fitness for publication. For this careful perusal and opinion, a preliminary fee of $10 is always required, whether the work to be examined be short or long—except, indeed, where manuscripts are of great length, in which cases, $20 is charged: and it is to be expressly understood, that after giving orally or in writing, his candid judgment of a work, the subscriber has discharged his duty.

If the author subsequently so desires, the work will be submitted to any publishers with whom an arrangement is likely to be effected; but the subscriber cannot be responsible for the delay or neglect of publishers. The author after a work shall have passed into their hands, must look to them for its safe return; although the subscriber will always be happy to serve those writers, who may request his friendly aid in ascertaining the fate of their manuscripts, or in any final disposition of them they may wish to make.

Should the subscriber succeed in selling any work to a publisher, an additional fee is charged.

If the author, not being able to obtain publication otherwise, determines on the expense of bringing out his book on his own account, the subscriber will make the necessary arrangements for the printing and issuing of the work, inclusive of the correcting of the manuscripts, the reading of the proofs, &c. &c., for which labor, a proper charge, proportionate to the time and effort required, will be made.

ADDRESS,

PARK BENJAMIN,

47, 7th Avenue, New York City.

P. S. Remittances should be made in letters duly registered at the places where they are posted. Manuscripts should be forwarded either by Post or Express, and always prepaid. Postage stamps should be inclosed in every letter.

PLATE 5

inson as publisher ended in failure, Benjamin resumed his literary agency; his announcement left no doubt that it would in the future be conducted as a business enterprise. A reading fee of $10 would be charged for examining all work submitted, regardless of whether or not it was successfully disposed of. Criticism would be given if desired, and every effort would be made to find a buyer for manuscripts that showed merit. All postal charges must be prepaid. The prospectus further stated that since the subscriber was being more or less constantly solicited for critical advice and assistance in placing manuscripts by persons from all parts of the country, he would endeavor to perform these services to the best of his ability. Benjamin requested that the advertisement be run for several weeks in the *Literary World;* in return he would render Duyckinck 'some literary service'. Insertions were made in other papers as well: the *Tribune,* the New York *Post,* and probably William Leete Stone's *Commercial Advertiser.*

To what extent Benjamin's literary agency actually contributed to his livelihood when he had no salaried editorial position, no one knows. But considering his widespread popularity as a poet and essayist and the incessant publicity surrounding his name during the *New World* years, we can safely suppose that he was moderately successful — if not in the way of financial returns, at least in the personal satisfaction derived from benefiting the authors he served. One example of the intangible rewards reaped by the agent has come to light: a published novel dedicated to Park Benjamin by the grateful author.

In 1849 a young man from the North spent seven months as a tutor in the family of a wealthy North Carolina plantation owner. Scotch Hall, the Capehart plantation house, was situated on Albemarle Sound in southeastern Bertie County. During that period the Capeharts, accompanied by the tutor, passed the summer months at Nag's Head, a resort of wealthy planters on the North Carolina Outer Banks in the vicinity of Cape Hatteras and Kitty Hawk. The young man, who adopted the pseudonym of 'Gregory Seaworthy' — his real name was George Higby Throop — wrote a novel based on his experience in the South, laying the scene at Nag's Head and Scotch Hall. He gave his book the title *Nag's Head, or, Two Months Among "The Bankers",* adding the descriptive subtitle, *A Story of Sea-Shore Life and Manners.* A discrepancy between the publication date as given on the title page, 1850, and the copyright recording, 1851, leaves the actual date of publication uncertain; but Richard Walser, who has tracked down a number of North Carolina 'firsts', including this edition, suggests that the 1851 date is either an error 'or else the publisher had planned purposely to delay registering the book.'[101] Mr. Walser designates *Nag's Head* and Throop's second work of fiction as the first local color North Carolina novels. (John Pendleton Kennedy's Revolutionary novel, *Horse-Shoe Robinson*, was nonetheless the first to employ a partial North Carolina setting, Walser notes.) Throop's dedication to Park Benjamin reads:

My Dear Sir: — When, at the idle suggestion of a friend, I had whiled away some of the else unoccupied hours of a five months' passage homewards, by writing *a book*, you were pleased to pat the shy bantling encouragingly on the head, and to say a friendly word to the Publisher. May I, in acknowledgment of that kindness, present another, the youngest, to your Burchell-like[102] caresses, in the belief of its fewer imperfections, and with the conventional, but hearty, assurance that I am Yours, always, GREGORY SEAWORTHY, Merry Hill, Bertie Co., N.C.

Benjamin's encouragement seems to have led Throop to continue writing. He produced two more novels, *Bertie, or, Life in the Old Field: A Humorous Novel by Capt. Gregory Seaworthy;* and *Lynde Weiss, An Autobiography by Geo. H. Throop, Author of "Nag's Head," "Bertie," Etc., Etc.* The second of these, dedicated to the publisher A. Hart, has an author's preface in which is incorporated a letter of praise from Washington Irving, to whom Throop had sent a copy of *Nag's Head.* The last, *Lynde Weiss,* to which he signed his own name, was issued by the Philadelphia house of Lippincott, Grambo & Co. Benjamin may have seen the second novel, but it is unlikely that he read all three.

VII

A short while before the birth of *Nag's Head,* Benjamin was writing Carey & Hart about doing a translation of Chateaubriand's *Memmoires d'outre-tombe.*[103] He had undertaken it, 'and seeing your name on the title page of the French edition, issued at the Bureau du *"Courier des Etats Unis,"* it occurred to me that you would like to issue a carefully prepared . . . *English* translation.' He could obtain advance

[101] Richard Walser, 'North Carolina Literary Firsts', *North Carolina Libraries,* VII (June 1949), [1]–3.
[102] The reference is to Mr. Burchell, the benevolent, kindhearted protector in Goldsmith's *The Vicar of Wakefield.*
[103] 7 December 1848, in the Duyckinck Collection.

sheets if necessary. 'At all events, I will execute the task with care and diligence for what you may deem a reasonable compensation — say $1, for each printed French page.' He asked the favor of an early answer, having already been approached by 'certain parties here'; he would prefer having his translation published by Carey & Hart. Only one other edition had thus far been announced, that of Williams Brothers; 'but it will doubtless wear the shabby appearance of their other books and be translated hastily to be first in the market. This is, however, a library book which will be always in demand, and it has no such immediate interest that the public will not prefer to wait for a good edition, backed by a responsible name.' Since no further mention is made of this translation elsewhere in Benjamin's known correspondence, the conclusion is that Carey & Hart declined publication and the project was abandoned. Benjamin, however, continued to seek other ways to live by producing words rather than by editing them.

In the previous summer of 1848, he was married to a young lady who admired his poetry and had collected in a scrapbook as many of the poems as she could find.[104] Mary Brower Western, the daughter of a New York lawyer, was strongly sympathetic to her new husband's desire to escape from the suffocating thralldom of editorial labor. It was she who first suggested to him that he take up lecturing before lyceum groups as a profession. Emerson was earning a comfortable living by that means. Others among Benjamin's friends, Dr. Holmes, Edwin Percy Whipple, Greeley, the Reverend Henry Ward Beecher, were finding it a valuable and dependable way of adding to their incomes. Why not he?

The lyceum movement began in Connecticut, with the first lecture by Josiah Holbrook in 1826, and soon spread to other states.[105] With branches established in all of the major cities and towns of the eastern seaboard, the South and West, it swept the country and continued at high speed until the coming of the Civil War temporarily dried up the lecture market. Local groups had representation in the state organizations, and these in turn joined in the formation of the National American Lyceum Association for the dissemination of

[104] The wedding was on 8 May 1848. The collection, added to over the years and hand-copied in a bound volume by Mary Brower Benjamin, is known as the 'M. B. B. Collection', in the Park Benjamin Collection. It became the basis for identifying many of Benjamin's poems.

[105] See John F. Noffsinger, *Correspondence Schools, Lyceums, Chautauquas* (New York: Macmillan, 1926).

information on the arts, sciences, history, and public affairs. Owing to the immense popularity of the lectures, the movement became an important countrywide adjunct to adult education. The return to peace brought a revival of interest in the lyceums, but the educational aspect was increasingly minimized as the rise of material prosperity stimulated the demand for entertainment; the association gradually merged with the Chautauqua movement, which was devoted almost exclusively to entertainment.

Acting on his wife's suggestion, Benjamin severed his 'disagreeable' connection with the *Metropolis* at the end of a twelvemonth, and announced in a letter to the *Literary World*, dated 30 March 1851, that he was leaving the city to take up residence temporarily in Newport, Rhode Island, and was discontinuing his literary agency. 'In consequence of my numerous engagements as a public lecturer, I have no longer time to act for those who are disposing of their manuscripts, or who seek information on subjects of literary or artistic interest.' To persons at a distance who sent him subscriptions or sought advice on which literary journal they should subscribe to, he said, after declaring that he was no longer connected with any journal as editor, 'I earnestly recommend to all who are interested in the cause of Art or Letters, the *Literary World*, as a paper eminently worthy of their approbation and support.' In the same column, a paragraph just above Benjamin's signed letter points admiringly to one of his public appearances:

We have received from Mr. Winchester, the publisher, a copy of Park Benjamin's excellent poem delivered before the Mercantile Library Association, at their anniversary in November last. In the recital this poem was the most effective we have ever listened to on any occasion; and the audience testified their approbation by the warmest and most prolonged plaudits. The style is satirical, and the author was allowed little time for elaboration; but it abounds in pointed satire and vigorous lines, evincing a perfect mastery of the heroic verse, in which it is written.

Had he heeded Benjamin's earlier advice on omitting 'extracts', Duyckinck might have been saved some embarrassment caused by the foregoing sample. But, evidently wishing to laud Benjamin as an accomplished speaker in return for the latter's public endorsement of the *Literary World*, Duyckinck, or one of his assitants, apparently delved into the morgue for an appropriate item; the uncovered notice was nine years old. The poem referred to, 'Poetry: A Satire', had been

Four Lectures of Entertainment,

AT THE

MUSICAL FUND HALL.

Mr. PARK BENJAMIN

Will have the honor to deliver Four Lectures of Humor and Satire, on the Evenings of

TUESDAY, WEDNESDAY, FRIDAY & SATURDAY,

Of this Week, the 24th, 25th, 27th and 28th of this Month.

TUESDAY,

FASHION—A Humorous and Satirical Poem.

WEDNESDAY,

AMERICANISMS—Or traits of Character—a Discursive Excursion in Prose.

FRIDAY,

MONEY AND LOVE—A Humorous and Satirical Poem.

SATURDAY,

MATRIMONY—A Prose Lecture for Wives and Husbands—Maids and Bachelors.

☞ Lecture to commence at 8 o'clock. ☜

TICKETS FOR EACH LECTURE, - 25 CENTS

To be obtained at the Musical Fund Hall, and at the principal Music and Book Store.

Philadelphia, Washington House, January 23, 1854.

Brown Pr. Ledger Building

PLATE 6

delivered at Clinton Hall on the twenty-second anniversary of the founding of the Mercantile Library Association, 9 November 1842.

Benjamin met with remarkable success on the lyceum platform, and in the next ten-year period gave brilliant expression to his gift for satire in a series of 'lectures in verse', a form he developed using Pope's heroic couplet for mock-heroic effect. As a satirist he was then without equal on the American scene, and these now undeservedly forgotten pieces probably represent his most notable achievement as a poet. With his fine voice and dramatic delivery, he drew capacity audiences wherever he went. Fees, including expenses, were on a sliding scale, according to the size and resources of the local lyceums and the expected attendance. He would never lecture for less than $25, plus hotel and railroad expenses, and then only if a series could be arranged for in adjacent territory. The average figure was $40–50, but in the big cities such as Baltimore, Philadelphia, and Boston he asked $100 and got it. Sometimes he was entertained in the homes of his many friends along the route, but whenever he stayed in a hotel he always asked for a room on the ground floor—if there was no elevator—on account of his difficulty in climbing stairs on crutches. His itinerary covered the entire Pennsylvania—New York State—New England area up into Canada, extending south as far as Washington, and west to Detroit, Chicago, St. Louis, and as far as Duluth. In the capital city he usually lectured at the Smithsonian. Advertising space was solicited and paid for, either in cash or in contributions from his pen, in various New York papers, the *Tribune, Evening Post,* Morris's *Evening Mirror* and *Home Journal,* and James Watson Webb's *Courier and Enquirer;* and in such magazines as *Graham's, Putnam's, Harper's New Monthly,* and *Gleason's Pictorial.* In all of the towns and cities where he lectured, outside of New York, on-the-spot advertising was of course handled by the local lyceum bureaus, who issued handbills and got publicity into the local newspapers. In the latter years of his lecturing career, the advertisements often combined notices of his public appearances with others publicizing his literary agency.

The cataclysmic depression of 1857, only slightly less severe than the one of twenty years earlier, did enormous damage to the economy and caused the lecture market, in general, to shrink by a half. Brought on by reckless expansion in internal improvements, with a vast overbuilding of canals and railroads for the enrichment of stockholders, in combination with the opening up of the western lands to speculators, the panic had a catastrophic effect: banks once more sus-

Lectures and Literary Agency.

1863

The subscriber, having resumed his residence in New York, renews his offers of service as a Public Lecturer and Literary Agent.

LECTURES.

He has prepared and is preparing new lectures in prose and verse, adapted to popular audiences, and will deliver them on acceptable terms, at the invitation of Young Men's Associations, Lyceums, and Institutes throughout the country. He will also deliver addresses on anniversary occasions for Colleges, other Seminaries of Learning, and public bodies political and social.

LITERARY AGENCY.

The subscriber will continue his Literary Agency. Its object is to assist authors. Manuscripts are critically read. A candid opinion is given. They are then, if approved, recommended to publishers. For this opinion, whether favorable or adverse, an advance fee of ten dollars is required. This should be remitted by Mail or Express, together with manuscripts, prepaid. Letters of inquiry or asking advice should always cover a small fee, to compensate time and trouble in replies.

Address,

PARK BENJAMIN,

75 West 45th St., New York.

Park Benjamin Dec./63

PLATE 7

pended specie payments and hundreds of thousands of workingmen in the cities and factories were thrown out of employment, their families thereby rendered destitute. So Benjamin, once again, turned to his agency as a stopgap.

This time a preliminary reading fee of $10 was specified, regardless of length, but if the manuscripts examined were longer than average—a novel, for example—the fee was doubled. After reading and criticizing work submitted, the agent's task was fulfilled; if at the author's request he undertook placement, entering into negotiations with editors and publishers, an additional amount would be charged, proportionate to the time and effort involved. Also, a commission would be added to the fees charged when a work was sold.

The onset of the Civil War killed off what was left of the lecture market, and the agency as well. Benjamin made several abortive attempts to resume editorial work, then was reduced to selling real estate in Manhattan and uptown Washington Heights. He applied for a position in the New York Customs House, where Hoffman and Edward S. Gould before him had served; but the place was a nest of party factionalism and intrigue, and Benjamin's lifelong refusal to align himself with either of the parties in power kept him out. His friend George Putnam was awarded a rich plum: an appointment as collector of Internal Revenue for the wealthiest residential district in Manhattan, extending from 18th Street north to 42nd, and the Hudson River east to Fifth Avenue; a nominating petition headed by Bryant, and signed by many other prominent persons, had been circulated in Putnam's behalf. Benjamin entreated his friend Sumner, then senator from Massachusetts and chairman of the important Foreign Relations Committee, to intercede with the president to get him appointed as a tax collector for the Washington Heights district, where he was then living. But Sumner, apparently influenced by the gossip spread by his enemies in the period of newspaper warfare, seems to have doubted Benjamin's reliability. He did, however, join with John Pendleton Kennedy and two other senators, Hale of New Hampshire and Cowan of Pennsylvania, in getting Benjamin's son Park, Jr., appointed to the Naval Academy; and Benjamin himself to the Academy's Board of Visitors, a purely honorary position. President Lincoln authorized Benjamin to write his biography, probably for use in the 1864 campaign for re-election. Lincoln wrote him, a strong supporter of the president: 'I should be pleased to see you any time. I would be glad to have you publish a biography of me — by *my authority*. I certainly can facilitate you.'[106] But burdened as the president then was with the cares and responsibilities of winning the war, and as Benjamin was in his own private war for survival, nothing came of it. Both men were dead before a meeting could take place.

Benjamin was too shrewd, too much the realist, not to know that he had sacrificed his career as a poet to the exigencies of newspaper journalism. Yet he was very far from being the embittered 'half-man, half-snake' his enemies reviled. He wrote Longfellow late in 1858, 'I write very little except in the way of business. The only productions I rejoice in are my children — Four boys on Earth — one in Heaven, and my daughter of a year.'[107] Two more were born before his death, which was caused by blood poisoning following surgery for the removal of a kidney stone, on 12 September 1864. A hearty man who loved laughter and fun, he would pile his children into his carriage and drive at a fast clip through Central Park on up to Bloomingdale, singing and reciting at the top of his rich baritone voice Holmes's poem 'Old Ironsides', for which he had a special fondness, or his own lyric 'Press On', which borrowed the theme of 'Excelsior'.

For what Park Benjamin accomplished in his life, however ephemeral some of it proved to be, and for much else that existed only in a farseeing vision, history owes him remembrance.

[106] 19 January 1863, in the possession of Henry Rogers Benjamin.
[107] 20 September 1858, in the Longfellow Manuscripts.

HAWTHORNE AND THE PIRATES

C. E. FRAZER CLARK, JR.

FOR SEVENTEEN YEARS NATHANIEL HAWTHORNE DID NOT GET A SHILL-ing out of the English publishers of his work.[1] His first English money came when James T. Fields sold Chapman and Hall the British rights to *The Blithedale Romance* for £200 – $1,000 at the then current rate of exchange. Five years later he comfortably reflected on the long years before:

[1] C. E. Frazer Clark, Jr., 'Hawthorne's First Appearance in England', *CEAA Newsletter*, No. 3 (June 1970), 10–11.

For a discussion of the negotiations on the English rights to *The Blithedale Romance*, see Roy Harvey Pearce, Introduction to *The Blithedale Romance and Fanshawe, The Centenary Edition of the Works of Nathaniel Hawthorne*, III (Columbus: The Ohio State University Press, 1964), xvii–xxvi.

So far as I have been able to discover, Hawthorne received no money for any of the various printings of his work in England prior to *The Blithedale Romance*. He did receive a royalty from Wiley and Putnam for titles they published. Although these would have included the right to distribute a portion of the American edition in England under their London imprint, I do not consider this income from England.

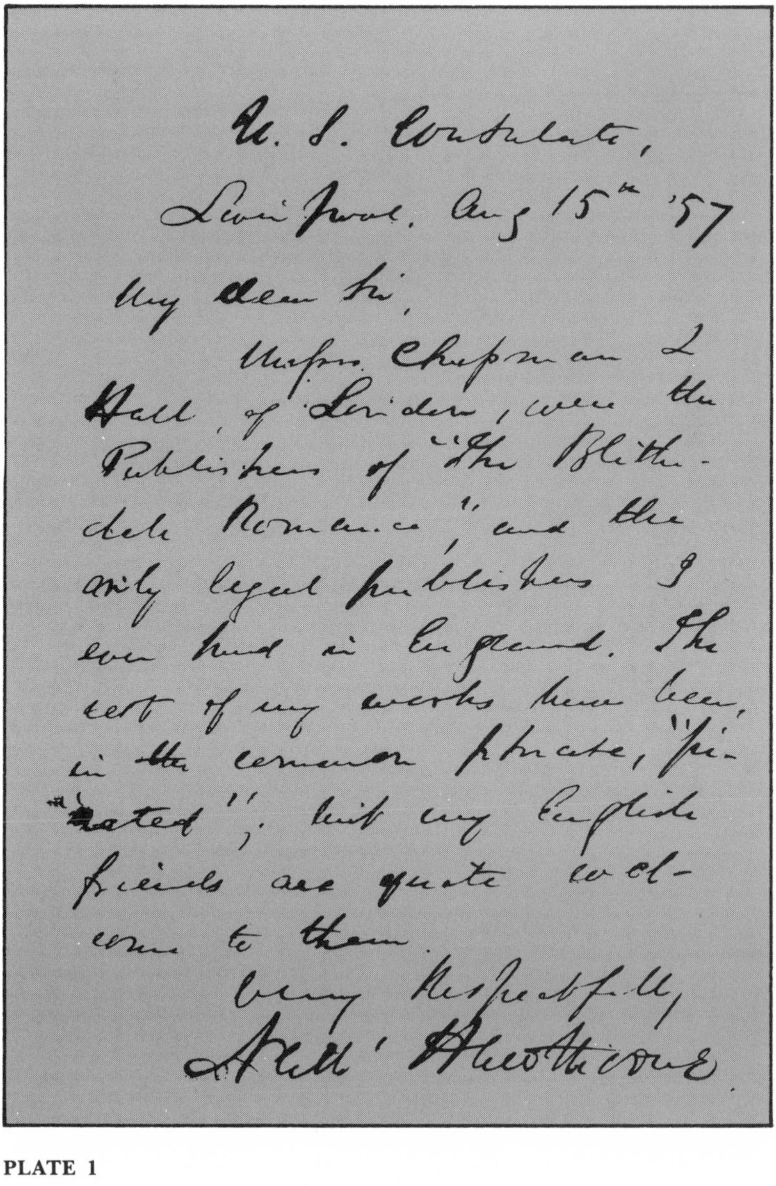

U. S. Consulate,
Liverpool. Aug 15ᵗʰ '57

My dear Sir,

Messrs. Chapman &
Hall, of London, were the
Publishers of "The Blithedale Romance", and the
only legal publishers I
ever had in England. The
rest of my works have been
in the common phrase, "pirated"; but my English
friends are quite wel-
come to them.

very Respectfully
Nathl Hawthorne.

PLATE 1

U. S. Consulate,
Liverpool.   Aug 15th '57

My dear Sir,

Messrs Chapman & Hall, of London, were the Publishers of "The Blithedale Romance," and the only legal publishers I ever had in England. The rest of my works have been, in the common phrase, "pirated"; but my English friends are quite welcome to them.

Very Respectfully
Nath[1] Hawthorne[2]

Immediately, and privately, however, it was another matter. Until he put his work into the hands of Fields, Hawthorne had little reason to feel that a satisfactory financial arrangement with any publisher was likely.[3] The lack of an international copyright law encouraged piracy on both sides of the Atlantic and gave publishers little reason to offer liberal terms to their authors. Although he knew these facts of publishing life, Hawthorne resented being victimized — particularly by the English pirates who plundered his work for their exclusive gain. On the eve of Fields's final negotiations for *The Blithedale Romance*, Hawthorne urged that the pirates owed him much:

It strikes me those London publishers are even greater skin flints than their American brethren. Ticknor tells me that Bogue and Routledge will neither of them advance on their original offering (£50.) which I do not feel at all inclined to accept. I had rather make an arrangement to share in the proceeds. Cannot you agree with Bentley to that effect? — or to any other effect? If you can get from any other publishers even as much as Routledge and Bogue offer, do not let them both have it. They ought to be more liberal, in consideration of having fleeced me heretofore.[4]

---

[2] This previously unpublished letter is from my collection. The addressee is unknown.

[3] Hawthorne's difficulties with S. G. Goodrich and other publishers and editors over payment for his work is well known; slow pay or no pay often was the case. Even his friend John L. O'Sullivan, editor of the *Democratic Review*, was unable to pay Hawthorne as much or as regularly as he wanted to. And Hawthorne had received promises to publish collections of his stories, only to experience delays in publication that obliged breaking up the collections and indiscriminate publishing of the individual stories. On this see Lillian Gilkes, 'Hawthorne, Park Benjamin, and S. G. Goodrich: A Three-Cornered Imbroglio', *The Nathaniel Hawthorne Journal*, I (1971), 83–112.

[4] Hawthorne to Fields, 3 May 1852, in the Berg Collection, NN.

'You have succeeded admirably in regard to the "Blithedale Romance",' Hawthorne congratulated Fields, 'and have got £150 more than I expected to receive.'[5] He had good reason to rejoice, even though Fields's deal with John Chapman did not include a share in the profits. It was not so much that the money came at a time when a new child and a new house both needed financing; rather it was the symbolic value in so large a sum. As Hawthorne passed the good news along to his old friend Horatio Bridge, 'Perhaps you have seen Blithedale before this time. I doubt whether you will like it very well; but it has met with good success, and has brought me (besides its American circulation) a thousand dollars from England, whence likewise have come many favorable notices. Just at this time, I rather think your friend stands foremost there, as an American fiction-monger.'[6]

But the English buccaneers had been largely responsible for this triumph. The unrestrained pirating of his work by a variety of presses gave Hawthorne English visibility he could have gotten from no one legitimate publisher, and the popularity of the piracies confirmed the insatiable demand of the English reader for his work. The freebooting English publications of *The Scarlet Letter* and *The House of the Seven Gables*, for example, 'made a greater sensation than any book since "Jane Eyre"', a friend told him.[7] For these reasons alone, a student of Hawthorne's reception must know the story behind the copyright notice on the Chapman and Hall edition of *The Blithedale Romance*. The following preliminary survey of the English piracies preceding that edition therefore is intended not only as a contribution to Hawthorne bibliography and the study of transatlantic publications of American books, but also as a key to recognizing Hawthorne's popularity in the English market.

That market was opened to Hawthorne in 1835 by Henry Chorley, a reviewer for the London *Athenæum*. In the issue for 26 September 1835 (p. 728), Chorley reviewed the *New-England Magazine* for 1835, concluding with a reprinting of 'A Rill from the Town-Pump' from it. Six weeks later, in reviewing the 1836 *Token* for the 7 November *Athenæum*, Chorley again singled out Hawthorne. 'My worshipful self is a very famous man in London', the American boasted to his

---

[5] Hawthorne to Fields, 17 June 1852, in the Berg Collection, NN.
[6] Hawthorne to Bridge, 18 October 1852, in MeB.
[7] Mrs. Kemble to Hawthorne, quoted in Hawthorne to Fields, 15 July 1851; see James T. Fields, *Yesterdays With Authors* (Boston: Houghton, Mifflin, 1882), p. 60.

sister, '—the Athenæum having noticed all my articles in the last Token, with long extracts.'[8] But the first book that could have entered that market with Hawthorne's name on the title page was an imported copy of *Twice-Told Tales* in 1837. It is advertised in the *Publishers' Circular and Booksellers' Record* (1 March 1838) as a 'new American publication.' However, few, if any, copies of that *Twice-Told Tales* seem actually to have made their way to England. There is no copy in the British Museum, and Chorley did not review the book — which, in view of both his and the *Athenæum's* continuing cordiality to Hawthorne, he presumably would have done had he seen it.

The story of Hawthorne's books in England, however, begins more properly with *Peter Parley's Universal History*, compiled for S. G. Goodrich by Hawthorne, aided by his sister Elizabeth. According to her, Goodrich paid Hawthorne $100 for the job. This book was fantastically successful, with an untold number of editions required in America. In England, it appeared first as an importation (Kennett): according to the trade press, copies of the two-volume 1837 American edition were brought in for sale. Almost immediately, though, the pirates moved in. John W. Parker brought out in 1837 a one-volume edition that was 'an entirely new production . . . reprinted from an unpublished copy, specially forwarded . . . for the purpose.' With the same plates, he reprinted the book again in 1839. Between the two Parker publications in 1838, Thomas Tegg brought out another one-volume edition, and this—if we accept the imprints on later Tegg title pages as evidence—was reprinted twenty-two times. Parker appears to have had no warrant for his publications. Tegg had had one in 1832, but had ignored it to the detriment of his relationship with Goodrich.[9] To all intents and purposes, then, the Tegg edition was as much a piracy as was Parker's. Since there is no evidence that Hawthorne's editorship of *Peter Parley's Universal History* was known in England (his name was not on the title page of either the American or English publications, although the editor of the Salem *Gazette* knew the secret),[10] this edition could have done little to contribute to Hawthorne's later popularity in England.

[8]Hawthorne to Elizabeth Hawthorne, 25 January 1835; see my 'Census of Nathaniel Hawthorne Letters: 1813–1849', in *The Nathaniel Hawthorne Journal*, I (1971), 257–82.

[9]S. G. Goodrich, *Recollections of a Lifetime* (New York and Auburn: Miller, Orton, 1857), II, 292.

[10]Caleb Foote identified Hawthorne as author in his review of *The Scarlet Letter* published in the Salem *Gazette*, 19 March 1850.

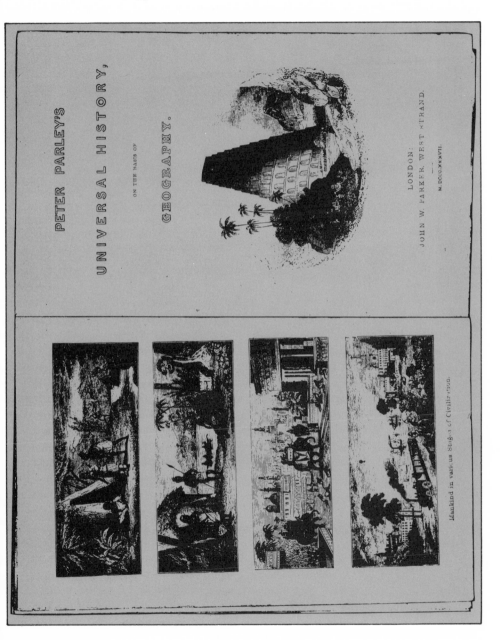

PETER PARLEY'S

UNIVERSAL HISTORY,

ON THE BASIS OF

GEOGRAPHY.

LONDON:

JOHN W. PARKER, WEST STRAND.

M.DCCC.XXXVII.

Mankind in various Stages of Civilization.

PLATE 2

PLATE 3

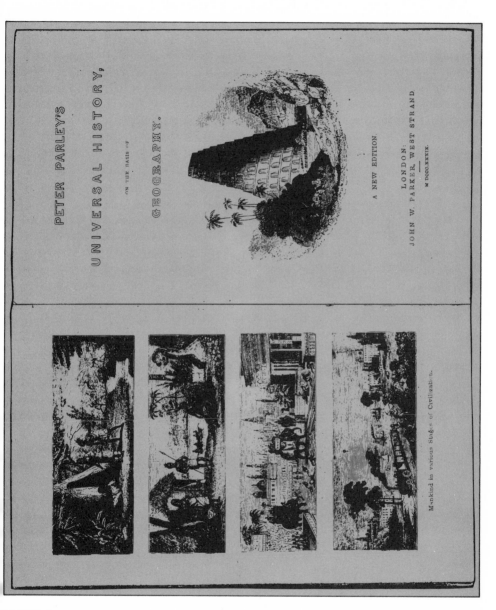

PLATE 4

The Gentle Boy: A Thrice Told Tale did have the author's name beneath its title, and an imported copy did make its way to England — the first such work known to have done so. A copy of the book distributed for sale in London by Wiley & Putnam reached the desk of a reviewer for the *Literary Gazette and Journal of Belles-Lettres*. The 22 June 1839 issue of that periodical carried a brief note stating that 'We confess we cannot tell what to make of this sentimental rhapsody. There is a pretty outline illustration.' Little harm was done by this because the circumstances under which the book was published and sold indicate no real expectations of the publisher for sale of the book.[11]

The 1842 *Twice-Told Tales*, on the other hand, was reviewed well in England in the 23 August 1845 *Athenæum* as it was in many American journals. Notice of the book did not appear in the *Publishers' Circular* between 1842 and 1845, however, so this boost could have been only the laying of the groundwork.

That groundwork began to pay off in 1845 when the London imprint of Wiley & Putnam appeared on the *Journal of an African Cruiser*, edited by Hawthorne from the diary of a voyage made by his friend Bridge. This was the first book bearing Hawthorne's name on the title page to be actively promoted and sold in England. Evert A. Duyckinck, whose laudatory notice had so pleased Hawthorne in 1841,[12] accepted the *Journal* as the first title in a new series he was editing for Wiley and Putnam, the Library of American Books. Hawthorne's book benefited both from the popularity of travel literature and the determination of the publisher to launch its new series successfully through its divisions in New York and London. These factors encouraged an initial printing large enough to include a substantial number of copies for the English market. 'The first edition

---

[11] George P. Putnam of Wiley and Putnam opened a London branch for the firm in 1838, the first for any American publisher. A first cousin of Sophia A. Peabody, Putnam may have known about the budding romance between Miss Peabody and Hawthorne. He also may have known about the circumstances surrounding the Wiley and Putnam publication of *The Gentle Boy*, with the frontispiece engraved from Sophia's drawing. The cost of engraving was paid for by her friend, Miss Burley. *The Gentle Boy* was mainly an ego publication, so it is unlikely that a large printing was ordered. But since the book was dedicated prominently to Putnam's cousin, and since it had her drawing, it is likely that he had distributed some friendly review copies when he received a shipment from America.

[12] Hawthorne to Cornelius Mathews and Evert A. Duyckinck, 22 December 1841, in the Berg Collection, NN.

JOURNAL

OF AN

AFRICAN CRUISER:

COMPRISING SKETCHES OF THE CANARIES, THE CAPE DE
VERDS, LIBERIA, MADEIRA, SIERRA LEONE, AND
OTHER PLACES OF INTEREST ON THE WEST
COAST OF AFRICA.

BY AN OFFICER OF THE U. S. NAVY.

EDITED BY
NATHANIEL HAWTHORNE.

LONDON:
WILEY AND PUTNAM, 6, WATERLOO PLACE.
1845.
[ENTERED AT STATIONERS' HALL.]

PLATE 5

will be two thousand copies,' Hawthorne wrote Bridge on 2 May 1845, 'five hundred of which will be sent to London.' Copies distributed in England were shipped in sheets with a cancel title leaf provided for binding up on arrival. The London publication was advertised as 'now ready' in the *Athenæum* (12 July 1845) and the *Publishers' Circular* (15 July 1845), and was reviewed in the *Literary Gazette* (2 August 1845) and the *Athenæum* (6 and 13 September 1845).

This book carried Hawthorne's name to a large readership. It evidently sold well. On 2 October 1845 Duyckinck wrote Hawthorne that 'The "Journal of the Cruiser" has just gone to a second edition of a thousand copies, the first, I believe, having been two thousand. . . . The English notices are bounteous in praise. No American book in a long time has been so well noticed.'[13] Presumably a portion of the second printing also went to London, the spate of notices suggesting the probability of early sales. Hawthorne answered Duyckinck that 'Bridge is greatly delighted, and not a little surprised, at his literary success, especially at the commendation from the other side of the water.'[14] He himself must also have been pleased, particularly if the sales reached the reported 5,000 and included a substantial proportion of English purchases.[15] That there was a significant demand for the American by the British reading public is suggested by a completely reset Aberdeen piracy in 1848.[16] Hawthorne took satisfaction in his growing reputation abroad; he also must have been struck by the potential of the English market.

Success of the *Journal of an African Cruiser* encouraged Wiley and Putnam to seek a third title from Hawthorne. *Mosses from an Old Manse* in two volumes was the result, Numbers XVII and XVIII in Duyckinck's growing Library of American Books. Here again Wiley and Putnam provided for English distribution by shipping sheets ready for binding with cancel title leaves for both volumes in England. *Mosses from an Old Manse* was listed as 'new' in the *Literary Gazette* (11 July 1846), *Publishers' Circular* (15 July 1846), *Athenæum* (18 July 1846), and relisted in the *Literary Gazette* (25 July 1846). Hawthorne's admirer, Henry Chorley, received it warmly in the 8

---

[13] Duyckinck to Hawthorne, 2 October 1845; as quoted in Horatio Bridge, *Personal Recollections of Nathaniel Hawthorne* (New York: Harper, 1893), p. 106.

[14] Hawthorne to Duyckinck, 10 October 1845, in the Berg Collection, NN.

[15] John D. Gordan, *Nathaniel Hawthorne: The Years of Fulfilment, 1845–1853* (New York: The New York Public Library, 1954), p. 27.

[16] Aberdeen: George Clark; London: S. Richardson, 1848.

MOSSES

FROM

AN OLD MANSE.

BY NATHANIEL HAWTHORNE.

IN TWO PARTS.

PART I.

LONDON:

WILEY & PUTNAM, 6, WATERLOO PLACE.

———

1846.

[ENTERED AT STATIONERS' HALL.]

PLATE 6

August 1846 *Athenæum*, but the reviewer for *Blackwood's Magazine* (November 1847) was colder. Nevertheless, the Wiley and Putnam publication was reprinted. Early in 1851, after he had become Hawthorne's publisher, James T. Fields tried to purchase the rights to the book, but Wiley and Putnam would not sell. They chose to retain the valuable property until they had no choice, selling it when financial trouble in 1854 forced them to do so.

The pirates knew a good thing too. The Aberdeen piracy of the *Journal of an African Cruiser* in 1848 had been anticipated by the treatment accorded *Mosses from an Old Manse*. In 1846, for example, Houlston and Stoneman of London reprinted one of the tales in that book from the *Baptist Magazine*. 'The Celestial Railroad' was a special favorite of editors on both sides of the Atlantic, so it is not surprising that it enjoys the distinction of being the most widely pirated of any of Hawthorne's works. The noteworthy thing may be that there was enough demand in England to warrant Houlston and Sons publishing a reprint of 'The Celestial Railroad' marked 'Twelfth Thousand'.

Soon after the publication of *Mosses from an Old Manse*, the pirates plundered with a vengeance. Hawthorne's writings were victims of a new situation. The Railway Mania of 1846 in England materially contributed to a revolution in English book marketing which necessitated the evolution of concepts of production, distribution, and pricing essential to the successful mass merchandising of books. In 1848 W. H. Smith opened his first bookstall at London's Euston Station. This began what was to become the chain of outlets through which a vast selection of titles was offered to the daily traffic of the mass transit reading public. Obviously, new product and pricing concepts were called for, and George Routledge was among the first to heed the call. Perceiving the new channels for distribution and understanding the need for increased inventory that they occasioned, Routledge launched his Railway Library of one-shilling 'paperbacks' in 1848. Anticipating the value of brand identification, he made his volumes easily recognizable: a cover design evolved with the title surrounded by an elaborate, standardized display panel completely filling the front cover; printing was in blue; boards were green. His methods were successful enough to encourage Henry G. Bohn, Routledge's arch competitor, to copy the format and the color scheme for his own Cheap Series of shilling books. Although there had been inexpensive one-shilling books on the market before his Railway

THE

CELESTIAL RAILROAD.

BY

NATHANIEL HAWTHORNE.

(REPRINTED FROM THE BAPTIST MAGAZINE.)

London:

HOULSTON AND STONEMAN,

65, PATERNOSTER ROW.

1846.

PLATE 7

THE

CELESTIAL RAILROAD

BY

NATHANIEL HAWTHORNE

TWELFTH THOUSAND

LONDON
HOULSTON AND SONS
65, PATERNOSTER ROW

PLATE 8

Library, Routledge's grasp of mass merchandising techniques made his series a runaway success:

The "Railway Library", confounding its critics, was a success from the first. Besides introducing Fenimore Cooper and other American romancers to a far wider audience than they had ever known before it brought a host of standard English novels—originally published for the most part in three volumes at a guinea-and-a-half—within the reach of the shilling public, hitherto too dependent for their literary entertainment on heavier or inferior fare. Where these tales had previously circulated in their hundreds through the libraries they now sold in their tens of thousands.[17]

Routledge and his competitors made the most of a rare business opportunity, exploiting to the fullest the new English mass market—readers who could own books at a shilling where before they could only borrow. The single problem facing the publishers was that of building saleable series quickly and cheaply. The obvious solution lay in taking full advantage of the unprotected American writer, who had no international copyright agreement under which to take shelter. English buccaneers promptly accelerated their plundering of American literature. They found a natural prey in Hawthorne, a defenseless writer whose reputation in England was growing and whose available books had been market-tested. So, for his Railway Library, Routledge stole *The Scarlet Letter* and *The House of the Seven Gables* in one volume each, and *Twice-Told Tales* in two volumes. Bohn went him one better for his Cheap Series: to these three titles he added another, *The Snow Image*. Routledge balanced his own offering by including *Mosses from an Old Manse* in his Popular Library, another one-shilling series.

A simple telling of titles and publishers does little to reveal the true extent to which the pirates cut up Hawthorne. The marketing concept of multiple-line merchandising so clearly grasped by Routledge and Bohn encouraged them to create what must vex bibliographers. These publishers packaged essentially the same merchandise in different styles to accommodate various classes of trade and to support different price structures. An important advantage of this concept was that the additional lines composed of the same material demanded more display space from the bookstall retailer, often crowd-

---

[17] F. A. Mumby, *The House of Routledge: 1834–1934* (London: George Routledge, 1934), p. 48.

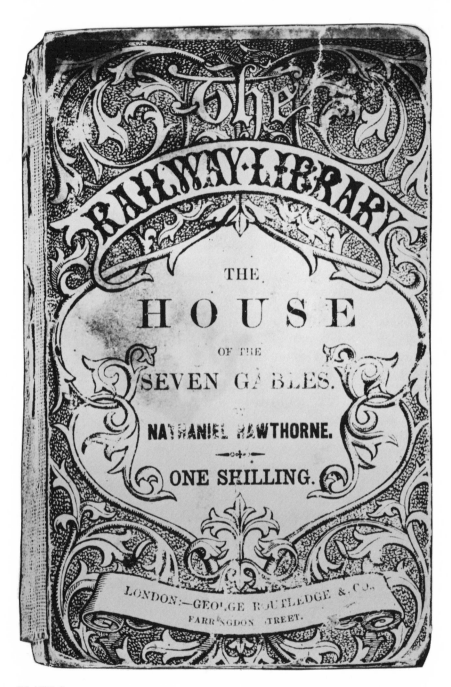

PLATE 9

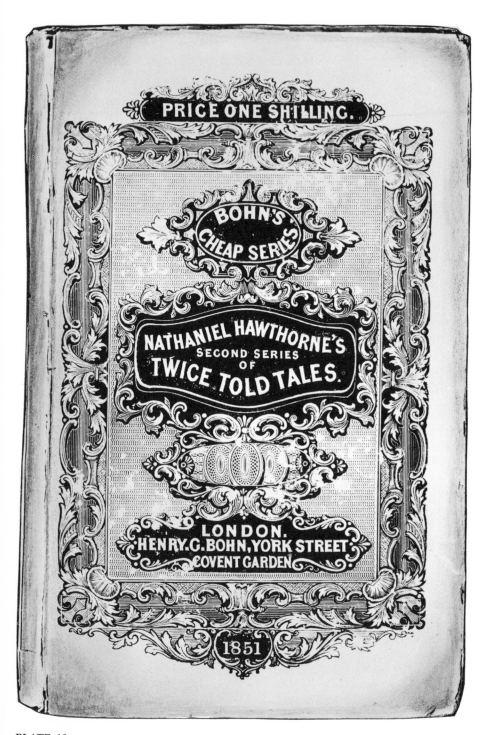

PLATE 10

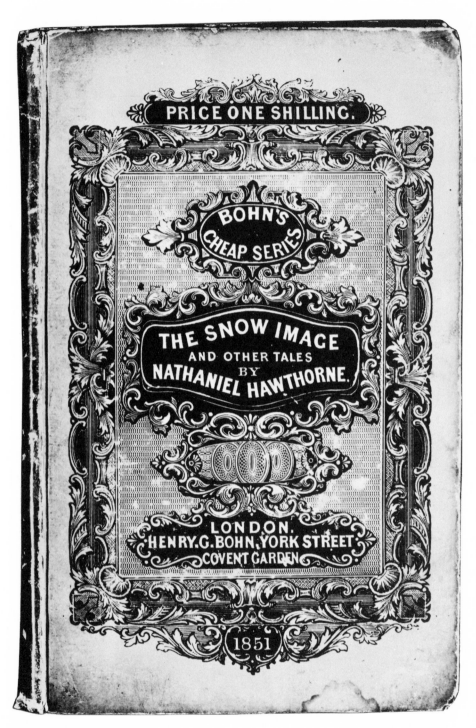

PRICE ONE SHILLING.

BOHN'S CHEAP SERIES

THE SNOW IMAGE
AND OTHER TALES
BY
NATHANIEL HAWTHORNE.

LONDON.
HENRY. G. BOHN, YORK STREET
COVENT GARDEN

1851

PLATE 11

THE

SCARLET LETTER:

A Romance.

BY

NATHANIEL HAWTHORNE.

LONDON:
(PUBLISHED FOR J. WALKER.)
DAVID BOGUE, FLEET STREET;
HAMILTON AND CO.; JOHNSTONE AND HUNTER; H. WASHBOURNE.
EDINBURGH: JOHNSTONE AND HUNTER; OLIVER AND BOYD.
DUBLIN: JAMES M'GLASHAN.

1851.

PLATE 12

ing competition into a corner—if not out of the stall. More important, however, were the economies involved. The publisher needed only one plating to make several products, and this meant production savings in longer press runs and the use of the same sheets bound as required for the different lines. The Routledge Standard Novels, for example, offered *The Scarlet Letter* and *The House of the Seven Gables*, as did the Railway Library. Both series used the same sheets. But where the Railway Library sold two volumes in boards for one shilling each, the Standard Novels bound both volumes in one cloth binding with a frontispiece at 2s. 6d. The Railway Library was disposable literature; the Standard Novels was bookshelf furnishing; conceivably a purchaser might buy both versions and pay 4s. 6d. for the same material, but certainly the publisher benefited from the double usage. Another example of the multiple-line approach is Bohn's publications of Hawthorne. He sold *Hawthorne's Tales* in two volumes at 3s. 6d., in a format uniform with Bohn's Standard Library: the first volume combines *Twice-Told Tales* and *The Snow Image*, and the second volume pairs *The Scarlet Letter* and *The House of the Seven Gables*. All four presumably use the sheets in Bohn's Cheap Series.

As W. H. Smith's chain of bookstalls spread because of prospering business, he decided to take greater advantage of his own distribution system by marketing his own line of books. For obvious reasons, Smith's books came to be called 'Yellow Backs'. These were 'branded merchandise' commissioned in special format from existing publishers: editions were ordered bound in a specified way for distribution, inventory, and sale by Smith's. In order to keep his publishers cooperative, Smith was careful to continue handling competing lines alongside his own. Bohn packaged *Twice-Told Tales* as a Yellow Back from the same germinal sheets used in his own lines; but this edition was Smith's property, packaged to his order, although carrying the Bohn imprint. Even Chapman and Hall—Hawthorne's rescuer—provided Smith with a number of Yellow Backs. Among these was *The Blithedale Romance*, appearing in the Select Library of Fiction at two shillings. Smith's stalls asked, and apparently got, more for their books than the competing publishers did for the same books in different packages. The Smith Yellow Back *Blithedale Romance* presumably was the first mass-marketed work by Hawthorne to appear in England under copyright privileges paid for by the publisher—if Chapman and Hall, publisher of the original sheets, can be considered publisher in fact of the Smith issue.

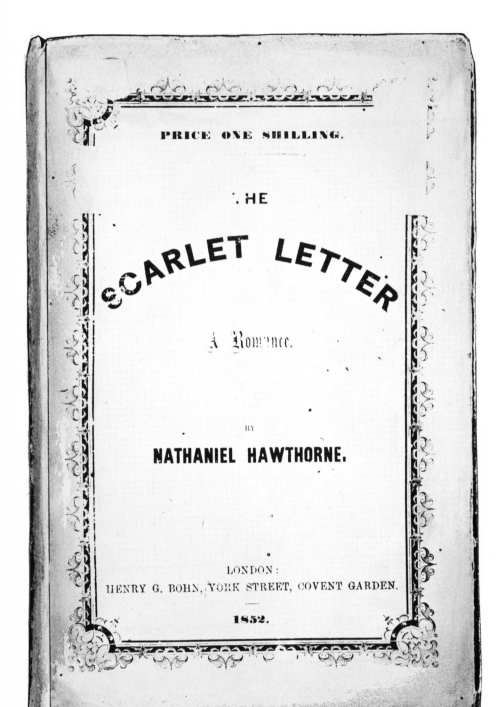

PRICE ONE SHILLING.

THE

SCARLET LETTER

A Romance.

BY

NATHANIEL HAWTHORNE.

LONDON:
HENRY G. BOHN, YORK STREET, COVENT GARDEN.

1852.

PLATE 13

A

WONDER-BOOK

FOR

GIRLS AND BOYS.

BY NATHANIEL HAWTHORNE.

WITH ILLUSTRATIVE ENGRAVINGS.

LONDON:
HENRY G. BOHN, YORK STREET, COVENT GARDEN.
1852.

PLATE 14

TANGLEWOOD TALES,

FOR

GIRLS AND BOYS:

Being a Second Wonder-Book.

BY

NATHANIEL HAWTHORNE.

WITH ILLUSTRATIONS.

LONDON:
CHAPMAN AND HALL, 193, PICCADILLY.

1853.

PLATE 15

Mass-market pirating was not, as one might expect in such a situation, the only way Hawthorne was exploited. Other English pirates sold their booty to a more select trade. David Bogue, for example, published an English edition of *The Scarlet Letter* for J. Walker in direct competition with at least two importations. The Bogue piracy was listed in the *Athenæum* (17 May 1851) and the *Publishers' Circular* (2 June 1851), and was on the street before the Routledge and Bohn piracies. Bohn also published an elaborately clothbound piracy of *A Wonder-Book*, listed in the *Athenæum* (27 December 1851) and the *Publishers' Circular* (1 January 1852).

But even luxury and mass-market piratings were not the only forms of exploitation. Like their American counterparts, English editors found that Hawthorne's work made attractive filler. His tales were pirated by such diverse periodicals as the *Athenæum*, the *Baptist Magazine*, and the *London Metropolitan*. The list of periodical piracies is long indeed.

Hawthorne was aware of what was happening, and was enraged by it. In his *American Notebook* he recorded one impression:

I left Mr. Thompson before 10, and took my way through the sloppy streets to the Athenæum, where I looked over the newspapers and periodicals, and found two of my old stories (Peter Goldthwaite and the Shaker Bridal) published as original in the last London Metropolitan. The English are ten times as unscrupulous and dishonest pirates as ourselves. However, if they are poor enough to perk themselves in such false feathers as these, Heaven help them! I glanced over the stories, and they seemed painfully cold and dull. It is the more singular that these should be so published, inasmuch as the whole book was republished in London, only a few months ago. Mr. Fields tells me that two publishers in London had advertised the Scarlet Letter as in press, each at a shilling.[18]

But that was in 1841. Hawthorne did not realize then that what was happening would benefit him later.

Trading across English bookstall counters in cheap and luxurious piracies proved to be the dynamic in the development of Hawthorne's English reputation. While the English pirates were plundering him of possible income, they also were establishing his saleability in their country. That was the asset enabling Fields to sell at high

---

[18] Randall Stewart, ed., *The American Notebooks by Nathaniel Hawthorne* (New Haven: Yale University Press, 1932), p. 247.

THE

BLITHEDALE ROMANCE.

BY

NATHANIEL HAWTHORNE,

AUTHOR OF " THE SCARLET LETTER," " THE HOUSE OF THE SEVEN
GABLES," &c.

IN TWO VOLUMES.

VOL. I.

LONDON:

CHAPMAN AND HALL, 193, PICCADILLY

1852.

PLATE 16

prices the British copyrights to *The Blithedale Romance* and later material. The pirates had helped Hawthorne fulfill the double-edged prophesy he made his mother when he departed for college: 'How proud you would feel to see my work praised by the reviewers as equal to the proudest productions of the Scribling Sons of John Bull. But authors are always poor devils and therefore Satan may take them.'[19] Or the pirates.

** *The English Copyright of this Romance is the property of* MESSRS. CHAPMAN *and* HALL.

PLATE 17

[19] Hawthorne to Elizabeth C. Hathorne, 13 March 1821; as quoted in Julian Hawthorne, *Nathaniel Hawthorne and His Wife* (Boston: James R. Osgood, 1885), I, 108.

APPENDIX

*Checklist of Hawthorne Title Pages Bearing English
Publishers' Imprints, 1837–1856.*

This Checklist represents a preliminary catalog of Hawthorne's
books and separate publications, 1837–1856, which bear an English
publisher's imprint on the title page. Both first printings and reprints
are listed.

The English publications of Hawthorne present special bibliographical problems. English publishers, exploiting mass merchandising techniques, 'packaged' the same sheets, or sheets from the
same plates, in a variety of ways. For example, Routledge published
The Scarlet Letter and *The House Of The Seven Gables* in his Railway
Library series (items 18 and 20), paired the two works under one
title page in his Standard Novel format (item 21), and issued the two
works bound together with separate title pages in a choice of bindings
(item 22). For the purposes of this Checklist, each such production
is listed separately because it represents a distinct offering by the
publisher, individually priced and advertised, and deliberately made
available in different formats.

I have included in this Checklist all the examples of English publications of Hawthorne present in my own collection (these are indicated by an asterisk following the listing), examples from other
collections, and other English Hawthorne where enough evidence
exists to warrant the listing. In four cases (items 27, 31, 35, and 39),
enough evidence exists even though there is as yet no knowledge of
the dates of publication.

This Checklist should be considered a working list; it is not a
bibliography, and it is not complete. I would be grateful for any additional information regarding the English publications of Hawthorne.

1837   1. *Peter Parley's Universal History, on the Basis of Geography.*
London: John W. Parker, 1837.*

1838   2. *Tales about Universal History on the Bases of Geography.* By
Peter Parley. London: Thos. Tegg, 1838.

1839 3. *Peter Parley's Universal History, on the Basis of Geography.*
London: John W. Parker, 1839. A New Edition.*

4. *Universal History, on the Basis Of Geography.* By Peter Parley. London: Thomas Tegg, 1839. Second Edition.*

5. *The Gentle Boy: a Thrice Told Tale.* Boston: Weeks, Jordan; New York & London: Wiley & Putnam, 1839.*

1845 6. *Journal of an African Cruiser.* New York & London: Wiley And Putnam, 1845. Cancel title leaf. No. 1 in Wiley And Putnam's Library Of American Books, and various other bindings.*

7. *Journal of an African Cruiser.* London: Wiley And Putnam, 1845. Cancel title leaf.*

8. *Journal of an African Cruiser.* New York & London: Wiley And Putnam, 1845. No. 20 in the Library Of Choice Reading.*

9. *Journal of an African Cruiser.* New York & London: Wiley And Putnam, 1845. (Bound with:) *Scenes And Thoughts In Europe.* New York: Wiley And Putnam, 1846.*

10. *Journal of an African Cruiser.* New York & London: Wiley And Putnam, 1845. (Bound with:) *Letters From Italy.* By J. T. Headley. New York: Wiley and Putnam, 1845.*

1846 11. *Mosses from An Old Manse.* London: Wiley & Putnam, 1846. Two volumes. Cancel title leaves.*

12. *The Celestial Railroad.* London: Houlston And Stoneman, 1846.* Reprinted: *The Celestial Railroad.* London: Houlston And Sons, (n.d.). Twelfth Thousand.*

1848 13. *Journal of an African Cruiser.* New York: John Wiley, 161 Broadway, And 12 Paternoster Row, London, 1848. Cancel title leaf. Library Of Choice Reading.*

118

14. *The Journal of an African Cruiser.* Aberdeen: George Clark; London: S. Richardson, 1848.*

1849 15. *Universal History, on the Basis Of Geography.* By Peter Parley. London: Thomas Tegg, (n.d.; contemporary inscription dated December 1849). The Fourth Edition.*

1850 16. *Twice Told Tales.* London: William Tegg, 1850.

1851 17. *The Scarlet Letter.* London: J. Walker, and others; Edinburgh: Johnstone And Hunter, and others; Dublin: James M'Glashan, 1851.*

18. *The Scarlet Letter.* London: George Routledge, 1851. No. 30 in The Railway Library, and various other bindings.*

19. *The House of The Seven Gables.* London: Henry G. Bohn, 1851. No. 31 in Bohn's Cheap Series, and various other bindings.

20. *The House of The Seven Gables.* London: George Routledge, 1851. No. 31 in The Railway Library, and various other bindings.*

21. *The Scarlet Letter, and the House Of The Seven Gables.* London: George Routledge, 1851. Routledge's Standard Novels.*

22. *The Scarlet Letter.* London: George Routledge, 1851. (Bound with:) *The House of The Seven Gables.* London: George Routledge, 1851. These two titles together in various bindings.*

23. *Twice-Told Tales.* London: Henry G. Bohn, 1851. A New Edition. No. 35 in Bohn's Cheap Series, and various other bindings.

24. *Twice-Told Tales.* London: Henry G. Bohn, 1851. Second Series. No. 36 in Bohn's Cheap Series, and various other bindings.*

25. *Twice-Told Tales.* London: Henry G. Bohn, 1851. A New Edition. (Bound with:) *Twice-Told Tales.* London: Henry G. Bohn, 1851. Second Series. Two volumes in one, Bohn's Popular Railway Literature series, and in various other two-in-one bindings.*

26. *The Snow-Image, and Other Tales.* London: Henry G. Bohn, 1851. No. 37 in Bohn's Cheap Series, and various other bindings.*

27. *Twice-Told Tales, And The Snow-Image.* London: Henry G. Bohn, [1851?]. Uniform with Bohn's Standard Library.

28. *Mosses from An Old Manse.* London: George Routledge, 1851. Bound singly and with other titles, in various bindings.*

1852 29. *Mosses From An Old Manse.* London: G. Routledge, 1852. British Museum deposit date: 19 May 1852. Bound singly and with other titles, in various bindings.

30. *Twice-Told Tales.* London: George Routledge, 1852. A New Edition. British Museum deposit date: 19 May 1852. Bound singly and with other titles, in various bindings.

31. *Twice-Told Tales.* London: Routledge, [1852?]. Two volumes. The Railway Library.

32. *The House of The Seven Gables.* London: G. Routledge, 1852. British Museum deposit date: 22 May 1852. Bound singly and with other titles, in various bindings.*

33. *The House of The Seven Gables.* London: Geo. Routledge, 1852. Bound singly and with other titles, in various bindings.*

34. *The Scarlet Letter.* London: Henry G. Bohn, 1852. No. 38 in Bohn's Cheap Series, and in various other bindings.*

35. *The Scarlet Letter, And The House Of The Seven Gables.* London: Henry G. Bohn, [1852?]. Uniform with Bohn's Standard Library.

36. *A Wonder-Book for Girls And Boys.* London: Henry G. Bohn, 1852.*

37. *True Stories From History And Biography.* London: S. Low, 1852.

38. *The Blithedale Romance.* London: Chapman And Hall, 1852. Two volumes. British Museum deposit date: 1 July 1852.*

39. *The Canterbury Pilgrims, And Other Twice-Told Tales.* London: Knight (n.d., 1852?).

1853 40. *Life Of Franklin Pierce.* London: George Routledge, 1853. British Museum deposit date: 29 December 1852.

41. *Tanglewood Tales, For Girls And Boys.* London: Chapman And Hall, 1853. British Museum deposit date: 24 August 1853.*

1854 42. *The Blithedale Romance.* London: Chapman And Hall, 1854. Second Edition. Chapman And Hall's Select Library Of Fiction.*

43. *The Blithedale Romance.* London: Chapman And Hall, 1854. Second Edition. (Bound with:) *The Bachelor Of The Albany.* London: Chapman And Hall, 1854.*

44. *The House of The Seven Gables.* London: G. Routledge, 1854. Twenty-sixth Thousand. The Railway Library.*

45. *Universal History, On The Basis Of Geography.* By Peter Parley. London: William Tegg, 1854. The Sixth Edition. British Museum deposit date: 3 November 1854.

1856 46. *The Scarlet Letter.* London: G. Routledge, 1856. Thirty-Seventh Thousand. The Railway Library.*

REFLECTIONS ON THE
FOUNDATIONS OF MODERN
TEXTUAL EDITING

MORSE PECKHAM

THE IMPRESSIVE ACHIEVEMENTS OF ANALYTICAL BIBLIOGRAPHY AND textual criticism under the admirable leadership of Fredson Bowers since World War II have been attacked and denigrated, notably by Edmund Wilson and James D. Thorpe, but not to any great effect. Wilson will be remembered as long as American literature is remembered, but *The Fruits of the MLA* was not his first foray into the cosmos of sheer downright silliness; it was preceded by a book on his encounter with the Internal Revenue Service. In 'The Aesthetics of Textual Criticism'[1] and 'The Ideal of Textual Criticism'[2] Thorpe has raised some questions and has most amusingly made some points against Bowers, but his answers are unsatisfactory and his points are mostly trivial. Nowhere does he show signs of an interesting analytical power. Others who have objected to the Centenary Hawthorne have

[1] *PMLA*, LXXX (1965), 465–82.
[2] In his and Claude M. Simpson, Jr.'s *The Task of the Editor* (Los Angeles: William Andrew Clark Memorial Library, 1969), pp. 3–27.

been pretty well disposed of by Bowers himself.[3] Nevertheless, the principles developed over the past thirty years (since Greg's *The Editorial Problem in Shakespeare*) are proving to be less satisfactory than they seemed to be ten years ago. Part of the difficulty lies in rhetoric, but much of it in the general truth that a great innovator's followers inevitably simplify and rigidify and sanctify their master's ideas. What is thrown out with the certainty of the excitement of discovery is taken for eternal truth, and careful qualifications of splendidly rotund statements are forgotten.

An example may be found in the increasingly vexing distinction between substantives and accidentals.[4] In the well-known 'Textual Criticism', written for the MLA, Bowers remarks on 'the common contractual practice of imposing a rigid house-style on an author's manuscript at the publisher's before copy is sent to the press.'[5] Now I have published with twelve different publishers, both commercial and academic, and also with more than forty different journals, scholarly and otherwise. Except for the presentation of notes in scholarly journals I have never encountered anything of the sort. Occasional suggestions, of course. But 'a rigid house-style' never. For this 'contractual' reason Bowers goes on to say that 'the dwindling authority of the accidentals may make Greg's distinctions of little account.' It seems to me highly unlikely that anyone is going to do a critical edition of any of my books, but if he does he can be sure that the overwhelming majority of the accidentals originated with me, and that most of the rest I accepted, ordinarily with pleasure. The tiny residue were compositorial errors which are quite obvious. They must be, since I found many of them myself. Several years later, in 'Today's Shakespeare Texts, and Tomorrow's', Bowers was more sensitive to

[3] See his 'The New Look in Editing', *South Atlantic Bulletin*, XXXV (1970), 2–10. I suspect the objections to the Centenary Hawthorne have been to a great extent occasioned by the fact that it is a clumsy and pretentious piece of bookmaking.

[4] See for example David J. Nordloh, 'Substantives and Accidentals vs. New Evidence: Another Strike in the Game of Distinctions', *CEAA Newsletter*, No. 3 (June 1970), 12–13.

[5] In *The Aims and Methods of Scholarship in Modern Languages and Literatures*, ed. James Thorpe (New York: Modern Language Association of America, 1963), p. 41. Bowers is apparently referring to a clause usually found in contracts in some such form as 'in such style and manner' or 'in such style' or 'in such style or styles' as the publisher deems best for the sale. The purpose of such expressions is principally to keep the author from trying to control format, binding, etc., and secondarily to provide by anticipation a legal foundation for settling arguments about styling.

the problem. He had begun to be aware that punctuation is somehow not quite just the form or the dress in which the substantives are presented.[6] Nevertheless, this distinction is commonly accepted as clear and unquestionable, or at least necessary. It is nothing of the sort.

In Greg's 'The Rationale of Copy-Text'[7] one finds the instructive note 4. 'It will, no doubt, be objected that punctuation may very seriously "affect" an author's meaning; still it remains properly a matter of presentation, as spelling does in spite of its use in distinguishing homonyms. *The distinction I am trying to draw is practical, not philosophic*' (italics mine). Greg, of course, was writing about Elizabethan and Stuart plays, and the justification for his making a practical distinction is the sparse and inconsistent punctuation in dramatic manuscripts *that have survived.* Does the practicality of his distinction apply to Jonson? Does it apply to Spenser? Does it apply to Bacon's philosophical works? Certainly by the eighteenth century, authors who took themselves seriously were making not a practical but a philosophical distinction. As Bowers has come to realize, punctuation does not merely ' "affect" an author's meaning'. Without punctuation it is frequently impossible to decide on that meaning. Punctuation is not a form or dress of substantives, something different from words. It is part of speech. Juncture, pitch, and stress are inseparable components in the semantic continuum of the spoken language. Their signs are punctuation. Admittedly punctuation marks are inadequate signs of these speech components, but that inadequacy is characteristic of all signs, which are signs of categories of discriminable phenomena, not of individual and unique phenomena. An author produces speech. When he writes it as he produces it, an educated author produces his punctuation as he produces his words; together they make up an unbroken semantic continuum. That he may revise his punctuation is true; but he also revises his words. And any author knows that if he revises many words he has to revise his punctuation. As Bowers points out himself, even spelling can have a substantive function. Again, any author knows this, since he often revises because he has inadvertently made a pun he does not want.

The lesson of this is clear. Greg needed to make a distinction for a specific class of texts at a specific and limited period of dramatic history. If anyone had told Tennyson that his punctuation was not part

[6] *On Editing Shakespeare* (Charlottesville: The University Press of Virginia, 1966), pp. 137–79.
[7] *Studies in Bibliography*, III (1950–51), 19–36.

of his 'thought', or that he had contractually surrendered his control over accidentals to his publisher, he would probably have thrown him out of the house. He certainly should have. Are we to imagine that the highly publicized editorial entrepreneurism of the eighteenth century, the occasion for immense publicity in the then small literary world and the stage for superb quarrels, had no effect on serious practicing authors? It seems to me that I could not have been more than eight when I first began to hear stories, in school and out of it, about how mispunctuation was responsible for decisional errors, not in literature but in government. The shift from rhetorical to syn-tactical punctuation in the first half of the nineteenth century re-flects a very old tradition of awareness that punctuation cannot be separated from words, especially in writing which is to be read se-riously and has some complexity of syntax. Greg's distinction rests upon the fact, which we know for other reasons, that nobody but Ben Jonson took writing for the public theater seriously.

Obviously, Greg's distinction is useless outside of his very special class of texts, and moreover, as his first sentence shows, he proposed a 'philosophic' justification for a distinction which he denied to be 'philosophic' in the very next sentence. And this is what we are sup-posed to take seriously for all different classes of authors of the nineteenth and twentieth centuries. It is not surprising, then, that the editors of the Centenary Hawthorne went back to the manu-scripts for the punctuation of *The House of the Seven Gables* and *The Blithedale Romance*, and went in for a great deal of compositorial analysis to recover as much as they could of the lost manuscript's punctuation for *Fanshawe*.

The point of all this is not whether or not there is a valid distinction between the strangely medieval terms 'accidentals' and 'substantives'. Does authorship transubstantiate language into divine utterance? A good many critics evidently think so, and among them are some textual critics. The point is that the textual critic is constantly being faced with a pseudo-problem that has arisen from converting into an editorial principle given the status of a scientific truth a distinction which Greg justified in an illogical and unhistorical note. Any disci-pline that develops rapidly in an atmosphere of excitement, enthusi-asm, and iconoclasm grabs its language from whatever is handy. In this case the iconoclasm included attacks on those dreadful establish-ment editors of the nineteenth century, and the language was at times grabbed from medieval theology. It was then pasted together with fine talk about science, laws of evidence, rigorous logic, and the rest of the rhetoric with which Thorpe has had such amusing fun. The time has come, it would seem, when some of this language should be subjected to analysis.

Bowers talks in various places about stripping away the veil of print and discovering the manuscript. Of course, sometimes, when you have nothing but a manuscript to begin with, as Bowers had with Dekker's *The Welsh Embassador,* and its sparse and inconsistent punctuation, you have to cover its indecencies with a veil of print. The Centenary Hawthorne editors, having discovered that in the manuscript of *The Blithedale Romance* Hawthorne used the same style of punctuation as that found in the manuscript for *The House of the Seven Gables,* although the printed form of the latter showed quite a different style, restored the manuscript punctuation. No doubt they were right in doing so, but it must also be remarked that by not recording the printed punctuation they have made it necessary for anyone who wants to study the history of punctuation in America in the nineteenth century to do the collation all over again. At least, I can find no statement that the collation has been preserved and deposited. But what if they had found that the punctuational style of the manuscript of *The Blithedale Romance* followed the printed style for *The House of the Seven Gables?* Precisely that happened in the case of another nineteenth-century book, *Paracelsus:* Browning saw the same work through the press four more times and corrected the final edition. Never again, either in this work or in subsequent works, did he revert to the style of that manuscript, from the publisher's or compositor's correction of which he learned how to punctuate. The lesson of this is that what to do about punctuation is an empirical matter, not a theoretical matter, not a matter of editorial principles or rules, as Greg pretentiously called them in *The Editorial Problem in Shakespeare.*[8]

The textual editor should do away with this theological terminology of accidentals and substantives, and talk simply and clearly about words, punctuation, spelling, capitalization, and whatever else he needs to talk about. These things are there, before our eyes; accidence and substance are not. They are high abstractions derived from a very different discipline. For an empirical problem one needs an empirical language. Yet it must be a language that can be philosophically justified and at the same time is founded on an examination of the phenomenally observable behavior of authors and their publishing cohorts.

[8] (Oxford: Oxford University Press, 1942, 1951, 1954), chap. 1.

I

It is desirable to begin with a clear and simple statement about what a textual editor actually does. Given a group of manuscript discourses, or of printed discourses, or of manuscript and printed discourses, which he asserts to be sufficiently alike to be categorized as versions of the same postulated work, and which he judges to be unsatisfactory versions, on whatever grounds, he adds to the group another version, which he asserts to be more satisfactory, on whatever grounds, than any existing member of that group.

Several points in this account need to be examined in some detail.

First, the textual editor decides that the group is sufficiently alike to be categorized together as versions of the same work. The decision is based on what kind of new discourse he wishes to add to the group. The differences may be such that he categorizes all versions together, or they may be such that he subdivides the group into two or more groups, each of which he decides are versions of two works—that is, two works with the same title and, to the best of his knowledge, authorship, but sufficiently different to be separated, as with the two versions of *The Rape of the Lock*. Obviously, his solution is not theoretical but empirical and rests upon his grounds for dissatisfaction with the group as it currently exists.

Second, he is making judgments about the relation of the versions to a *postulated* work. This status of the work as a postulation cannot be too strongly emphasized nor too clearly comprehended. It is vital for the textual editor to rid his theory of the notion that the object of his discourse is an empirical entity which now exists or ever existed. It certainly does not exist now, or he would have no problem. And even if it did exist in the past, that which has ceased to exist cannot be recovered. It can only be constructed. Talk about stripping the veil of print from a manuscript that no longer exists constitutes a fairy tale. Such a process merely reveals a Neoplatonic nonentity. (Indeed, the current language of textual criticism is surprisingly Neoplatonic at that school's worst.) This process is recognizable in the frequently encountered distinction between the work and the text of that work. The use of the expression 'categorized as versions' indicates clearly enough that the subsumption of the group of versions under 'work' is a linguistic process, not a non-linguistic or empirical observation. The distinction between 'work' and 'text' derives, like 'accidentals' and 'substantives', from an ontology that is in its ultimate pattern incarnationalist. Such language incarnates the metaphysical 'work' in the physical 'text', which in fact has now no physical existence and may never have had a physical existence. Both 'work' and 'text'—in the sense of '*the* text'—are constructs. For example, there is not now, and apparently there never was, something properly called *the* 'Ode on a Grecian Urn'. Further, the use of the same word, 'text', for two quite different semantic functions—the text and a group of texts, that is, empirically observable discourses—begs the question and introduces confusion. We can get this kind of confusing statement: 'The text is to be found in a number of texts.' To say, 'The work is to be found in a number of texts', is merely to conceal the issues, to bury them out of sight in obfuscating language. That is why Thorpe's yammering about 'the integrity of the work of art' and 'aesthetic integrity' makes it impossible for him to bring any light to a situation into which he has some insight. He murks further the waters of an already stagnant pond. Far from clearing up the language of textual criticism, he confuses it further by introducing the language of an extremely dubious and at best unsatisfactory philosophical aesthetic. Hence his complacency about scoring points against Bowers, and hence Bowers's quite justifiable refusal to take him seriously. The consequence of all this is that talk about 'transmission of the text' and 'recovery of the text' is abstract language which reifies words into nonexistent entities. We need not wonder at this; it is the norm of language behavior. It needs to be clearly understood that the textual critic neither recovers a text nor studies the transmission of that text. Either he constructs a new version to replace a postulated lost version, or he constructs a new version to fulfill a set of constructed conditions which he believes never to have been fulfilled by any version, existent or postulated. The result may be either a diplomatic version or an extreme conflated, sophisticated, and eclectic version; but the critic and the reader must always be aware that all versions, including the textual editor's own, are versions of a *postulated* work, that is, of a construct.

Third, there is the problem of the grounds for the textual editor's decision that the existing versions are unsatisfactory and for his assertion that his new or constructed version is more satisfactory than any existing version. Clearly, both these grounds rest on the further grounds for constructing a new version. Here again we encounter not a theoretical problem but an empirical one. The grounds for construction are a continuum, not a point. At one extreme of the continuum is the desirability of ridding a group of versions of an accumulation of changes that are the consequence of the necessarily incomplete success in repeating a version in manuscript or printed form. At the other extreme is the desirability of constructing into a single version all versions which are in themselves more or less satisfactory, as, for example, with Mill's *Logic*. At one end of the continuum lies repetition; at the other end is revision. When revising, the editor's purpose may be merely to put together into one version all typographically corrected versions so that the reader may study ideological change among the versions of the work (in this case very obviously postulated). Moreover the factor of repetition extends throughout the continuum as a continuum in its own right, from very poor success in attempted repetition to very great success, while revision extends into the primary continuum only to that point at which the subdivision of the category 'work' into two or more 'works' is, in the critic's judgment, no longer useful. It has been the practice of *Hamlet* editors to construct a version based upon both Q2 and F; thus we read a *Hamlet* which came into existence long after Shakespeare's death. For a long time the decision has been that *Hamlet* lies beyond the point at which the distinction between 'work' and 'works' is no longer useful. I should like, however, to see published in a single volume a Q2 version in which F additions are in footnotes or smaller print within the text, and a F version which reverses this. It seems to me very surprising that so far as I know this has never been done. At any rate the textual editor selects a point between the extremes of repetition and revision and does so on the grounds of what reader's purpose he wishes his version to serve. Thus his decision is on several grounds empirical and not theoretical. There is no 'best' point and consequently there can be no 'best' or 'definitive' edition. There can only be a best or definitive edition for the purposes of a constructed class of readers.

One further consideration is clear. In order to make this selection of a point on the continuum the textual editor must first construct his group of versions into a series of versions, whether he is concerned with the extreme of repetition or revision or both. Obviously the more revision is involved, the easier the construction of the series. The textual editor cannot even assume that several versions were not constructed simultaneously, as is shown in the now well-known case of *The Spectator*. That is, he is concerned with constructing a historical series. (By 'series' is meant, of course, directly, divergently, and convergently related versions.) This creation of a historical construct to explain the relation among versions of a postulated work is of course the area of analytical bibliography (which had perhaps better been called 'bibliology'). To deny that its achievements in the past thirty years have been anything but magnificent or to assert that Fredson

Bowers is anything but an extraordinary human being and an equally extraordinary scholar is to utter propositions not to be countenanced for a moment. Those who feel that their dignity as humanists is somehow compromised by analytical bibliography or by the inclusion in their ranks of analytical bibliographers have only to stay away from the subject and keep their mouths shut. To temper self-indulgence in this profession we need more 'Gradgrinds', not fewer. And if Bowers is a Gradgrind—well, I myself have a sneaking admiration for Mr. Gradgrind, at least before his conversion. Anyone who forces the noses of humanists onto the grindstone of hard, immutable fact has a genuinely redemptive function. Unfortunately, many of Bowers's hard, immutable facts are neither so hard nor so immutable as he says they are. An examination of two terms in analytical bibliography will reveal this clearly enough. They are the terms 'mechanical' and 'scientific'.

In what was perhaps an unguarded moment, Bowers once called the turning of a manuscript into a book a mechanical process. This has entered deeply into the theory, because he and others every now and then warn about the 'human factor', without however indicating very precisely what that human factor is. Roughly, I suppose they mean that an individual workman can always show a degree and character of independent judgment and error which can scramble the most carefully worked out series-construct; which can, in short, suspend the rather too optimistically named 'laws' of 'textual transmission', a concept the inadequacy of which I hope I have sufficiently demonstrated. Actually there is very little in version repetition which can be called mechanical; it is *mostly* the human factor. What any tool or machine does is to stabilize and increase the productivity of a human behavioral pattern. Any behavioral pattern which is not innovated by an individual has to be learned from another individual or other individuals. For reasons to be discussed in some detail later, no behavioral process can ever be perfectly learned. In the production of printed matter only that can be called 'mechanical' which happens between the operator's punching of a key in a mechanical or electronic typesetting machine and which happens in a mechanically operated printing press between the operator's giving the machine the impulse to perform and the ejection of the printed paper. Even in these operations, however, the term 'mechanical' has to be qualified. Type, for example, disintegrates under continuous pressure not because of any inherently mechanical process but because the design and manufacture of a machine has to be learned, because

130

neither design or manufacture can be learned perfectly, and because every machine is the consequence of the unavoidable divergence from a behavioral norm when an attempt is made to fulfill the conditions of that norm. To think of version repetition by printing as a mechanical process is to put oneself in a position of constantly having to remind oneself that the 'human factor' can enter in; it is to construct a series by ignoring as much as possible the salient factor in the historical emergence of that series. To think of version repetition, however, as requiring the editor to create a theoretical construct of a very complex sequence of interlocking behavioral patterns, in which the patterns cannot be perfectly executed and in which the machines are but an error-prone supplement to that behavior, is to avoid the peril of ignoring and constantly being surprised by something which can be explained only by dragging in the 'human factor'. To construct an explanation of version repetition in terms of mechanical process merely requires one to introduce an extra-explanatory term, 'human factor', which actually explains nothing, which only admits that the explanation has broken down. What the analytical bibliographer does, then, whether he realizes it or not, is, on the basis of certain artifacts which are the consequence or deposit of various behaviors, to make a theoretical reconstruction or construct of the behaviors responsible for the historical emergence of those artifacts. This is so obvious that it would scarcely need saying were it not for the constant appearance of the term 'human factor' in both the theoretical and problem-directed discourse of analytical bibliography. The 'human factor' is not something that occasionally enters into the bibliographer's thinking when he finds himself in a spot; it is almost exclusively all that he is concerned with. The analytical bibliographer is a historian, and he should not forget it for a moment. The object of his inquiry is not printed artifacts as physical objects but human behavior in the past, human behavior that no longer exists and cannot now be examined.

The recognition of this permits us to go on to the next problem. What is the scientific status of the behavioral-historical discipline of analytical bibliography? It is with a gentle smile that one reads in Bowers's *Bibliography and Textual Criticism*[9] of demonstrable, probable, and possible interpretation of evidence. He is in fact only talking about degrees of probability: not, however, degrees of probability of what happened, but, strictly speaking, degrees of the probability

[9](Oxford: Oxford University Press, 1964).

of generating a coherent verbal construct of what might have happened. Somewhere he says that Baconian induction and deduction are good enough for him. Well, Baconian induction and deduction are not good enough for anybody who proposes to be scientific. What it comes down to is this. The scientific status of analytical bibliography is the scientific status of any historiographical construct. Whether or not historiography can be a science is still, of course, unsettled, but something can be said on the subject which is possibly of sufficient interest to be included in this discussion.

The heart of science is the experimental method, of course, but this innocent proposition conceals a great many traps. The full implications of the statement are in fact rarely understood, particularly by humanists. Darwin put the problem well when he said that a scientific law is a mental convenience.[10] Today it is more accurate to call it a verbal convenience. This is the heuristic concept of scientific theory. But Darwin was also making the point that scientific law is not constitutive; it neither describes the data it subsumes, nor organizes them. This may not seem Darwinian, but considering his probable philosophical source in Dugald Stewart, it is reasonably correct. As 'convenience' emphasizes, the relation of the law to its data is instrumental. More precisely, it is a tool that operates *through* human behavior upon its data. It is rather instructional than instrumental. The link between scientific discourse and the empirical data it deals with is conventionally stabilized and formalized behavior, which, using the discourse as a set of directions, follows the directions to manipulate the empirical in such a way as to produce a predicted or unpredicted consequence, as the case may be. This is why to be a good scientist one must have laboratory training. The behavior conventionally linked to the discourse is never completely stabilized or formalized. It must be learned paradigmatically as well as linguistically. As a result of the empirical nonverbal manipulation the discourse is further stabilized, or is corrected, or is abandoned. This verbal behavior consequent upon the nonverbal behavior can affect a low level of abstraction or a high level.

It is easy to see where historiography fits into this model—the area of discourse. Insofar as it purports to discuss events which have ceased to exist, it is literally talking about nothing at all; it is not talking

---

[10] I use Darwin because his science was a historical one and because his philosophical position on science was much more advanced than that of most scientists of his day, Huxley's, for example.

about anything which is empirically, phenomenally, observable *now*, about anything which lies outside discourse. By examining documents and artifacts it constructs a coherent theory about how those documents and artifacts are related and a coherent explanatory theory of how they came into existence. But in so doing it remains inside its own discourse, in this being no more scientific than astrology or phrenology. To convert astrology into a science one must move the stars in their courses and see what happens to men on earth. That the logic of postdiction is the same as the logic of prediction may be true and interesting if we are studying logic, but it has no effect on the scientific status of history, which so far is no more scientific than astrology. Of both astrology and of the historical constructs of analytical bibliography, at best we can but say, 'It may be.' The fact that one can generate a logically coherent construct of the behavior responsible for the historical emergence of manuscript and printed artifacts does not make that construct scientific. The situation is as it is with the interpretation of a poem. The fact that you have uttered a coherent interpretation of the poem does not mean that the poem is coherent, only that the interpretation is. Not even that, really. It only means that your interpretation is coherent according to current conventionalized standards of coherence, as you understand those standards.

All is not lost, however, because in fact the historian does not remain inside of his historiographical language. He does not get outside it, however, merely by producing discourse about documents and artifacts; in doing that he is still inside his discourse. Rather, he gets outside of it just as any scientist gets outside of his discourse: he predicts. But his predictions can scarcely be about events which no longer exist. Rather, he predicts about where he is going to find documents and artifacts and what their attributes are going to be. Thus the proper object of the historian's investigations is not, as he usually imagines, the events of the past, but rather documents and other artifacts whose existence is concurrent with his own. And like any scientist, having performed this manipulation (which involves taking himself someplace and looking for something) he stabilizes, corrects, or abandons his theoretical construct—that is, the coherent explanation from which he derived his nonverbal behavioral instructions.

A simple example will clarify this. The Centenary Hawthorne editors of *Fanshawe* predicted that bibliographical analysis of the first printing would reveal sequences of composition discriminable in such a way that, on the basis of current theory, the best explanation was by postulating and constructing several compositors. From this they constructed a 'synthetic' version which, they believe, is closer to the manuscript than is the printed version. Some of their steps do seem a little too confident. Perhaps one wonders why only five copies of *Fanshawe* were collated and only eleven by spot-checking. Are these all that are known? We are not told. No doubt if there are more, their theoretical construct led them to the conclusion that further collation would be unproductive. Such a conclusion may be logical and coherent, but it is incomplete science. In short, an historiographical discourse modeled on scientific discourse does not make the discipline of that discourse into a science. Consequently the Bowers claim that analytical bibliography is a science is justifiable, though analytical bibliography certainly is not a very highly developed science. However, his justification is misplaced. Analytical bibliography belongs not in the area of historiographical discourse, in which he has placed it, but in the area of predictions about documents and other artifacts and the nonverbal behavior which responds to the directions given by that prediction.

The consequences of this misplacement of the scientific justification for analytical bibliography have not been happy. The reason for this is two-layered. The first, of course, is a misunderstanding of the nature of science. Actually the scientific model at work has been a late nineteenth-century model, in origin a seventeenth-century model. It was still dominant not only when Bowers went to graduate school but also even when I did in the 1930s. In fact, when we consider current a critical discourse which offers endless quotations as evidence for an interpretation—as they cannot be, since their evidential value depends upon interpretation—it is obviously still dominant in humanistic studies. However, this scientific model was thrown into confusion by the work of Einstein and Heisenberg and has in fact been abandoned. It is not, possibly, incumbent upon every humanist to know anything about the philosophy of science, but it is incumbent upon any humanist who proposes to found and develop a scientific discipline. This error of misplacement has made it possible to ignore the patent fact that the modern theories of analytical bibliography and textual criticism have been erected on the astonishingly narrow basis of the characteristics of a very special class of books from the late sixteenth and early seventeenth centuries. It is worth repeating that the result has been the establishment of a great many 'laws' and 'rules' and 'principles' that are reasonably useful in working on the kind of bibliographical data to which they were an appropriate generalizing or theoretical response. But such rules and principles are at best but exceedingly vague directions offering only very questionable advice when the bibliographical data are of a different sort, either in class or in time. What is useful for the very careless Shakespeare is pretty useless for the very careful Tennyson, and often enough misleading. What can be applied to a novelist in the first steps towards popularity cannot be applied to a poet at the height of his fame. The famous and puzzling intralinear spaces of Wallace Stevens were not, we now know, supposed to have been repeated in print, but his prestige as a serious poet was such that his copy was but too carefully followed by his house editor.

The consequence of this two-layered error has been an exaggerated confidence. The establishment of a definitive text means, after all, only the construction and presentation of a version which is asserted to be better for some purpose than any version currently in existence. Thorpe says that 'the ideal of textual criticism is to present the text which the author intended. The knowledge that this ideal is unattainable in any final and complete and detailed sense can perhaps help us to avoid the pedantry of vainly trying to attain it by a glorification of method.[11] One may be permitted to wonder if to entertain an ideal which cannot be reached is not the result of missing the problem. Bowers's corresponding definition is, 'The recovery of the initial purity of an author's text and of its revision (insofar as this is possible from the preserved documents), and the preservation of this purity despite the usual corrupting process of reprint transmission, is the aim of textual criticism.'[12] On the basis of the preceding analysis and discussion, it should now be clear that the fundamental difficulty lies not in the assumption that the task is 'to present the text the author intended', nor that it is to recover 'the initial purity of an author's text', but rather in the assumption that there *is* a text to be recovered and presented. There is no such text. Textual criticism with the aid of analytical bibliography constructs a text out of a group of versions. Even if all versions but one are rejected as unserviceable, the principle remains the same, for the selection of a version requires the historiographical construct of an explanatory theory of the relations of those versions to each other. To combine the two definitions, the recovery and presentation of the text the author intended in its original purity requires the ascription of existence to the nonexistent. Such a notion

[11] 'The Ideal of Textual Criticism', p. 27.
[12] 'Textual Criticism', p. 24.

creates an impossible goal and automatically generates pseudo-problems.

But there are yet further difficulties here. What is meant by 'intended'. And what is an 'author'? 'Intention' is a very puzzling word indeed, and 'author' may very well be as much a reification as 'text' in the sense just discussed. Is an author an entity? Is he a monad? But to analyze these problems it is necessary to subject the production of a printed discourse to careful examination.

II

Before that examination can be begun it is necessary to rid our minds of certain assumptions which lie in the way of any clarity of analysis. These notions emerge most clearly in Thorpe's essays, particularly 'The Aesthetics of Textual Criticism'. Let us be perfectly clear about at least one aspect of our subject. Textual editing and its assistant, analytical bibliography, are logically independent of problems of aesthetics. The fact that both are ordinarily applied to what are known as literary works of art is a matter of no importance, as the current editions of John Stuart Mill and John Dewey make perfectly evident. The textual critic and the analytical bibliographer are theoretically indifferent as to whether they are concerned with Shakespeare or with Fanny Farmer, and in practice they should be indifferent. Yet even Bowers feels it necessary, or at least advisable, to justify his discipline by an appeal to what it does for our literary culture. This is not surprising, since he emerged from a background of literary humanism and still, apparently, perceives himself against that background. The phrase 'the purity of an author's text' is sufficient indication of his culturally derived assumptions about an author.

In the theology and hagiography of literary humanism the term 'author', like the term 'work of art', is a sacred term. I use 'sacred' neither carelessly nor metaphorically. Literary humanists employ the term 'author' in a way that cannot be distinguished from the language of hagiology. 'Purity' is an attribute of sainthood. The term indicates a link with the doctrine of plenary inspiration. God inspired the authors of the Bible, and in the *Phaedrus* is a locus classicus for the notion that poets also are divinely inspired. To be sure, Plato was being ironic: since poets do not know what they are talking about, the only rational explanation for the oddity of their utterances and their ignorance of what they are doing is divine inspiration. But this irony has been traditionally ignored by literary humanists and on the whole still is. Literary inspiration, then, descends upon the poet as grace

136

descends upon the saint. 'Imagination' in literary theory is the equivalent of 'grace' in hagiology. Wordsworth manfully tried to develop and promulgate a non-hagiological conception of the poet, but the tradition and especially the Coleridgean doctrine of the imagination defeated him. The hagiological and generally religious character of literature subsequently has been given greater power by the disappearance of religious belief from a culturally central position. It is, therefore, revealing to see how many literary humanists have been impelled by the hagiographical character of their interests to reverse this cultural direction and to enter an established church and accept an established faith. The explanation is that in literary theory the substitution for such terms as 'God' and 'the divine' of such terms as 'unconscious', 'subsconscious', 'depths of being', 'innermost spirit', 'imagination', and 'self' does nothing to change the pattern of what might well be called the hagiolatrous syndrome. In short, in literary humanism the term 'author' (the intensive is 'poet') ascribes to a human organism conceived of primarily as producer of language the gift of God's grace, or charisma. Although charismatic cognition is no doubt a human universal, the ascription by masses of youngsters of charisma to The Beatles seems almost certainly the consequence of the penetration of the hagiology of literary and aesthetic humanism into lower culture levels by means of mass education.

Individuals whose cultural background has been literary humanism and who take up textual criticism and analytical bibliography justify their activity hagiologically. Thorpe's complaint really amounts to a protest that the Bowers school is not worshipful enough. And, of course, there are innumerable literary humanists for whom textual criticism and especially analytical bibliography are services so far from the divine light of the altar of literature that to engage in them is rather degrading, since they might be after all really in the service of the forces of darkness. Such silliness is really too painful to contemplate. All of this would be harmless enough did it not prevent the textual editor from understanding how his hagiology interferes with his comprehension of what he is doing and of the kinds of materials he is working with. In this context, the justification for literary hagiolatry is that it provides the textual critic with cultural propulsion as well as with cultural justification or validation. No doubt he can scarcely do without it, since charismatic cognition does appear to be a universal necessity for human existence. There is no reason, however, why he cannot perceive that the necessary can also be the intellectually damaging. The syndromatic equivalence of the two patterns, God-grace-saint-works and imagination-inspiration-author-works, has been responsible for the hypostatization of the word 'text' in place of the phenomenally observable and existent 'versions subsumed under the category "postulated work".' It has been responsible for Thorpe's urging us to pursue an unattainable ideal; this is true hagiolatry. It has been responsible for the hypostatization of the term 'author' into an unchanging entity, into a fixed monad who emanates 'works' instead of a man like other men whose existence is cultural and semiotic.[13] Of course, language behavior itself is responsible for an almost irresistible tendency to hypostatize terms, but resistance to that tendency is frustrated by various cultural forces, of which in the study of literature humanistic hagiolatry is the most important. It must be said for Thorpe that at least he sees that by the time a work is published it is to a certain extent 'a collaborative enterprise' but his aesthetic hagiology forces him to back away from his insight and prevents him from pursuing its implications or seeing where the collaboration begins. To do that will take considerable description and analysis.

An author produces a series of utterances, the assemblage of which he judges to be a discourse; and, by making it available to another or others, proposes that they too judge it to be a discourse — a sequence of utterances (no matter how broken down into their linguistic elements) which can be appropriately examined together. He does not, of course, ordinarily produce the utterances in an unbroken behavioral sequence. The ordinary process is to combine the production with revision of the production, so that he alternates between production and revision. Nor is this a unique characteristic of authorship. Revising, or amending, or editing one's utterances before one produces fresh utterances, is a norm of verbal behavior. However, to use such terms as 'revise', 'amend', and 'edit' is already to say too much, since such terms bear with them the attribute of 'improvement'. To be sure, *revisere* meant merely to look at again, but 'revise' now

---

[13] This point has been recently well analyzed by Paul Watzlawick, Janet Helmick Beavin, and Don D. Jackson, *Pragmatics of Human Communication* (New York: W. W. Norton & Company, 1967). The authors' identification of communication with behavior is the position I have long held myself, though for somewhat different reasons and in different terms. Their analysis of communication as a system is better than anything I have been able to achieve. However, their denial that the organism is an individual or monad does not include a discussion of why the notion of individuality should have emerged; this seriously distorts much of what they have to say.

generally means to change for the better. We can say, 'He revised it but did not improve it', but when we use 'revise' in the simple sense of change, it is the norm to add the qualification in order to forestall the attribution of improvement which is the norm of response to the word. But even to say 'change' is to say too much. The only way to know that the discourse has been changed is to observe a statistically significant series of responses by a number of individuals before and after the change has been made. It is, for one thing, a common experience in spoken conversation that the speaker changes his utterance but the responder insists that nothing has been changed, or nothing 'essential' has been changed, a term which begs so many questions that it is better not to think about it, at least very seriously. More precisely, in spoken utterance the speaker instructs the listener to make a substitution in his remembrance of what the speaker has uttered. He can do this only because he himself is listener as well as speaker. The results are of course, since the utterance no longer exists, bound to be a source of uncertainty. It is one of the principal sources of human troubles. In writing, however, the speaker is not listener; he is reader. The utterance is recorded, and the substitution does not depend upon remembrance. The term 'substitution', however, though it can include putting words in place of a juncture and a juncture in place of words, is strained if it is used to cover insertion and elimination of words at points in the utterance at which there is no juncture. 'Change' can subsume all cases.

A writer proceeds, then, by producing utterances until he judges he has come to the end of a discourse, and then by producing changes within the discourse; or by alternating the production of utterances with the production of changes; or by combining the two modes of producing a discourse. An author can continue change-production for a given discourse indefinitely, until he dies.

Before proceeding further, it is necessary to dwell a moment upon the word 'produce' and its implications. A writer produces utterances because he is a human being. It is a condition of being human. We do not know why human beings produce utterances, nor even how. It is a primitive, or surd, with which we begin and, to make matters worse, within which we must operate. To talk about self-expression, or projections, or mental ideas being expressed in language, is at worst to cover up our ignorance with pseudo-explanations, and at best to use a verbal category to subsume the production of language and the production of nonverbal behavior. But of course we do not produce behavior; we behave. Even 'produce' carries with it more attributional quality than is desirable. Here it is justified because it is useful in making a distinction between producing an utterance and producing a change for some or all of an already produced utterance. Strictly, we do not produce utterances; we utter. Moreover, the term is useful in making another distinction: one between an utterance which is in response to a situation *which does not* include a discourse of which the utterer judges his utterance to be a part, and an utterance which is in response to a situation *which does* include a discourse to which the utterer judges he is responding by producing a change.[14]

Ultimately an author arrives at a point in time at which he judges his production of the discourse to be complete and likewise judges his production of changes to be complete, or judges he has taken the production of changes as far as he ever can—or can for the time being, or judges that the discourse cannot be considered complete until not only himself but others have produced changes. Once he shows his discourse to someone else he has created a situation which is a situation-with-discourse. Such a situation is one in which the normal response is the production of changes. In normal spoken verbal behavior it is not only true that the utterer alternates between producing utterances and producing changes, but it is also the norm for the responder to produce changes for the utterances to which he is responding. It is the norm of any conversation. It is the norm of any reader's response to a published discourse, even if he confines himself to marginal corrections of typographical errors or limits himself still further to covert correction. The range of change extends from this all the way to total change by rejection and the production of complete new discourse as change, and even beyond this to the attempt to destroy all copies of the discourse, and further still to the attempt to destroy all individuals whom one considers probable candidates for uttering discourses, or any utterance similar to the utterances within these discourses. The explanation for this is that the only way to get rid of the kind of utterance you do not like is to kill everybody who is likely to produce it. This perhaps is one source

[14] It should not be imagined that I am proceeding on a simple stimulus-response theory, as the word 'situation' should make apparent. A stimulus is definable; a situation is not. But since a stimulus for the responder is necessarily a part of a situation, a stimulus cannot be isolated from a situation. When it is isolated and placed in a laboratory situation it is thus no longer the same stimulus. This is one of the reasons why some of the most brilliant work of experimental psychology is also so inconclusive.

of the vanity of authors; they see all too clearly where the process of change can end—elimination not only of their discourses but also of themselves. As Hegel pointed out, since there are no negatives to propositions but only alternatives, a proposition cannot be disproved, only transcended.

Situationally, then, anyone other than the author is in exactly the same situation as the author vis-à-vis the discourse. The fact that the author may or may not encourage the production of changes is not to the point. And the fact that he can accept or reject proposed changes is not much more to the point, since the acceptance or rejection of changes which he produces himself is a norm in the production of a discourse. His behavior in response to proposed changes by others can range all the way from determined resistance to all changes to complete indifference to what changes others make. Factors in his response to proposed changes are the kind of discourse involved and his status either in an authorial or a non-authorial role. The factor of the degree of his resistance to proposed changes and the more stable factors of kind of discourse, role, and status are of crucial importance to the textual editor, since such factors make his problem of accepting or rejecting changes he himself produces an empirical problem, not one to be solved on theoretical or a priori grounds.

Thus the activities of all those who respond to the discourse from the time the author surrenders it to the time it appears in print are in the same category. Editor, author, copy editor, author, copy editor, compositor, compositor's proofreader, corrector of composition, publisher's proofreader, author, corrector of composition, repairer of damaged or otherwise disintegrated composition, author (who always finds something wrong if he is so courageous and foolish as to read the printed version of his own discourse), reader, re-compositor, re-compositor's proofreader, re-corrector of composition, reader of the reprint version (these last four to be repeated indefinitely, as can authorial revision, which involves the entire process all over again), and *textual editor* (under which I subsume both analytical bibliographer and textual critic)—each of these proposes changes, not for the same discourse but for the version he is responding to. Any one of these, even inadvertently, even the compositor or the repairer of broken type, can make a change acceptable to the author or to anyone else involved. This clarifies further the notion of 'text' vs. 'text postulated from versions'. Not even in those cases in which an author produced a text and did not subsequently produce changes can we say that there is a text, since there is always the possibility that the discourse was produced covertly and changes were produced and accepted covertly before the discourse was uttered overtly and written down. (This was Wordsworth's practice.) Since covert behavior cannot be recovered with any accuracy more than a few moments later or be recovered at all after a greater lapse of time, the textual editor must assume that even the first rough draft, if he happens to have it and has documentary evidence that it *was* the first rough draft, is a version.

At this point a crucial difficulty arises. Granted that the author responds not to the discourse either while producing the discourse or after he judges the discourse is complete, but to versions of the discourse, can a distinction be made between authorial change and change by anyone else? The distinction cannot be made on the grounds of the distance in time between the author's response to his own discourse and another's, since the author himself is separated in time from the original production of the utterance to which he is now responding. That the author is in the same relation to his discourse as even so late a comer as the textual editor can also be shown. The distinction between responses to an utterance is to be made on the grounds of whether the response is immediate or mediated. An immediate response is one in which no further instructions, verbal or nonverbal, intervene between the utterance and the response to the utterance—that is, no instructions beyond those of the utterance and the situation in which it appears. A mediated response is, of course, just the reverse: additional instructions are offered. Now it frequently happens that an author engaged in the production of changes does not understand—that is, know how to respond to—his own previously written utterance. To decide whether or not a change is required he reconstructs as best he can the situation in which he produced the utterance. That is, he engages not merely in response but in interpretation, which consists of instructions on how to respond appropriately to a discourse. Whether or not he decides to produce a change is here a matter of indifference. Now the textual editor does precisely the same thing. Occasionally, innumerable textual critics have endeavored to reconstruct the author's total cultural situation in order to decide upon an emendation—that is, a change—in some version. (This is necessarily a task beyond completion, since situations are indefinable and since an individual's perception and cognition of a situation are inaccessible as well as irrecoverable. Since the amount of information-plus-inter-

142

pretation of the past is either infinite or might as well be, the effort can be expanded and extended indefinitely. For some famous cruxes it certainly looks as if it were going to be.) Like the author, the textual editor produces a change and then decides either to accept it or reject it.

Nor can a distinction be made between authorial change and anyone else's change on the grounds that the author was engaged in an aesthetic activity, was producing a work of art. In the first place, the activity of producing an artistic discourse is no different from producing any other kind of discourse. The fact that the discourse itself may be categorized as a work of art has nothing to do with the process of producing it. To think otherwise is to succumb to literary hagiolatry. This is sufficiently indicated by recalling borderline cases; it is always worth remembering that for a long time Pope was not a poet. In the second place, the textual critic, as we have seen, is completely indifferent to what category of discourse he is concerned with or what category the discourse easily falls into or is more or less arbitrarily assigned to by the categorical conventions of the critic's own cultural situation. Furthermore, the attempt to make a distinction is made even more difficult by the fact that the author, like anyone else, accepts proposed changes and actually uses them in changing his discourse.

The question of the possible distinction between changes by the author and by someone else comes down, then, to the question of whether the author is an organism engaged in the production of utterances, an activity which as a human organism he cannot avoid, even when alone and engaged in covert utterance, or whether he is an individual. So far there have appeared no grounds, save linguistic hypostatization and literary hagiolatry, for considering him an individual. The notion to be understood here is that he is but an organism and not an individual or monad or entity which can be differentiated from other similar entities. Two ways of comprehending this may be proposed, a general and a restricted. The general way is to conceive of the human organism as not human until and unless it becomes part of the communicational interactional system which by now has had an unbroken existence for an unknown number of tens of millions of years. From this point of view, personality, for example, is not something that emanates from an organism in a Neoplatonic manner but something that happens between organisms. The restricted way is the fact that the works of a particular period at a particular cultural level can be categorized together as sharing a common style. This can be put more precisely by pointing out that we can successfully predict that evidence will be found that will enable us to verify a hypothesis of the historical location of an anonymous work. The fact that such predictions sometimes fail is of no significance: all predictive behavior is marked by partial and repeated failure. The fact that it can be attempted with frequent success is all that is necessary here. Furthermore, if literature were as original, as creative, as individual, as unique as literary humanists are constantly saying it is, we would not be able to understand a word of it, let alone make emendations. In short, behavior is communication (see note 13). This notion that the individual is but an organism playing its part in a communication system which exists perfectly well without him, or, to put it a little differently, that individuality happens between organisms, that individuality is a mode of communication, is at least seventy years old, and since it derives from Hegel, nearly a hundred years older than that. The notion that individuality is not an existent is, of course, to be found in a number of religions, some of them very ancient.

All this does not mean, of course, that the textual editor is engaged in something he has no reason or right to be engaged in. It simply means that he, whose existence like the author's is a function of the human communicational system — of the same system as the author's, though in a historically different state — is simply continuing an activity initiated by the author. It is not necessary, therefore, that in order to perform his task he should have a justification for the notion of individuality. However, if he does have available such a notion he will be able to understand better what he is doing, he will have firmer theoretical foundations, and he will be able to extend his activities over materials beyond the area he as yet has some control over. In short, the account of individuality just offered is incomplete unless the emergence of the notion of individuality is accounted for, since it does appear to be a human universal, so deeply ingrained that it takes a fearful effort to divest oneself of it.

The problem, however, requires a much wider frame of reference and explanation than has yet been offered, though it is one that is perhaps best derived from the very phenomena the textual critic is concerned with, the versions of a postulated text. The problem may be sharpened by focusing on the compositor. Why cannot he repeat a version perfectly in type? But it is equally puzzling that he can repeat it at all, especially with such astounding success. Precisely analogous is the performance of music. A composer does not compose music; he composes a set of directions for a performer. No performer, however skilled, can perform the same piece of music in precisely the same way, even on the same instrument. Moreover, even the composer, no matter how skilled a performer he may be, cannot do it either, since he also is responding to a set of directions. One reason for this is that musical directions are never complete. Exactly how much slowing down does *rallentando* indicate? It is necessary therefore for the performer to supplement the directions on the printed sheet before him with directions and behavioral patterns he has learned from his training, a training which blends imperceptibly into a far richer cultural background from which further directions for performance are also derived. For the compositor the copy is a set of directions the meaning of which is not immanent but depends upon his previous training. Since, however, he is part of a cultural situation, what we may call 'cultural noise' frequently intervenes and furnishes him with inappropriate directions for governing his behavior. So he composes 'sallied' into 'solid'. Moreover, just as in this century the performing musician has been required to reduce his substitutions to the minimum, 'to follow the score', so too for quite different reasons the compositor has been required with steadily increasing insistence to set to the best of his ability only what lies before him, whether it makes any sense to him or not. That is, in setting Elizabethan and Stuart plays he was allowed a considerable degree of mediated response and openness to cultural noise, but now every effort is made to train him so and to control him so that he performs only immediate response.

This gives us some insight into two oddities of human behavior: behavioral divergence and behavioral convergence, both of which are quite puzzling, whether taken together or separately. Responsible for divergence are the human inability to repeat any behavioral pattern exactly, and what I have called 'cultural noise'—inappropriate directions, interpretation, or inappropriate mediation. Responsibility for convergence is pressure on the behaving organism to resist the forces making for the divergence. These pressures are the cultural norms. I shall call the applications of such pressure 'policing'. (Strictly, 'cultural norm' is an abstraction from and an explanation for observed policing behavior and its results.) Further insight into the first reason for divergence can be found in recent studies of the brain. It is now reasonably certain that it is impossible to make 'any meaningful statement about the relation between an individual response and a particular single stimulus'. The brain is not to be conceived of on the older model of a telephone exchange but on the model of a computer. Brain activity is not to be understood causally but stochastically, as a random system to be comprehended statistically. This is why above 'situation' was substituted for 'stimulus'. This new model provides some explanation for the norm of human behavior, constant innovation, which is another way of saying that the human organism cannot repeat anything perfectly except for extremely brief behavioral patterns (such as a name, a date, or a phrase).[15] Innovation, then, is divergence from a learned behavioral pattern. To account for the fact that behavior can be repeated well enough to be recognized as repeated, and for the fact that the organism can be instructed to repeat behavior to the same degree, the new model also uses the term 'memory'. For the time being, however, all that 'memory' means is merely 'the repetition of behavioral patterns'.

Within this frame of reference it is possible to explain in two ways how the notion of individuality emerged. Both are highly pertinent to textual criticism. The first derives from the fact that response is not only mediated but also self-mediated. Thus the organism can not only produce instructions to others but also produce them for itself. Policing has been responsible for the increasing reliability of compositors and the increasing convergence of their behavior, but this result could not have been possible if compositors were not capable of self-policing. The establishment of cultural norms through policing, therefore, can be internalized. This internalization of policing is one of the principal tasks of education, and on the whole is quite successful. Generally speaking, people do exactly what you tell them to do if it is in line with a well-policed cultural norm, as it almost always is. The second source of the notion of individuality is divergence itself. Primary divergence is the norm of innovation. The consequence is the opposite of policing. It is the delta effect. A behavioral pattern ineffectively transmitted and poorly policed brings about a range of deviations from a cultural norm, and the range is ordinarily repeated in each generation of transmission. It is not necessary to postulate a genetic factor. College teaching is an excellent example, since the delta effect is evident in each year's crop of college teachers as they proceed through their teaching life; but on the whole they are neither the offspring of college teachers nor are their own offspring college teachers. Secondary divergence derives once again from self-

[15] See B. Delisle Burns, *The Uncertain Nervous System* (London: Edward Arnold, 1968). The quotations above come from a review of this work by M. A. Boden, *Mind,* LXXVIII (1969), 313.

mediated response, since the organism can produce instructions to itself not only to obey instructions but also to disobey or to modify them. The condition for this possibility is the incoherence of cultural norms, an incoherence which can be increased by interpretation. This is the condition which makes cultural revolutions possible.

One other factor needs to be isolated before it is appropriate to proceed. The term 'individuality' is not, at least ordinarily, applied simply to divergence, but rather to what is judged to be self-mediated divergence from a cultural norm, evasion of the pressures which make for convergence. The term can also be applied pejoratively, neutrally, and honorifically. Thus individuality can be socially invalidated, simply pointed out, or socially validated. When individuality is socially validated it is currently called creativity. In the past it was called divine inspiration; with the disappearance of God the attribute of creativity has been transferred to the artist, and from thence to the scientist, the businessman, and the denizens of kindergartens. Actually, today there is an interesting and widespread social and cultural norm to call any divergence 'creative'. To call something 'creative', then, is a value judgment on what is judged to be socially validated divergence which had been judged to be self-mediated. The recognition of these three successive layers of judgmental behavior is of the greatest importance, for it forces upon us the awareness that creativity is not an attribute of the process of the production of an utterance but an attribute of the process of responding to it. The writer himself, in going over a discourse with a view to changing it, makes judgments about divergence, decides whether or not a particular divergence is marked by individuality, and decides in that case whether or not it should be validated or invalidated. If the latter, he produces a change. To type 'teh' instead of 'the' is a simple divergence. To use 'cognit' (which does not appear in Webster's Second or Third) instead of 'know', deriving it analogically from 'cognition', the writer may judge to be the result of self-mediated individuality and may decide to invalidate it by changing it to 'know', or may decide to let it stand and thus validate it. This process is what makes it possible for the author or anyone else to validate a compositor's divergence. It is likewise what makes the notion of a definitive text an idle dream and the establishment of it as an ideal to be striven for a very great mistake. When human organisms produce for others or themselves verbal instructions which cannot be carried out, those who attempt to do so sooner or later find themselves in inextricable difficulties — in a labyrinth from which there is no exit. There are strong indicators that textual editing is becoming just such a labyrinth.

The proposition, then, that individuality is what happens between organisms is correct as far as it goes, since it is the consequence of a judgment of a behavioral process or the judgment of such a process now lost in the past but constructed from the deposit of the process: manuscripts and printed discourses are the deposits of processes. However, the source of individuality is behavioral divergence, and the distinction between immediate and mediated divergence is so difficult to make, particularly when it is based upon the deposit of a process, that the two are constantly being fused. When we apply this notion to a literary discourse, it is evident that the total amount of divergence can vary from small to great; but even when it is great the amount of divergence in comparison with the amount of convergence is comparatively small. This is true even of *Finnegans Wake*, about the validation of which there is still considerable doubt.

To comprehend this it is necessary to make a distinction, previously but hinted at, between simple divergence and deviation. To use once more college teaching as an example, when one is inside of that situation, there appears to be a great amount of divergence, an impression intensified by the almost universal unwillingness as well as inability of teachers to talk about what they actually do in the classroom except in the most vague, general, and validating language. When one is outside of the situation, however, it is obvious that the range of divergence is quite narrow. Deviance, then, is patterned divergence from a cultural norm, but it often becomes a cultural norm. Thus a young criminal may be judged deviant by those who disapprove of criminality, and it is equally obvious to them that it is a very common and easily recognizable pattern of deviancy. To his fellow criminals, however, he may be a very ordinary criminal indeed, insufficiently creative, lacking in the power to produce divergencies by the validation of which the cultural norm of criminality may be made more effective. Thus *Finnegans Wake* shows the consequences of a high degree of divergence but its patterns of divergence are limited. In comparison with the degree of convergence in the work, the range of deviance is rather narrow.[16] The same point can be made of the

[16] David Hayman's 'From *Finnegans Wake:* A Sentence in Progress', *PMLA*, LXXIII (1958), 136–54, shows not only the narrow range of deviancy but the tremendous effort necessary to achieve even that much. Human organisms are not capable of very much divergence and can likewise tolerate very little of it.

Cantos; once the patterns of divergence are grasped as lying within a narrow range of deviancy the poem loses much of its difficulty. Obviously it is only because divergence tends to fall within a range of deviancy that the textual editor can operate at all. If in all the typescript and printed matter in the English language there were but one 'teh' it would be a puzzle of divergence. Since in actuality it is a very common deviancy, it very rarely presents difficulties.

With this analysis of the notion of individuality it is now possible to understand why the notion of individuality to be found in literary hagiolatry creates unnecessary difficulties for the textual editor.[17] The first step in hagiolatry is the acceptance of the discourses, all of which are believed to have been, in origin, produced by the same writer. The name which subsumes these works now becomes a hagiological entity. The works have been judged canonical; the author is canonized; literary sainthood is conferred upon him. This is why no matter how disgusting an author's private life may have been his sainthood remains valid. The basis of the canonization is not the man, but the discourses. The hypostatized entity said to be responsible for the discourses is distinguished from the hypostatized entity be-

---

[17] I have no interest in the total invalidation of literary hagiolatry. Textual editing is an act of hagiolatry. Literary hagiolatry is the cultural norm which is the pressure upon the textual editor. It makes it possible for him to undertake his heroic activities. Since, however, those activities are indifferent to the character of the discourse, textual editing can be an act of scientific or philosophical hagiolatry. The first example of editing a modern scientific classic I know of is James Strachey's edition of Freud's *The Interpretation of Dreams* (New York: Basic Books, 1955). The second I am aware of is my own edition of Darwin's *The Origin of Species* (Philadelphia: University of Pennsylvania Press, 1959). The editions of Mill and Dewey now being prepared and published are more recent examples. (The editing of Plato and Aristotle from manuscript is of course an old story.) The value for cultural history of editing works of great importance which the author put through many revisions over a considerable period of time, revisions which responded to continuing changing cultural conditions, is to my mind greater than the value, for example, of editing Hawthorne. Valuable as the Centenary Edition is, the editors have not changed the picture much, though one should be grateful for the punctuation in *The House of the Seven Gables* and *The Blithedale Romance.* Unhappily the stupidity of the attacks on analytical bibliography has driven its practitioners, quite understandably, to misplaced claims for the importance of their work. *Whether an edition has a high yield or not has nothing to do with whether or not it should have been done.* The discovery that most versions are reliable enough save for the most exacting purposes is just as important as the discovery that all of them show extreme degeneration and are unreliable for any purpose.

lieved to have been responsible for the invalidated non-authorial behavior. The proper name and the canonization now confer individuality upon the author, though not upon the man. The same distinction is made for religious saints, whose activities after the descent of grace, or conversion, are validated, but not those before. For writers, of course, there are many befores and afters, since the descent of literary grace is intermittent, not continuous once it has descended. (To be sure, some religious saints have been backsliders and have needed a couple of conversions.) Moreover, some discourses produced by the identical writer are validated as the justification for canonization, and some are not, though with very high literary saints, everything is. Even worse, it frequently happens that only sections of discourses are so validated; literary hagiolators who do this are said to be very discriminating critics and tend to be much admired. This creates a severe difficulty for the textual editor, since the greater the discrimination the less the validational consensus. However, the textual editor can if he wishes mediate his behavior by the cultural norms of such extreme discriminatory hagiolatry, given the assumptions of uncomprehended hagiology. Nothing is to prevent him from asserting that only 250 lines of *Paradise Lost* are truly creative, and since only these exhibit the stigmata of creativity, and hence only these can be said to be really by Milton, therefore only these *can* be edited. However, once he accepts the author as canonical he is condemned to giving all that author's discourses the same status. The obscurely felt instability of highly discriminatory canonization is probably responsible for the textual editor's taking the safe way out. One never knows what literary critic is going to have the next divergent canonizational revelation.

Thus the textual critic emerging from a cultural context of humanistic literary hagiolatry is saddled with a notion of 'author' which is not even a notion of personality, since a full notion of personality requires a random sample of an organism's full range of behavior, not just the portion of that range involving the production of utterances assembled into what are judged to be discourses. Since on the whole discourses tend to be continuously canonical over a long period of time because they manifest the stigmata of creativity (or, to use an older term, 'inspiration'), and since to the categorizing term 'author' is ascribed the attribute of 'creativity', everything that the author has written is called 'creative'. Divergence, deviance, and convergence are all fused together. The textual editor is thus in an im-

150

possible position. He is faced with a group of versions which, as best he could, he has ordered into a series. He now desires to produce by change a new version. To do so he must discriminate among the divergencies, the deviations, and the convergences of each of the versions. The notions, however, of text and author prevent him from doing so by requiring him to produce a definitive edition, which he cannot do, instead of producing a new version more satisfactory for some specific purpose than any existing version, which he can do. This cultural incoherence comes out clearly in the work of Fredson Bowers. On the one hand he insists on the 'recovery of the initial purity of an author's text and of its revision', and on the other hand he insists that a textual editor who knows his business will have no hesitation in creating an eclectic and synthetic text by conflation. As we have seen, convergence does not confer individuality, creativity, and sacred authorship and charisma; the author exists as an individual only to the degree his discourses are the deposit of immediate and mediated divergence, the difference between which cannot be recovered by examination of behavioral deposits. Consequently, as we have also seen, the textual editor continues the process of producing changes, a process begun by the author. When he incorporates a change previously to be found in no known version, he implies, 'If the author were here, he would accept this substitution.' This, of course, is a condition contrary to fact, and nothing can make it factual. Since it is a change derived from a verbal construct (only a verbal construct can have the 'rigorous logic' Bowers so often recommends), it is not scientific because science requires nonverbal behavior leading through manipulation of nonverbal material to a predicted or unpredicted result. The only way to convert his contrafactual conditional into a scientific instruction is to say, 'If we were to find a version which incorporates the author's final changes and *only* his final changes, then there is a probability that this change would be found among them.' The chances of verifying such a prediction certainly seem to be remote. The notions of text and author have been responsible for the fact that a discipline which came into existence as a reaction against textual eclecticism has returned to textual eclecticism, as in the Centenary *Fanshawe*. Nor is it surprising that a discipline based on a very small and very special class of printed documents should find itself unable to handle even those documents by obeying the instructions in the laws, principles, and rules it itself has produced. The lesson of this is that the textual editor may, if he feels that his purposes so require, limit himself only to what his construct tells him are utterances and changes of the postulated author, but he need not do so; in practice he rarely so limits himself; and given the limitations on behavioral accuracy, cannot do so.[18]

[18] This is the place to say a word about Thorpe's conundrum and his solution, which is not worth discussing in the body of this paper. His position is that the discourse is an aesthetic object 'which must be protected in order to preserve the work from becoming a collaborative enterprise' ('The Aesthetics of Textual Criticism', sec. 4). If we ask what an 'aesthetic object' is, we learn that it is one that elicits an aesthetic response. If we ask what an aesthetic response is, we learn that it is a response elicited by an aesthetic object. This sort of thing, though common, has never gotten anybody very far, and it does not get Thorpe very far either. Unable to solve the conundrum of collaborative enterprise, which it is his chiefest merit to have observed, he falls back on the emanator of the aesthetic object, the author, and then falls back on the (sacred) intentions of the author. This is a splendid example of how to organize an argument on the hagiolatrous model. He does not tell us what an 'intention' is. Two semantic functions for 'intention' may be discriminated: mediated intention and immediate intention. Mediated intention is a statement or other sign. Immediate intention not only is inaccessible, it does not exist. It has come into existence by metaphorical extension of mediated intention into the area of 'mind', which does not exist either, being a categorial term at a high abstract level. Mediated intention, further, is a statement or other sign that we interpret to mean that the organism producing the sign is going to behave in a particular way. Mediated intention does not exist either. It is an interpretation. When we ask, 'What is the intention of the behavior?', we are asking for further instructions for interpreting it. When we say that we know the intention of the behavior, we are asserting that on demand we can produce such instructions. This can easily be seen. You can ask me my intention in saying something which puzzles you for some reason; I can reply by a statement of my intention; you can reply that my intention was something other than what I have proposed; and I can agree with you. Statements of intention about past behaviors are constructs. (For a more detailed discussion of this see my 'The Intentional? Fallacy?' reprinted in *The Triumph of Romanticism: Collected Essays* [Columbia, S.C.: University of South Carolina Press, 1970], pp. 421–44.) Consequently Thorpe's solution that the textual critic must 'undertake to discover all that he can, from whatever source, about the linguistic intentions of the artist' is quite useless. There are no such sources. Even an author's statements of intention before producing the discourse or the changes leaves completely open the question as to whether or not he fulfilled them. Even an intentional statement that the author proposed to produce a particular class of divergences does not mean that a divergence of that class was intended by the author — that is, is a fulfillment of his intentional statement — even if found in manuscript in his own hand. The case is clearer for deviancies but still uncertain.

III

The textual editor is engaged in continuing the process begun by the author, the production of changes. This can now be put with greater accuracy and also in more general terms, terms which indicate the continuity of the textual editor's behavior with other verbal behavior and with human behavior in general. Like the author he is engaged in policing and validating. As bibliographical analyst he organizes a group of versions of a postulated discourse into a series and determines whether or not it is a complete series, and whether or not the effort to determine its completeness as a series is worth the trouble. Who is going to collate all the surviving copies of even the first edition of *Ulysses*? Obviously, since not all copies of all printed versions have survived and since it cannot be known how many have survived, no series can be complete. Therefore the statement should read, 'As bibliographical analyst he organizes a group of versions of a postulated discourse into a series which he asserts either to be complete enough, or to be as complete as he can make it.' At this point his task as bibliographical analyst ends. As one who has created an historiographical construct of a lengthy and complex series of behaviors involving a number of different organisms and a number of different social roles, he can do no more. Now the textual editor becomes the textual critic. Bibliographical analysis has eliminated some divergencies. Sometimes it has provided a probabilistic basis for validating some. Henceforth the editor is engaged in three activities: policing, validating, and substituting. In all three, once again, he is continuing the process begun by the writer. What the writer does that the textual critic does not is to produce utterances. Like the writer, the textual critic produces changes both immediately and mediately. Working probabilistically from his necessarily incomplete, partial, and on the whole uncontrollable knowledge of the convergencies of the cultural conditions during which were produced the versions of the postulated text, he polices by eliminating what he judges to be divergences, he validates divergences and deviancies which he judges to be indications of individuality and cultural mode, and produces and incorporates changes which he judges to be coherent with individuality and cultural mode. The result—let it once again be said—is a version added to the existent group of versions, but not, however, to an existent series of versions, since a series is a construct.

In producing that new version by policing, validating, and changing he may mediate his behavior by a wide range of aims. He may decide to eliminate all changes to the original utterance, or what he takes to be the original utterance, for given the phenomenon of covert change he can never be sure whether he has an original utterance or not. To do this is the simplest thing he can do and the most certain, since he disengages himself from policing, validating, and changing. The result may be, however, a version that nobody has any use for. Or, mediating his behavior by instructions about the possible use for his version, he may produce a version based upon any stage of the writer's change-production, upon change-production by author + editor, or author + editor + copyreader, or editor + copyreader + compositor, and so on, mediating his behavior in each version-production by policing, validating, and changing. Or he can produce his version by eliminating any segment or segments of the production sequence, as in producing a version of Hamlet Q2 or F. For some purposes he may produce a version of the manuscript of *Look Homeward, Angel;* for others he may produce a version of the published version edited by Perkins and who knows how many copyreaders. If we ever have a printed version of *Flags in the Dust,* an edited version of *Sartoris* will always be needed; it is part of literary and cultural history. In recording variants, he can record none or, if he wishes, can record all of them. If he does the latter for a nineteenth-century work which was frequently reworked by the author and was frequently set in type from new authorial manuscript versions, from authorial and editorial changes in a copy of a printed version, and directly from a printed version, he has not perhaps done much that the literary scholar will thank him for, but he has accumulated a mass of related material invaluable for the student of the history of spelling and punctuation, for the student of historical linguistics, and above all for the student of human behavior. The production of versions of a postulated text is the best historical evidence we have for the fine grain of human behavior. Students of human behavior have not learned to use it; most of them scarcely know of its existence. But it is so rich and so exquisitely revealing that a theory of the foundations of behavior could very possibly be constructed solely from the evidence it has to offer. There is no reason that textual editors should be governed solely by the cultural norm of literary hagiolatry.

Such further uses of the results of his work bring out the easily neglected fact that the textual editor must take full responsibility not merely for the thoroughness and care of his work but above all for the decision on what use he foresees for his efforts, since everything he does subsequently depends on that. He must engage not only in self-policing but also in self-mediation. Like all human beings, from the depths of his animal background he longs for both immediacy of response and convergence. This alone confers that feeling of cultural validation which is the source of certainty and truth—in his case, for the definitive edition. But he must be aware that his decision involves the divergence and deviation brought about by his physiology and his self-mediation. He must choose among cultural incoherences, yet knowing that his choice is at best barely individual and is itself merely a consequence of his own unavoidable cultural ethnocentricity. For all he knows, in the future may emerge uses he cannot foresee and techniques he cannot imagine. No misplaced confidence in inadequately based theory can justify his evasion of the problems of an empirical situation.

To conclude, the task of the textual editor is to produce a new version from a series of a postulated text by a postulated author by making up for the policing, validating, and changing deficiencies in the long, complex, and interlocking series of behaviors the consequence of which was the production of that series. There is no 'definitive' version at which he must or can arrive. There is no one set of instructions which can mediate his behavior to the exclusion of all other sets. His activities are multi-purposeful; his problem is empirical; it cannot be solved a priori. His situation is open.[19]

[19] Nothing in this paper should be construed as an attack on Professor Bowers. As a hagiolator myself, I have a tendency to canonize great scholars, perhaps because they are so much rarer than great artists. As a man of achievement and as a human being built on the grand scale, he is necessarily the object of the free-floating resentment which seems to be more prevalent in the academic world then elsewhere. As for his detractors, it is best but to quote Swinburne: 'Silence is most noble till the end.'

MELVILLE AND THE CONCEPT OF 'AUTHOR'S FINAL INTENTIONS'

HERSHEL PARKER

ONE OF THE DOGMAS OF MODERN TEXTUAL EDITING IS THAT THE 'author's final intentions' must be respected. In its present form this concept can be traced to 'The Rationale of Copy-Text' (1950–51), where W. W. Greg posed two questions an editor should ask himself whenever variant readings occur: '(1) whether the original reading is one that can reasonably be attributed to the author, and (2) whether the later reading is one that the author can reasonably be supposed to have substituted for the former.'[1] Greg was unequivocal about an editor's duty when both questions are answered affirmatively: 'the later reading should be presumed to be due to revision and admitted into the text, whether the editor himself considers it an improvement or not.' The phrase 'author's final intentions', which was only implicit in Greg's essay, has been given wide currency by Fredson Bowers and others. In his superbly condensed 'Textual Criticism' (1963), Bowers's definition of the aim of the editor of a critical edition

---

[1] *Studies in Bibliography*, III (1950–51), 19–36; the quotation is from p. 32.

was 'to recover the author's final intentions more faithfully than these can be found in any preserved document.'[2] In the Centenary Edition of *The Marble Faun* (1968), Bowers argued that any of Hawthorne's revisions in the proofs of the first (English) edition of that book 'would represent his final intentions and would become more authoritative than the corresponding manuscript readings.'[3] Furthermore, any hypothetical 'afterthoughts'—readings Hawthorne might have 'sent to Boston for inclusion in the first American edition'— would 'also come in the class of his final intentions and would be adopted as more authoritative than the original readings either of manuscript or of first edition.' In these formulations, 'final intentions' means simply last known intentions, the underlying notion in Bowers as in Greg being that an author knows what he wants and has a right to do it. Yet recent editors, including Bowers, have begun to interpret 'author's final intentions' in various ways and to modify the phrase itself. Among editors who explicitly commit themselves to following Greg's theory of copy-text appear such variations as 'full intentions', 'true intentions', 'original intention', 'final artistic intentions', and 'concept of the book as an artistic whole'.[4] Far from being mere elegant or careless variations, these wordings seem to reflect attempts of the editors to deal with problems which Greg did not entirely anticipate.

For most classes of authorial changes, of course, Greg's dictum obviously applies, as when the first edition or editions contain misprints that an author later corrects. Where in the Revised Edition of *Typee* Melville had individual lines or parts of lines reset to correct single words, an editor welcomes restorations like that of 'red' instead of the erroneous 'rich' and 'liberally' instead of 'literally'. *The Whale* contains several similar changes stemming from Melville's revision of the Harper proofs before he sent them to England. No one but the author would have corrected a quotation to read 'her mere appearance' rather than the plausible 'her near appearance' or would have restored the tragic quality to the phrase 'fullest sweep and direst

---

[2] *The Aims and Methods of Scholarship in Modern Languages and Literatures*, ed. James Thorpe (New York: Modern Language Association of America, 1963), pp. 23-42; the quotation is from p. 25.

[3] P. lxxiv, also the source for the quotations in the following sentence.

[4] The first quotation is from Bowers's 'Textual Criticism', p. 25. The others are from volumes of CEAA editions—the Centenary Hawthorne, the Northwestern-Newberry Melville, and the Virginia Crane: *The Scarlet Letter*, p. xxxvi; *Typee*, p. 309; *Maggie*, p. xcvii; *White-Jacket*, p. 455.

swing' that was printed in *Moby-Dick* as 'fullest sweep and direct swing'. In a copy of the third impression of *Israel Potter* Melville made several corrections, most strikingly changing Israel's comment about Benjamin Franklin's 'sort of wild slyness' to 'sort of mild slyness'. An editor accepts the change whether Melville made it soon or many years after the book was printed. Similarly, any editor would accept the correction 'but that is treating the poor fellow like an ex-king indeed' from the printing of 'Benito Cereno' in *The Piazza Tales* rather than 'but that is treating the poor fellow like an ex-king denied', as the *Putnam's Monthly* text reads. In all these instances, and many more in Melville, whose handwriting was notoriously bad, the author's final intentions are identical with his original intentions, and the editor is merely restoring what the author first wrote or meant to write.

Nor does a challenge to Greg arise with most small stylistic revisions made soon after a work was completed. Toward the end of chapter 76 of *Omoo* the Harper edition has this sentence: 'The appearance of the Leviathan herself was quite pleasing. Like all large, comfortable old whalers, she had a sort of motherly look:—broad in the beam, flush decks, and four chubby boats hanging at the breast.' The English edition, which normally has later readings than the American, contains the jarringly masculine synonym 'whalemen' instead of 'whalers'. In the Harper text the word 'she' is spaced unusually far from the word on either side, leading to the suspicion that the author noticed the awkwardness and had the correction made after the proofs had been prepared for shipment to England. An alert reader at Harper's could have made the change, but it is easy to attribute so superior a reading to Melville himself. Some simple examples in *White-Jacket* are even more certainly Melville's, made on a set of the Harper proofs which served as the printer's copy for the English edition.[5] In chapter 6, Mr. Pert, the aptly named midshipman, is sent after the boatswain—a routine chore that is sarcastically called a 'perilous errand' in the American edition and a 'dignified errand' in the English, which must be presumed to be later. The revision blunts the irony, but apparently only to avoid weakening the word 'perilous' in another ironic scene in chapter 28

[5] The theoretical possibilities for priorities of readings in *White-Jacket* are extremely complex, as explained in the Northwestern-Newberry Edition, pp. 451–56. Aside from Melville's late changes in the 'Note' to the American edition, however, there is no reason for thinking any American variant is later than the English variant.

some one to come on deck. I liked his voice. Hearing it was as good as a look at his face. It betokened a true sailor, and no taskmaster.

The appearance of the Leviathan herself was quite pleasing. Like all large, comfortable old whalers, she had a sort of motherly look :—broad in the beam, flush decks, and four chubby boats hanging at the breast. Her sails were furled loosely upon the yards, as if they had been worn long, and fitted easy ; her shrouds swung negligently slack ; and as for the "running rigging," it never worked hard as it does in some of your "dandy ships," jamming in the sheaves of blocks, like Chinese slippers, too small to be useful ; on the contrary, the ropes ran glibly through, as if they had many a time traveled the same road, and were used to it.

When evening came, we dropped into our canoe, and paddled ashore ; fully convinced that the good ship never deserved the name which they gave her.

PLATE 1

where Mr. Pert is again sent to summon the boatswain and finishes by going below 'to the surgeon with an alarming wound, gallantly received in discharging his perilous duty on the forecastle' — having been 'struck on the nose with a snow-ball of wondrous compactness.' In chapter 37 of the American edition, the ship sights 'five goodly puncheons' of oporto united lengthwise by ropes so that they 're-semble a long sea-serpent'. In the more imaginatively visualized English reading, they 'resemble a section of a sea-serpent'. When Melville revised the *Putnam's* printing of 'Benito Cereno' for book publication he made many small but good revisions. In a famous sen-tence of the fourth paragraph he changed 'except on extraordinary and repeated excitement' to 'except on extraordinary and repeated incentives'. In *Putnam's* as the *San Dominick* glides away from the sealer, the blacks are seen with upthrown gestures hailing the now 'dusky expanse of ocean', while in the revision they are more evoca-tively hailing 'dusky moors of ocean'. According to Greg's formula, it does not matter whether or not an editor thinks such revisions are improvements. In fact, however, as Greg mentioned elsewhere in the essay,[6] any editor will make a literary judgment before deciding to call them authorial.

No serious challenge to Greg arises with simple corrections of fact, as in the following example from *White-Jacket*. In his descrip-tion of the wardroom in chapter 6, Melville first wrote: 'I never had a good interior look at it but once; and then the Chaplain was seated at the table in the centre, playing chess with the Lieutenant of Ma-rines.' The first English edition reads: 'The first time I had a look at it, the Chaplain was seated at the table in the centre, playing chess with the Lieutenant of Marines.' There seems to be no way of know-ing which, if either, was literally true of Melville himself on board the *United States*. The revision was not made for the sake of consis-tency, for there are no eyewitness descriptions of the wardroom elsewhere in the book. While one might find some slight literary dif-ference (arguing that the American version makes the segregation of officers and men more pronounced), the chances are that the concern behind the alteration was one of factual truth, not a desire to improve the literary quality of the sentence, and there is little an editor can do but accept the English reading, without knowing precisely why it was made.

Even authorial additions may often pose no challenge to Greg.

[6] P. 29.

Melville made several additions—small and large—on the Harper proofs of *White-Jacket* he was marking as the basis for the English edition; they were not subsequently added to the American edition. In chapter 45 he added a sentence which makes it more plausible for Lemsford to have entrusted his roll of poetry to the tube of a gun on the main deck: 'Little Quoin, the quarter-gunner, was on the "sick-list" then.' To the end of chapter 68, 'A Man-of-War Fountain, and Other Things', Melville added three delightful paragraphs on the ritual in which Old Coffee submits the day's salt beef or pork to the judgment of the officer of the deck—an addition that makes up a full page in the Northwestern-Newberry Edition. In *Typee* Melville had seized somewhat awkwardly on the omnium-gatherum chapter as a handy device for an unorganized author; by *Redburn* he was able to invest the form with something of the charm of Charles Lamb; and in this chapter of *White-Jacket* he was the triumphant master of the form. The three added paragraphs are altogether in keeping with the earlier sections of the chapter, each of which is set off casually by asterisks. Any editor who finds such additions will happily conflate them into his critical text.

After these clear-cut kinds of authorial restorations of the original readings, of minor stylistic improvements, of corrections of fact, and of additions that enhance the original work, an editor of Melville finds a series of more ambiguous textual situations in which he may decide, contrary to Greg, that the author's final intentions should not be obeyed.

The most obvious authorial changes which an editor may reject are simple expurgations. No editor need debate for long about the advisability of printing a *Typee* which follows the Revised Edition in omitting three dozen pages and in bowdlerizing many other passages throughout the book. Melville agreed to the expurgations (which John Wiley demanded) and even rationalized that they improved the book, but he knew that 'Expurgated' was an 'Odious word!' and showed in his next book—for a less straitlaced publisher—just how unrepentant he was for his risqué situations and his indictments of missionaries. Nor does an editor necessarily obey Melville's instructions—made shortly before his death—that the last paragraph of chapter 2 be omitted ('Our ship was now wholly given up to every species of riot and debauchery. . . .') and that the blithe homosexual joke in chapter 4 be removed by substituting 'Desolate Island' for 'Buggerry Island'. The Northwestern-Newberry editors in effect disputed the concept of author's final intentions when they rejected the instructions:

> these few isolated changes requested by Melville half a century after the composition of the work do not stem from the same conception of a coherent whole that existed at the time the manuscript was completed; whether they result from Melville's altered notions of propriety in his old age or from the persuasion of someone else, certainly the omission of a paragraph and the change of "Buggerry" represent the same kind of weakening which was made under external pressure in the "Revised Edition."

Without directly challenging Greg, the editors went so far as to postulate one possible time limit on an author's revisions—in this case, 'the time the manuscript was completed.'

More difficult editorial problems are created in the Revised Edition of *Typee* by authorial changes which may have been made in response to external pressures, though they are not mere expurgations. Conspicuous among these are three changes which remove allusions that could only have been made by a man of some education. Where the first English and American editions (chapter 4) mention some youths who 'forced by the united influences of Captain Marryatt and hard times, embark at Nantucket for a pleasure excursion to the Pacific,' the Revised Edition substitutes 'a roving spirit' for 'Captain Marryatt'. Where Melville had described the Marquesan damsels as looking 'like a band of olive-colored Sylphides on the point of taking wing' (chapter 20), the Revised Edition says merely that 'one would almost think that they were about to take wing'. The word 'Teniers'' in this passage of chapter 29 was changed to 'the olden': 'one of those monstrous imps that torment some of Teniers' saints'. These can hardly have been dictated by John Wiley, but they may have originated in the doubts about the authenticity of *Typee* that had been expressed by the English publisher, John Murray, and by many reviewers. As Leon Howard has suggested, Melville may have been trying to make 'the book read more like the work of a common sailor.'[7] By aesthetic standards, the later readings are inferior, and they are hardly successful in making the author appear uneducated, since the prose of the book as a whole remains self-consciously literary in an old-fashioned, eighteenth-century manner. To complicate the editorial problem, it is impossible to decide posi-

[7] *Typee*, p. 291.

162

tively whether Melville intended to make these changes even before he knew Wiley wanted to expurgate the whole book or whether he thought of making them during the course of the expurgation, after he realized that the Revised Edition would be a very different book from the one he had written.

Other complex editorial problems, not solvable by simple recourse to Greg, were created when Melville tried to bring certain references up to date as of the preparation of the Revised Edition of *Typee*. In the first English edition, chapter 1, Melville had included these three sentences:

Among these [general narratives], there are two that claim particular notice. Porter's 'Journal of the Cruise of the U. S. frigate Essex, in the Pacific, during the late War,' is said to contain some interesting particulars concerning the islanders. This is a work, however, which I have never happened to meet with; and Stewart, the chaplain of the American sloop of war Vincennes, has likewise devoted a portion of his book, entitled 'A Visit to the South Seas,' to the same subject.

When Melville wrote that he had 'never happened to meet with' Porter's book (probably early in 1845), those words may have been true. They were not true by the time he finished the book, and his 'final' and honest intention (though the motive may not have been honesty) was to omit what had become an error of fact. Possibly (but not certainly) in the process of correcting that error, he omitted the rest of the passage on Stewart, whose book had become one of his more important sources. It is impossible to tell whether or not a motivation in all or part of the deletion was to reduce the number of 'learned' references in the book or whether the deletion of the reference to one of the writers was a mere by-product of the deletion of the reference to the other. A somewhat similar example is in the original chapter 4. Melville had declared on his 'faith as an honest man' that the vessel he abandoned at Nukuheva 'still continues in the Pacific, and but a few days since I saw her reported in the papers as having touched at the Sandwich Islands previous to going on the coast of Japan.' This could hardly have been true, especially since by his own rather suspect dating, the passage was written after 9 July 1845, two months after the *Acushnet* had returned to Fairhaven. For the Revised Edition Melville substituted the following: 'some time after arriving home from my adventures, I learned that this vessel was still in the Pacific, and that she had met with very poor success in the fishery. Very many of her crew also, left her, and her voyage lasted about five years.' Even here Melville's accuracy is in doubt, since the voyage lasted only four years and four and one-half months. After the veracity of *Typee* had become an internationally debated issue, Melville had special reason for wanting to eliminate obvious errors of fact. From the freewheeling exaggeration of the first edition he had retreated—in certain passages though by no means in all— to an incompatibly cautious position. An editor could argue that both these instances of updating could hardly have been initiated by any- one but Melville and that one should adopt them as his revisions while excluding Wiley's expurgations. The editors of the North- western-Newberry Edition decided that both instances were inex- tricably part of the many changes that made the Revised Edition a quite different book from the one Melville wrote. In these circum- stances, Melville's original intention took precedence in their minds over what may well have been his 'final' intention.

Some of Melville's corrections of matters of fact have clear literary effects and create special editorial problems. *White-Jacket* provides good examples. In the first American edition, White-Jacket reclines high up on the main-royal-yard (chapter 19):

Eight bells had struck, and my watchmates had hied to their ham- mocks, and the other watch had gone to their stations, and the *top* below me was full of strangers, and still one hundred feet above even *them* I lay entranced; now dozing, now dreaming; now thinking of things past, and anon of the life to come.

The moment is dangerous as well as dreamy, for the superstitious sailors—thinking they have seen the ghost of the cooper—drop the yard from under him. In the English edition, one substantive change is made: 'still one hundred feet' becomes 'still almost one hundred feet'. Later, in chapter 21, Melville attacked the precedents that kept hammocks stowed in the nettings all day: 'such a thing as sailors sleeping in their hammocks in the daytime, after being eight hours exposed to a night-storm, was hardly ever heard of in the navy.' The English edition substitutes 'is not a regular thing' for 'was hardly ever heard of'. Still later, in chapter 22, the Harper edition calls the gen- eral discipline of American ships 'the most arbitrary' while the Bent- ley edition calls it 'perhaps the most severe'. In these instances, the aesthetic—and editorial—question is whether or not the revisions, in three particular sentences, counteract in a quite random, haphazard way the extravagancies which characterize the rhetoric of *White-Jacket* as a whole, even in the English edition. An editor who thinks they are erratic and anomalous may well decide he is not bound by an impulsive author's sober-headed afterthoughts. But any editorial decision is complicated by the fact that Melville's style was already becoming progressively more cautious, though it was far from the noncommital intricacies of *The Confidence-Man.* While these changes may be out of keeping with the general tone of the American — and even the English — edition of *White-Jacket*, they may be in keeping with this developing tendency of his style. Seeing no simple and satisfying course of action, an editor may be driven to theorizing about the precise time at which a given writer may be said to have the most 'authoritative' sense of his intentions and accomplishments for a particular work.

Some additions also create serious editorial problems. At the end of chapter 27 of *White-Jacket* the English edition has two new short paragraphs:

But if there is good reason to believe, that there are some incompetent officers in our navy; we have still better, and more abundant reason to know, that there are others, whom both nature and art have united in eminently qualifying for it; and whom the service does not so much honour, as they may be said to honour it.

And the only purpose of this chapter is, to point out as the peculiar desert of individuals, that generalized reputation, which most men, perhaps, are apt to ascribe in the gross, to one and all the members of a popular military establishment.

These pious paragraphs contradict the vein of democratic protest which infused the chapter as originally written and printed, where the question for discussion, twice posed, is, 'Are there incompetent officers in the American navy?' No one asked to define 'the only purpose' of the chapter could conceivably come up with anything like the one which Melville added in what seems like a perfunctory retrenchment from political radicalism. Another instance is in chapter 90 of the American edition, where Melville made this conclusion to a hortatory footnote on British impressment of American sailors during the Napoleonic Wars:

These things should be known; for in case the English government again goes to war with its fleets, and should again resort to indiscriminate impressment to man them, it is well that both Englishmen

and Americans, that all the world be prepared to put down an
iniquity outrageous and insulting to God and man.

This is in Melville's most fervent manner of oratorical 'gas and glory'
(Horace Greeley's term for Melville's brother Gansevoort's rhetoric).[8]
For the English edition, he expanded the passage at both ends:

It is not intended to revive old feuds. In one sense, let by-gones be
by-gones. But these things should be known; for in case the English
government again goes to war with its fleets, and should again resort
to indiscriminate impressment to man them, it is well that both
Englishmen and Americans, that all the world be prepared to put
down an iniquity outrageous and insulting to God and man. It is
hardly to be anticipated, however, that in case of war the English
government would again attempt to revive measures, which some of
its own statesmen must have deplored from the beginning; and
which, as [i.e., at] the present day, must surely seem iniquitous to
the great body of Englishmen. Indeed, it is perhaps to be doubted,
whether Englishmen could again be brought to submit even to domestic impressment.

This milder version obviously derives from a different attitude than
the earlier one. Presumably the additions were motivated less by Melville's own spontaneous literary impulses than by his desires to adapt
the book to a British publisher and a British audience. He may have
made the changes either before he sailed for England or on the boat
there but he also — and more likely — may have made them during the
frustrating weeks during which he 'wearily hawked this book from
Piccadilly to Whitechapel'.[9] When he came to terms with Bentley,
he had every reason for wishing to mollify the British in any con-
venient way. No editor following Greg's injunctions can feel entirely satisfied with himself, for the attitudes in these additions are
in varying degrees out of keeping with both the immediate contexts
and the book as a whole.

Another instance of an addition made with a different audience in
mind occurs in one of the most famous chapters of *Moby-Dick*, 'The
Grand Armada', where in preparing the American proofs for shipment to England Melville added a footnote to the word '*gallied*'. The
footnote was restyled and respelled in England and printed this way:

[8] *The Melville Log*, ed. Jay Leyda (New York: Gordian Press, 1969), I, 186.
[9] *The Melville Log*, I, 362.

To *gally*, or *gallow*, is to frighten excessively,—to confound with fright. It is an old Saxon word. It occurs once in Shakspere:—
"The wrathful skies
Gallow the very wanderers of the dark,
And make them keep their caves."
Lear, Act iii. sc. 11.
To common land usages, the word is now completely obsolete. When the polite landsman first hears it from the gaunt Nantucketer, he is apt to set it down as one of the whaleman's self-derived savageries. Much the same is it with many other sinewy Saxonisms of this sort, which emigrated to the New-England rocks with the noble brawn of the old English emigrants in the time of the Commonwealth. Thus, some of the best and furthest-descended English words—the etymological Howards and Percys—are now democratised, nay, plebeianised—so to speak—in the New World.

The literary merit of the footnote can hardly be at issue, but an editor must consider the fact that the topic and the treatment were both incidental to the process of tidying up the American sheets for the British publisher. One can argue that Melville may have thought the note enhanced the book as some kind of ideal whole, yet it was all but surely written with only English readers in mind. The editor who admires the footnote and prints it in a critical edition is choosing the reward of a fine authorial addition at the cost of printing something which was probably conceived for a more limited audience than was the rest of the book.

Of the several works which Melville revised at all extensively after they were first set in type, the only one to which Greg's conclusions fully apply is 'Benito Cereno', the revisions of which constitute merely a final polishing. Some of the authorial changes in other books—especially *Typee*, *White-Jacket*, and *Moby-Dick*—create textual problems too complex to be settled by the automatic acceptance of all the latest revisions into a critical text. In *Pierre* Melville grotesquely parodied his own situation as a weak-eyed, frantic proofreader:

As every evening, after his day's writing was done, the proofs of the beginning of his work came home for correction, Isabel would read them to him. They were replete with errors; but preoccupied by the thronging, and undiluted, pure imaginings of things, he became impatient of such minute, gnat-like torments; he randomly corrected the worst, and let the rest go; jeering with himself at the rich harvest thus furnished to the entomological critics.

Melville may occasionally have been this desperate, as when he proof-read *Redburn* while writing *White-Jacket*, or when he proofread early pages of *Moby-Dick* while writing some later sections. However, many of his revisions, as opposed to simple corrections, were the product of more sober if still hasty and unmethodical scrutinies of proofs or the first printings. Many of them are, in the phrase of his time, 'sober second thoughts' — more temperate but often less forceful than the first 'thronging, and undiluted, pure imaginings of things'. An editor may well feel that the impassioned Melville who writes a passage is more to be respected than the deliberate Melville who later tones down certain parts of that passage. The example of Melville suggests that for at least one type of writer — a Melville if not a Haw-thorne, a Faulkner if not a Trollope — original intentions may often be more valid than final intentions.[10] It suggests, in short, that quali-fication is needed to the textual dogma that an 'author's final inten-tions' are always the most 'authoritative'.

[10] I mention Faulkner on the basis of a conversation with James B. Meri-wether. A study by Professor Meriwether, with examples from Faulkner, would greatly enlighten the whole matter of 'author's final intentions'.

SOME REMARKS ON
BIBLIOGRAPHICAL NON-PROLIFERATION

G. THOMAS TANSELLE

JOHN CARTER, AT THE END OF HIS COMPREHENSIVE AND ENTERTAINING
Presidential Address to the Bibliographical Society (now published
as an epilogue to a new impression of *Taste and Technique in Book
Collecting*), comments on Warner Barnes's *Bibliography of Elizabeth
Barrett Browning* (Austin: University of Texas Press, 1968) as a
pioneer example of the use of the Hinman Collator in preparing an
author bibliography.[1] He remarks that Barnes occasionally falters,
as might 'an infantry subaltern suddenly entrusted with a squadron
of tanks armed with quick-firing atomic cannon'. But, he goes on,

---

[1] The Hinman Collator had previously been used for Matthew J. Bruccoli's *Notes on the Cabell Collections at the University of Virginia* (Charlottesville:
University of Virginia Press, 1957), Vol. II of Frances Joan Brewer's bibliography, *James Branch Cabell*; and for William W. Kelly's *Ellen Glasgow: A
Bibliography*, ed. Oliver L. Steele (Charlottesville: University Press of Virginia, 1964). But Barnes's is probably the first full-scale descriptive bibliography systematically to employ complete machine collations of all first
editions.

'the stark fact remains that these war-heads are now freely available, with no arrangements for non-proliferation'.[2] In characteristic fashion, Carter has touched on a basic question which bibliographers must face—an old question, really, but one which, as he recognizes, the Hinman machine poses with particular urgency. Essentially the problem is how detailed a descriptive bibliography ought to be; and, though it has been discussed many times before, new weapons always call for a reassessment of old strategies. Formulating some tentative answers to Carter's 'awkward but inevitable question' is facilitated by splitting it into two parts. First: Is 'non-proliferation' a desirable thing? Second: If so, what 'arrangements' can be made for it?

The word 'proliferation' often connotes uncontrolled multiplication and, taken in this sense, loads the question so that only one answer is possible, for no one wants to be in a position of favoring chaos over discipline. On the other hand, if 'proliferation' means the continual emergence of new techniques for extracting relevant information, the balance is swung in the opposite direction, since no one admits to standing in the way of the discovery of truth. The answer to the question clearly depends on the kind of proliferation involved. The second kind must be accepted intellectually, even though emotionally it may be regarded with distaste; thus the value of the Hinman machine having been amply demonstrated, we cannot now do without it, however much some collectors (and bibliographers too) may wish to perpetuate the older, simpler days. The first kind of proliferation, however—the undisciplined recording of all manner of details uncovered by the machine—is capable of destroying the very search for facts which it is presumably intended to foster. The cogency of Carter's military metaphor is obvious.

When we read in Barnes's preface that he has collated on the machine an average of six copies of every book and that 'a variant state or concealed impression was discovered for every volume so examined', we may at first be startled to think that each *copy* represented a different state; then we realize that it is each edition or 'book' that yielded a previously unknown state or impression. Nevertheless, the first thought is not as unlikely as it may seem. No two physical objects—including machine-printed books—are precisely

[2]*Taste and Technique in Book Collecting* (London: Private Libraries Association, 1970), p. 241. Carter's remarks, in slightly different form, also appear in his review of Barnes's bibliography in the *Book Collector*, XIX (1970), 101–4.

the same, and the Hinman Collator makes it easily possible, if one were so inclined, to record differences between every single copy of a book and thus to make of every copy a separate state. (Of course, one could have achieved this result in pre-Hinman days as well, given sufficient patience, but the point is that it is now much more comfortably manageable.) If Barnes has brought to light, on the average, one new state or impression for every six copies collated, we may well ask (as Barnes himself does) what the result would have been if still more copies of each book had been examined. Surely it stands to reason that the six copies chosen (and what basis is there for choosing, in many cases, before collation has been performed?) do not, except through remote coincidence, represent all the significant variations present in the edition as a whole.[3] A bibliographer following Barnes could examine six more copies of every title (when they exist) and probably come up with a few new states, if not impressions. And the process could be continued — with diminishing returns, it is true — until all surviving copies had been collated. In the case of some books — though perhaps none of Elizabeth Barrett Browning's — there is no doubt that every copy would need to be examined in order to discover, and note the incidence of, all significant variations. The key issue is not so much deciding on the number of copies to be examined (though that is difficult enough) but rather determining what variations are to be considered 'significant'. As lesser and lesser points are deemed worth recording, more and more copies have to be looked at in an effort to find a pattern (diminishing returns, that is, will be later setting in); and the ultimate result could be the situation in which no pattern at all is discernible because the criteria for groupings are so demanding that each copy forms a separate category, with no other copy able to qualify for inclusion in its select company.

Obviously this vision of bibliographical horror is an extreme, but it serves to define the problem. Since every physical object is unique, classifying every copy of a book as a separate state is no doubt a truer physical picture than the usual one presented in bibliographies — but, one hastens to add, not necessarily a truer *bibliographical* picture. For 'physical bibliography', though it may deal with the physical rather than the literary aspects of books, is not interested, for the most part,

[3] Barnes is well aware of this point: 'There has been an unfortunate tendency of late by some American bibliographers', he says, 'to assume that every variant of every book has been seen by them' (p. 12).

in the same physical characteristics which would attract the attention of a physicist, say, or a chemist. And the bibliographer who moves to this extreme is not merely being overzealous; he is—what amounts to the same thing—being irresponsible by allowing the minutiae of his job to obscure its essential features. This is not to say that what his industry has unearthed may not be useful to someone; but if it is not useful (and is, indeed, distracting) to those for whom it is intended, then it can hardly be considered a responsible performance. A bibliographical description cannot be other than a selection of details from the infinity of details available; but if the selection is to be more than a random accumulation of miscellaneous facts, it must be based on a firm conception of the purposes it is to serve. That some users of descriptive bibliographies do not know what they ought to expect until they are told by the bibliographer only increases his own obligation to understand what he is doing and to keep it under control. The bibliographer's duty—any scholar's duty—is to find that spot along the continuum of possible details which is most appropriate for his undertaking: if he moves in one direction from that location, he is oversimplifying, not reporting relevant facts which are obtainable; if he moves in the other direction, he is indulging in the display of details for their own sake, making a situation seem more complex than necessary, and therefore obfuscating rather than clarifying. Proliferation of this kind is not a new danger, for many scholars have always found it difficult to judge the relevance of a detail without thinking of the amount of research that was involved in procuring it. But it is well to recognize that in all fields technological aids (such as the Hinman machine, which is after all a very simple device and represents only a beginning) are continually making possible more rapid and more efficient accumulation of details and that the temptation to present raw data as finished research is correspondingly stronger.

The answer to our first question, then, is that non-proliferation is indeed desirable if it means a retardation, at the least, of this kind of proliferation. It is easy enough, however, to agree on what is desirable without knowing how to bring it about, and 'arrangements for non-proliferation' are notoriously difficult in any area. Treaties can sometimes be passed for limiting the proliferation of arms; whether or not they do much good, an official position has been stated. Such an approach to scholarship, though, is worse than the evil it is aimed at eradicating. We may sometimes wish that we could institute a moratorium on various kinds of pseudo-scholarship which are motivated more by personal ambition than the search for truth, but we know, at the same time, that we could not really tolerate any such thing. If the problem cannot be solved by edict, is there any way to make arrangements for bibliographical non-proliferation? Worded in that manner, the answer would have to be no, because we cannot 'make' intellectual endeavor turn in any particular direction. But if we ask, instead, whether arrangements in fact exist for controlling proliferation, I think we can reply that several do.

If I were to say that one of these controls is common sense, I would surely be regarded as naïvely optimistic about human judgment—and would be reminded that scholarly performance in the past does not seem to lend support to this optimism. Yet I have now said it, and I think there is some point to it. One of the principal ingredients of common sense, by anyone's recipe, must be a sense of proportion. We say that someone has lost his common sense (or his good judgment, or whatever we wish to call it) if his behavior about a given matter shows that he has allowed one aspect of it to loom larger than it ought to in terms of the overall configuration of the problem; his conception of the whole, in other words, has gone awry through a failure to keep in balance the various elements involved. Now just what constitutes proper balance is not always immediately apparent, and it may happen that what seems today a disproportionate amount of attention to a given detail will in the long run be proved an eminently sensible amount. This long-run common sense is precisely what I have in mind: the common sense of an accumulated tradition consisting of the individual judgments of numerous people over a period of time and providing a context to give meaning to such words as 'relevant', 'disproportionate', and 'eccentric'. Experimentation and departure from tradition are of course to be encouraged, since they may result in something better; but the value or relevance of any given innovation often cannot be accurately assessed without the perspective which time offers. A new technique which proves to be useful and productive, even if it is scorned at first, will eventually become standard procedure; but a technique which is not fruitful, even if it has a vogue for a considerable period, will eventually be abandoned. I think it can be said, for example, that the Greg-Bowers formulary for signature collation is now an accepted part of bibliographical practice; we are beyond the point where those who resist it offer constructive arguments, and thus it is their resistance, and not the technique itself, which seems eccentric. But if a bibliographer were to include in a descriptive bibliography long lists of variations discovered through the use of a Hinman Collator, we could not easily label the procedure either relevant or eccentric because we do not yet have a context which would offer guidelines as to what constitutes an excessive or disproportionate amount of detail in this area. One bibliographer, after examining the use to which this information is put and the proportions of the description as a whole, may conclude that it is not relevant (at least for a bibliography conceived on this particular scale); he may even express this opinion in a review, and his review may be influential. But it is still only one opinion and will not necessarily prevent others from following the practice. In the long run, however, if this view is acknowledged to be correct, few will persist in employing the technique. This whole process may operate more inefficiently in the field of bibliography than in some other fields because there are relatively few people engaged in it and because the users of bibliographies are often extraordinarily incapable of evaluating bibliographical merit; nevertheless, the kind of common sense which I have described here is surely one of the controls which will prevent an excessively luxuriant growth of bibliographical data.

Although this common sense ultimately manifests itself in a tradition, it necessarily shows itself first in the attitudes of particular individuals. Another control, therefore—if it is not tautological to say so—lies in the degree of intelligence and perceptiveness of those who choose to write bibliographies. At the risk of repeating what I have said before,[4] I believe that anyone undertaking a descriptive bibliography should have thought about what he is doing sufficiently to recognize that each of his descriptions must necessarily consist of only a selection of details and that, if it is to be a coherent piece of research, the selection must be based on a clear understanding of the aims it is intended to accomplish. This much could be said, of course, about any kind of historical research; but apparently the fact that bibliographies in general do not assume a narrative form has caused some people to regard them simply as compendiums of data rather than as historical studies. It is true that some of the earlier handbooks for collectors consisted of mere listings of the 'points' which were supposed to distinguish 'first editions' of a particular author's books. But this kind of guide is totally dissimilar in approach from a *bibliography*, conceived of as a history of the forms in

[4] Particularly in 'Tolerances in Bibliographical Description', *Library*, 5th ser., XXIII (1968), 1–12.

which a given group of books was presented to the public. All who use works of this kind — collectors, dealers, librarians, historians, literary scholars, as well as bibliographers — have come increasingly to see that bibliographies must supersede collectors' handbooks, for they can serve the same purposes for which the handbooks were designed but in a less oversimplified and more historically accurate way. (Any collector who is at all serious in his interest — even if he limits himself to 'firsts' — recognizes the foolishness of not learning as much as he can about the books he collects, though the result may be that the quality of 'firstness' is less clear-cut than he had supposed.) If, then, bibliographies are agreed to be works of history — not only the history of the forms and the publication of individual books, but also inevitably the partial history of printing and publishing in certain periods — they should be held to the same basic requirements as other finished pieces of historical research.

An intelligent and perceptive bibliographer who has examined a large number of copies of the books he is investigating and performed whatever associated research seems required will be in a position to judge what details are relevant for the audience he is aiming at, as well as what degree of accuracy is appropriate. There will still be various levels on which he can properly operate — just as a short and a long history can be written on the same subject — but on any of these levels he will know what the relative proportions of the parts to the whole ought to be. He will know that normally he should not go into great detail about bindings, for instance, if he has not gone into such detail for typography and paper; but more than that, he will know when circumstances demand what might otherwise seem a disproportionate treatment of bindings. In the same way, he will know what details discovered through machine collation are relevant and important within the contours of his descriptions and which details do not belong there. Obviously, some bibliographers will lack the judgment necessary to make these decisions wisely, just as other historians have been known to produce books with strange excrescences and biases; and these eccentric treatments may even be stimulating and productive by provoking reaction. But the fact remains that an important control over the indiscriminate publication of bibliographical details lies in the mind of the responsible bibliographer, thinking through the problems of producing, from the data of a particular case, a bibliography which is coherent and meaningful and not simply a collection of undigested notes.

Any discussion of the selection of details in descriptive bibliography raises the troublesome issue of the so-called degressive principle, which has come to mean the reduction in the number of details offered in the descriptions of later editions of particular books (or editions deemed, for whatever reason, less important). Some sort of degressive procedure is inevitable: no description of anything can be so detailed that it is impossible to add further details, and every description therefore represents a 'degression' from the abstract and unattainable ideal of 'complete description'. The most elaborate description which a bibliographer employs in a given bibliography is presumably not the most elaborate of which he is capable but rather that form of description which he has concluded to be most appropriate for the occasion; when he then proceeds to make his account of certain later editions still less detailed, he is not introducing a new principle but only applying to his whole bibliography the same concern with proportion and subordination which he has directed to the composition of individual descriptions. There may be some bibliographies in which the nature of the material treated and the purposes to be served do not allow much flexibility in the number of details presented; but the existence of such a possibility does not alter the fact that varying the number of details provided for different categories of material is a natural part of the process of turning out a finished piece of historical research. Of course, there is no detail that is not potentially of use to someone, and every description (like every historical essay) is the outcome of a process of weighing relative values: the bibliographer (or historian), using his specialized knowledge of the situation, makes a judgment about which details, given the scope and aims of the investigation, are most important in terms both of proved usefulness and of potential significance for future research. It may happen that he omits details which are later shown to be more relevant than some of those included; but what he includes, if he performs his task responsibly, represents his best judgment at the time as to what constitutes a balanced presentation. The number of details finally included—it goes without saying—has nothing to do with the thoroughness of the research necessary to make judgments about those details, just as a short history, if it is to be reliable, cannot be based on any less comprehensive research than a long history. Bibliographers have not always recognized the basic fact that neither the omission of details nor the automatic inclusion of them reduces one's responsibility for pursuing what Fredson Bowers calls the 'qualitative' part of bibliographical research—and certainly no bibliographer can afford to be unacquainted with his important discussion of this point in 'Bibliography Revisited'.[5] A consideration of the 'degressive principle' only reinforces the view that an essential curb on the unbridled proliferation of bibliographical details is individual scholarly integrity.

One other control may be mentioned, and it, too, is an obvious one: the amount of work required to discover details. Although the Hinman Collator has reduced the drudgery involved in the multiple collation of copies of books belonging to the same edition, drudgery it remains. It is not a job to be undertaken lightly; when it is so undertaken, it is not likely to be pushed to completion. This is not to say that certain persons, strong in industry and weak in judgment, may not amass a large quantity of such data without knowing what to do with it; but in general the sheer effort of acquiring and manipulating it will serve as some deterrent. The real concern should be the opposite one—that the deterrent may be so strong as to result in a shortage of bibliographical data. This problem is less serious in connection with those authors whose texts are likely to be established in full-scale scholarly editions, for the process of mechanical collation which must be carried out in preparing the texts serves at the same time to provide many of the details to be recorded in the descriptive bibliographies. In fact, editing and descriptive bibliography are so complementary and interrelated that it is difficult to do an adequate job of one without amassing much of the information for the other.

Editing requires a knowledge of the sequence of editions and impressions, and descriptive bibliography presumes an understanding of the textual relationships among those editions and impressions. This interdependence is being dramatically demonstrated by the work now in progress under the auspices of the MLA Center for Editions of American Authors: descriptive bibliographies have been announced in conjunction with several of the editions, and, until they appear, by far the most thorough and reliable bibliographical information available about these authors is to be found in the textual essays included in the individual volumes of the editions. Although Barnes's Browning bibliography is not connected with an edition, it seems safe to say that most of the descriptive bibliographies to be published in the near future utilizing evidence obtained through machine collation will emerge from larger projects for editions. The question which suggests itself, therefore, is not whether the Hin-

[5] *Library,* 5th ser., XXIV (1969), 89–128.

man machine will produce a surfeit of bibliographical data but whether the productive use of the machine in a series of important author bibliographies (connected with editions) will prove so intimidating to the potential bibliographer (but not editor) of another author as to stifle whatever urge he originally had to undertake the task. Put another way, the issue is simply this: If machine collation of multiple copies is necessary for dependable bibliographies, can we realistically expect such bibliographies to be produced in the future except in conjunction with the research for editions?

We may wish that the answer could be yes, since there are many authors in need of bibliographies who are not likely to be edited for a very long time indeed. But there is no reason to suppose — however fashionable machines may be — that the Hinman Collator is going to cause the ranks' of descriptive bibliographers to be swelled with hordes of industrious, intelligent, and reliable workers. That being the case, another question arises: Is a poor bibliography better than no bibliography at all? One may be tempted to feel that it is, for it provides something to go on and may stimulate the reporting of more reliable information. Nevertheless, incorrect facts or misleading discussions, once they appear in print, are notoriously difficult to dislodge from people's minds; and we have already had to wait so long for bibliographies of many major figures that the inconvenience of having to wait still longer for really good bibliographies is well worth enduring. It is in the nature of scholarship, of course, that good books may be superseded by even better books; but there is no excuse for producing a book which can be recognized as outdated at the time of its publication.

The fact is inescapable: bibliographical research is becoming more demanding. Robert Donaldson expressed many people's feelings when he remarked, in a review of the 1969 volume of *Studies in Bibliography*, that several of the essays leave the reader 'somewhat apprehensive of the size, complexity, and expense of the effort necessary for the study of textual [or descriptive, one may add] bibliography in view of the expanded vistas that continue to open before us'.[6] Apprehensive, perhaps, and even dismayed — but surely not disapproving, if the effort is fruitful. Rigor of investigation is not a matter open to objection; but thoroughness of research naturally produces a large quantity of data, and if these data are published indiscriminately a real cause for objection does exist. The

[6] *Library*, 5th ser., XXV (1970), 160.

problem of proliferation ultimately turns on a recognition of the requirements of historical research. Bibliography cannot be 'scientific' in the same way that the natural sciences are; but it can be regarded as *analogous* to them—or to any other scholarly pursuit—in its discipline, its control of detail, its responsibility of conclusion. Those who understand that bibliographies are histories—it is strange that the point even needs to be made—know that bibliographies of the future will not necessarily be more complex in outward form than many of the past; but the research they entail will necessarily be more involved. Carter's infantryman does have new weapons at his command; but he cannot win the battle if he squanders them in an ostentatious display of power instead of making them an integrated part of his total strategy.

179

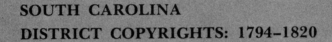

SOUTH CAROLINA
DISTRICT COPYRIGHTS: 1794–1820

WILLIAM S. KABLE

A DISBOUND FOLIO VOLUME BOLDLY INSCRIBED 'RECORD OF COPY
Rights' has recently come to light in the Manuscript Division of the
South Caroliniana Library at the University of South Carolina. This
volume has proven to be the original ledger kept by the Clerk of
the District of South Carolina and contains all of the entries covering
items entered for copyright in that district from 8 July 1794 to 12
November 1858. The provenance of the ledger from the time it
ceased to be used for copyright entries until recent times is a complete mystery; nothing whatsoever is known about its whereabouts
until it was discovered in the South Caroliniana Library by Mr. E. L.
Inabinet, who kindly called it to my attention.

Presented on the following pages is a distillation of the bibliographical evidence which this ledger contains for the period 1794
through 1820 – the first period covered by Shaw and Shoemaker.
There are 115 entries, which range among the various genres of
printed materials. Numerous legal, medical, religious, and scientific

works are to be found as are a lesser number of works of a purely literary nature. There is but a single work of prose fiction, Edmund Botsford's *The Spiritual Voyage* (1814), seven volumes of poetry, and, providing remarkable evidence of the dramatic activity in Charleston at the time, twelve dramas. Also included are several non-book entries which cover engravings and the like.

The value of the information presented in the ledger is seen in an entry like No. 97, *Essays: Religious, Moral, Dramatic & Poetical* (1818). Shaw and Shoemaker list this volume under its title only. Turnbull, in his *Bibliography of South Carolina 1563–1950*, and Hill, in *American Plays Printed 1714–1830*, boldly assign the volume to one Maria Henrietta Pinckney. Nonetheless, the copyright entry listing 'Miss Pogson . . . as author and proprietor' supplies direct evidence for a more convincing attribution of this work to Sarah Pogson.

The form of the entry in the ledger itself is condensed in this listing to give four facts:

(1) date of entry for copyright;
(2) the party who entered the volume for copyright and, where it is given in the ledger, the role in which the party was acting (as author, proprietor, or both);
(3) a transcription of relevant parts of the title page as given in the entry—in most cases, only as much of the title as is needed for positive identification, though where no record of the existence of the item can be found, a somewhat fuller form of the title-page transcription is given (the author's name, if given in the ledger as appearing on the title page, is always included in the transcription); and
(4) a single identifying reference to one of the standard bibliographies of the period or to a single extant copy of the work represented by the entry. (No attempt has been made to verify this information; it is simply evidence for the existence of the item outside the copyright ledger itself. A number of items could not be located outside the ledger; information concerning the existence of these items will be appreciated by the compiler.)

The following sigla are used in supplying identifying references:

Evans—Charles Evans, *American Bibliography* (Chicago: For the Author, 1903—and various imprints).
Shaw & Shoemaker—Ralph R. Shaw and Richard H. Shoemaker, compilers, *American Bibliography: A Preliminary Checklist for*

1801[-1819] (New York: The Scarecrow Press, Inc., 1958–66).

Shoemaker (1820)—Richard H. Shoemaker, compiler, *A Checklist of American Imprints for 1820* (New York & London: The Scarecrow Press, Inc., 1964).

Turnbull—Robert James Turnbull, *Bibliography of South Carolina 1563–1950* (Charlottesville: University of Virginia Press, 1956–60).

Hill—Frank Pierce Hill, *American Plays Printed 1714–1830: A Bibliographical Record* (Stanford, Calif.: Stanford University Press, 1934).

McMurtrie—Douglas C. McMurtrie, 'Some Nineteenth Century South Carolina Imprints 1801–1820', *The South Carolina Historical and Genealogical Magazine,* XLIV (1943), 87–106, 155–72, 228–46.

Wolfe—Richard J. Wolfe, *Secular Music in America 1801–1825* (New York: The New York Public Library, 1964).

No. 1 8 July [1794][1]
William Price Young
An Oration, delivered in St. Michaels Church . . . on the fourth of July, 1794 . . . . By David Ramsay . . . .
Evans 27590

No. 2 17 March 1795
Thomas Mills
A Compendium of Latin Syntax . . . . By Thomas Mills . . . .
Evans 29084.

No. 3 8 July [1795]
Timothy and Mason, printers
An Oration, delivered in St. Michaels Church . . . on the 4th July, 1795 . . . . By Thomas Tuder Tucker . . . .
Evans 29663.

No. 4 26 October [1795]
Charles Lining, in Trust for the Orphan-house
An Oration delivered at the Orphan-house . . . October 18th, 1795 . . . . By the Reverend George Buist . . . .
Evans 28369.

[1] From this entry through entry 42 the Clerk of the District of South Carolina was Thomas Hall.

No. 5   7 July [1796]
William Price Young . . . as proprietor
An Oration, delivered in St. Philips Church . . . on the fourth July, 1796 . . . . By William Smith . . . .
Evans 31210.

No. 6   6 September 1796
The honorable Judge John Faucheraud Grimké
The Rules and Orders of the Courts of Sessions and Common pleas, of the Court of Equity and the Federal Court, in South Carolina.
Evans 31220.

No. 7   20 March [1797]
William Parker, druggist . . . the titles of two several books or rolls
The domestic Dispensary or complete family and plantation Chest; corresponding with Buchans domestic medicine and particularly adapted to the diseases of the southern States; And The Seaman's Dispensary or complete ship medicine chest.
Not located; probably not in book format.

No. 8   6 May 1797
John Beete . . . as author
The Man of the times, or a Scarcity of Cash; a farce . . . . By Mr. Beete Comedian.
Evans 31790.

No. 9   20 January 1798
the Honorable John Faucheraud Grimké . . . as Author
The duty of Executors and Administrators. By J. F. Grimké.
Evans 32214; New-York: T. & J. Swords, 1797.

No. 10   29 August 1798
the Honorable Elihu Hall Bay . . . as Author
Reports of Cases argued and determined . . . in . . . South Carolina since the Revolution. By Elihu Hall Bay . . . .
Evans 33382.

No. 11   21 March 1799
Amos Pilsbury . . . as Author
The United States Sacred Harmony . . . . By Amos Pilsbury . . . .
Evans 36119.

No. 12   22 January 1800
         Doctor David Ramsay . . . as Author
             An Oration on the Death of . . . Washington . . . . By
             David Ramsay . . . .
         Evans 38358.
No. 13   25 March 1800
         John B. Williamson Esquire . . . as Author
             Preservation; or, the Hovel of the Rocks: A Play . . . . By
             John B. Williamson . . . .
         Evans 39110.
No. 14   6 May 1802
         Major General William Moultrie . . . as Author
             Memoirs of the American Revolution. By William
             Moultrie . . . .
         Shaw & Shoemaker 2704; New-York: Longworth, 1802.
No. 15   23 September 1802
         his Excellency John Drayton Governor and Commander in
         Chief in and over the State of South Carolina . . . as Author
             A View of South Carolina . . . . By John Drayton.
         Shaw & Shoemaker 2159.
No. 16   27 February 1803
         J. J. Negrin
             Negrin's Public Guide of Carolina and Georgia, Directo-
             rial Register For 1803 the 27–28th of American Inde-
             pendence.
         Not located; Turnbull (I, 392) lists *The Georgia and South
         Carolina Almanac, for the Year of our Lord 1803, and the 27–28
         of American Independence* (Augusta [Georgia]: Printed by
         John Erdman Smith, 1802).
No. 17   7 March 1803
         [William] Stewart
             An Easy Introduction to Geography . . . . By a Friend of
             Youth . . . .
         Shaw & Shoemaker 4128.
No. 18   4 June 1803
         Doctor John Mackey
             A Treatise on the Cow-Pox containing The History of its
             discovery; Mode of performing the inoculation; The
             Progress and Medical Treatment of the Disease; Method
             of taking & preserving matter for Inoculation; And A

Collection of Testimonies In favor of the Cow-Pox. By John Mackey M:D: . . . .

Not located.

No. 19   2 April 1804
James Workman
    Liberty in Louisiana, A Comedy. By James Workman. Shaw & Shoemaker 7804, which gives: '2d ed., Charleston: Query and Evans, 1804.'

No. 20   12 April 1804
David Cromwell
    The Ocean Spectre, An Entire New Grand MeloDrame: In five Acts. Interspersed with Songs Chorusses &c. Translated from the French of Le Spectre De L'ocean. Written by Flareau.

Not located. Hill 213 lists a New York, 1795, publication with this title and adds a note: 'Both William Dunlap and James Rees attribute a play with this title to "Cromwell."'

No. 21   26 May 1804
Joel Bliss
    The American Orator or New Guide to Oratory Containing Orations on various select subjects. Being a Selection from the most approved Authors. With considerable additions and improvements interspersed throughout the work. Designed for the use of Grammar Schools. By Joel Bliss.

Not located.

No. 22   26 May 1804
Joel Bliss
    The Prompter or Federal Arithmetic containing A very large variety if not all of the useful rules that occur in business and particularly applied To the Federal Currency. Designed and calculated for the use of Schools throughout the United States. By Joel Bliss.

Not located.

No. 23   26 January 1805
Lucius Bellinger
    Poems. By the late George Hartwell Spierin of Charleston, South Carolina, Student of Law.

Shaw & Shoemaker 9410.

No. 24   7 February 1805

Stephen Cullen Carpenter Esqr.
Report of The Trial of Richard Dennis the Younger For the Murder of James Shaw . . . . By S. C. Carpenter.
Shaw & Shoemaker 8139.

No. 25   25 April 1805
William Ioor Esquire
Independence, or which do you like best, The Peer or The Farmer? a Comedy . . . . By William Ioor . . . .
Shaw & Shoemaker 8684.

No. 26   2 July 1805
Stephen Cullen Carpenter Esqr.
The Monthly Register and Review of the United States. By Samuel C. Carpenter.
Shaw & Shoemaker 8918, which gives the first issue as January 1805. The Union List of Serials gives the complete run as January 1805 to December 1807, with publication suspended from September 1805 to March 1806 and from September to November 1806.

No. 27   8 January 1806
Doctor L. E. W. Shecut
Flora Carolinæensis . . . . In Two Volumes. By John L. E. W. Shecut. Vol. I.
Shaw & Shoemaker 11351, Vol. I—all that was published.

No. 28   12 February 1806
William Stewart
A new Selection of Arithmetical Tables with a Short and easy Explanation of the Principal Rules, &c. For the use of Schools, and Private Tuition.
Not located.

No. 29   19 February 1806
John B. White Esquire
Foscari, or the Venetian Exile, A Tragedy . . . . By John B. White.
Shaw & Shoemaker 11867.

No. 30   1 May 1806
John L. E. W. Schecut Doctor of Medicine . . . an Engraving Plan for a Botanic Garden according to Linnaeus's System.
Not located.

No. 31   16 August 1806
Thomas A. Whitney

A print from the Engraving of Revd. Richard Furman, Pastor of the Baptist Church in Charleston. By Thomas A. Whitney.

Not located.

No. 32   17 March 1807

John B. White Esquire

The Mysteries of the Castle . . . A Drama . . . . By John B. White Esqr.

Shaw & Shoemaker 14215.

No. 33   28 July 1807

John Hoff . . . (as proprietor)

The Female Enthusiast, A Tragedy . . . . By a Lady . . . .

Shaw & Shoemaker 13409, attributed to Sarah Pogson.

No. 34   10 March 1808

Miss Eliza Crawley

Poems. By a Young Lady of Charleston.

Shaw & Shoemaker 15965.

No. 35   1 July 1808

William P. Young

Military System of South Carolina

Shaw & Shoemaker 15606, as 'Ed. 2.'

No. 36   6 July 1808

William P. Young

The Book of Common Prayer . . . .

Copy in the South Caroliniana Library (s.c./264.03/B64).

No. 37   day of   1808 [blank spaces]

George Logan, Doctor of Medicine

Medical Pocket-Book. By George Logan, M.D.

Not located.

No. 38   1 December 1808

James M. Elford . . . a Print from an Engraving

James M. Elford's Polar Tables. For finding the Latitude at any time of night in the northern hemisphere by an altitude of the Pole Star.

Not located. In Elford's *Marine Telegraph* (Charleston: Archibald E. Miller, 1823), he calls himself 'Teacher of Navigation and Nautical Astronomy, Author of the Polar Tables, Universal and Perpetual Tide Tables, and Proprietor of the Longitude Tables, No. 119 East-Bay.' See also Nos. 45, 79, 95, and 98 below.

No. 39   3 February 1809

Alexander Macomb Esquire
A Treatise on Martial Law and Courts Martial . . . . By
Alexander Macomb . . . .
Shaw & Shoemaker 17964.

No. 40   3 February 1809
W. P. Young . . . as Proprietor
The Gardner's Calendar for North Carolina, South
Carolina, and Georgia. By Robert Squibb.
Shaw & Shoemaker 18679. Pasted to this page of the ledger
is a slip recording the transfer of the rights to *The Gardner's
Calendar* by Dinah Young, executrix to the estate of W. P.
Young, to Mr. Edwin Gibbes, dated 15 February 1826.

No. 41   9 March 1809
Amos Pilsbury . . . as Author
The Sacred Songster or a Collection of Hymns . . . . By
Amos Pilsbury . . . .
Shaw & Shoemaker 18395.

No. 42   17 March 1809
Doctor David Ramsay . . . as author
The History of South Carolina . . . . By David Ramsay,
M.D.
Shaw & Shoemaker 18474.

No. 43   15 August 1809[2]
Richard Hrabowskie . . . as author
Directory for the District of Charleston . . . . Collected
by Richard Hrabowskie.
Shaw & Shoemaker 17390.

No. 44   20 August 1809
the Honorable Elihu Hall Bay . . . as author
Reports of Cases argued argued [*sic*] and determined
. . . South Carolina . . . . By Elihu Hall Bay . . . . Second
Edition.
Sabin 87459; Turnbull, I, 448.

No. 45   8 February 1810
Henry Bremar . . . a print from an Engraving
A New Lunar Table, whereby the true distance of the
Sun and Moon or Star is ascertained in a concise and
accurate Method. Invented by Francis Bremar Jun. decd.

[2] From entry 43 through entry 115 the Clerk of the District of South
Carolina was James Jervey.

Not located. An additional entry, dated 14 July 1818, transfers this copyright to James M. Elford.

No. 46   20 March 1810
E. Morford Willington & Co. . . . as Proprietors
The Weekly Monitor. A Series of Essays on Moral and Religious Subjects. By a Layman.
Shaw & Shoemaker 21993.

No. 47   19 April 1810
John H. Sargent . . . as author
A Treatise upon Wines. By Mons. Chaptal. Translated from the French by John H. Sargent.
Note: Probably a preliminary entry for the item entered as No. 53 (see below).

No. 48   10 May 1810
The Reverend Solomon Halling
The Messiah. From the German of . . . Mr. Klopstock. By Solomon Halling . . . .
Shaw & Shoemaker 20504.

No. 49   5 July 1810
William P. Young . . . as Proprietor
A Report in part of the trial of Thomas Gayner . . . . Byone of the Counsel for the defense.
Shaw & Shoemaker 21390.

No. 50   17 July 1810
Amos Pilsbury . . . as Author
The Sacred Songster . . . . Second Edition, improved and enlarged.
Not located; see entry No. 41 for the first edition.

No. 51   23 November 1810
Doctor John R. Witherspoon . . . as Editor and proprietor
The Works of the Revd. Daniel McCalla, D.D. . . .
Shaw & Shoemaker 20613.

No. 52   4 February 1811
John Waldo of Georgetown . . . as author
Rudiments of English Grammar. By John Waldo.
Shaw & Shoemaker 24354.

No. 53   16 February 1811
John H. Sargent . . . as author
A Treatise upon Wines. By M. Chaptal . . . . Translated from the French by John H. Sargent.

Shaw & Shoemaker 22513; see No. 47 for anticipatory (?) listing.

No. 54   15 July 1811
Eleanor Henry Laurens Ramsay, Martha Henry Laurens Ramsay, Catharine Henry Laurens Ramsay, and Sabina Elliott Ramsay . . . as proprietors
   Memoirs of the Life of Martha Laurens Ramsay . . . .
   By David Ramsay, M.D.
Shaw & Shoemaker 23784.

No. 55   7 August 1811
Doctor David Ramsay . . . as Author
   The History of the American Revolution. By David Ramsay, M.D.
Shaw & Shoemaker 23780, as 'Trenton, N.J.: James J. Wilson, 1811.'

No. 56   12 September 1811
The Honorable John Faucheraud Grimké . . . as Author
   The Public Laws of South Carolina . . . . By the Honorable John Faucheraud Grimké Esq.
No 1811 edition located; see Evans 22897 for the original 1790 edition.

No. 57   16 April 1812
John B. White Esquire . . . as Author
   Modern Honor. A Tragedy . . . . By John B. White . . . .
Shaw & Shoemaker 27535.

No. 58   29 April 1812
John H. Woodward . . . as Author
   The Poetical Works of John H. Woodward.
Shaw & Shoemaker 27604.

No. 59   26 October 1812
John Waldo . . . as author
   The Child's Pronouncing Spelling Book . . . . By John Waldo . . . .
Not located.

No. 60   26 October 1812
John Waldo . . . as author
   The Youth's Pronouncing and Defining Spelling Book . . . . By John Waldo . . . .
Not located.

No. 61   20 March 1813
Benjamin James

A Digest of the Laws of South Carolina . . . . By Benjamin James.
Turnbull, I, 502.

No. 62 20 May [1813]
W. P. Young . . . as Proprietor
Rules of the District Court of the United States, for the District of South Carolina.
Not located.

No. 63 4 November [1813]
Philip Muck . . . a song . . . as Proprietor
The Light House. Written by Thomas Moore Esqre. Music composed by Arnold Remoussin.
Not located.

No. 64 30 March 1814
Edmund Botsford, A.M. . . . as Proprietor
The Spiritual Voyage . . . . By Edmund Botsford . . . .
Shaw & Shoemaker 30970.

No. 65 28 April 1814
W. H. Timrod . . . as Author
Poems on Various Subjects. By W. H. Timrod . . . .
Turnbull, I, 503.

No. 66 20 September 1814
John Hoff . . . as Proprietor
An Alphabetical Digest of the Public Statute Law of South Carolina. In Three Volumes. By Joseph Brevard.
Shaw & Shoemaker 32822.

No. 67 1 October 1814
John Hoff . . . as Proprietor
The Drill and Excercises issued to the United States Troops of the Sixth Military District.
Shaw & Shoemaker 33234.

No. 68 29 May 1815
John Mackey . . . as Author
The American School Manual, or A Sure and easy Guide to Correct Pronunciation. By John Mackey.
Not located.

No. 69 20 September 1815
John Hoff . . . as Proprietor
A Compend of Domestic Midwifery for the use of Female Practitioners. Being an Appendix to Buchan's Domestic Medicine.

Not located.

No. 70 26 October 1815

John L. E. W. Shecut . . . as Author

Elements of Medicine or Universal Doctrine of Disease. Being a New and complete system of the Theory and Practise of Physic . . . . By Doctor John L. E. W. Shecut . . . .

Not located.

No. 71 4 March 1816

Benjamin Hollinshead . . . as Author

A Sermon Explaining the Christian Religion, wherein the Sacrament of Baptism and the Lord's Supper of the New Testament instituted by Christ is the fulfilment of the Old Testament Sacraments . . . . By the Revd. Dr. Benjamin Hollinshead.

Not located.

No. 72 4 March 1816

Benjamin Hollinshead . . . as Author

An Example of plain Catechism upon the Assembly's Shorter Catechism humbly offered . . . . By the Revd. Mr. John Willison . . . . First American Edition. The Corrections & additions of the secõnd Philadelphia Edition. By the Revd. Dr. Benjamin Hollinshead . . . .

Not located; see Shaw & Shoemaker 27570 for the '2nd Philadelphia edition' of Willison's work (Philadelphia, 1812).

No. 73 6 March 1816

Abraham Motte . . . as Proprietor

Charleston Directory and Stranger's Guide for 1816 . . . . By A. M.

Shaw & Shoemaker 37213.

No. 74 8 March 1816

John Waldo . . . as Proprietor

A Latin Grammar . . . . By John Waldo . . . .

Shaw & Shoemaker 39697.

No. 75 13 April 1816

Jacob Eckhard Senr. . . . as Author and Proprietor

Choral Book. Containing Psalms, Hymns, Anthems and Chants as used in the Episcopal Church of St. Michael in Charleston . . . . Selected, arranged and composed by Jacob Eckhard Senr. . . .

Not located; possibly a preliminary entry of No. 77 below.

No. 76 3 May 1816

John Waldo . . . as Author and Proprietor
The Child's Pronouncing Spelling Book. By John
Waldo . . . .
Shaw & Shoemaker 42804, which gives the imprint:
'Georgetown, S.C., 1817.'

No. 77 20 May 1816

Jacob Eckhard Senr. . . . as Author and Proprietor
Choral Book. Containing Psalms, Hymns, Anthems and
Chants used in the Episcopal Churches of Charleston
. . . . By Jacob Eckhard Senr. . . . .
Turnbull, II, 8, which gives the imprint as: 'Boston: Printed
by James Loring for the Author, [co. 1816].'

[From this point on, the entries in the original ledger are unnumbered.]

No. 78 3 June 1816

John Waldo . . . as Author and Proprietor
The Child's First Lessons. By John Waldo . . . .
Not located.

No. 79 21 June 1816

James M. Elford . . . the title of an Engraving . . . as
Author and Proprietor
James M. Elford's Universal and Perpetual Circular
Tide Tables . . . .
Shaw & Shoemaker 37500.

No. 80 3 July 1816

John Waldo . . . as Author and Proprietor
The Dictionary Spelling Book . . . . By John Waldo . . . .
Shaw & Shoemaker 39696.

No. 81 3 July 1816

John Mackey . . . as Author and Proprietor
The American Analytical Spelling Book, and Initial
Standard of Pronunciation. By John Mackey . . . .
Not located.

No. 82 2 September 1816

Eleanor H. L. Ramsay, Martha H. L. Ramsay, Catharine
H. L. Ramsay, Sabina E. Ramsay, David Ramsay, James
Ramsay, Nathaniel Ramsay, and William Ramsay . . . as
Proprietors

> The History of the United States. By David Ramsay, M.D.
> Shaw & Shoemaker 38753, which states: 'Philadelphia: Printed by M. Carey, 1816–17. 3 vols.'

No. 83   21 September 1816
> Stephen Elliott Esquire . . . as Author and Proprietor
>> A Sketch of the Botany of South Carolina & Georgia. By Stephen Elliott.
> Shaw & Shoemaker 40749, as 'Charleston, S.C.: Printed by J. Hoff, 1817.'

No. 84   12 December 1816
> William King . . . as Author and Proprietor
>> A new and easy method for finding the Longitude at Sea . . . . By William King of Greenville District, So. Carolina.
> Not located.

No. 85   9 January 1817
> Charles Motte Lide . . . as author and proprietor
>> Forensic Speeches . . . . By Charles Motte Lide, Barrister at Law.
> Not located.

No. 86   9 January 1817
> Charles Motte Lide . . . as Author and Proprietor
>> A Vocabulary of English Words. By Charles Motte Lide Esqre.
> Not located.

No. 87   25 April 1817
> The Honorable Henry William DeSaussure . . . as author and Proprietor
>> Reports of Cases argued and determined in the Court of Chancery . . . . In Three Volumes. By Henry William DeSaussure . . . .
> Shaw & Shoemaker 42176, as 'Columbia, S.C.: Printed by Cline & Hines, 1817–19. 4 vols.' See No. 94 below.

No. 88   13 May 1817
> Levi Walbridge . . . as author and proprietor
>> School Dictionary on a scale of arithmetical progression from one Letter to the highest number of Letters in a word . . . . By Levi Walbridge . . . .
> Not located.

No. 89   13 May 1817
Levi Walbridge . . . as author and proprietor
A new American Spelling Book on a scale of arithmetical progression from one letter to the highest number of Letters in a word . . . By Levi Walbridge . . . .
Not located.

No. 90   3 July 1817
John Mackey . . . as Author and proprietor
Walker improved. A Critical Pronouncing Dictionary & Expositor of the English Language . . . . By John Mackey.
Not located.

No. 91   9 August 1817
Barnwell Deveaux . . . as author and Proprietor
The Cotton Planter's & Farmer's Companion or, A Treatise on the improved Cultivation of Cotton . . . . By a Gentleman of South Carolina.
Not located.

No. 92   16 January 1818
Edwin C. Holland . . . as Author and Proprietor
The Corsair. A Melo-Drama . . . . By Edwin C. Holland Esqr. . . .
Shaw & Shoemaker 44361

No. 93   3 March 1818
"The Protestant Episcopal Society for the advancement of Christianity in South Carolina"
Sermons on Confirmation and An Address . . . . By the late Right Revd. Theodore Dehon, D.D.
Shaw & Shoemaker 43827, as 'New York: Printed by T. and J. Swords, 1818.'

No. 94   1 June 1818
The Honorable Henry William DeSaussure . . . as Proprietor
Reports of Cases . . . . By Henry Wm. DeSaussure . . . . Volume the 4th.
Shaw & Shoemaker 42176; see No. 87 for Vols. I–III.

No. 95   23 July 1818
James M. Elford . . . a Print from an Engraving
Second Edition of Longitude Tables . . . . Improved. By James M. Elford . . . .

Shaw & Shoemaker 43926.

No. 96   26 September 1818

The Reverend Andrew Fowler . . . as Proprietor

The Lessons of the Protestant Episcopal Church in the United States of America. Selected from the Holy Scriptures with an Exposition of all the Sundays & principal Holydays throughout the Year. By Andrew Fowler, A.M.

Not located.

No. 97   28 October 1818

Miss Pogson . . . as Author and Proprietor

Essays: Religious, Moral, Dramatic & Poetical . . . . By a Lady.

Shaw & Shoemaker 43956, under title only. Turnbull, II, 35, assigns the volume to Maria Henrietta Pinckney, as does Hill 238.

No. 98   31 October 1818

James M. Elford . . . as Proprietor

The Universal Signal Book . . . . By N. Squire. With improvements adapted to the Vessels of the United States of America. By James M. Elford . . . .

McMurtrie P591.

No. 99   30 November 1818

Ebenezer Thayer and W. P. Young . . . as Proprietors

The Juvenile Pupil's Companion. A collection of Tables, useful and interesting.

Copy in the South Caroliniana Library (s.c./p510.2/J98).

No. 100   19 January 1819

Archibald E. Miller . . . as Proprietor

The Sea Serpent or Gloucester Hoax. A Dramatic Jeu d'esprit.

Shaw & Shoemaker 47744, attributed to William Crafts.

No. 101   20 March 1819

P. A. Faber . . . as Proprietor & Author

System of Medical-Jurisprudence. By P. A. Faber.

Not located.

No. 102   3 April 1819

John Blake White Esquire . . . as Author and proprietor

The Triumph of Liberty or Louisiana preserved. A National Drama . . . . By John Blake White . . . .

Shaw & Shoemaker 50101.

No. 103   3 April 1819

J. L. E. W. Shecut . . . as Author and Proprietor

Shecut's Medical and Philosophical Essays . . . . By J. L. E. W. Shecut . . . .

Shaw & Shoemaker 49406.

No. 104   20 May 1819

Eugene Guilbert . . . a Book of Music . . . as author and Proprietor

Twelve Selected English Songs with an accompaniment for the Spanish Guitar or Lyre. By Mr. Eugene Guilbert . . . .

Wolfe 3239.

No. 105   15 July 1819

John Mill . . . as Proprietor

Reports of Judicial Decisions . . . .

Shaw & Shoemaker 49464.

No. 106   2 October 1819

Eleanor H. L. Ramsay, Martha H. L. Ramsay, Catharine H. L. Ramsay, Sabina E. Ramsay, David Ramsay, James Ramsay, Nathaniel Ramsay and William Ramsay . . . as Proprietors

Universal History Americanised; or, An Historical View of the World from the earliest records to 1808 . . . . By David Ramsay, M.D. In Twelve Volumes.

Shaw & Shoemaker 49234, as 'Philadelphia: Printed by M. Carey & son, 1819. 12 vols.' Note: entry unsigned.

No. 107   21 October 1819

James Simmons . . . as Author and proprietor

The Exile's Return. A Tale in three Cantos. With other pieces. By A South Carolinian.

Shaw & Shoemaker 49418. Note: entry unsigned.

No. 108   8 January 1820

Eugene Guilbert . . . a Print from an Engraving . . . as Author & Proprietor

President Munroe's March. By Mr. E. Guilbert.

Wolfe 3246.

No. 109   15 March 1820

the Reverend Frederick Dalcho . . . as Author and proprietor

An Historical Account of the Protestant Episcopal Church in South Carolina . . . . By Frederick Dalcho

Shoemaker (1820) 941.

No. 110 13 May 1820
A. E. Miller . . . as Proprietor
Particulars of the Piracies; committed by the Commander
and Crews of the Buenos Ayrian Ship Louisa . . . .
Shoemaker (1820) 2660 lists 'Ed. 3.'

No. 111 18 May 1820
T. B. Stephens . . . as Proprietor
Sullivan's Island. The Raciad. And Other Poems Re-
printed.
Turnbull, II, 53, attributed to William Crafts.

No. 112 23 August 1820
The Reverend Frederick Dalcho . . . as Author and Pro-
prietor
Evidences of the Divinity of Jesus Christ . . . . By Fred-
erick Dalcho . . . .
Shoemaker (1820) 940.

No. 113 4 October 1820
The Reverend Frederick Dalcho . . . as Author and pro-
prietor
The Evidence from Prophecy, for the Truth of Chris-
tianity . . . . By Frederick Dalcho . . . .
Shoemaker (1820) 939.

No. 114 13 October 1820
Daniel Faust, of Columbia . . . as Proprietor
Reports of Cases . . . . By Henry Junius Nott, & David
James McCord. Vol. 1.
Shoemaker (1820) 3280 lists as 2 vols., the second of which
was entered for copyright on 26 September 1821.

No. 115 14 December 1820
William I. Street . . . as Author and Proprietor
The Juvenile Penman's Analytical Guide . . . . By an
American.
Not located.

THE LIBRARY OF STEPHEN
AND CORA CRANE

JAMES E. KIBLER, JR.

THE BOOKS CATALOGED HERE ARE A LIBRARY ONLY IN THE SENSE THAT they belonged to Stephen Crane and his wife Cora.[1] They never were assembled under one roof. Brede Place, the Cranes' Sussex residence from February 1899 to June 1900, evidently was to have housed some kind of formal library built not only of the books they acquired in England but also of those to which they were attached earlier in their lives. There are, however, some volumes in this catalog which Crane signed before he left the United States in early 1897 but which never reached England, and some bought by Cora after Stephen's death in June 1900 when she left Brede for other homes. Doubtless there are still other books not recorded here. From time to time items once owned by the Cranes turn up on the rare book market. One purpose of this article is to bring together the

[1] I would like to thank Kenneth A. Lohf and the staff of the Rare Books Division of the Butler Library at Columbia University, and Edmund Berkeley at the Alderman Library at the University of Virginia.

titles that they are known to have possessed, and another is to encourage the missing to emerge into light.

I

One suspects that Stephen and Cora intended a formal library at Brede because they attempted a formal catalog of the books they owned there. After an abortive try by Stephen to record them in one of Cora's notebooks, she took over the task some time between February 1899 and 2 August 1900 and prepared her own 'List of Books | Brede Place' in a ledger measuring $4\frac{1}{2}$ by $6\frac{3}{4}$ inches. Both are in the Butler Library of Columbia University. Cora's List is an eccentric work which runs only from 'A' to 'T', ordering the books alphabetically by title—including initial articles as the first word.[2] There are 205 entries in the List, but not all of them can be tied down to particular editions or printings: the entries are by short title, with no publication information, with only uneven indications of authors, and with a number of errors. The incorrect titles and misspellings, the method of alphabetizing, the erratic manner of listing authors' names, the many inconsistencies, and the fact that the catalog went unfinished may very well suggest the state of mind of its compiler. This project is indicative of the many small, unfinished, frantic attempts at domesticity which, as their notebooks reveal, occupied the Cranes during Stephen's last year. The evidence is that Cora had not even cataloged all of the Brede Place books within the 'A–T' category—not if the inscriptions in some surviving volumes are to be trusted. The known bulk of the Cranes' papers owned by her when she died in 1910 is at the Butler Library; in it are seventy-five books and several remains of books. Twenty-one of the volumes are inscribed 'Milborne Grove, The Boltons': this was Cora's London address from September 1900 to 28 April 1901, so books marked in this way may have been acquired after she left Brede. Twenty others, however, are marked in ways that suggest they once were at Brede: four are indisputably signed by Stephen, six are marked 'Brede Place', and ten are marked both 'Brede Place' and 'Milborne Grove'. Of these twenty, only six are on Cora's List. And only sixteen of the entire seventy-five appear there. The natural suspicion

[2] In his *Stephen Crane: A Biography* (New York: George Braziller, 1968), pp. 12, 471, and 619, R. W. Stallman writes that Crane made the List. It is definitely in Cora's handwriting, however. The revised second printing, which corrects some of the errors in the first, leaves this one uncorrected.

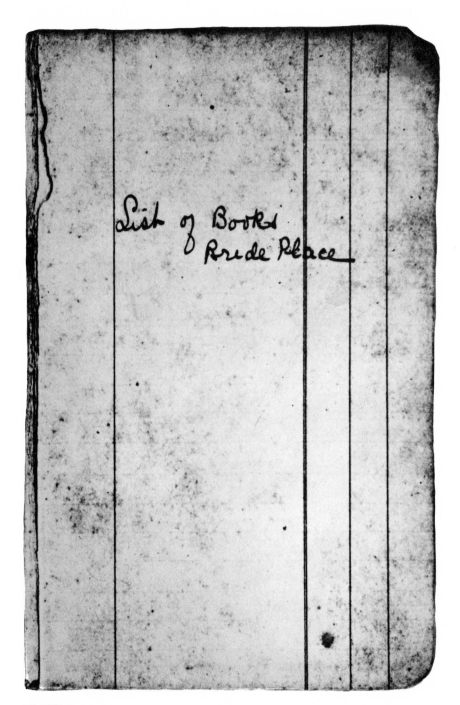

PLATE 1

A Book about Roses   By   S. Reynolds Hole
Antony and Cleopatra   "   Shakespeare
A Winters Tale   "   '
A Midsummer Nights' Dream   "   "
All's Well that Ends Well   "   "
As You Like It   "   "
Amiel's Journal   translated by Mrs Humphry Ward
A Lear of the Steppes Ect.   By   Ivan Turgenev
An Outcast of the Islands   "   Joseph Conrad
Almayers Folly   "   "
A Street in Suburbia   "   E. W. Pugh
A Passionate Pilgrim   "   Percy White
An Imaginative Man   "   R.S. Hichens
At the Cross Roads   "   Montresor
A Pair of Blue Eyes   "   Thomas Hardy
A Son of Israel   "   Rachel Penn
A Window in Thrums   "   J. M. Barrie
A Child in the Temple   "   Frank Mathews
An Altruist   "   Ouida
An Almanac with words   "   Kipling

PLATE 2

is that Cora had omitted books in some rooms of the large house at
Brede, perhaps even the volumes in Stephen's study.

A reconstruction of the Cranes' library, therefore, must necessarily be only tentative. This catalog comprises 277 titles in four sections. Section I is a list of copies once owned by the Cranes—with
the exception, of course, of presentation copies of Stephen's own
works, unless they were for some reason retained by him or Cora.
Sections II and III are redactions of Cora's List: Section II presents,
alphabetically by author instead of in Cora's individual manner, those
titles which could be identified through standard references; Section
III lists, in Cora's form, those titles which could not be identified

further. Section IV records unlocated copies for which there is some evidence of the Cranes' ownership.

II

The Crane library must be a Platonic concept because the Cranes moved about so frequently. Stephen lived with his family from his birth in 1871 until the fall of 1892. Even after that his base was the home of one or another of his brothers until he left for England with Cora in 1897. For a large part of this time such library as he had was the library of his father, the Reverend Jonathan Townley Crane, a Methodist minister who inveighed against novels and frivolous literature. Stephen's father died in 1880, his mother in 1891. In her will she left him most of the family books; but since Stephen then had no house in which to place them, physical possession was assumed by his brother William. Of course Stephen acquired books of his own — some of these survive — but they were casual acquisitions casually discarded in the main.

Then, as one result of his open boat adventure, he met Cora Howorth Stewart in Jacksonville late in 1896. With her he left the United States to report the Greco-Turkish War. They stopped briefly in England, returning there that June to take up residence at Ravensbrook. Crane evidently intended to make this his home, for in October he wrote William Crane instructions for sending him the books he had left behind: 'I have been wanting to write you for some time about the library but have been quite too busy. For my part I would gladly give to you power to choose my part . . . . Take an encyclopaedia and as many histories as possible and then let the others have a chance.'[3] Stephen and Cora lived at Ravensbrook, except for Stephen's absence to report the Spanish-American War, until February 1899, when they moved to Brede Place. And there they stayed until Crane's final illness in May 1900. After he died on 5 June 1900, Cora accompanied his body to America. Brede she had to relinquish. In July she sailed back to London and on her arrival, roomed at 47 Gower Street. But her belongings remained at Brede until the beginning of August. Then she collected them and moved to South Kensington, to 6 Milborne Grove, staying there until she left for America in April 1901.

[3] R. W. Stallman and Lillian Gilkes, eds., *Stephen Crane: Letters* (New York: New York University Press, 1960), p. 146.

Cora's possessions were in storage until early 1903 when her English creditors permitted their removal. Around that time she was back where she had begun when she met Crane — operating an establishment where men came to meet women. When she began managing The Court in 1904 the books came there. According to Lillian Gilkes, they were placed 'under lock and key', while 'an assortment of the latest popular works, and novels in profusion . . . were available to the girls or to clients'. These had an injunction on their flyleaves:

Please return to book case in sitting room so that others may enjoy
Cora Taylor[.][4]

Only eighteen titles entered in Cora's List reached the Butler Library. A total of 186 volumes are thus unaccounted for. The number is likely far higher because, as will be remembered, Cora did not carry her catalog from 'U' to 'Z' and perhaps did not enter even all the 'T' titles. In addition, as shown, she did not list some of the other books in the first place. When Cora died, the inventory for the public sale of her belongings held on the steps of the Jacksonville courthouse in April 1911 contained a lot of 176 books. This information may go far in explaining what happened to many of the books from Brede. Some of what remained after the auction went to the Butler Library in 1952. Others still find their way to the marketplace.

III

A history of the movement of the books in the Cranes' library is implicitly a history of their dispersal. But although dispersal forms a necessary background to this catalog, the Cranes' acquisition of them is both more interesting and more important. Somewhat hastily, R. W. Stallman has exclaimed that the titles on Cora's List formed 'An odd collection!'[5] More thought, however, indicates that it was not at all an unusual assemblage for a man who was a professional writer but an amateur reader and who was living with a highly literate woman. Gifts account for at least ten books. Joseph Conrad, Henry James, Charles Whibley, Robert Barr, Burr McIntosh, and Frank Harris — friends and acquaintances of the Cranes — inscribed ones to

[4] Lillian Gilkes, *Cora Crane* (Bloomington: Indiana University Press, 1960), p. 320. I have relied on this book heavily for information on the Cranes' movements.

[5] Stallman, *Stephen Crane: A Biography*, p. 554.

Stephen and Cora. In addition, Harold Frederic contributed Batten-
berg's *Men-of-War Names,* and Mrs. Pease, Sharp's *The Sin-Eater.*[6] H. G.
Wells calls attention to another important source when he reports:

There had been many Cranes who wrote before him. He has shown
me a shelf of books, for the most part the pious and theological works
of various antecedent Stephen Cranes. He had been at some pains
to gather together these alien products of his kin. For the most part
they seemed little, insignificant books, and one opened them to read
the beaten *clichés,* the battered, outworn phrases, of a movement
that has ebbed. Their very size and binding suggested a dying impulse . . . .[7]

Fifteen books in these lists were written by Crane's father and by his
mother's family—his uncle George M. Peck,[8] his granduncle Jesse T.
Peck, and his great-granduncle J. K. Peck.[9] And many of the forty-
seven titles published before either Stephen or Cora likely was old
enough to have purchased them probably came from one family or

[6] According to Stallman, *Stephen Crane: A Biography,* p. 340, before Crane
moved to Brede, Frederic wrote, 'I ran across a little book on Naval Names
yesterday which impressed me at once as having been made expressly for
you—and it leaves by this same post for Ravensbrook.'
 In *Stephen Crane: Letters,* p. 210, there is a note from Cora to Mrs. Edward
Pease dated from Brede Place in February 1899: 'Mr. Crane was so much
pleased with the book. He has heard a great deal about Fiona MacCleod
[*sic*] but has never seen this book of hers.' 'Fiona Macleod' was William
Sharp, and the only Sharp title on Cora's List is *The Sin-Eater.*
[7] H. G. Wells, 'Stephen Crane From an English Standpoint', in Edmund
Wilson, ed., *The Shock of Recognition* (New York: Farrar, Strauss, 1955), p. 671.
[8] George Peck's *Wyoming* is a familial work twice again: a copy in the collection of Joseph Katz reveals a drawing by Crane's mother on p. 192; and
chapter 14, 'A View from Campbell's Ledge', on pp. 344–48 is by the Reverend L. W. Peck, her brother.
 In *Stephen Crane: A Biography,* p. 12, R. W. Stallman says that Stephen's
brother Wilbur owned a copy of *Wyoming,* brought it to Stephen in 1899, and
'must also have taken it back home with him; it is not listed in Crane's [*sic*]
"List of Books at Brede Place" [*sic*].' Stallman may be correct in saying that
Wilbur loaned Crane a copy. However, he is wrong in assuming that because
the title does not appear in Cora's List Crane did not have it. For in the Butler
Library are two copies of the book which were at Brede. The reason that
neither is on the List is obvious: *Wyoming* begins with 'W', but the List ends
at 'T'.
[9] In *Stephen Crane: A Biography,* p. 555, Stallman attributes *Luther Peck and
His Five Sons* to Luther Peck. It is, however, by the Reverend J. K. Peck. Only
if Reverend Peck's nickname was 'Luther' would Stallman be correct.

the other. One presumes that at least five of them came from his side because they are sermons or books on morals, the kinds of books one expects of ministerial Cranes and Pecks rather than artistic Howorths. So it is probable that *A Pastoral Letter from a Minister*, Dixon's *Personal Narrative*, Bishop Horne's *Memoirs*, the *Life of the Rev. J. B. M. Vianney*, *Discourse Concerning the Divine Providence*, the *History of European Morals*, and others came to Brede as links to Crane's background. In October of 1897, Crane had written to his brother to take as part of the family's library 'an encyclopaedia and as many histories as possible.' Two multivolumed encyclopedias appear in the List: *Lloyd's* and the *Popular Encyclopedia*. And extant at the Butler Library are several histories published prior to 1880.

Four volumes once housed at Brede are more direct links between Stephen and his youth. He inscribed three with the year 1881: *Atwood's Country and Suburban Houses*, Dixon's *Personal Narrative*, and his granduncle's *What Must I Do to Be Saved?* At the age of nineteen he signed the fourth, Gardiner's *The French Revolution*, dating it 1891 from Syracuse University and affixing the name of his fraternity.

Still more books are souvenirs of his friends. In addition to the presentation copies from James, Conrad, and others, there are books Crane might have bought or borrowed because they were written by people he knew. Edwin Pugh played handball with Stephen at Ravensbrook and had a standing invitation to Brede: the Cranes owned his *King Circumstance, The Man of Straw, A Street in Suburbia*, and *Tony Drum*. Similarly, there are two books by Robert Barr, a close friend while Crane lived and a collaborator after he died, and two by Harold Frederic, at least equally close while he was alive. Crane reviewed one of them, *March Hares*, in an article that reveals his knowledge of *In the Sixties, Seth's Brother's Wife, In the Valley, The Lawton Girl*, and *The Damnation of Theron Ware*.[10] He also knew *Gloria Mundi*.[11] The Cranes owned four books by Hamlin Garland, who had befriended Crane early, and Stephen had doubtless read others. Elizabeth Robins corresponded with Cora about the children of Kate Lyon and Harold Frederic and with Cora was invited to join the Society of American Women in London: there are four of her books. George Gissing was sufficiently an acquaintance to contribute to *The Ghost*: the Cranes owned one of his books. And there are eight volumes from other

[10] Crane, 'Harold Frederic', *Chap Book*, VIII (15 March 1898), 358–59.
[11] A manuscript London newsletter dispatch at Columbia reveals that both Stephen and Cora read the novel under the working title *Strawberry Leaves*. Information supplied by Joseph Katz.

acquaintances: James Barrie, Anthony Hope Hawkins, Swinburne, Henley, Clemens, Chanler, McIntosh, and Hubbard.

It is not 'odd' to find books by popular contemporaries on a writer's shelves. Seventeen by Marie Corelli, Hall Caine, F. Marion Crawford, A. Conan Doyle, Hardy, Trask, Shaw, Westcott, Wister, Stevenson, Yeats, Ouida, and Fitzgerald were there. Some of them may have come from publishers who hoped for a blurb. Crane had, after all, paid his respects not only to Frederic but also to Ouida.[12] Kipling, immensely popular, accounts for the largest number of titles by one author on the List — eleven. Crane admired him much at one time. Tolstoi was another of his admirations, but only one book concerning him was at Brede.

This leads to a necessary caution: the books recorded here constitute only one access to Stephen Crane's reading career. For that purpose they more accurately reflect interests of either Stephen or Cora through June 1900, and after that they give a clue to the kind of person Cora had become. Crane's interest in the Spanish-American War seems to be reflected in the four books by Bonsal, Clarke, McIntosh, and Somerville which treat either the war or some aspect of Spanish culture. His bent towards history and his interest in its possibilities for literature may be seen in the books by Page, Armstrong, Baring-Gould, Chambers, Hodgkin, Comte de Ségur, and Thomson. Preparation for his later war pieces, including *Great Battles of the World*, may have involved Dredge, Maclay, Roosevelt, and Robinson. Zangwill's *Children of the Ghetto* fits readily into the library of the man who wrote *Maggie*. Baedeker's *London* was a practical acquisition in Athens before settlement in England. The books on roses by Hibberd and Hole, along with Darwin's work on cross-pollination, reflect Cora's interest in gardening once their home had been begun. And children's books by Fröbel, Grimm, and Lear, as well as *Two Little Girls in Green*, were probably entertainment for the Frederic children on rainy days at Ravensbrook or Brede.

More generally significant, perhaps, is the Cranes' apparent commitment to standard authors like Shelley, Byron, Scott, Burns, Gray, Ossian, Moore, Lamb, Longfellow, Heine, George Eliot, Browning, Carlyle, Meredith, Rossetti, Lowell, Shakespeare, Dryden, and Boswell. They suggest the need for immediate revision of the theory that Crane was ignorant of literary tradition. Far from being an untu-

---

[12] Crane, 'Ouida's Masterpiece', *Book Buyer*, XIII (January 1897), 968–69. The subject was *Under Two Flags* — not on the List.

tored genius or the man Howells imagined as having sprung into life fully armed, Crane evidently was an avid reader. He was not bookish; yet he nevertheless grew up with books. For as Melvin Schoberlin reports, Stephen's sister, a schoolteacher who herself aspired to be an author, directed 'to a great extent' his childhood reading; it 'was she who gave direction to his early years.'[13] When at Syracuse University, according to a friend, Stephen 'sat up late at night diligently poring over the masterpieces of literature.'[14] Although the books recorded here must represent only the top of an iceberg of indeterminate size, they suggest that after college he could have spent more late nights in the same way.

[13] Melvin Schoberlin, ed., *The Sullivan County Sketches of Stephen Crane* (Syracuse, N.Y.: Syracuse University Press, 1949), p. 3.
[14] Stallman, *Stephen Crane: A Biography,* p. 30.

I. Copies Located

*Books preceded by an asterik (*) are on
Cora Crane's List, Section II.*

Alcott, W. A. *The Young Man's Guide.* Boston: T. R. Marvin, 1842. Fifteenth Edition. 360 pp. Inscribed by Cora on the front pastedown: 'This book belongs to | Mr̲s̲ Stephen Crane | July, 1900'. There are many penciled underlinings. NNC.

Allan, James. *Under the Dragon Flag. My Experiences in the Chino-Japanese War.* London: William Heinemann, 1898. 122 pp. Inscribed by Cora on the front pastedown: 'Mr̲s̲ Stephen Crane | 6. Milbourne [*sic*] Grove | The Boltons | S.W.' Cora has written on the title page beneath the subtitle beginning '*My Experiences*': 'A fat lie!! An | impossible journey | C. C.' NNC.

Anon. *Abrége de L'histoire Romaine. À L'usage des Elèves de L'école Royale Militaire, à Paris.* Baltimore: 'Se trouve chez Philippe Nicklin', 1812. 'Première Édition Américane. À L'usage des Écoles.' 249 pp. NNC.

Anon. [*The Book of Conversations; A Guide for the Tongue* . . . . Charleston: S. Babcock & Co., 1837.] 251 pp. The title page and first sixty pages are missing. NNC.

Anon. *The British Imperial Calendar for the Year of Our Lord 1824:* . . . *Containing a General Register of the United Kingdom* . . . . London: W. Clowes [1823]. 430 pp. Signed by Cora on the front pastedown: 'Mrs. Stephen Crane | 6. Milborne Grove | The Boltons | SW'. NNC.

Anon. *Conversations on Common Things; or, Guide to Knowledge: with Questions.* 'By a Teacher'. Boston: Munroe and Francis, 1824. 'For the Use of Schools'. 263 pp. NNC.

Anon. [*Executive Reports, at the Second Session of the Seventeenth Congress, 1822–1823.* Washington, D.C.: 1823.] The pages are not numbered consecutively. NNC.

Anon. *Flora and Thalia; or, Gems of Flowers and Poetry: Being an Alphabetical Arrangement of Flowers, with Appropriate Poetical Illustrations . . . to Which is Added, a Botanical Description of the Various Parts of a Flower, and the Dial of Flowers.* 'By a Lady'. Philadelphia: Carey, Lea, and Blanchard, 1836. 240 pp. NNC.

Anon. *The Globe Trotter the Medium of Inter-communication of the Cosmopolitan Correspondence Club (January 1910. No. 32).* Milwaukee, Wisconsin: 1910. 124 pp. NNC.

Anon. *The National Gallery British Art Catalogue with Descriptions, Historical Notes . . . .* London: His Majesty's Stationery Office, Darling & Son, 1908. Sixteenth Edition. Inscribed to Cora on its paper cover: 'Mrs McNeil with Mrs Harvey Brabazon Co[illegible] | kind regards | See P 19.' Page 19 contains a sketch of the life of H. B. Brabazon, painter, born 1821, died 1906.[15] NNC.

Anon. *A Pastoral Letter from a Minister to His Parishioners, Being an Earnest Exhortation to Them to Take Care of Their Souls. . . .* London: 1700. 16 pp. Inscribed in either Stephen's or Cora's hand: 'Stephen Crane | Brede Place | [illegible] 30th 1899 | [torn]d for this book.' NNC.[16]

Anon. *Rules of the Saint Andrew's Society, of the City of Charleston, in South-Carolina: Established in the Year of Our Lord One Thousand Seven Hundred and Twenty-Nine.* Charleston: J. S. Burges, 1830. 46 pp. NNC.

Anon. *The Tablet of Memory, Shewing Every Memorable Event in History, from the Earliest Period to the Year 1790, Classed Under Distinct Heads, with Their Dates: Comprehending an Epitome of English History, with an Exact Chronology of Painters and Eminent Men. To Which Are Annexed, Several Useful Lists.* London: 1790. Seventh Edition. 295 pp. NNC.

---

[15] Cora was Mrs. Hammond McNeil from 1 June 1905 until her divorce 18 October 1909. (See Gilkes, *Cora Crane*, pp. 330 and 352.) Cora's involvement with the studio set while she lived at Milborne Grove (Gilkes, p. 295) might explain the presence of this title.
[16] See also in this list Fleetwood, Leslie, Moore, Sewell, Sharp, Stanley, Tenison, and Williams, all of whom wrote works bound in the same volume with *A Pastoral Letter.*

Anon. *Who's Who 1898 Second Year of New Issue* . . . . London: 1898. 60 pp. Inscribed on the front pastedown by Cora: 'Mrs Crane. | 6 Milborne Grove The Boltons'. On the front free endpaper in either Cora's or Stephen's hand is: 'Crane'. NNC.

Atwood, Daniel T. *Atwood's Country and Suburban Houses.* New York: Orange Judd & Company, [1871]. 287 pp. Inscribed by Stephen on the front free endpaper: 'Stephen Crane | 1881'. On the frontispiece Cora has written: 'This book belongs to Mrs Stephen Crane.' There are penciled X-marks throughout. NNC.

Baedeker, K. *London and Its Environs, Including Excursions to Brighton, The Isle of Wight, etc.* London: Dulau and Co., 1878. 366 pp. Cora has written on the front free endpaper: 'Property of Mrs Stephen Crane | Brede Place | Sussex | 1898'; and then in darker ink: '6. Milborne Grove | The Boltons | SW.' There are also two other indecipherable signatures in Greek. Stephen and Cora likely acquired this copy when they were in Greece during the Greco-Turkish War in 1897. The book is stamped in purple: 'ΒΙΒΛΙΟΠΩΛΕΙΟΝ · Γ. ΛΑΜΠΡΟΥ · ΕΝ ΑΘΗΝΑΙΣ'.[17] NNC.

Bancroft, George. *History of the United States, from the Discovery of the American Continent.* Volume II only. Boston: Little, Brown, 1838. Third Edition. 468 pp. NNC.

[Black, Adam and Charles.] *Black's Guide to South Wales.* London: Adam and Charles Black, 1896. Ninth Edition. 132 pp. Cora has written on the front pastedown: 'Property of Mrs Stephen Crane | Brede Place. Sussex | Bought going to Ireland in 1899.' Then on the next line in darker ink: '6. Milborne Grove. The Boltons South Kensington.' On the fly title in either Cora's or Stephen's hand is: 'Crane | Brede Place | Sussex | Oct. 1899.' NNC.

Boswell, James. *British Essays in Favour of the Brave Corsicans: by Several Hands.* London: Edward and Charles Dilly, 1769. 136 pp. NNC.

[17] Translates 'G. Lampros, Bookseller in Athens'. The Cranes reached Oxted, Surrey, in early June 1897, and so must have purchased the book some time before this date. At the time of the inscribed date (1898), the Cranes lived at Ravensbrook, not Brede; thus the date does not match the place.

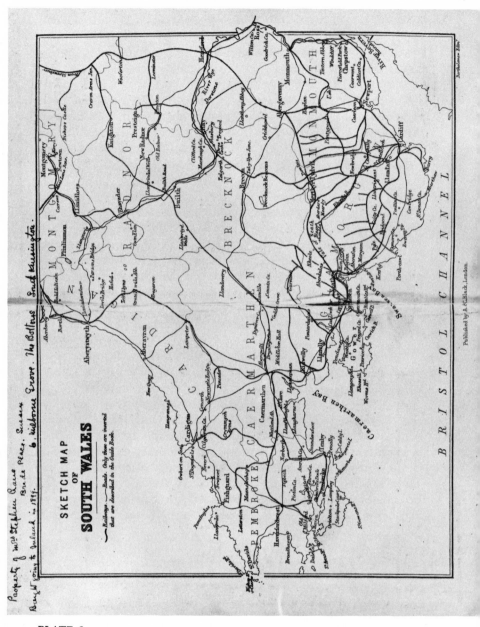

SKETCH MAP
OF
SOUTH WALES

Railways.——Roads. Only those are inserted
that are described in the Guide Book.

BRISTOL CHANNEL

Published by A.&C.Black, London.

PLATE 3

Chanler, William Astor. *Through Jungle and Desert: Travels in Eastern Africa.* New York: Macmillan, 1896. On the front free endpaper is the record of its owners: 'Hamlin Garland | 141 East 25th St. | New York. | Stephen Crane | Hartwood | Sullivan Co., | N.Y. | Frank [surname illegible; begins with an 'S'] | -Players- | book presented by Chanler.'[18] InU Lilly.

Cheever, G[eorge] B[arrell]. *The American Common-place Book of Prose, a Collection of Eloquent and Interesting Extracts from the Writings of American Authors.* Boston: Russell, Shattuck, and Co., [1828]. 468 pp. Signed: 'Antonia Alvarez [or Aliary] | St. Augustine'. NNC.

Crabb, George. *English Synonyms Explained in Alphabetical Order with Copious Illustrations and Examples.* London: George Routledge and Sons, 1898. 638 pp. Inscribed by Cora on the front pastedown: 'This book belongs to | Mrs ['s' is erased] Stephen Crane. | 6. Milborne Grove | The Boltons | South Kensington | July, 1899'.[19] NNC.

*Crane, Rev. J[onathan] T[ownley]. *Arts of Intoxication. The Aim, and the Results.* New York: Phillips & Hunt, [1870]. Fourth Thousand. 264 pp. Inscribed by Cora on the front pastedown: 'Mrs Stephen Crane | 6. Milborne Grove | The Boltons | S.W.' NNC.

Crane, Stephen. *Active Service.* London: William Heinemann, 1899. Pp. 1–64, 83–94.[20] NNC.

_____. *Active Service. A Novel.* New York: Frederick A. Stokes Company, [1899]. 345 pp. NNC.

[18] Transcribed from [Joseph Katz], '*Ex Libris* Stephen Crane', *Stephen Crane Newsletter*, II (Fall 1967), 5–6. Stallman, *Stephen Crane: A Biography*, p. 585, note 8, says the missing name is 'Snathis'. Stallman's version of how Crane got the book differs from the reconstruction offered by Katz, who has Crane receive the book from Garland who got it from the Player's Club; Stallman has 'Snathis' give the volume to Crane and Crane in turn passing it on to Garland. Unlikely.

[19] The date is in darker ink. The Cranes were living at Brede Place at this time, the date thus not belonging to the place.

[20] This is an incomplete proof copy bound in a blue paper cover.

————. *Active Service. A Novel.* New York: IANA, 1901. 345 pp. Inscribed in what appears to be Cora's hand: 'For Mark.'[21] NNC.

*————. *George's Mother.* New York: Edward Arnold, 1896. 177 pp. Initials on the fly-title page are erased: the last one is 'M.' and the first is either 'J.', 'L.', or 'I.' After these is written in a hand unknown to me: 'Lansing | Xmas 1901.' NNC.

*————. *George's Mother.* New York: Edward Arnold, 1896. 177 pp. In Stephen's hand: 'Nov. 4, / 96 | To an unnamed sweetheart | Stephen Crane'. NhD.[22]

————. *The Little Regiment and Other Episodes of the American Civil War.* London: William Heinemann, 1897. Paper cover; Pioneer Series. 150 pp. Inscribed in either Cora's or Stephen's hand on the front free endpaper: 'Crane | Brede Place'; and then below this: 'This book belongs to | Mrs Stephen Crane | Brede Place | Sussex | 1897'.[23] NNC.

*————. *Maggie. A Girl of the Streets.* New York: D. Appleton and Company, 1896. 158 pp. Inscribed by Crane on the page preceding the fly title: 'To Lyda | From her friend | Stephen Crane | Jacksonville, Fla. | February 18, | 1897.'[24] Tipped in this copy is David Belasco's article 'The Genius of Stephen Crane', which appeared in the *Metropolitan Magazine* after Crane's death. NNC.

*————. *Maggie das Strassenkind.* Leipzig: Georg H. Wigand's Verlag, 1897. 126 pp. There are two copies, one bound in paper, the other hardcover. The paper-covered copy has unopened leaves and is inscribed by Cora on its cover: 'Mrs Stephen Crane | 6. Milborne Grove | The Boltons | South Kensington'. Either Stephen or Cora has also written on the fly title: 'Crane | Brede

[21] Likely Mark Barr, husband of Kate Frederic's niece.

[22] Stallman and Gilkes, *Letters*, p. 132, reports that the book was inscribed to Cora. Its presence at Brede would point toward this conclusion, but, as in the *Maggie* inscribed to Lyda de Camp (see note 24), it is not certain evidence. See also *Letters*, p. 132, for a discussion of the dating of the inscription. The transcription here is from Herbert Faulkner West, *A Stephen Crane Collection* (Hanover: Dartmouth College Library, 1948).

[23] The Cranes were not yet at Brede at this date; thus the date does not match the place.

[24] Lyda is Lyda de Camp, madam of another brothel 'down the line' from Cora Taylor's.

Place'. The hardcover copy is unsigned, but someone has begun translation: P. 2 bears three penciled words in English. NNC.

————. *The Monster and Other Stories.* New York: Harper & Brothers, 1899. 189 pp. NNC.

————. *The Monster and Other Stories.* London: Harper & Brothers, 1901. 252 pp. NNC.

————. *The Open Boat and Other Stories.* London: William Heinemann, 1898. Paper cover; Colonial Library. 295 pp. Inscribed by Cora on the title page: 'This book belongs to Mrs Stephen Crane | 6. Milborne Grove. The Boltons | S.W.' The copy has two title pages. The one which is signed is not bound with the volume. Cora has also signed the cover: '[tear] Stephen Crane | 6. Milborne Grove | The Boltons. S.W.' NNC.

*————. *Pictures of War. The Red Badge of Courage. The Little Regiment, Etc. with an Appreciation by George Wyndham, M.P.* London: William Heinemann, 1898. Paper cover; Colonial Library. 344 pp. Inscribed by Cora on the cover: 'Mrs ['s' is erased] Stephen Crane | 6. Milborne Grove | The Boltons | S.W.' NNC.

*————. *Pictures of War.* [without the appreciation by Wyndham.] London: William Heinemann, 1898. Paper cover; Colonial Library. 344 pp. Inscribed by Cora on the cover: 'Mrs. Stephen Crane. | 6. Milborne Grove | The Boltons | S.W.' NNC.

————. *The Red Badge of Courage. An Episode of the American Civil War.* New York: D. Appleton and Company, 1895. 233 pp. Inscribed by Cora on the front pastedown: 'This book belongs to | Mrs Stephen Crane | 6. Milborne Grove | The Boltons | South Kensington'. A printed biography of Crane is tipped in. NNC.

————. *The Red Badge of Courage. An Episode of the American Civil War.* London: William Heinemann, 1900. Paper cover. 194 pp. Inscribed by Cora on the fly title: 'This book belongs to | Mrs Stephen Crane | 6. Milborne Grove | The Boltons | South Kensington.' NNC.

*————. *The Third Violet.* New York: D. Appleton, 1897. 203 pp. Stephen's calling card is pasted inside the front cover. Cora has written on the front pastedown: 'This book belongs to | Mrs

Stephen Crane | 6. Milborne Grove | The Boltons | South Kensington'; and on the front free endpaper either Cora or Stephen has written: 'Crane | Brede Place'. NNC.

*_____. *The Third Violet.* London: William Heinemann, 1897. 220 pp. NNC.

_____. *War is Kind.* London: William Heinemann, 1899. 96 pp. Stephen's calling card is pasted on the inside cover. The copy is marked: 'File copy | Published April 28th | 1899' with the date canceled in purple pencil. Cora has written on the front pastedown: 'This book belongs to | Mrs Stephen Crane | 6. Milborne Grove | The Boltons | South Kensington.' NNC.

_____. *Whilomville Stories.* New York: Harper & Brothers, 1900. 199 pp. Crane's signature is pasted in. NNC.

_____. *Wounds in the Rain.* London: Methuen, 1900. Inscribed on the front pastedown and partially obscured by a crayon are these words in Cora's hand: 'This book belongs to | Mrs. Stephen Crane | 6 Milborne Grove | The Boltons | South Kinsington [*sic*].' Affixed beneath the inscription is the following note in Crane's hand: 'Wounds in the Rain. | A collection of stories relating to the Spanish-American war of 1898 | By Stephen Crane. | [rule] | Note: The intermediate descriptive phrase should certainly appear on the cover of the book as well as on the title page. Otherwise, rain rhymes atrociously with Crane and ruins the entire effect of the singular and sinister brutality of the title. The intermediate sentence should also be made to appear in any advertisement. | S. C.' Mr. Richard S. Williams, Jacksonville, Florida.[25]

[25] The transcription, information, and description come from George W. Hallam, 'Some New Stephen Crane Items', *Studies in Bibliography*, XX (1967), 263–66. Hallam also reports the presence in this copy of a commercial photograph of Crane and a 'small, heavily addressed envelope' which contained a Kipling letter. The envelope is postmarked 14, 15, 17, and 18 September and has the following addresses: (1) 'Mrs. Crane | c/o Methuen Co. | 36 Essex St | Strand | London W.C.', (2) 'Mr. Alfred Plant, Esq. | 18 Bedford Row | Greys Inn', and (3) '47 Gower Street'. According to Hallam, 'The envelope is affixed to the second front flyleaf. Alfred T. Plant was the Cranes' solicitor' (264n). Hallam also quotes a Kipling letter which acknowledges Cora's presentation of a copy of *Wounds in the Rain.*

_____ and Robert Barr. *The O'Ruddy. A Romance*. London: Methuen & Co., 1904. 356 pp. NNC.

Dixon, James. *Personal Narrative of a Tour Through a Part of the United States and Canada: with Notices of the History and Institutions of Methodism in America. Containing Also the Fifth Part, Heretofore Omitted in the American Editions*. New York: Lane & Scott, 1850. Third Edition. 556 pp. Inscribed by Crane on the front pastedown: 'Stephen Crane | 1881 – '. NNC.

*[Dunne, Finley Peter.] *Mr. Dooley In Peace and In War*. London: Grant Richards, 1899. 'Reprinted, March (three times), 1899'. 260 pp. Inscribed by Cora on the front pastedown: 'This book belongs to | Mrs Stephen Crane | Brede Place | Sussex | 1899 | 6. Milborne Grove | The Boltons | S.W.' There is a clipping entitled 'Mr Dooley on the Future in China' mounted on the front free endpaper. NNC

Fasig-Tipton Co. *Catalogue of the Rancocas Stock Farm Thoroughbred Yearlings . . . To be Sold By Public Auction at Fasig-Tipton Co.'s Paddocks Sheepshead Bay, N.Y. Monday, July 9, Tuesday, July 10, 1906 . . . Wm. Easton, Auctioneer*. New York: [1906]. Unnumbered pages. There are marginal notations throughout.[26]

Fénelon, François de Salignac de La Mothe-. *The Adventures of Telemachus: the Son of Ulysses. Translated from the French . . . by John Hawkesworth*. Cooke's Edition. Books I–IV; XII–XV; and part of XVI: pp. 1–73; 13–84. No covers present. London: W. Pople, [n.d.] NNC.

Fielding, Henry. *The History of Tom Jones. A Foundling*. London: George Bell and Sons, 1880. Volume I only of a two-volume edition. 498 pp. Inscribed by Cora or Stephen on the flyleaf: 'Crane | Brede Place'; and beneath this in Cora's hand: 'This book belongs to | Mrs Stephen Crane | Brede Place. | Sussex | 1895.'[27] On the front pastedown in Cora's hand is: 'Mrs Stephen Crane | 6. Milborne Grove | The Boltons'. NNC.

[26] According to Gilkes, *Cora Crane*, p. 355, the presence of this title is probably owing to Ernest Budd, a friend of Cora's in her last years who played the horses.
[27] The 1895 date is puzzling. Since the Cranes did not move to Brede until February 1899, this is perhaps the date the book was acquired.

[Fleetwood, William.] *Four Sermons: I. On the Death of Queen Mary, 1694. II. On the Death of the Duke of Gloucester, 1700. III. On the Death of King William, 1701. IV, On the Queen's Accession to the Throne, in 1703.* London: 1712. 84 pp. Bound with *A Pastoral Letter.* See note 16. NNC.

Frederic, Harold. *The Young Emperor William II of Germany. A Study in Character Development on the Throne.* London: T. Fisher Unwin, 1892. Second Edition. 251 pp. Inscribed by Cora on the front pastedown: 'Mr<u>s</u> Stephen Crane | 6. Milborne Grove. | The Boltons | South Kensington'. On the front free endpaper is the signature of Cora's traveling companion in Greece and attendant at Brede: 'Ruedy | <u>Brede Place</u>'. NNC.

Gardiner, Bertha Meriton. *The French Revolution. 1789–1795.* London: Longmans, Green, and Co., 1889. Fourth Edition. Epochs of Modern History. 262 pp. Inscribed twice by Stephen. In his large scrawl on the front free endpaper is: 'Stephen Crane | Delta Upsilon | Lafayette Chapter' and on the fly title appears: 'Stephen Crane | Syracuse NY | Jan 13th, 1891. | Stephen Crane'. On the front pastedown Cora has written: 'This book belongs to | Mr<u>s</u> Stephen Crane. | July, 1900.' There are several pencil marks in the Index. NNC.

[Germain, Walter.] *The Complete Bachelor Manners for Men.* New York: D. Appleton and Company, 1896. 211 pp. Inscribed by either Stephen or Cora on the front free endpaper: 'Crane | Brede <u>Place</u>'. NNC.

Gleig, Rev. G[eorge] R[obert]. *The Life of Major-General Sir Thomas Munro, Bart. And K. C. B. Late Governor of Madras. With Extracts from His Correspondence and Private Papers.* London: Henry Colburn and Richard Bentley, 1830. Volume II only of a two-volume edition. 454 pp. Inscribed by Cora on the front pastedown: 'Mr<u>s</u> Stephen Crane | 6. Milborne Grove | The Boltons | SW.' Many leaves unopened. NNC.

[Golovin, Ivan.] *Russia under Nicholas the First. Translated from the German by Captain Anthony C. Sterling, 73rd Regiment.* London: John Murray, 1841. 202 pp. Inscribed by Cora on the front pastedown: '6. Milborne Grove | The Boltons | SW'. There is also an inscription on the front free endpaper in either Stephen's or

Cora's hand: 'This book belongs to | Stephen Crane | Brede Place | Sussex | 1900. March'. NNC.

*Hardy, Thomas. *Jude the Obscure.* New York: Harper & Brothers, 1896. The Wessex Novels, Vol. VIII. Inscribed in Cora's hand on the front pastedown: 'Property of | "The Court" | Ward and Davis St— | Jacksonville Fla | Please return to bookcase in sitting room so that | others may enjoy | Cora Taylor'. ViU, Barrett.

*Harris, Frank. *Elder Conklin and Other Stories.* London: W. Heinemann, 1895. Second Edition. 241 pp. Inscribed by the author: 'To Stephen Crane | from the author. | June '97.' Inscribed by Cora on the front free endpaper: 'This book belongs to | Mrs Stephen Crane | 6. Milborne Grove | The Boltons | South Kensington'. Stephen's autograph is pasted inside the front cover. NNC.

Hawkesworth, John. See 'Fénelon, François'.

Howorth, George. *The Restoration of Oil Paintings: With a Few Practical Hints to the Owners of Pictures.* Boston: Press of Geo. C. Rand & Avery, 1859. 'Cora Crane | Brede Place | Sussex'. NNC.[28]

Hunt, Leigh. *The Autobiography of Leigh Hunt, with Reminiscences of Friends and Contemporaries.* New York: Harper & Brothers, 1850. Vol. I only of a two-volume edition. 299 pp. NNC.

*James, Henry. *The Bostonians. A Novel.* London: Macmillan and Co., 1886. 449 pp. Inscribed by Cora on the front pastedown: 'Mrs Stephen Crane | 6. Milborne Grove | The Boltons | SW'. NNC.

*———. *The Spoils of Poynton.* London: William Heinemann, 1897. 286 pp. Inscribed by either Stephen or Cora on the front free endpaper: 'Crane | Brede Place'; and by Cora on the front pastedown: 'Mrs Stephen Crane | 6. Milborne Grove | The Boltons | S.W.' NNC.

*———. *Stories Revived. First Series* . . . . London: Macmillan and Co., 1885. 428 pp. Inscribed by Cora on the front pastedown: 'Mrs Stephen Crane | 6. Milborne Grove | The Boltons | SW'. NNC.

[28] George Howorth was Cora's father.

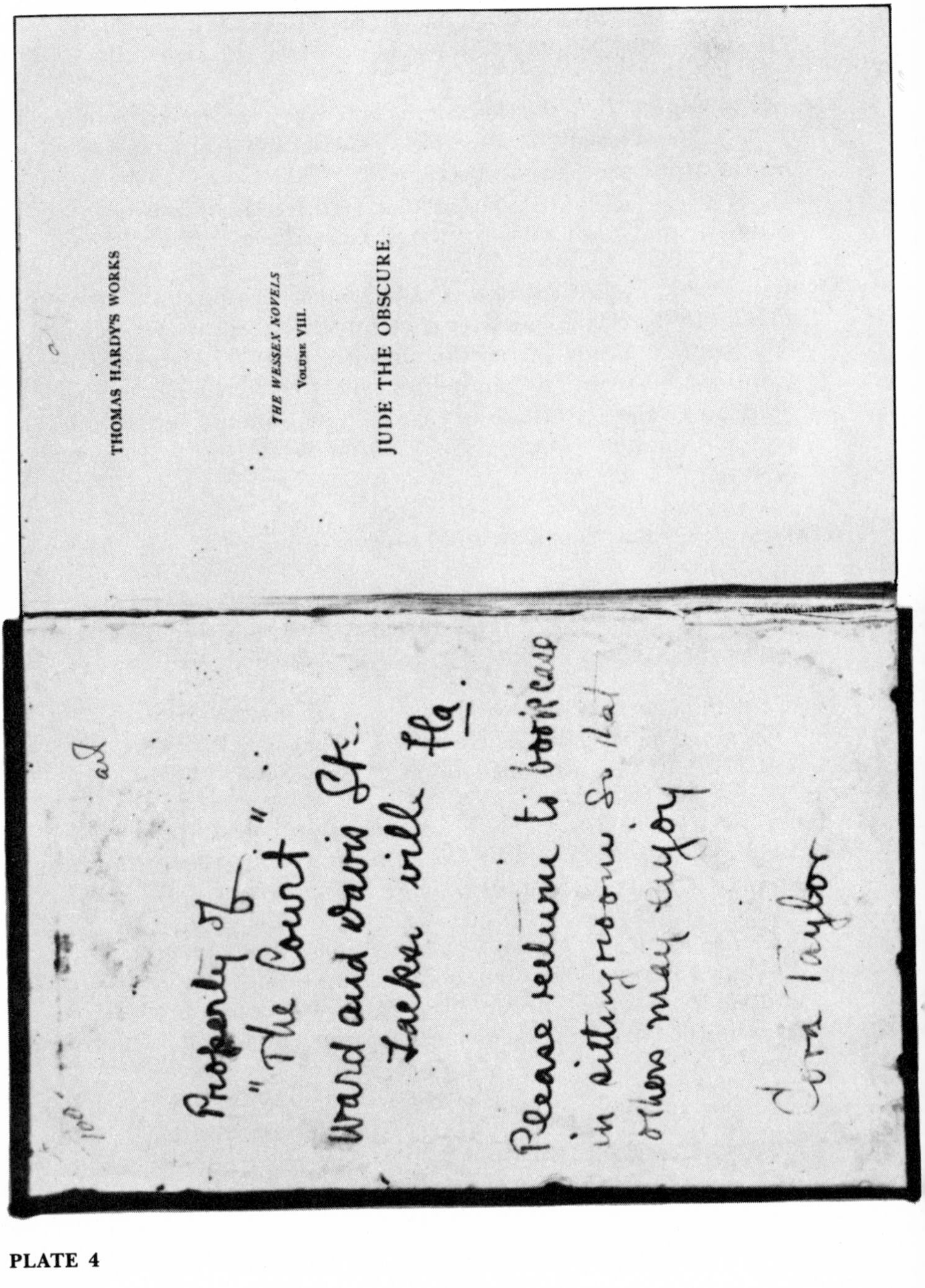

THOMAS HARDY'S WORKS

THE WESSEX NOVELS
VOLUME VIII.

JUDE THE OBSCURE.

Property of
"The Court"
Ward and Davis Sts.
Zacher ville fla.

Please return to bookcase
in sitting room so that
others may enjoy

Cora Taylor

PLATE 4

*_____. *Stories Revived. Second Series* . . . . London: Macmillan and Co., 1885. 401 pp. Inscribed by Cora on the front pastedown: 'Mrs Stephen Crane | 6. Milborne Grove | The Boltons | SW'. NNC.

Jones, William. *Memoirs of the Life, Studies, and Writings of the Right Reverend George Horne, D.D. Late Lord Bishop of Norwich to Which Is Added His Lordship's Own Collections of His Thoughts on a Variety of Great and Interesting Subjects.* London: Robinson, 1795. 418 pp. Inscribed by Cora on the front pastedown: 'Mrs Stephen Crane | 6. Milborne Grove | The Boltons | SW.' NNC.

*Kipling, Rudyard. *The Seven Seas.* New York: Appleton, 1896. Inscribed by Cora on the front pastedown: 'The first thing my mouse ever gave me was this book. | 1896 | This book belongs to | Mrs Stephen Crane | [Brede Place] | [Sussex] | 6, Milborne Grove | The Boltons | South Kensington.' The front free endpaper has Kipling's signature and address pasted in over another inscription, which Matthew J. Bruccoli feels is 'almost certainly' Cora's: 'Cora | Jacksonvill 1896'.[29] Matthew J. Bruccoli, Columbia, South Carolina.

*_____ and Wolcott Balestier. *The Naulahka: a Story of West and East.* London: William Heinemann, 1895. Third Edition. 276 pp. Inscribed by Cora on the front pastedown: 'This book belongs to | Mrs Stephen Crane | 6. Milborne Grove | The Boltons | South Kensington | 1898'. Wolcott Balestier's picture is pasted in. The verso reads: 'Crane, Brede Place'. NNC.

Kock, [Charles] Paul de. *The Good Fellow . . . Translated from the French, by a Philadelphian.* Philadelphia: E. L. Carey & A. Hart, 1837. Volume II only. 182 pp. NNC.

Lamb, Charles. *Detached Thoughts on Books and Reading.* Boston: Privately printed for Herbert Copeland and F. H. Day and their friends, Christmas, 1894. Inscribed 'Stephen Crane' on front wrapper.[30] NSyU.

---

[29] From Matthew J. Bruccoli, 'Cora's Mouse', *Papers of the Bibliographical Society of America*, LIX (1965), 188–89.
[30] Copeland & Day published *The Black Riders and Other Lines* in 1895.

[Leslie, Charles.] *A Short and Easie Method with the Deists Wherein, the Certainty of the Christian Religion Is Demonstrated by Infallible Proof: from iv. Rules . . . .* London: 1701. 57 pp. Bound with *A Pastoral Letter.* See note 16. NNC.

Mace, Frances L. *Under Pine and Palm.* Boston: Ticknor and Company, 1888. 222 pp. Inscribed by Stephen and his nephew, George Archer Crane on the front free endpaper: '<u>Stephen</u> <u>Crane.</u> | December 2, 1890 | G. Archer Crane, | Nov. 20, 1904.' Joseph Katz, Columbia, South Carolina.[31]

*McIntosh, Burr [William.] *The Little I Saw of Cuba.* London: F. Tennyson Neely, [1899]. 173 pp. Inscribed by Cora on the front pastedown: 'This book was given by the author to | Mr<u>s</u> Stephen Crane | Brede Place | Sussex | 1899. There is a correction by Stephen in his handwriting on p. 99. There is a picture of Stephen on p. 165. NNC.

[Mitchell, Donald Grant.] *Dream Life: A Fable of the Seasons.* by Ik Marvel [pseud.] Philadelphia: Henry Altemus, 1893. 299 pp. NNC.

Monnin, Abbé Alfred. See 'Piot, Rev. B. S.'

[Moore, John.] *Of Religious Melancholy. A Sermon Preach'd Before the Queen at White-Hall, March 6. 1691/2 . . . .* London: [n.d.] Fifth Edition. 16 pp. Bound with *A Pastoral Letter.* See note 16. NNC.

Niles, John M. *The Life of Oliver Hazard Perry. With an Appendix, Comprising a Biographical Memoir of the Late Captain James Lawrence. . . .* Hartford: Oliver D. Cooke, 1821. 372 pp. Several early signatures are illegible. NNC.

*Peck, George. *Our Country: Its Trial and Its Triumph. A Series of Discourses Suggested by the Varying Events of the War for the Union.* New York: Carlton & Porter, 1865. 300 pp. Inscribed by Cora on the front pastedown: 'Mr<u>s</u> Stephen Crane | 6. Milborne Grove | The Boltons | SW'. Either Stephen or Cora has written on the front free endpaper: 'Stephen Crane | Brede Place'. NNC.

[31] From [Joseph Katz], 'Ex Libris Stephen Crane: *Under Pine and Palm*', *Stephen Crane Newsletter,* III (Summer 1969), 8.

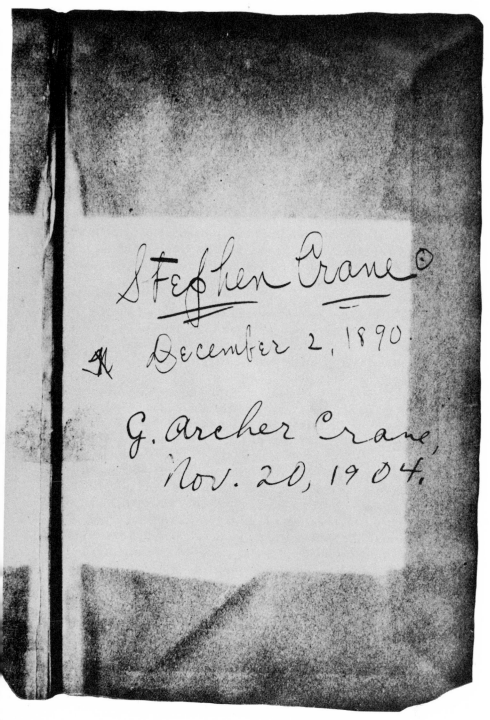

PLATE 5

_____. *Wyoming: Its History, Stirring Incidents, and Romantic Adventures.* New York: Harper & Brothers, 1858. 430 pp. Inscribed in either Stephen's or Cora's hand: 'Stephen Crane | Brede Place | Sussex'. NNC.

_____. *Wyoming: Its History, Stirring Incidents, and Romantic Adventures.* New York: 1860. Third Edition. 432 pp. Inscribed by Cora on the front pastedown: 'This book belongs to | Mrs Stephen Crane | 6. Milborne Grove | The Boltons | South Kensington.' NNC.

Peck, Jesse T. *What Must I Do to Be Saved?* New York: Carlton & Porter, [1858]. 192 pp. Inscribed by the author on the front free endpaper to Stephen's father: 'Rev. Dr. Crane | With the respects of | The Author'. Stephen has also inscribed this page: 'Stephen Crane | 1881 – '. NNC.

Percival, Emily, ed. *The Garland; or, Token of Friendship. A Christmas and New Year's Gift for 1853.* Boston: Phillips, Sampson and Company, [1853]. 287 pp. Inscribed: 'Miss Kezia Cranford | A Christmas Gift | from S. V. P.' NNC.

Piot, Rev. B. S. *The Life of the Rev. J. B. M. Vianney, the Celebrated Parish Priest of Ars (France) . . . by the Abbé Alfred Monnin. Abridged from the French, by Rev. B. S. Piot.* Baltimore: Kelly & Piet, 1867. 216 pp. NNC.

*Robertson, William. *The History of Scotland, During the Reigns of Queen Mary, and of King James VI. Till His Accession to the Crown of England, with a Review of the Scottish History Previous to that Period; A Critical Dissertation on the Murder of King Henry, and an Appendix Containing Original Papers.* Edinburgh: 1814. Volume I only of two volumes. 374 pp. Inscribed by Cora on the front pastedown: 'Mrs Stephen Crane | 6. Milborne Grove | The Boltons | SW.' NNC.

*Scott, Sir Walter. *Kenilworth.* London: Richard Edward King, Limited, [n.d.] 376 pp. Inscribed by Cora on the front pastedown: 'Mrs Stephen Crane | 6. Milborne Grove | The Boltons | South Kensington | 1898'.[32] NNC.

[32] The date likely marks when the book was acquired. Mrs. Crane did not live at 6 Milborne Grove until after Stephen's death.

[Sewell, George.] *Remarks Upon a Pamphlet Intitul'd [Observations Upon the State of the Nation, in January, 1712/13.]* London: 1713. 29 pp. Bound with *A Pastoral Letter.* See note 16. NNC.

[Sharp, John.] *The Government of the Thoughts: A Sermon Preach'd Before the King and Queen, at White-Hall. The 4th of March, Being the 2d Sunday in Lent, 1693/4* . . . . London: [n.d.] 15 pp. Bound with *A Pastoral Letter.* See note 16. NNC.

Sherlock, William. *A Discourse Concerning the Divine Providence.* London: D. Browne, 1725. Sixth Edition. 452 pp. NNC.

[Stanley, William.] *The Faith and Practice of a Church of England Man.* London: 1713. 78 pp. Bound with *A Pastoral Letter.* See note 16. NNC.

Sterling, Anthony C. See 'Golovin, Ivan.'

[Tenison, Thomas.] *Concerning Holy Resolution. A Sermon Preach'd Before the King, at Kensington, Decemb. 30, 1694* . . . . London: [n.d.]. 16 pp. Bound with *A Pastoral Letter.* See note 16. NNC.

Treeby, S. *The Elements of Astronomy; with Methods for Determining the Longitudes, Aspects, Etc. of the Planets for any Future Time; and an Extensive Set of Geographical and Astronomical Problems on the Globes.* New York: Samuel Wood & Sons, 1826. Second Edition Revised by M. Nash. 216 pp. NNC.

*Westcott, Edward Noyes. *David Harum. A Story of American Life.* New York: D. Appleton and Company, 1899. 392 pp. Inscribed by Cora on the front pastedown: 'Mrs̲ Stephen Crane | 6. Milborne Grove | The Boltons | S.W.'; and by Stephen's niece: 'Helen Crane | June 9, 1899 – '. NNC.

Whitaker, Joseph. *An Almanack for the Year of Our Lord 1900 . . . Containing an Account of the Astronomical and Other Phenomena. A Large Amount of Information Respecting the Government Finances Population Commerce and General Statistics of the British Empire* . . . . London: [1899]. 155 pp. Inscribed by Cora on the front pastedown: '6.

Milborne Grove The Boltons SW'; and on the front free end-
paper in either Cora's or Stephen's hand is: 'Crane. Brede
Place'. NNC.

[Williams, John.] *A Brief Exposition of the Church-Catechism. With Proofs
from Scripture.* London: 1699. 64 pp. Bound with *A Pastoral Letter.*
See note 16. NNC.

II. CORA CRANE'S
LIST OF BOOKS BREDE PLACE

Books preceded by a dagger (†) are located in Section I.

A. BOOKS AND SEPARATE PUBLICATIONS

[Adams, Henry Brooks.] *Democracy*[,] *an American Novel* [At least three publications of the novel before 1900: New York: Henry Holt, 1880; London: Macmillan, 1882; and London: Ward, Lock & Co., 1882.]

[Amiel, Henri-Frédéric.] *Amiel's Journal*[, *the Journal of Henri-Frédéric Amiel*] *translated by Mrs Humphry Ward* [Cora usually notes the fact that a book has more than one volume. This title was published in one volume by London: Macmillan, 1889, 1891, 1898; two-volume sets in 1885 and 1893.]

Armstrong[, Edward.] *Lorenzo de*['] *Medici* [*and Florence in the Fifteenth Century.*] [Pre-1900 publications: New York and London: G. P. Putnam's Sons, 1896.]

Balestier, Wolcott. *The Average Woman*[, *with a Biographical Sketch by Henry James.*] [Published Leipzig: Heinemann and Balestier; London: Heinemann and Balestier Ltd.; London: Heinemann; New York: U.S. Book Company. All 1892.]

————. See also 'Kipling, *The Naulahka*'.

Baring[-]Gould[, Sabine.] *Germany Past and Present* [Published as a one-volume reprint of the London, 1879, first edition: London: Kegan Paul & Co., 1881; New York: H. Holt and Co., 1882.]

Barr, Robert. *The Countess Tekla* (2 copies) [The flyleaf and title page of one of the copies are at the Butler Library. The title page identifies the edition as 'Methuen's Colonial Library' which was published in London by Methuen & Co. in 1899. It is inscribed by Barr to Cora and by Cora herself. See Section IV under 'Barr'. There was also an American publication by Frederick A. Stokes in 1898.]

_____. *A Woman Intervenes*[*; or, The Mistress of the Mine.*] [Published New York and London: Frederic A. Stokes and Chatto & Windus. Both 1896.]

Barrett, Wilson, *The Sign of the Cross* [Published Philadelphia: J. B. Lippincott Company, 1897; London: John Macqueen, 1897.]

Barrie, J[ames] M[atthew.] *A Window in Thrums* [Published in London by Hodder & Stoughton: 1889, 1892, 1898. Various American publications: 1894, 1895, 1896, 1897, and 1900.]

[Battenberg, Prince Louis of.] *Men-of-war Names*[*: Meaning, Origin.*] [Published London: Stanford, 1897.]

[Beattie, William (?).] [*The*] *Castles and Abbeys of England*[. . . .] [Published London: G. Virtue and J. Mortimer, 1842, 1844.]

Bonsal, Stephen. *The Fight for Santiago*[*; The Story of the Soldier in the Cuban Campaign, from Tampa to the Surrender.*] [Published in New York and London by Doubleday & McClure Co., 1899.]

[Boswell, James.] *Boswell's Life of Johnson* (6 vols) [Published in six volumes by Oxford: Clarendon Press, 1887; New York: Harper & Brothers, 1891; and Westminster: A. Constable and Co., 1896.]

Brailsford[, Henry Noel.] *The Broom of the War God* [Published New York: D. Appleton and Company; London: William Heinemann—both in 1898.]

Browning, Robert. *Poems* [Published at least once in London in 1849 and twice in 1897. Two Boston publications in 1850 and 1866.]

[Burns, Robert.] *Burns*['] *Poetical Works* [Published frequently from the 1870s to 1900.]

Caine, [Sir Thomas Henry] Hall. *The Christian* [Published New York: D. Appleton and Company, 1897; London: William Heinemann, 1897; Toronto: Morang, 1897.]

_____. *The Scapegoat*[*, A Romance and a Parable.*] [Published London: William Heinemann, 1891, two volumes; one-volume publica-

228

tions by D. Appleton and Company in New York in 1899 and Heinemann in London in 1892.]

Carew, George, Earl of Totnes. See 'O'Grady'.

Carlyle[, Thomas.] *Heroes and Hero-worship* [Published New York: J. W. Lovell Company, 1885; Chicago: W. B. Conkey, 1900.]

Chambers, Robert [William.] *Ashes of Empire* [Published New York: F. A. Stokes Company, 1898; London: Macmillan, 1898.]

Clarke[, Henry Butler.] *The Cid* [*Campeador and the Waning of the Crescent in the West.*] [Published New York: G. P. Putnam's Sons, 1897.]

[Clemens, Samuel L.] Mark Twain. *A Yankee in King Arthurs Court* [*A Yankee at the Court of King Arthur* published London: Chatto & Windus, 1889 (?).]

[Clifford, Lucy Lane.] [W. K.] Clifford. *Aunt Anne* (2 vols) [At least two two-volume publications: London: R. Bentley & Son, 1892, 1893.]

Conrad, Joseph. *Almayers Folly*[*, A Story of an Eastern River.*] [At least two pre-1900 publications: New York and London: Macmillan and Co., 1895; London: T. Fisher Unwin, 1895. See also 'Conrad', Section IV.]

————. *The Nigger of the* ['']*Narcissus*['.] [At least two pre-1900 publications: London: William Heinemann, 1897, 1898. See also 'Conrad', Section IV.]

————. *An Outcast of the Islands* [Published New York: D. Appleton and Company, 1896; London: T. Fisher Unwin, 1896.]

————. *Tales of Unrest* [Published New York: C. Scribner's Sons, 1898; London: T. Fisher Unwin, 1898.]

Corelli[, Marie.] *Thelma* [One-volume publications: New York: W. L. Allison and Company, 1895; London: Richard Bentley & Son, 1888.]

†Crane, [Rev.] J[onathan] T[ownley] D.D. *Arts of Intoxication*[. *The Aim, and the Results.*]

_____. [*An*] *Essay on Dancing* [Published New York: Carlton & Porter, 1849.]

_____. *Holiness the Birthright of all God's Children* [Published New York: Nelson & Phillips; Cincinnati: Hitchcock & Walden, 1874.]

_____. *Methodism and Its Methods* [Published New York: Nelson & Phillips; Cincinnati: Hitchcock & Walden, 1876.]

Crane[, Rev. Jonathan Townley] D.D. *Popular Amusements* [*with an Introduction by Bishop E. S. Jones.*] [Published Cincinnati: Hitchcock and Walden; New York: Carlton & Lanahan, 1869.]

Crane, Stephen. *The Black Riders* (Lines, 3 copies)

†_____. *George's Mother*

†_____. *Maggie*

†_____. *Maggie* (German) 3 copies [Cora has canceled a '2' with '3'. Two copies located.]

†_____. *Pictures of War* (4 copies) [Cora has canceled a '2' with the '4'. Only one copy located.]

†_____. *The Third Violet* (4 copies) [Two copies located.]

Crawford[, Francis] Marion. *Casa Braccio* (2 vols) [Two-volume publications: New York and London: Macmillan and Co., 1894; London: Macmillan, 1895.]

Darwin, Charles [Robert.] [*The Effects of*] *Cross and Self Fertilisation* [*in the Vegetable Kingdom*] *of Plants* [London and New York publications before 1900: 1876, 1877, 1878, 1892.][33]

[33] The English spelling of 'Fertilisation' in Cora's title is present also in the New York publication and is thus not a key to the copy at Brede. Also, Cora's habit of writing 'Mr', 'Mrs', and 'St' without periods removes this as a possible source for determining whether the publication was American or British.

[De la Ramée, Mary Louise.] Ouida. *An Altruist* [Published London and New York: F. T. Neely, 1897; London: T. F. Unwin, 1897.]

Doyle[, Sir] A[rthur] Conan. *Round the Red Lamp*[*; Being Facts and Fancies of Medical Life.*] [Published New York: D. Appleton and Company, 1894; London: Methuen & Co., 1894.]

Dredge[, James.] *Modern French Artillery*[*: (the St. Chamond, De Bange, Canet and Hotchkiss Systems) with Illustrations of French War-Ships.*] [Published London: Office of Engineering; New York: J. Wiley & Sons, 1892.]

Dryden[, John.] *Poetical Works* [Numerous pre-1900 publications.]

†Dunn[e, Finley Peter.] *Mr. Dooley In Peace and War*

[Evans, Marian.] George Eliot. *The Mill on the Floss* (2 vols) [Two two-volume publications: Edinburgh and London, 1860; Edinburgh and London, 1862.]

Fitzgerald, Edward. See 'Omar Khayyám.'

Frederic, Harold. *Illumination* [Published London: W. Heinemann, 1896.]

―――. *March Hares* [Published New York: D. Appleton and Company, 1896; London: John Lane, 1896.]

[Fröbel, Wilhelm August.] *Mother*['*]s Songs*[*, Games*] *and Stories* (for chrildren [*sic*]) [Published London: W. Rice, 1885, 1888, 1890.]

Garland, Hamlin. *Jason Edwards*[*, An Average Man.*] [Published New York: D. Appleton and Company, 1897.]

―――. *A Little Norsk*[*; or, Ol' Pap's Flaxen.*] [Published New York: D. Appleton and Company, 1892; London: T. Fisher Unwin, 1892.]

―――. *A Member of the Third House* [Published Chicago: F. J. Schulte & Company, 1892; New York: D. Appleton and Company, 1897.]

————. *A Spoil of Office*[. *A Story of the Modern West.*] [Published Boston: Arena Publishing Company, 1892; New York: D. Appleton and Company, 1897, revised edition.]

Gissing, George. *In the Year of Jubilee* [Published one-volume edition: New York: D. Appleton and Company, 1895; three-volume edition: London: Lawrence & Bullen, 1894.]

Graham, R[obert Bontine] Cunningham[e.] *The Ipané* [*and Other Sketches and Tales*] [Published London: T. Fisher Unwin, 1899, the Overseas Library.]

Gray, Maxwell, pseud. See 'Tuttiett, Mary'.

[Gray, Thomas.] *Greys* [*sic*] *Elegy* (Fine Edition) [Numerous 'fine' publications in the 1880s and 1890s.]

Green, Anna Katharine. See 'Rohlfs, Anna Katharine'.

Grim[m, Jakob Ludwig Karl.] [*Grimm's*] *Fairy Tales* [Numerous publications.]

†Hardy, Thomas. *Jude the Obscure*

————. *A Pair of Blue Eyes* [Published New York and London: 1873, 1877, 1885, 1889, 1895; Leipzig, 1884.]

†Harris, Frank. *Elder Conklin* [*and Other Stories.*]

[Hawkins, Sir] Anthony Hope. [*The*] *Chronicles of Count Antonio* [Published New York: D. Appleton and Company, 1895; London: Methuen & Co., 1895.]

[Heine, Heinrich.] *The Works of Heinrich Heine* 2 sets of 8 vols. each [No eight-volume sets identified.]

Henley, W[illiam] E[rnest.] *Lyra Heroica*[; *a Book of*] *Verse* [*for Boys* selected and] *Arranged by W. E. Henley* [Published New York: C. Scribner's Sons, 1891; London: D. Nutt, 1892.]

Hibberd, Shirley. *The Amatur's* [*sic*] *Rose Book*[, *Comprising the Cultivation of the Rose in the Open Ground* . . . .] [Published London:

Groombridge and Sons, 1878; London: W. H. and L. Colling-ridge, 1894.]

Hichens, Robert [Smythe.] *By[e]ways* [Published New York: Dodd, Mead and Company, 1897; London: Methuen & Co., 1898 (1897).]

Hichens R[obert] S[mythe.] *An Imaginative Man* [Published New York: D. Appleton and Company, 1895; London: W. Heine-mann, 1895.]

Hodgkin[, Thomas.] *Theodoric [the Goth . . . .]* [Published New York: G. P. Putnam's Sons, 1891, 1897; London: G. P. Putnam's Sons, 1890.]

Hogan, E[dmund.] *[The History of] The Irish Wolfdog* [Dublin: Sealy & Co., 1897.]

[Hole] Holt, S. Reynolds. *A Book About Roses[. How to Grow and Show Them.]* Numerous publications from 1869 to 1896.

Hope, Anthony. See 'Hawkins, Sir Anthony Hope.'

[Hubbard, Elbert.] *Little Journeys to the Holmes [sic] of Great Men (Rubens) | (Meissonier) | (Michael Angelo) | (Rembrandt)*[34] *[Little Journeys to the Homes of the Great, V. Eminent Painters*, New York and London: G. P. Putnam's Sons, [1899?] Separate pamphlets for these men published under series title.]

†James, Henry. *The Bostonians*

———. *The Princess Casamassima* [Published London and New York: Macmillan and Co., 1886.]

———. *The Real Thing[, and Other Tales.]* [Published London and New York: Macmillan and Co., 1893.]

†———. *The Spoils of Poynton*

---

[34] Cora dittoed the *Little Journeys to the Holmes [sic] of Great Men* preceding the names of each painter.

†_____. *Stories Revived*[. *First Series* . . . .]

†_____. *Stories Revived*[. *Second Series* . . . .]

_____. *Tales of Three Cities* [Published Boston: J. R. Osgood and Company, 1884; London: Macmillan and Company, 1884.]

_____. *The Two Magics*[. *The Turn of the Screw; Covering End.*] [Published London: W. Heinemann, 1898; London: Macmillan and Co., 1898.]

_____. See 'Balestier'.

Jones, Bishop E. S. See 'Crane, Rev. Jonathan Townley. *Popular Amusements*'.

Kipling[, Rudyard.] *An Almanac, with words* [*An Almanac of Twelve Sports. By William Nicholson. Words by R. Kipling.*] [London, 1898.]

Kipling, Rudyard. [']*Captains Courageous*['. *A Story of the Grand Banks.*] [Published New York: The Century Co., 1897; Leipzig: B. Tauchnitz, 1897; London: Macmillan and Co., 1897.]

Kipling[, Rudyard.] *The Day*[']*s Work* [Published London: Macmillan & Co., 1898, 1899; Toronto: Morang, 1898; New York: Doubleday & McClure Co., 1898; or Leipzig: B. Tauchnitz, 1898 [1900].]

_____. *Departmental Ditties, Barrack-room Ballads and other verse*[*s.*] [This is the exact title of the New York: United States Book Company, 1890 publication which was reissued Philadelphia: H. T. Coates, 1900. The next closest title introduces '*and Ballads*' after '*Ditties*' — New York: Doubleday and McClure Co., 1899.]

_____. *The Jungle Book* [Publications in New York, London, and Leipzig: 1894, 1897, 1898, 1899, 1900.]

_____. *Many Inventions* [Publications in London and New York: Macmillan and Co., 1893; New York: D. Appleton and Company, 1893.]

_____. *Reccessional* (Poem) [Published London: 1897; New York: Frederick A. Stokes, 1897, 1898, 1899.]

_____. *The Second Jungle Book* [Published London: Macmillan, 1895, 1899; New York: The Century Co., 1895, 1899.]

† Kipling, Rudyard. *The Seven Seas* (Poetry)

Kipling[, Rudyard.] *Soldiers Three* [Published Allahad: 1888; London: Sampson Low & Co., 1890, 1893. Various other publications New York and London: 1890, 1895, and 1899.]

†_____ and Balistier [*sic*] [, Wolcott.] *The Naulahka*]*: a Story of West and East.*]

Lamb, Charles. *Essays of Ella* [*sic (Elia)*] (Fine Edition) [Numerous publications from the 1860s to 1900. New York: Frederick A. Stokes Company, 1894, edition is illustrated with 31 full-page illustrations.]

[Lear, Edward.] *The Book of Nonsense* For Children [Published London: F. Warne & Co., 1866, 1889.]

Lecky[, William Edward Hartpole.] *History of European Morals* [*from Augustus to Charlemagne*] (2 vols) [The most recent pre-1900 publication — two volumes, New York: D. Appleton and Company, 1879.]

Le Gallienne, Richard. *The Quest of the Golden Girl* [Published London and New York: John Lane, 1896, 1897.]

[Longfellow, Henry Wadsworth.] *Poetical Works of Longfellow* [Numerous one-volume publications.]

Lowell[, James Russell.] *Poems* [Numerous publications.]

†McIntosh, Burr [William.] *The Little I Saw of Cuba*

Maclay[, Edgar Stanton, A.M.] [*A*] *History of* [*the*] *U*[*nited*] *S*[*tates*] *Navy* [*from 1775 to 189–*] (2 vols) [Published New York: D. Appleton and Company, 1894; revised and enlarged edition carrying the history to 1898 rather than 1893, 1898; London: Bliss, Sands and Co., 1894.]

Macleod, Fiona, pseud. See 'Sharp'.

[Macpherson, James.] Ossian. *Ossian* (Poems) [Volumes of Macpherson's poetry appeared in 1884, 1888, and 1896. Only one title—*Ossian; His Principle Poems*—Edinburgh: 1858, is close to Cora's entry.]

Mark Twain, pseud. See 'Clemens'.

Marlas, Ben. *Brer Mortal* (2 copies) [Published London: T. F. Unwin, 1896.]

[Mathew] Mathews, Frank [James.] *A Child in the Temple* [Published London and New York: J. Lane, 1897.]

Meredith[, George.] *Poems* [A number of one-volume publications of *Poems* in the 1880s and 1890s.]

Montrésor[, Frances Frederica.] *At the Cross*[-]*Roads* [Published London: Hutchinson & Co., 1897; New York: D. Appleton and Company, 1897.]

[Moore, Thomas.][35] *Irish Melodies* [Published 1844, 1873, 1887, 1888, and 1890.]

Murray, [David] Christie. *My Contempor*[*ar*]*ies in Fiction* [Published London: Chatto & Windus, 1897.]

Nicholson, William. See 'Kipling. *An Almanac*'.

O'Grady, Standish [James, ed.] *Pacata Hibernia* [*Ireland Appeared and Reduced . . . compiled by George Carew, Earl of Totnes*] (2 vols) [Published London: Downey & Co., 1896.]

[Omar Khayyám.] *Rubáiyat of Omar Khayyám* Fitzgerald's translation [Numerous publications; one is East Aurora: Roycrofters, 1898.]

Ossian, pseud. See 'Macpherson'.

Ouida, pseud. See 'De la Ramée'.

[35] Cora mistakenly placed Moore's name after *Ingersteid Hall* (authored by Routledge).

Page, Thomas Nelson. *Red Rock* [Published New York: C. Scribner's Sons, 1898, 1899; London: W. Heinemann, 1898; Toronto: Publishers' Syndicate, 1899.]

Peck, Geo[rge] D.D. *Early Methodism from 1788 to 1828* [Not identified.]

†_____. *Our Country*[*:*] *Its Trial and Its Triumph* [. *A Series of Discourses Suggested by the Varying Events of the War for the Union.*]

[Peck, George.] [*The Scripture Doctrine of*] *Christian Perfection* [*Stated and Defended . . . .*] [Published New York: 1842, 1845, 1848, 1851, 186–?.]

Peck[, J. K.][36] *Luther Peck and His Five Sons* [, *by Rev. J. K. Peck*] (2 copies) [Published New York: Eaton & Mains; Cincinnati: Curts & Jennings, 1897.]

_____. [*The*] *Seven Wonders of the New World* [Published New York: Phillips & Hunt; Cincinnati: Cranston & Stowe, 1885.]

Peck, Jesse [Truesdell] D.D. [*The*] *Central Idea of Christianity* [Published Boston: H. V. Degen, 1856; New York: Carlton and Porter, 1857; Boston: H. V. Degen and New York: Carlton and Porter, 1858; Boston: H. V. Degen & Son, 1860; and New York: Nelson & Phillips; Cincinnati: Hitchcock & Walden, 1876.]

Peck, Jesse [Truesdell.] [*The*] *History of the Great Republic* [, *Considered From a Christian Stand-Point.*] [Published New York: Broughton and Wyman, 1868.]

_____. See '*County Families of the United Kingdom 1868*' in Section III.

Peck[, Jesse (?)] D.D. *Rule of Faith* [Not identified.][37]

Penn, Rachel, pseud. See 'Willard, Caroline'.

[36] See note 8.
[37] Stallman, *Stephen Crane: A Biography*, p. 555 attributes this title to Jesse Peck; however, he may be as incorrect here as when he gives *The Seven Wonders of the World* to George rather than J. K. Peck.

Pugh, Edwin [William.] *King Circumstance* [Published New York: Henry Holt and Company, 1898; London: W. Heinemann, 1898.]

_____. *The Man of Straw* [Published London: W. Heinemann, 1896.]

Pugh, E[dwin] W[illiam.] *A Street in Suburbia* [Published New York: D. Appleton and Company, 1895; London: W. Heinemann (Pioneer Series), 1895.]

Pugh, Edwin [William.] *Tony Drum* [, *A Cockney Boy.*] [Published New York: H. Holt and Company, 1898; London: W. Heinemann, 1898.]

†[Robertson] Robinson[, William.] [*The*] *History of Scotland* [. . . .]

Robins, Elizabeth. *Below the Salt* [Published London: W. Heinemann, 1896.]

_____. *George Mandeville's Husband* [Published New York: D. Appleton and Company, 1894; London: W. Heinemann, 1894.]

_____. *The New Moon* [Published London: W. Heinemann (Pioneer Series), 1894; New York: D. Appleton and Company, 1895.]

_____. *The Open Question* [Published London: W. Heinemann, 1898, 1899; New York and London: Harper & Brothers, 1899.]

[Robinson, C. N., ed.] *The Navy and Army* [*Illustrated*] [Cora listed this title twice] [A four-volume publication of this title published London: George Newnes, 1896–1897. There is also a similar title: Charles Napier Robinson, ed. '*Navy and Army Illustrated*' *Library.* (*Stories of Our National Heroes.*) *Wellington and Waterloo*, by Major Arthur Griffiths (One volume) London: G. Newnes, 1898.]

[Rohlfs, Mrs.] Anna Katharine Green. *Behind Closed Doors* [Published London: G. Routledge & Sons, 1888; New York and London: G. P. Putnam's Sons, 1888.]

Roos[e]velt[, Theodore.] *The Naval War of 1812* [*; or, The History of the United States Navy During the Last War with Great Britain.*] [The title of the New York: G. P. Putnam's Sons, 1882 publication.

New York: G. P. Putnam's Sons, 1889 fourth edition appends 'an Account of the Battle of New Orleans.']

Rossetti, D[ante] G[abriel.] *Poetical Works* [*The Poetical Works of Dante Gabriel Rossetti*, William Rossetti, ed. (One volume) published London: Ellis and Elvey, 1891, 1893.]

Routledge[, James.] *Ingerstein*[38] Hall [*and Chadwick Rise. A Story of the Thirty Years' War.*] [Published in three volumes London: 1878.]

Scott, Sir Walter. *Ivanhoe* [Numerous publications in the 1890s, 1880s, and earlier.]

†———. *Kenilworth*

———. *The Talisman* [Numerous publications.]

[Ségur, Philippe Paul, comte de] [Cora entered the name as 'Count De Segur'] *Napoleon's Expedition to Russia* (2 vols) [*History of the Expedition to Russia, Undertaken by the Emperor Napoleon, in the year 1812.* New York: Harper & Brothers, 1842, 1845 — the most recent two-volume issue of this title.]

Shakespeare[, William.] [The following titles are entered separately in Cora's List:]
All's Well That Ends Well
Antony and Cleopatra
As You Like It
The Comedy of Errors
Coriolanus
Cymbeline
Hamlet
Julius Ceasar
King Henry |IV|
King Henry |V|
King Henry |VI| (3 vols)
King Henry |VIII|
King John
King Lear

[38] Cora wrote *Ingersteid.* See also note 34. Cora mistakenly placed Routledge's name after *In the Land of Tolstoi.*

King Richard /II/
King Richard /III/
Love's Labour's Lost
Macbeth
The Merry Wives of Windsor
A Midsummer Nights' Dream
Much Ado About Nothing
Othello
Pericles
The Rape of Lucrece
Romeo and Juliet
The Sonnets
The Taming of the Shrew
The Tempest
Timon of Athens
Titus Andronicus
Twelfth Night
Two Gentlemen of Verona
A Winter[']s Tale
[Three large multivolumed sets, all consisting of forty volumes: London: Sands & Co., 1898; London: Dent & Co., 1894–96 Macmillan, 1893–95.]

[Sharp, William.] Fiona Macleod. *The Sin[-]Eater [and Other Tales.]* [Cora wrote *Eaters.*] [Published Chicago: Stone & Kimball, 1895; Edinburgh: Patrick Geddes & Colleagues, [1895].]

Shaw[, George Bernard.] *The Quintessence of Ibsenism* [Published London: Walter Scott, 1891; Boston: B. R. Tucker, 1891.]

Shelley[, Percy Bysshe.] *Poems* [Several *Poems* or *Poetical Works* published London and New York in the 1880s and 1890s.]

Sienkiewicz, Henryk. *Quo Vadis* [Several London, New York, and Boston publications in the 1890s.]

Somerville[, Alexander.] *History of the British Legion [and War in Spain, from Personal Observations and Other Authentic Sources, Containing a Correct Detail of the Events of the Expedition Under General Evans.]* [Published London: 1839.]

Steel[, Mrs.] F[lora] A[nnie (Webster).] *From the Five Rivers* [(*The Punjaub, Stories and Songs of the People.*)] [Published New York: D. Appleton and Company, 1893.]

———. *On the Face of the Waters* [Published London: W. Heinemann, 1897 [1896]; New York: Macmillan Company, 1897; Rahway, New Jersey: Mershon Company, 1896.]

Steele[, Joel Dorman.] [*The Story of the Rocks:*] *Fourteen Weeks in* [*Popular*] *Geology* [Published New York and Chicago: A. S. Barnes & Company, 1873, 1877; New York and Cincinnati: American Book Company, 1898.]

Stevenson, Robert Louis. *A Child*[*'*]*s Garden of Verse*[*s.*] [Published London: Longmans, Green, & Co., 1885; New York: Charles Scribner's Sons, 1885, 1895, 1897; Boston: L. C. Page & Company, 1900; New York: R. H. Russell, 1900; London: John Lane, 1896 [1895].]

———. *The Ebb-Tide*[*; A Trio & Quartette.*] [Published Chicago & Cambridge: Stone & Kimball, 1894.]

———. *St Ives*[39] [Published New York: Scribner's, 1897; Leipzig: B. Tauchnitz, 1898; London: W. Heinemann, 1898.]

Strahan[, Samuel Alexander Kenny] M.D. *Marriage and Disease* [*. A Study of Heredity and the More Important Family Degenerations.*] [Published London: K. Paul, Trench, Trübner, & Co., Ltd., 1892.]

Swinburne[, Algernon Charles.] *Poems and Ballads* [Several publications New York and London: 1870–1900.]

Thomson[, Harry Craufuird.] *The Outgoing Turk*[*; Impressions of a Journey Through the Western Balkans*] [Published London: W. Heinemann, 1897; New York: D. Appleton and Company, 1897.]

Trask, Katrina [Mrs. Kate Nichols Trask.] *John Leighton*[*,*] *Jr* (2 copies) [Published New York and London: Harper & Brothers, 1898.]

[39]See note 33.

Turgenev, Ivan [Sergeevich.] *A Lear of the Steppes Ect.*[40] [*and Other Stories.*] [Published London: W. Heinemann, 1898.]

[Tuttiett, Mary Gleed.] Maxwell Grey [*sic* (Gray).] *The Last Sentence* [One-volume publication: New York: Tait, Sons & Company, 1893. Three-volume publication: London: Heinemann, 1893.]

Ward, Mrs. Humphry. See 'Amiel, Henri-Frédéric.'

Werner, A[lice.] *The Captain of the Locusts* [Published London: T. F. Unwin, the Overseas Library, 1899.]

†Westcott[, Edward Noyes.] *David Harum*[. *A Story of American Life.*]

White, Percy. *A Passionate Pilgrim* [Published New York: D. Appleton and Company, 1898; London: Methuen & Co., 1897.]

Wilcox, [Mrs.] Ella Wheeler. *Poems of Passion* [Published Chicago: W. B. Conkey Company, 1883; Chicago: Morrill, Higgins & Co., 1892; London: Gay & Bird, 1900.]

[Willard, Caroline McCoy White ('Mrs. E. S. Willard').] Rachel Penn. *A Son of Israel* [Published Philadelphia: J. B. Lippincott Company, 1898; London: J. Macqueen, 1898 [1897].]

Wister, Owen. *Lin McLean* [Published New York and London: Harper & Brothers, 1898.]

Yeats[, William Butler.] *The Secret Rose* [Published London: Lawrence & Bullen, Ltd., 1897.]

Zangwill[, Israel.] *Children of the Ghetto* [Published Philadelphia: Jewish Publication Society, 1892; New York and London: Macmillan and Co., 1895, 1899; London: Heinemann, 1892 (three volumes); and London: Heinemann, 1893.]

B. PERIODICALS AND SERIALS

The Bookman for year '96 '97 [The American *Bookman* in February, October, and December of 1896 has Crane poems and commen-

[40] Cora presumably meant *Etc.*

tary on Stephen. There is no contribution in 1897. However, the English *Bookman* for that year does contain a review of *The Third Violet* in its June issue.]

Lloyd's Encyclopaedia (7 vols) [Not identified.]

The Popular Encyclopedia (15 vols[)] [Fourteen-volume publication of this title edited by C. Annandale, London: Blackie & Son, 1890–93.]

The Times Atlas [Not identified.]

Town Topics bound [XXXVI (1 October 1896) contains Stephen's 'In the Tenderloin'.]

III. UNIDENTIFIED TITLES
LISTED BY CORA CRANE

The Book of Job (2 vols rare edition)

County Families of the United Kingdom 1868[41]

Hark the Angels Sing

History of Germany

In the Land of Tolstoi[42]

Practical Methods of Utilizing Boiled Beef

Two Little Girls in Green (For children)

---

[41] Stallman, *Stephen Crane: A Biography*, p. 555, attributes this to George Peck. However, he may have misinterpreted the juxtaposition of authors and titles in Cora's List.

[42] The juxtaposition is confused in Cora's List. Routledge is incorrectly given as the author. I have been unable to locate the real one.

IV. OTHER COPIES

This section includes four books known to have belonged to the Cranes, but the actual copies of which I have not located. One of these Stallman refers to without giving its location. Listed here are also three inscribed fly titles or title pages from identified titles and five inscribed pages from unidentified titles.

Barr, Robert. *The Countess Tekla.* Methuen's Colonial Library. This publication information is given on a torn-out flyleaf and title page. The *British Museum Catalogue of Books* lists only one entry with this title: London: Methuen, 1899. On verso of flyleaf in Cora's hand is: 'This book belongs to Mrs̲ Stephen Crane. | Brede Place. Sussex.'; on the title page, Barr has written: 'To my valued friend | Mrs̲ Cora Crane | With the best wishes of | Robert Barr | London March 15 '99'. See also 'Barr', Section II. NNC.

Conrad, Joseph. *Almayer's Folly.* Remains of a copy of this title inscribed by Conrad: 'To Stephen Crane with the greatest regard and most sincere admiration from | Jph Conrad | 9th Nov. 1897'. Cora has inscribed the flyleaf: 'This book belongs to Mrs. Stephen Crane 6. Milborne Grove Boltons South Kensington 1898'. Cora was at Ravensbrook, not Milborne Grove, at this date. See also 'Conrad', Section II. NNC.

James, Henry. *In the Cage.* Stallman (*Stephen Crane: A Biography,* pp. 465–66 and 555) reports the following without giving source: James 'presented Stephen with a copy of his book *In the Cage,* with an elaborate and affectionate inscription in French. Crane later sent the book to a friend, with instructions to "please be very careful of it, as you see that the inscription makes it a personal affair. Hope that you find it interesting. I got terribly tired half way through and just reeled along through the rest. You will like some of it a lot. But I do not think that this girl in the cage is exactly an underclass clerk in love with a 'man about town.' Women think more directly than he lets this girl think. But notice the writing in the fourth and fifth chapters when he has really got started."'

Whibley, Charles. *A Book of Scoundrels.* Only the flyleaf and fly title are extant. The *British Museum* and *Library of Congress* catalogs list only one publication under this title: London: W. Heinemann, 1897. Whibley inscribed fly title: 'To Stephen Crane | with the regard of | his [word hard to decipher, but most likely *confrère*]'. Cora inscribed flyleaf: 'This book belongs to | Mrs. Stephen Crane | Brede Place | Sussex | Oct. 1899 | 6. Milborne Grove | The Boltons | SW.' The Milborne Grove address is added in darker ink. Not entered in Cora's List. Letter from Whibley pasted on flyleaf and dated from Heath Edge, Haslemere, 17 November. NNC.

Unidentified title: Undated letter from unknown correspondent pasted to a torn-out flyleaf on which Stephen or Cora has written: 'Crane, Brede Place.' NNC.

Unidentified title: Letter from Hamlin Garland dated 8 May 1894 pasted to a torn-out flyleaf on which either Stephen or Cora has written: 'Crane, Brede Place.' NNC.

Unidentified title: Letter from Irving Bacheller dated 13 July 1900 pasted to a torn-out flyleaf on which is written in Cora's hand: 'This book belongs to Mrs. Stephen Crane   6. Milborne Grove, The Boltons,   South Kensington, July, 1900.' NNC.

Unidentified title: Inscribed by Joseph Conrad on a torn-out flyleaf: 'To | Stephen and M[torn here] with the author's | affectionate regard | 2 Feb. 1898'. NNC.

Unidentified title: Inscribed by Henry James on a torn-out flyleaf: 'To Stephen Crane. Henry James.   Sept. 6th, 1899.' Inscribed also by Cora on both sides of the flyleaf: 'This book belongs to Mrs. Stephen Crane,   Brede Place,   Sussex. 1899.' NNC.

Addendum:

A bill dated 2 April 1888 from Claverack College was sent to Stephen's mother for these books bought for him:[43]

March 6	Physology	1.25
March 6	English Literature	1.40
March 10	English History	1.25
March 20	Tempest	.35

[43] [Joseph Katz], 'Stephen Crane at Claverack College and Hudson River Institute', *Stephen Crane Newsletter*, II (Summer 1968), 3.

THE PUBLICATIONS OF
THEODORE DREISER: A CHECKLIST

DONALD PIZER

THE INTENT OF THIS CHECKLIST IS TWOFOLD: TO PROVIDE A PRELIMINARY
account of Dreiser's publications in order to encourage progress
toward a definitive bibliography; and to make available in concise
form a list of Dreiser's published writings for scholars and critics
interested in particular phases of his work and career. I hope that it
is understood that the checklist is a tentative effort and that it does
not presume to be a final listing of Dreiser's publications. Although
I have built on the previous efforts of bibliographers and scholars —
Edward D. McDonald, Vrest Orton, John F. Huth, Robert H. Elias,
Walter Blackstock, Robert Saalbach, W. A. Swanberg, Ellen Moers,
and Richard Lehan — and though I have found many new items and
discarded many ghosts, there is still much work to be done in Dreiser
bibliography. The difficulty of listing Dreiser's writings can be easily
appreciated if one recalls that he was a professional writer for over
fifty years, that much of his early work appeared anonymously or
pseudonymously, and that during his later career he was a frequent

247

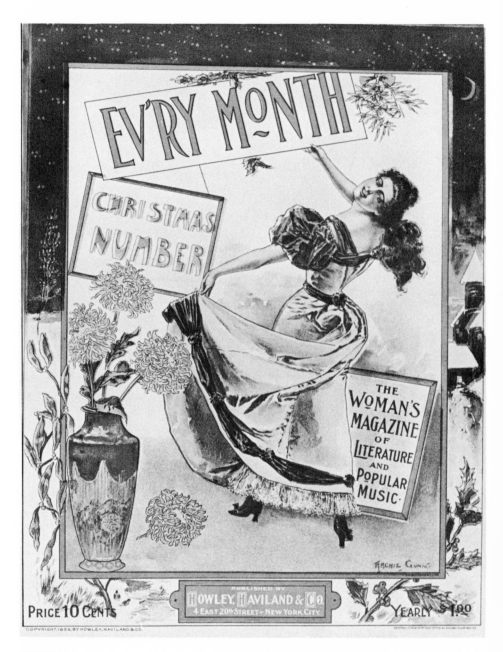

PLATE 1

contributor to obscure and ephemeral radical journals. The present list attempts in particular to bring together all that is presently known about Dreiser's periodical publications and their relation to his published books. It is not concerned with two important areas of Dreiser bibliography which require especial attention: a descriptive bibliography of his books and a checklist of translations.

The following guides are supplied for the use of this checklist. **1.** I have seen all items included. Many of these can be found only in the New York Public Library, the Library of Congress, or the Dreiser Collection of the University of Pennsylvania Library. Since I have not attempted to make this checklist a census, I cite location in only a few instances.
2. Titles under 'A' are separate publications and contributions to separate publications. Place of publication is New York unless otherwise noted. I list initial publication only, except when a work is known to have been substantially revised in a later publication. The order of listing is alphabetical, since it is often impossible to date the publication of broadsides and pamphlets. Titles under 'B' are contributions to journals and newspapers. I have included letters to the editor and articles containing Dreiser letters but have omitted interviews not signed by Dreiser.
3. Republication of periodical items is noted for first republication. Second republication is noted only if it is a first book appearance. Periodical items are noted only once, at the time of initial publication. Thus a 1916 item republished in another journal in 1920 and in a book in 1923 is cited only in 1916, with the 1920 and 1923 republication information immediately following this citation. I have not listed changes in the text of republished items, though many such changes occur.
4. I have noted contents only when such information is not apparent from the title. Remarks on attribution and on other matters requiring comment are footnoted.
5. All items are signed by Dreiser unless I have indicated otherwise. However, Dreiser's contributions to the Chicago *Globe*, St. Louis *Globe-Democrat*, St. Louis *Republic*, Toledo *Blade*, and Pittsburg *Dispatch* are unsigned but are not so indicated by me. In addition, Dreiser's editorial notes and columns in *Smith's*, the *Broadway*, and the *Delineator* are unsigned but are not so indicated by me.
6. I use the following abbreviations and short titles.

BAM: A Book About Myself (1922)
Chains: Chains (1927)
Color: The Color of a Great City (1923)
Free: Free and Other Stories (1918)
GW: A Gallery of Women, 2 vols. (1929)
HRDD: Hey Rub-A-Dub-Dub (1920)
HTS: How They Succeeded, ed. O. S. Marden (1901)
Letters: Letters of Theodore Dreiser, ed. Robert H. Elias, 3 vols. (Philadelphia, 1957)
LVGA: Little Visits with Great Americans, ed. O. S. Marden (1903)
Moods (1926): *Moods, Cadenced and Declaimed* (1926)
Moods (1928): *Moods, Cadenced and Declaimed* (1928)
Moods (1935): *Moods, Philosophical and Emotional* (*Cadenced and Declaimed*) (1935)
PD: Pittsburg *Dispatch*
Plays: Plays of the Natural and Supernatural (1916)
SLGD: St. Louis *Globe-Democrat*
SLR: St. Louis *Republic*
TM: Twelve Men (1918)
Traveler: A Traveler at Forty (1913)
TWGW: Talks with Great Workers, ed. O. S. Marden (1901)

1892

A: None.
B:

1. 'The Return of Genius', Chicago *Daily Globe*, 23 October, p. 4. (Signed 'Carl Dreiser'.)[1]

2. 'Fakes', Chicago *Daily Globe*, 25 October, p. 1.

3. 'Labor Leaders Here. To-Day's National Assembly — A Talk with Powderly', SLGD, 15 November, p. 9.

4. 'Greatest in the World. Inception and Progress of the St. Louis Union Depot Scheme', SLGD, 11 December, p. 28.

[1] My knowledge of Dreiser's contributions to the Chicago *Daily Globe*, SLGD, SLR, and PD depends primarily on Dreiser's recollections in *BAM* and on clippings preserved in the Dreiser Collection. I was unable to locate a number of pieces which he recalled writing — the interview of John L. Sullivan for the SLGD, for example. The 'Heard in the Corridors' column and the theater review section of the SLGD have been discarded as Dreiser items. Both reveal the work of more than one hand during the period Dreiser was on the SLGD staff.

1893

A: None.

B:

1. 'Mr. Watterson on Politics', SL*GD*, 6 January, p. 4.
2. 'Water Works Extension', SL*GD*, 15 January, p. 31.
3. 'Theosophy and Spiritualism', SL*GD*, 20 January, p. 12.
4. 'Burned to Death', SL*GD*, 22 January, pp. 1-2.
5. 'Sixteen Dead', SL*GD*, 23 January, p. 10.
6. 'Twenty Dead', SL*GD*, 24 January, p. 11.
7. 'Behind the Scenes', SL*GD*, 26 February, p. 30.[2]
8. 'Black Diva's Concert', SL*GD*, 1 April, p. 8.
9. 'His Own Story', SL*R*, 4 June, pp. 1-2.
10. 'Fast Mail Train', SL*R*, 19 June, pp. 1, 3.
11. 'The Trouble Still On', SL*R*, 20 June, p. 4.
12. 'Got It In For the Owls', SL*R*, 28 June, p. 12.
13. 'The O. and E. Baseball Game', SL*R*, 30 June, p. 12.
14. 'No More Monkeying', SL*R*, 1 July, p. 11.
15. 'Portentous Pointers', SL*R*, 14 July, p. 7.
16. 'A Presage of Disaster', SL*R*, 15 July, p. 11.
17. 'Monday the Day', SL*R*, 16 July, p. 2.
18. 'To Leave To-Day', SL*R*, 16 July, p. 11.
19. 'Pictures from Real Life', SL*R*, 16 July, p. 24.
20. 'Teachers at the Fair', SL*R*, 18 July, p. 7.
21. 'The Republic Teachers', SL*R*, 19 July, p. 6.
22. 'Third Day at the Fair', SL*R*, 20 July, p. 4.
23. 'Will See Everything', SL*R*, 21 July, p. 2.
24. 'Fifth Day at the Fair', SL*R*, 22 July, p. 2.
25. 'Almost a Riot', SL*R*, 11 August, pp. 1-2.
26. 'They Met—and Lunched', SL*R*, 12 August, p. 4.
27. 'Blindfolded He Drove', SL*R*, 18 August, p. 1.
28. 'Jules Wallace, Fake, Fraud, Medium, Healer!', SL*R*, 9 September, pp. 1-2.
29. 'Wallace on Wallace', SL*R*, 10 September, p. 6.
30. 'A Spiritualist Fraud', SL*R*, 11 September, p. 3.
31. 'Unprovoked Murder', SL*R*, 24 September, p. 2.
32. 'A Deep Mystery', SL*R*, 25 September, p. 1.
33. 'Will Wear the Medal', SL*R*, 1 October, p. 29.
34. 'Mystery of a Murder', SL*R*, 19 November, pp. 9-10.

[2] Not recalled by Dreiser in *BAM*; attributed to him on the basis of internal evidence.

35. 'Bloodshed May Result', SL*R*, 30 December, p. 5.
36. 'Miltenberger's Scheme', SL*R*, 31 December, p. 12.

1894

A: None.
B:

1. 'That Football Fracas', SL*R*, 2 January, p. 8.
2. 'Charity Teams Chosen', SL*R*, 4 January, p. 5.
3. 'Armed for the Battle', SL*R*, 5 January, p. 2.
4. 'The Strike Today', Toledo *Blade*, 24 March, pp. 1, 6.[3]
5. 'No Union Men', Toledo *Blade*, 24 March, p. 6.
6. 'As If in Old Toledo', Toledo *Blade*, 28 March, p. 7.
7. 'Hospital Violet Days', *PD*, 12 May, p. 2.[4]
8. 'And It Was Mighty Blue', *PD*, 15 May, p. 2.
9. 'After the Rain Storm', *PD*, 19 May, p. 2.
10. 'A Tale About Two Cats', *PD*, 20 May, p. 2.
11. 'An Hour Among Sinners', *PD*, 21 May, p. 2.
12. 'Funny Man's Gala Day', *PD*, 23 May, p. 2.
13. 'Is Not Down on the List', *PD*, 25 May, p. 2.
14. 'Gathering the Shekels In', *PD*, 27 May, p. 2.
15. 'The Weather Man's Woes', *PD*, 31 May, p. 2.
16. 'How It All Came About', *PD*, 3 June, p. 2.
17. 'Frank Bruin in a Pig', *PD*, 3 June, p. 3.
18. 'An Emblem of Socialism', *PD*, 7 June, p. 3.
19. 'A Novelty of Its Kind', *PD*, 8 June, p. 3.
20. 'Swearing as a Fine Art', *PD*, 9 June, p. 2.
21. 'Where Humanity Fails', *PD*, 10 June, p. 2.
22. 'Cool Spots Were Found', *PD*, 12 June, p. 2.
23. 'Wheels Went 'Round'', *PD*, 13 June, p. 2.
24. 'Hoodwinking Uncle Sam', *PD*, 16 June, p. 2.
25. 'Some of Baby's Spheres', *PD*, 17 June, p. 2.

[3]This article and the two which follow are the only *Blade* items which can be attributed to Dreiser, given his account in *BAM* and his 1945 recollections in letters to Elias.

[4]Dreiser's *PD* period involves a special problem in attribution. In *BAM* he recalled his success as a daily columnist but mentioned only a few pieces specifically. In addition, a few columns are in the Dreiser Collection. For the most part, therefore, *PD* items are attributed to Dreiser principally on the basis of the consistent location of the column he claims to have written — initially almost always page 2, and later page 3 — and of consistency in tone and content in these columns.

26. 'Three Ways to Get Rain', P*D*, 19 June, p. 2.
27. 'Cupid's Bargain Day', P*D*, 21 June, p. 2.
28. 'River Alive with Fish', P*D*, 24 June, p. 2.
29. 'A Midsummer Mania', P*D*, 25 June, p. 2.
30. 'The Fresh Air Funders', P*D*, 26 June, p. 2.
31. 'Fooled Him Every Time', P*D*, 27 June, p. 2.
32. 'Lemonade 1 Cent a Glass', P*D*, 29 June, p. 2.
33. 'Bade Defiance to Law', P*D*, 30 June, p. 2.
34. 'Along the River Shore', P*D*, 2 July, p. 9.
35. 'Soldiers of Morganza', P*D*, 5 July, p. 3.
36. 'Reapers in the Fields', P*D*, 6 July, p. 2.
37. 'Odd Scraps of Melody', P*D*, 7 July, p. 3.
38. 'Triumph for the Toby', P*D*, 8 July, p. 3.
39. 'This Girl Is a Puzzle', P*D*, 11 July, p. 3.
40. 'Charity in the Woods', P*D*, 12 July, p. 3.
41. 'The Spirit of the Spire', P*D*, 13 July, p. 3.
42. 'See the Graphomaniac', P*D*, 14 July, p. 3.
43. 'Patrons of the Springs', P*D*, 16 July, p. 3.
44. 'Views the Passing Show', P*D*, 17 July, p. 3.
45. 'In Old Hancock Street', P*D*, 18 July, p. 3.
46. 'Fenced Off the Earth', P*D*, 19 July, p. 3.
47. 'The Cat Became Woolly', P*D*, 20 July, p. 3.
48. 'Billy Boy's Bad Habit', P*D*, 21 July, p. 3.
49. 'With the Nameless Dead', P*D*, 23 July, p. 3.
50. 'It Was Hoax All Around', P*D*, 27 July, p. 3.
51. 'Confound the Mosquito!', P*D*, 28 July, p. 3.
52. 'Sleep During Hot Nights', P*D*, 31 July, p. 3.
53. 'This Settles the Japs', P*D*, 1 August, p. 3.
54. 'Woes of Dog Catchers', P*D*, 2 August, p. 3.
55. 'Isobars and Isotherms', P*D*, 3 August, p. 3.
56. 'Spoiled by a Meek Cow', P*D*, 6 August, p. 3.
57. 'Relics of a Bygone Age', P*D*, 7 August, p. 3.
58. 'Some Dabbling in Books', P*D*, 14 August, p. 3.
59. 'Here's to the Sadder Men', P*D*, 16 August, p. 3.
60. 'They Are Passing Away', P*D*, 17 August, p. 2.
61. 'Snap Shots at Pleasure', P*D*, 18 August, p. 3.
62. 'Now the Pill Doctrine', P*D*, 20 August, p. 3.
63. 'The Baby Autographer', P*D*, 23 August, p. 3.
64. 'Survival of the Unfittest', P*D*, 24 August, p. 3.
65. 'Where Sympathy Failed', P*D*, 25 August, p. 3.

66. 'Our Fleeting Shekels', P*D*, 26 August, p. 2.
67. 'Sweet Corn on the Cob', P*D*, 27 August, p. 3.
68. 'Tramps in Convention', P*D*, 3 September, p. 3.
69. 'In a Rambling Sort O' Way', P*D*, 13 September, p. 3.
70. 'Telegraphy Now Upon Us', P*D*, 23 September, p. 3.
71. 'September in the Park', P*D*, 24 September, p. 3.
72. 'The Last of the Season', P*D*, 28 September, p. 3.
73. 'Mushrooms in Season', P*D*, 1 October, p. 3.
74. 'The Last Fly of Fly Time', P*D*, 3 October, p. 3.
75. 'Uncle Simon Sees Frost', P*D*, 7 October, p. 3.
76. 'Study of Spider Webs', P*D*, 13 October, p. 3.
77. 'General Booth Says Farewell', P*D*, 12 November, pp. 1–2.

1895

A: None.
B:

1. 'Review of the Month', *Ev'ry Month*, I (December), 2–9. (Signed 'The Prophet'.)[5]

2. 'We Others', *Ev'ry Month*, I (December), 15–16. Sketch. (Signed 'S. J. White'.)[6]

3. 'The Gloom Chasers', *Ev'ry Month*, I (December), 16–17. Sketch. (Signed 'The Cynic'.)

[5] Dreiser probably contributed this column to *Ev'ry Month* from the publication of the first number of the magazine in October 1895. However, the Library of Congress file of *Ev'ry Month* for the period of Dreiser's editorship is missing. The extant numbers of *Ev'ry Month* for this period are those of II (September 1896)–IV (July 1897) on film at Yale University Library and the Dreiser Collection, of II (April, June–August 1896) in the Dreiser Collection, and of all but the October and November 1895 issues in the Joseph Katz Collection. In 1973 the University of South Carolina Press will publish a facsimile edition of the extant *Ev'ry Month* issues edited by Dreiser, with an introduction by Joseph Katz.

[6] Dreiser produced *Ev'ry Month* with very little aid and therefore adopted several pseudonyms to disguise this fact. 'Edward Al' is based on the first names of two of his brothers, and 'S. J. White' derives from Sallie White, his fiancée. In addition, most of the contributions signed 'V. D. Hyde' appear to be by Dreiser, since he later reused much of this material when a free-lance writer during the period 1897–1901. Attribution of three unsigned *Ev'ry Month* contributions made on the following grounds: (1) item B-3 (1895) similar to sketch published in the P*D*, 20 August 1894; (2) item B-3 (1896) attributed to 'Edward Al' on the cover of the issue; and (3) item B-7 (1896) comprised of drama reviews, a responsibility of Dreiser during this period of his editorship of *Ev'ry Month*.

4. 'The Literary Shower', *Ev'ry Month*, I (December), 18. Reviews. (Signed 'Edward Al'.)

5. 'The Drama', *Ev'ry Month*, I (December), 22–23. Reviews.

1896

A: None.

B:

1. 'Reflections', *Ev'ry Month*, I (January), 2–11. (Signed 'The Prophet'.)

2. 'Dramatic', *Ev'ry Month*, I (January), 16–17. Reviews.

3. 'The Literary Shower', *Ev'ry Month*, I (January), 21–22. Reviews. (Unsigned.)

4. 'Reflections', *Ev'ry Month*, I (February), 2–6. (Signed 'The Prophet'.)

5. 'The Literary Shower', *Ev'ry Month*, I (February), 10–11. Reviews. (Signed 'Edward Al'.)

6. 'Winter Landscapes', *Ev'ry Month*, I (February), 18. Sketch. (Signed 'S. J. White'.)

7. 'Dramatic', *Ev'ry Month*, I (February), 23. Reviews. (Unsigned.)

8. 'Reflections'. *Ev'ry Month*, I (March), 2–6. (Signed 'The Prophet'.)

9. 'As to the Jucklins', *Ev'ry Month*, I (March), 10. Review of Opie Read's *The Jucklins*. (Signed 'Edward Al'.)

10. 'Cometh in as a Lion', *Ev'ry Month*, I (March), 16. Sketch. (Signed 'S. J. White'.)

11. 'Dramatic', *Ev'ry Month*, I (March), 22. Reviews.

12. 'Reflections', *Ev'ry Month*, II (April), 2–7. (Signed 'The Prophet'.)

13. 'The Day of Their Wedding', *Ev'ry Month*, II (April), 11. Review of the novel by W. D. Howells. (Signed 'Edward Al'.)

14. 'Dramatic', *Ev'ry Month*, II (April), 22. Reviews.

15. 'Reflections', *Ev'ry Month*, II (May), 2–6. (Signed 'The Prophet'.)

16. 'Literary Notes', *Ev'ry Month*, II (May), 11–12. Reviews. (Signed 'Edward Al'.)

17. 'I Shall Pass Through This World But Once', *Ev'ry Month*, II (May), 17. Poem. (Signed 'S. J. White'.)

18. 'Conditioned Ones', *Ev'ry Month*, II (May), 18. Poem.

19. 'The Drama', *Ev'ry Month*, II (May), 22. Reviews.

20. 'Reflections', *Ev'ry Month*, II (June), 2–6. (Signed 'The Prophet'.)

21. 'The Madding Crowd', *Ev'ry Month*, II (June), 17. Poem.

22. 'The Literary Shower', *Ev'ry Month*, II (June), 21–22. Reviews. (Signed 'Edward Al'.)

23. 'Dramatic', *Ev'ry Month*, II (June), 26. Reviews, (Signed 'S. J. White'.).

24. 'Reflections', *Ev'ry Month*, II (July), 2–6. (Signed 'The Prophet'.)

25. 'Some Notable Women in New York Society', *Ev'ry Month*, II (July), 10–11. (Signed 'V. D. Hyde'.)

26. 'Chevalier', *Ev'ry Month*, II (July), 18. (Signed 'S. J. White'.)

27. 'The Literary Shower', *Ev'ry Month*, II (July), 24–25. Reviews. (Signed 'Edward Al'.)

28. 'Reflections', *Ev'ry Month*, II (August), 2–7. (Signed 'The Prophet'.)

29. 'Woes of Cats', *Ev'ry Month*, II (August), 10–11. (Signed 'S. J. White'.)

30. 'Forgotten', *Ev'ry Month*, II (August), 16–17. Story.

31. 'The Literary Shower', *Ev'ry Month*, II (August), 21–22. Reviews. (Signed 'Edward Al'.)

32. 'Reflections', *Ev'ry Month*, II (September), 2–7. (Signed 'The Prophet'.)

33. 'A Royal Abdication', *Ev'ry Month*, II (September), 16–17. [Queen Victoria.] (Signed 'S. J. White'.)

34. 'The Literary Shower', *Ev'ry Month*, II (September), 22–23. Reviews. (Signed 'Edward Al'.)

35. 'Reflections', *Ev'ry Month*, III (October), 2–7. (Signed 'The Prophet'.)

36. 'Reflections', *Ev'ry Month*, III (November), 2–7. (Signed 'The Prophet'.)

37. 'A Metropolitan Favorite', *Ev'ry Month*, III (November), 22. [R. F. Outcault.]

38. 'Reflections', *Ev'ry Month*, III (December), 2–7. (Signed 'The Prophet'.)

39. 'Caricatures and a Caricaturist', *Ev'ry Month*, III (December), 10. [Homer Davenport.] (Signed 'S. J. White'.)

1897

A: None.

B:

1. 'Reflections', *Ev'ry Month*, III (January), 2–7. (Signed 'The Prophet'.)

2. 'William Gillette', *Ev'ry Month*, III (January), 17. (Signed 'S. J. White'.)

3. 'The Woman Journalist', *Ev'ry Month*, III (January), 24–25. (Signed 'V. D. Hyde'.)

4. 'Reflections', *Ev'ry Month*, III (February), 2–7. (Signed 'The Prophet'.)

5. 'Reflections', *Ev'ry Month*, III (March), 2–6. (Signed 'The Prophet'.)

6. 'Where Grant Is to Rest', *Ev'ry Month*, III (March), 18–19. (Signed 'V. D. Hyde'.)

7. 'Mary E. Tillingast: Stained Glass Artist', *Ev'ry Month*, III (March), 20–21. (Signed 'V. D. Hyde'.)

8. 'A Social Samaritan: Rose Hawthorne Lathrop's Mission to the Afflicted', *Ev'ry Month*, III (March), 25. (Signed 'S. J. White'.)

9. *Ev'ry Month*, IV (April), 20–21. (Unsigned.)[7]

10. *Ev'ry Month*, IV (May), 20–21. (Unsigned.)

11. 'Portia Come Again', *Ev'ry Month*, IV (May), 8. [Mrs. Clara Foltz.] (Signed 'V. D. Hyde'.)

12. *Ev'ry Month*, IV (June), 20–21. (Unsigned.)

13. *Ev'ry Month*, IV (July), 20. (Unsigned.)

14. 'New York's Art Colony. The Literary and Art Retreat at Bronxville', *Metropolitan*, VI (November), 321–26. (Signed 'Theodore Dresser'.)[8]

15. 'Our Women Violinists', *Puritan*, II (November), 34–35.

16. 'On the Field at Brandywine', *Truth*, XVI (6 November), 7–10.

1898

A:

1. 'Exordium', in *Spanish-American War Songs*, ed. Sidney A. Witherbee, pp. 276–77: S. A. Witherbee (Detroit).

B:

1. 'The Haunts of Bayard Taylor', *Munsey's*, XVIII (January), 594–601.

---

[7]From April to July the 'Reflections' column was transferred to the back of *Ev'ry Month* and was untitled and unsigned, but it is nevertheless clearly the work of Dreiser.

[8]During his career as a free-lance magazine writer between 1897 and 1901 Dreiser frequently reused material. For example, compare this article with the one in *Demorest's* of August 1899: 'A Notable Art Colony: Artistic and Literary People in the Picturesque Bronx'. I have not noted these borrowings unless one item is essentially a republication of the other.

2. 'A Talk with America's Leading Lawyer', *Success*, I (January), 40–41. [Joseph Choate.] *LVGA*.[9]

3. 'A High Priestess of Art', *Success*, I (January), 55. [Alice B. Stephens.] (Signed 'Edward Al'.)

4. 'Henry Mosler, a Painter for the People', *Demorest's*, XXXIV (February), 67–69.

5. 'The Art of MacMonnies and Morgan', *Metropolitan*, VII (February), 143–51.

6. 'A Photographic Talk with Edison', *Success*, I (February), 8–9. *HTS*.

7. 'Historic Tarrytown', *Ainslee's*, I (March), 25–31.

8. 'Work of Mrs. Kenyon Cox', *Cosmpolitan*, XXIV (March), 477–80.

9. 'Virtue', *Demorest's*, XXXIV (March), 100. Poem.

10. 'Anthony Hope Tells a Secret', *Success*, I (March), 12–13. *TWGW*.

11. 'A Vision of Fairy Lamps', *Success*, I (March), 23. [H. Barrington Cox.] (Signed 'Edward Al'.)

12. 'Benjamin Eggleston, Painter', *Ainslee's*, I (April), 41–47.

13. 'A Prophet, But Not Without Honor', *Ainslee's*, I (April), 73–79. (Signed 'Edward Al'.)

14. 'The Harp', *Cosmopolitan*, XXIV (April), 637–44.

15. 'Resignation', *Demorest's*, XXXIV (April), 137. Poem.

16. 'Art Work of Irving R. Wiles', *Metropolitan*, VII (April), 357–61.

17. 'How William Dean Howells Climbed Fame's Ladder', *Success*, I (April), 5–6. *HTS*.

18. 'A Great American Caricaturist', *Ainslee's*, I (May), 336–41. [Homer Davenport.]

19. 'The American Water-Color Society', *Metropolitan*, VII (May), 489–93.

20. 'Of One Who Dreamed: W. Louis Sonntag, Jr., Obit., May 11, 1898', *Collier's*, XXI (28 May), 2. Poem.

21. 'A Painter of Travel', *Ainslee's*, I (June), 391–98. [Gilbert Gaul.]

---

[9] At one time during his career as a magazine writer, Dreiser unsuccessfully attempted to publish a collection of his articles on prominent personalities of the day. He was unaware that O. S. Marden, the editor of *Success* (the magazine in which most of these articles appeared), had republished many of them, unattributed to Dreiser, in a series of volumes issued in the early 1900s. Dreiser's contributions to these collections—*TWGW*, 1901; *HTS*, 1901; and *LVGA*, 1903—were first noted by John F. Huth, Jr.

22. 'Where Battleships Are Built', *Ainslee's*, I (June), 433–39. (Signed 'Edward Al'.)

23. 'Artists' Studios', *Demorest's*, XXXIV (June), 196–98.

24. 'With Whom Is Shadow of Turning', *Demorest's*, XXXIV (June), 189. Poem.

25. 'The Making of Small Arms', *Ainslee's*, I (July), 540–49.

26. 'Scenes in a Cartridge Factory', *Cosmpolitan*, XXV (July), 321–24.

27. 'Carrier Pigeons in War Time', *Demorest's*, XXXIV (July), 222–23.

28. 'Night Song', *Ainslee's*, II (August), 73. Poem.

29. 'The Harlem River Speedway', *Ainslee's*, II (August), 49–56.

30. 'The Sculpture of Fernando Mirando', *Ainslee's*, II (September), 113–18.

31. 'Brandywine, the Picturesque', *Demorest's*, XXXIV (September), 274–75.

32. 'Mortuarium', *Demorest's*, XXXIV (September), 279. Poem.

33. 'Thou Giant', *Success*, I (September), 16. Poem.

34. 'Fame Found in Quiet Nooks', *Success*, I (September), 5–6. [John Burroughs.] *HTS*.

35. 'The Haunts of Nathaniel Hawthorne', *Truth*, XVII (21 September), 7–9.

36. 'The Haunts of Nathaniel Hawthorne', *Truth*, XVII (28 September), 11–13.

37. 'American Sculptors', New York *Times Illustrated Magazine*, 25 September, pp. 6–7.

38. 'The Return', *Ainslee's*, II (October), 280. Poem.

39. 'Great Problems of Organization. III. The Chicago Packing Industry', *Cosmpolitan*, XXV (October), 615–26.

40. 'Supplication', *Demorest's*, XXXIV (October), 302. Poem.

41. 'The Smallest and Busiest River in the World', *Metropolitan*, VII (October), 355–63.

42. 'Life Stories of Successful Men — No. 10, Philip D. Armour', *Success*, I (October), 3–4. *HTS*.

43. 'The Real Zangwill', *Ainslee's*, II (November), 351–57.

44. 'Through All Adversity', *Demorest's*, XXXIV (November), 334. Poem.

45. 'Birth and Growth of a Popular Song', *Metropolitan*, VIII (November), 497–502.

46. 'Life Stories of Successful Men — No. 11, Chauncey M. Depew', *Success*, I (November), 3–4, *TWGW*.

47. 'And Continueth Not', *Ainslee's*, II (December), 477. Poem.

48. 'When the Sails Are Furled: Sailors Snug Harbor', *Ainslee's*, II (December), 593–601. New York *Tribune Sunday Magazine*, 22 May 1904, pp. 3–5, 19. *Color.*

49. 'The Treasure House of Natural History', *Metropolitan*, VIII (December), 595–601.

50. 'Life Stories of Successful Men — No. 12, Marshall Field', *Success*, II (8 December), 7–8. *HTS.*

51. 'More Cargoes', *Saturday Evening Post*, CLXXI (10 December), 384. Review of the stories by W. W. Jacobs. (Unsigned.)[10]

52. 'A Leader of Young Mankind, Frank W. Gunsaulus', *Success*, II (15 December), 23–24. *TWGW.*

1899

A: None.

B:

1. 'Who Wills to Do Good', *Ainslee's*, II (January), 667. Poem.

2. 'The Making of Stained-Glass Windows', *Cosmopolitan*, XXVI (January), 243–52.

3. 'In Keeping', *Demorest's*, XXXV (January), 37. Poem.

4. 'Electricity in the Household', *Demorest's*, XXXV (January), 38–39.

5. 'A Golden Sorrow', *Saturday Evening Post*, CLXXI (28 January), 496. Review of the novel by Marion L. Pool. (Unsigned.)[11]

6. 'He Became Famous in a Day', *Success*, II (28 January), 143–44. [Paul W. Bartlett.] *TWGW.*

7. 'The Chicago Drainage Canal', *Ainslee's*, III (February), 53–61.

8. 'A Painter of Cats and Dogs', *Demorest's*, XXXV (February), 68–69. [J. N. Dolph.]

9. 'Karl Bitter, Sculptor', *Metropolitan*, IX (February), 147–52.

10. 'E. Percy Morgan and His Work', *Truth*, XVIII (February), 31–35.

11. 'His Life Given Over to Music', *Success*, II (4 February), 167–68. [Theodore Thomas.] *HTS.*

12. 'America's Greatest Portrait Painters', *Success*, II (11 February), 183–84.

13. 'The Career of a Modern Portia', *Success*, II (18 February), 205–6. [Mrs. Clara Foltz.]

[10] Attribution based on correspondence in the Dreiser Collection.
[11] Attribution based on correspondence in the Dreiser Collection.

14. 'Literary Lions I Have Met', *Success*, II (25 February), 223–24. James B. Pond.]

15. 'The Town of Pullman', *Ainslee's* III (March), 189–200.

16. 'Amelia E. Barr and Her Home Life', *Demorest's*, XXXV (March), 103–4.

17. 'Edmund Clarence Stedman at Home', *Munsey's*, XX (March), 931–38.

18. 'The Real Choate', *Ainslee's*, III (April), 324–33.

19. 'Bondage', *Ainslee's*, III (April), 293. Poem.

20. 'Japanese Home Life', *Demorest's*, XXXV (April), 123–25.

21. 'Women Who Have Won Distinction in Music', *Success*, II (8 April), 325–26.

22. 'The Horseless Age', *Demorest's*, XXXV (May), 153–55.

23. 'Woodmen', *Demorest's*, XXXV (May), 159. Poem.

24. 'The Home of William Cullen Bryant', *Munsey's*, XXI (May), 240–46.

25. 'Human Documents from Old Rome', *Ainslee's*, III (June), 586–96.

26. 'Concerning Bruce Crane', *Truth*, XVIII (June), 143–47.

27. 'A Monarch of Metal Workers', *Success*, II (3 June), 453–54. [Andrew Carnegie.] *HTS*.

28. 'A Master of Photography,' *Success*. II (10 June), 471. [Alfred Stieglitz.] *TWGW*.

29. 'The Foremost of American Sculptors', *New Voice*, XVI (17 June), 4–5, 13. [J. Q. A. Ward.]

30. 'American Women as Successful Playwrights', *Success*, II (17 June), 485–86.

31. 'American Women Who Play the Harp', *Success*, II (24 June), 501–2.

32. 'The Log of an Ocean Pilot', *Ainslee's*, III (July), 683–92. *Color.*

33. 'An Important Philanthropy', *Demorest's*, XXXV (July), 215–17.

34. 'From New York to Boston by Trolley', *Ainslee's*, IV (August), 74–84. (Signed 'Herman D. White'.)[12]

35. 'A Notable Colony: Artistic and Literary People in the Picturesque Bronx', *Demorest's*, XXXV (August), 240–41.

36. 'If Force Transmutes', *Demorest's*, XXXV (August), 243. Poem.

37. 'John Burroughs in His Mountain Hut', *New Voice*, XVI (19 August), 7, 13.

38. 'Christ Church, Shrewsbury', New York *Times Illustrated Magazine*, 27 August, pp. 11–12.

[12] Attribution based on correspondence in the Dreiser Collection.

39. 'C. C. Curran', *Truth*, XVIII (September), 227–31.

40. 'It Pays to Treat Workers Generously', *Success*, II (16 September), 691–92. [John H. Patterson.] *TWGW*.

41. 'American Women Violinists', *Success*, II (30 September), 731–32.

42. 'The Camera Club of New York', *Ainslee's*, IV (October), 324–35.

43. 'Curious Shifts of the Poor', *Demorest's*, XXXVI (November), 22–26. *Sister Carrie*.

44. 'The Unrewarded', *Demorest's*, XXXVI (November), 5. Poem.

45. 'American Women Who Are Winning Fame as Pianists', *Success*, II (4 November), 815.

46. 'Our Government and Our Food', *Demorest's*, XXXVI (December), 68–70.

1900

1. Chapter XIII of *A Princess of Arcady*, by Arthur Henry: Doubleday, Page.[13]

2. *Sister Carrie:* Doubleday, Page.

B:

1. 'The Trade of the Mississippi', *Ainslee's*, IV (January), 735–43.

2. 'Atkinson on National Food Reform', *Success*, III (January), 4. (Signed 'Edward Al'.)

3. 'The Story of a Song-Queen's Triumph', *Success*, III (January), 6–8. [Lillian Nordica.] *HTS*.

4. 'The Railroad and the People', *Harper's Monthly*, C (February), 479–84.

5. 'Little Clubmen of the Tenements', *Puritan*, VII (February), 665–72.

6. 'The Real Howells', *Ainslee's*, V (March), 137–42. *Americana*, XXXVII (April 1943), 274–82.

7. 'New York's Underground Railroad', *Pearson's*, IX (April), 375–84.

8. 'Good Roads for Bad', *Pearson's*, IX (May), 387–95.

9. 'Champ Clark, the Man and His District', *Ainslee's*, V (June), 425–34.

10. 'The Descent of the Horse', *Everybody's*, II (June), 543–47.

11. 'Thomas Brackett Reed: The Story of a Great Career', *Success*, III (June), 215–16.

[13] Dreiser frequently claimed to have written the final chapter of Henry's novel.

12. 'The Transmigration of the Sweat Shop', *Puritan*, VIII (July), 498–502.

13. 'Apples: An Account of the Apple Industry in America', *Pearson's*, X (October), 336–40.

14. 'Fruit Growing in America', *Harper's Monthly*, CI (November), 859–68.

15. 'Whence the Song', *Harper's Weekly*, XLIV (8 December), 1165–66a. *Color.*

1901

A:

1. 'How an Agricultural Society Markets Fruits and Vegetables', *The Success Library*, ed. Orison S. Marden, IX, 5215–17. *Choosing a Career*, ed. Orison S. Marden (Indianapolis, 1905).

B:

1. 'Why the Indian Paints His Face', *Pearson's*, XI (January), 19–23.

2. 'When the Old Century Was New', *Pearson's*, XI (January), 131–40. *Free.*

3. 'Delaware's Blue Laws', *Ainslee's*, VII (February), 53–57.

4. 'Rural Free Mail Delivery', *Pearson's*, XI (February), 233–40.

5. 'Lawrence E. Earle', *Truth*, XX (February), 27–30.

6. 'The Story of the States: No. III — Illinois', *Pearson's*, XI (April), 513–43.

7. 'The Shining Slave Makers', *Ainslee's*, VII (June), 445–50. *Free.*

8. 'Plant Life Underground', *Pearson's*, XI (June), 860–64.

9. 'Nigger Jeff', *Ainslee's*, VIII (November), 366–75. *Free.*

10. 'A True Patriarch', *McClure's*, XVIII (December), 136–44. *TM.*

11. 'Butcher's Rogaum's Door', *Reedy's Mirror*, XI (12 December), 15–17. *Free.*

12. 'The Color of Today,' *Harper's Weekly*, XLV (14 December), 1272–73. *TM* (as 'W. L. S.')

1902

A: None.

B:

1. 'The New Knowledge of Weeds', *Ainslee's*, VIII (January), 533–38.

2. 'A Cripple Whose Energy Gives Inspiration', *Success*, V (February), 72–73.

3. 'A Touch of Human Brotherhood', *Success*, V (March), 140–41, 176.

4. 'The Tenement Toilers', *Success*, V (April), 213–14, 232. New York *Call Magazine*, 24 August 1919, pp. 6–7. *Color.*

5. 'A Remarkable Art', *Great Round World*, XIX (3 May), 430–34. (Unsigned.) [Alfred Stieglitz.] A reworking of Dreiser's 10 June 1899 article in *Success.*

6. 'A Doer of the Word', *Ainslee's*, IX (June), 453–59. *TM.*

7. 'Christmas in the Tenements', *Harper's Weekly*, XLVI (6 December), 52–53. *Color.*

1903

A: None.

B:

1. 'True Art Speaks Plainly', *Booklover's Magazine*, I (February), 129. *Modernist*, I (November 1919), 21.

2. 'Scared Back to Nature', *Harper's Weekly*, XLVII (16 May), 816. (Unsigned.)[14]

3. 'A Mayor and His People', *Era*, XI (June), 578–84. *TM.*

4. 'The Problem of the Soil', *Era*, XII (September), 239–49.

1904

A: None.

B:

1. 'Just What Happened When the Waters of the Hudson Broke into the North River Tunnel', New York *Daily News* (Magazine Section), 23 January, pp. 6–7. (Unsigned.)[15]

2. 'The Cradle of Tears', New York *Daily News* (Magazine Section), 27 March, p. 4. (Unsigned.) *Tom Watson's Magazine*, I (May 1905), 349–50. *Color.*

3. 'The Sowing', *Ainslee's*, XIII (April), 135. Poem.

4. 'The Story of a Human Nine-Pin', New York *Daily News* (Magazine Section), 3 April, p. 3. (Unsigned.) *Tom Watson's Magazine*, I (June 1905), 502–3 (as 'The Track Walker'). *Color.*

5. 'The Love Affairs of Little Italy', New York *Daily News* (Magazine Section), 10 April, p. 3. (Unsigned.) *Color.*

[14] A sketch of Muldoon, who appears as 'Culhane, the Solid Man' in *TW.*
[15] The basis for 'St. Columba and the River' in *Chains.*

6. 'Hunting for Swordfish', New York *Daily News* (Magazine Section), 24 July, pp. 11–12. (Unsigned.)[16]

7. 'The Voyage', *Ainslee's*, XIV (October), 136. Poem.

1905

A: None.

B:

1. 'The Old 10:30 Train', *Tom Watson's Magazine*, I (March), 96. Poem. (Signed 'Marion Drace'.)[17]

2. 'The Rivers of the Nameless Dead', *Tom Watson's Magazine*, I (March), 112–13. *Color.*

3. 'The Publisher's Word', *Smith's*, I (April), 12.[18]

4. 'The Publisher's Word', *Smith's*, I (May), i–iii.

5. 'A Word to the Public', *Smith's*, I (June), i–iii.

6. 'A Word to the Public', *Smith's*, I (July), i–iv.

7. 'What the Editor Has to Say', *Smith's*, I (August), i–ii.

8. 'What the Editor Has to Say', *Smith's*, I (September), i–ii.

9. 'The Silent Worker', *Tom Watson's Magazine*, II (September), 364.

10. 'What the Editor Has to Say', *Smith's*, II (October), i–ii.

11. 'The City of Crowds', *Smith's*, II (October), 97–107.

12. 'The Loneliness of the City', *Tom Watson's Magazine*, II (October), 474–75.

13. 'What the Editor Has to Say', *Smith's*, II (November), i–iii.

1906

A: None.

B:

1. 'A Lesson from the Aquarium', *Tom Watson's Magazine*, III (January), 306–8.

2. 'What the Editor Has to Say', *Smith's*, II (March), i–ii.

3. 'What the Editor Has to Say', *Smith's*, III (May), i–ii.

4. 'The Beauty of the Tree', *Broadway*, XVI (June), 130.[19]

---

[16] Attributed to Dreiser on the basis of a clipping in the Dreiser Collection.

[17] Attributed to Dreiser on the basis of a clipping in the Dreiser Collection.

[18] Dreiser edited *Smith's Magazine* from April 1905 to April 1906 and was responsible for its contents up to and including the July 1906 number.

[19] Dreiser edited the *Broadway Magazine* from April 1906 to June 1907. Many of the issues during his editorship contain brief squibs on current and coming articles, but there is nothing which identifies these as by Dreiser.

5. 'New York and the New Broadway', *Broadway*, XVI (June), vii–ix.[20]

6. '$5,000 for Short Stories', *Broadway*, XVI (August), iv.

7. 'The Poet's Creed', *Broadway*, XVI (August), 353. Poem.

8. 'The Peace of the Thousand Islands', *Smith's*, III (August), 769–84.

1907

A: None.

B:

1. 'Fruitage', *Broadway*, XVII (February), 566. Poem.

2. 'Concerning Us All', *Delineator*, LXX (October), 491–92.[21]

3. 'Concerning Us All', *Delineator*, LXX (November), 732–33.

4. 'Interviews with the Editor', *Delineator*, LXX (November), 649–50.

5. 'Concerning Us All', *Delineator*, LXX (December), 927–28.

6. 'Your Magazine in 1908', *Delineator*, LXX (December), 865.

1908

A: None.

B:

1. 'Concerning Us All', *Delineator*, LXXI (January), 67–68.

2. 'Just You and the Editor', *Delineator*, LXXI (January), 5–7.

3. 'Concerning Us All', *Delineator*, LXXI (February), 221–22.

4. 'Just You and the Editor', *Delineator*, LXXI (February), 161–63.

5. 'Concerning Us All', *Delineator*, LXXI (March), 397–98.

6. 'Just You and the Editor', *Delineator*, LXXI (March), 335–37.

7. 'Concerning Us All', *Delineator*, LXXI (April), 575–76.

8. 'Concerning Us All', *Delineator*, LXXI (May), 775–76.

9. 'Just You and the Editor', *Delineator*, LXXI (May), 710–11.

10. 'Concerning Us All', *Delineator*, LXXI (June), 971–72.

11. 'Concerning Us All', *Delineator*, LXXII (July), 77–78.

12. 'Concerning Us All', *Delineator*, LXXII (August), 223–24.

13. 'Concerning Us All', *Delineator*, LXXII (September), 369–70.

14. 'Concerning Us All', *Delineator*, LXXII (October), 537–38.

[20] Both this and the next article are unsigned but appear to be the work of the editor.

[21] Dreiser was editor of the *Delineator* from June 1907 to October 1909, though he did not become fully responsible for the magazine until the October 1907 number. All the *Delineator* items included in this list are unsigned but are designated as by the editor.

THE DELINEATOR
LONDON · PARIS · NEW YORK
THEODORE DREISER, EDITOR

October 1st, 1909.

My dear Sir:

Your name has been suggested to me as that of some one who is interested in the sociological progress of America, and particularly in matters
which concern the development and well-being of the on-coming generation of
Americans. I am the editor-in-chief of the three publications, The Delineator,
The Designer and The New Idea which have a combined circulation of 1,800,000.
It is the object of these magazines to be useful in an educational and instructive way - presenting to the average person those subjects which will demonstrate
the practical workings of life. We endeavor to teach at every turn new ways,
new theories in all that relates to the well-being of the individual and the
family. Naturally it is necessary to be aware of the advisable things to discuss at any time, and I write to ask if you will not make some suggestions for
subjects which could be discussed either by you or by some one who may dwell in
your mind as the ideal person to present a certain phase of life in a helpful
way. I should very much appreciate it if you would give this proposition your
serious consideration, and if there is any subject you have in mind which you
could present personally let me know.

Very truly yours,

Theodore Dreiser

Editor.

Mr. Frederick Tuckerman,
Amherst, Mass.

PLATE 2

15. 'Just You and the Editor', *Delineator*, LXXII (October), 468–69.

16. 'Concerning Us All', *Delineator*, LXXII (November), 739–40.

17. 'Just You and the Editor', *Delineator*, LXXII (November), 659–61.

18. 'Just You and the Editor', *Delineator*, LXXII (December), 881–83.

1909

A: None.

B:

1. 'Concerning Us All', *Delineator*, LXXIII (January), 69–70.

2. 'Concerning Us All', *Delineator*, LXXIII (February), 211–12.

3. 'Concerning Us All', *Delineator*, LXXIII (March), 391–92.

4. 'Concerning Us All', *Delineator*, LXXIII (April), 556.

5. 'Concerning Us All', *Delineator*, LXXIII (May), 672.

6. 'Concerning Us All', *Delineator*, LXXIII (June), 766.

7. 'Concerning Us All', *Delineator*, LXXIV (July), 33.

8. 'Concerning Us All', *Delineator*, LXXIV (August), 113.

9. 'Concerning Us All', *Delineator*, LXXIV (September), 193.

10. 'The Man on the Sidewalk', *Bohemian*, XVII (October), 422–23. (Unsigned.)[22]

11. 'In the Matter of Spiritualism', *Bohemian*, XVII (October), 424–25. (Unsigned.)

12. 'The Day of the Great Writer', *Bohemian*, XVII (October), 426–27. (Unsigned.)

13. 'The Defects of Organized Charity', *Bohemian*, XVII (October), 429–31. (Unsigned.)

14. 'The Cruise of the Idlewild', *Bohemian*, XVII (October), 441–47. *Free.*

15. 'The Flight of Pigeons', *Bohemian*, XVII (October), 494–96. (Signed 'Edward Al'.) *Color.*

16. 'Concerning Us All', *Delineator*, LXXIV (October), 292.

17. 'The Waterfront', *Bohemian*, XVII (November), 633–36. (Signed 'Edward Al'.) *Color.*

---

[22] Dreiser acquired a financial interest in the *Bohemian Magazine* in September 1909 and helped edit the October, November, and December issues. One of the monthly features of the magazine was 'At the Sign of the Lead Pencil', a series of unsigned editorial and descriptive items. Attribution to Dreiser of this column is based on correspondence in the Dreiser Collection and on internal evidence.

18. 'Concerning Us All', *Delineator*, LXXIV (November), 400.

19. 'Our National Literary Debt', *Bohemian*, XVII (December), 705–7. (Unsigned.)

20. 'Pittsburgh', *Bohemian*, XVII (December), 712–14. (Unsigned.)

21. 'The Red Slayer', *Bohemian*, XVII (December), 793–95. (Signed 'Edward Al'.) *Color.*

22. 'Concerning Us All', *Delineator*, LXXIV (December), 494.

1910

A: None.

B:

1. 'Six O'Clock', *1910*, No. 4 (n.d., n.p.). *Color.*
2. 'The Factory', *1910*, No. 5 (n.d., n.p.).

1911

A:

1. *Jennie Gerhardt:* Harper.

B:

1. 'The Mighty Burke', *McClure's*, XXXVII (May), 40–50. *TM.*

1912

A:

1. *The Financier:* Harper.

B:

1. 'The Men in the Dark', *American*, LXXIII (February), 465–68. *Color.*

2. 'Deeper Than Man-Made Laws', *Hearst's Magazine*, XXI (June), 2395.

1913

A:

1. *A Traveler at Forty:* Century.

B:

1. 'Lilly Edwards: An Episode', *Smart Set*, XL (June), 81–86. *Traveler.*

2. 'Letter to the Editor', St. Louis *Star*, 11 July, p. 2.

3. 'The Toil of the Laborer', New York *Call*, 13 July, p. 11. *Reconstruction*, I (October 1919), 310–13. *HRDD.*

4. 'The First Voyage Over', *Century*, LXXXVI (August), 586–95. *Traveler.*

5. 'An Uncommercial Traveler in London', *Century*, LXXXVI (September), 739–49. *Traveler.*

6. 'Paris', *Century*, LXXXVI (October), 904–15. *Traveler.*

7. 'The Girl in the Coffin', *Smart Set*, XLI (October), 127–40. *Plays.*

8. 'The Man on the Bench', New York *Call*, 16 November, p. 9. *Color.*

9. 'Three Sketches of the Poor', New York *Call*, 23 November, p. 10.[23]

1914

A:

1. Foreword to *Life in a Garrison Town*, by Lieutenant [Fritz] Bilse, pp. v–xiii: John Lane.

2. *The Titan:* John Lane.

B:

1. 'My Uncompleted Trilogy', New York *Evening Sun*, 30 May, p. 7.

2. 'The Blue Sphere', *Smart Set*, XLIV (December), 245–52. *Plays.*

1915

A:

1. *The "Genius":* John Lane.

B:

1. 'In the Dark', *Smart Set*, XLIV (January), 419–25. *Plays.*

2. 'Laughing Gas', *Smart Set*, XLV (February), 85–94. *Plays.*

3. 'The Saddest Story', *New Republic*, III (12 June), 155–56. Review of Ford Maddox Ford's *The Good Soldier.*

4. 'Neither Devil Nor Angel', *New Republic*, III (10 July), 262–63. Review of Robert Steele's *One Man.*

5. 'The Spring Recital', *Little Review*, II (December), 28–35. *Plays.*

6. 'As a Realist Sees It', *New Republic*, V (25 December), 202–4. Review of W. Somerset Maugham's *Of Human Bondage.*

1916

A:

1. *A Hoosier Holiday:* John Lane.

[23]Of the three sketches, 'The Man Who Bakes Your Bread' was republished in the New York *Call Magazine*, 13 April 1919, pp. 1, 6; and 'The Men in the Snow' in *Color.*

2. *Plays of the Natural and Supernatural:* John Lane.

B:

1. 'The Light in the Window', *International,* X (January), 6–8, 32. *Plays.*

2. 'Freedom for the Honest Writer', Cleveland *Leader,* 16 March, p. [7]. A contribution to the symposium 'Literature and Art from the Point of View of American Ideals', syndicated by Newspaper Enterprise Associates.

3. 'The Lost Phoebe', *Century,* XCI (April), 885–96. *Free.*

4. 'Four Poems', *Smart Set,* XLIX (May), 277–78. *Moods* (1926).

5. 'Change', *Pagan,* I (September), 27–28. New York *Call Magazine,* 26 January 1918, p. 1. *HRDD.*

6. 'America's Foremost Author Protests Against Suppression of Great Books and Art by Self-Constituted Moral Censors', Los Angeles *Record,* 7 November, p. 4. Syndicated by Newspaper Enterprise Associates.

1917

A:

1. *Life, Art and America.*[24]

B:

1. 'Symposium on the Medical Profession', *Medical Review of Reviews,* XXIII (January), 8–9.

2. 'Life, Art and America', *Seven Arts,* I (February), 363–89. *Life, Art and America* and *HRDD.*

3. 'Mister Bottom', *The Social War,* I (April), 2.

4. 'A Man and His House', *Hoggson Magazine,* III (June), 107.

5. 'The Dream', *Seven Arts,* II (July), 319–33. *HRDD.*

6. 'Our Greatest Writers Tells What's Wrong with Our Newspapers', *Pep,* II (July), 8–9.

7. 'Married', *Cosmopolitan,* LXIII (September), 31–35. 112–15. *Free.*

8. 'Our Amazing Illusioned Press', New York *Call Magazine,* 16 December, p. 3.

1918

A:

1. *Free and Other Stories:* Boni and Liveright.

2. *The Hand of the Potter:* Boni and Liveright.

[24]Pamphlet republication of Dreiser's February 1917 *Seven Arts* article.

3. *Twelve Men:* Boni and Liveright.

B:

1. 'The Second Choice', *Cosmopolitan,* LXIV (February), 53–58, 104, 106–7. *Free.*

2. 'Free', *Saturday Evening Post,* CXC (16 March), 13–15, 81–89. *Free.*

3. 'The Right to Kill', New York *Call Magazine,* 16 March, pp. 1, 12–13.

4. 'Dreiser Sees World-Hope in Change', Chicago *Examiner* (Fine Arts Supplement), 30 March, p. 1. *HRDD* (as 'Change').

5. 'I Hope the War Will Blow Our Minds Clear of the Miasma of Puritanism', Philadelphia *Press,* 13 April, p. 12.

6. 'The Country Doctor', *Harper's Monthly,* CXXXVII (July), 193–202. *TM.*

7. 'The Old Neighborhood', *Metropolitan,* XLIX (December), 27–30, 46, 48–50. *Chains.*

8. 'Rural America in War-Time', *Scribner's,* LXIV (December), 734–46.

1919

A: None.

B:

1. 'To Make It Safe for Art', *Reedy's Mirror,* XXVIII (21 February), 101–2. A contribution to a symposium.

2. 'The Standard Oil Works at Bayonne', New York *Call Magazine,* 16 March, pp. 3, 5. *Color* (as 'A Certain Oil Refinery').

3. 'The Pushcart Man', New York *Call Magazine,* 30 March, pp. 1, 7. *Color.*

4. 'Love', New York *Tribune,* 18 May, Part VII, pp. 2–3. *Live Stories,* XXV (December 1920), 3–19. *Chains* (as 'Chains').

5. 'The Hand', *Munsey's,* LXVI (May), 679–88. *Chains.*

6. 'Ashtoreth', *Reedy's Mirror,* XXVIII (10 July), 456–57. *HRDD.*

7. 'Life Is to Be Learned from Life', New York *Call Magazine,* 27 July, p. 2.

8. 'Man and Romance', *Reedy's Mirror,* XXVIII (28 August), 585. New York *Call Magazine,* 14 September 1919, p. 9.

9. 'Hey Rub-A-Dub-Dub', *Nation,* CIX (30 August), 278–81. *HRDD.*

10. 'Sanctuary', *Smart Set,* LX (October), 35–52. *Chains.*

11. 'More Democracy or Less?: An Inquiry', New York *Call Maga-*

zine, 30 November, pp. 6–7. *Reconstruction,* I (December 1919), 338. *HRDD.*

1920

A:

1. Introduction to *Caius Gracchus,* by Odin Gregory (pseudonym of J. G. Robin), pp. 3–9: Boni and Liveright.

2. *Hey Rub-A-Dub-Dub:* Boni and Liveright.

3. Statement in *Jurgen and the Censor* (Report of the Emergency Committee Organized to Protest Against the Suppression of James Branch Cabell's *Jurgen*), p. 47: Privately printed.

4. *Notice.* A broadside containing letters by Annie N. Meyer and Dreiser, Dreiser's dated 16 May 1920.[25]

B:

1. 'Mr. Dreiser and the Broadway Magazine', *The Review,* II (5 June), 597. Letter to the Editor. *Notice.*

2. 'Marriage and Divorce', *Forum,* LXIV (July), 26–36. *HRDD.*

1921

A: None.

B:

1. Letter to Frank Harris, dated 3 November 1920, *Pearson's,* XLVI (January), 234. *Letters,* III, 294–95.

2. 'Phantom Gold', *Live Stories,* XXVI (February), 3–23. *Chains.*

3. 'Dreiser Sees No Progress', New York *Globe,* 22 February, p. 6. Letter to the Editor.

4. 'Americans Are Still Interested in Ten Commandments—For the Other Fellow', New York *Call Magazine,* 13 March, p. 7.

5. 'A Word Concerning Birth Control', *Birth Control Review,* V (April), 5–6, 12–13. New York *Call Magazine,* 1 May 1921, p. 4.

6. 'Hollywood Now', *McCall's,* XLVIII (September), 8, 18, 54.

7. 'Why Not Tell Europe About Bertha M. Clay?', St. Paul *Daily News,* 11 September, Section 2, p. 6. Letter dated 25 August 1921 to Thomas A. Boyd. New York *Call,* 24 October 1921, p. 6.

8. 'Hollywood: Its Morals and Manners', *Shadowland,* V (November), 37, 61–63.

---

[25]The first of Dreiser's privately printed broadsides or leaflets. Reproduced in Vrest Orton, *Dreiserana: A Book about his Books* (Chocorua Bibliographies, 1929), p. [ii].

9. 'A Letter About Stephen Crane', *Michigan Daily* (Ann Arbor), 27 November, Magazine Section, p. 1.

10. 'Out of My Newspaper Days', *Bookman*, LIV (November), 208–17. *BAM*.

11. 'Hollywood: Its Morals and Manners', *Shadowland*, V (December), 51, 61.

1922

A:

1. *A Book About Myself:* Boni and Liveright.[26]

B:

1. 'Out of My Newspaper Days', *Bookman*, LIV (January), 427–33. *BAM*.

2. 'Hollywood: Its Morals and Manners', *Shadowland*, V (January), 43, 67.

3. 'Out of My Newspaper Days', *Bookman*, LIV (February), 542–50. *BAM*.

4. 'Hollywood: Its Morals and Manners', *Shadowland*, V (February), 53, 66.

5. 'Out of My Newspaper Days', *Bookman*, LV (March), 12–20. *BAM*.

6. 'Out of My Newspaper Days', *Bookman*, LV (April), 118–25. *BAM*.

7. 'The Scope of Fiction', *New Republic*, XXX (12 April), Part II, pp. 8–9.

1923

A:

1. *The Color of a Great City:* Boni and Liveright.

2. Preface to *Ebony and Ivory*, by Llewellyn Powys, pp. vii–ix: Harcourt, Brace.

3. 'Marriage—For One', in *Marriage*, pp. 238–58: Doubleday, Page. *Chains*.

B:

1. 'A Letter from Vienna to Theo. Dreiser—And His Reply', *Tempest* (Ann Arbor), I (2 April), 3.

2. 'Applied Religion—Applied Art', *Survey*, L (1 May), 175.

3. 'Oddments and Remainders', by Percy Hammond, New York

[26]Reissued in 1931 as *Newspaper Days*.

Tribune, 14 May, p. 8. Contains an undated letter by Dreiser to Sidney Kirkpatrick.

4. 'Dreiser Refuses to Help Films Reach "Higher Level"', New York *Globe and Commercial Advertiser*, 16 May, p. 5. Contains an undated letter by Dreiser to Rex Beach.

5. 'Ida Hauchawout', *Century*, CVI (July), 335–48. *GW*.

6. 'Reina', *Century*, CVI (September), 695–716. *GW*.

7. 'Indiana, Her Soil and Light', *Nation*, CXVII (3 October), 348–50. *These United States: A Symposium, Second Series*, ed. Ernest Gruening, 1924: Boni and Liveright.

8. 'Sombre Annals', New York *Post Literary Review*, 17 November, p. 255. Review of *Undertow* by Henry K. Marks.

1924

A: None.

B:

1. 'Four Poems', *American Mercury*, I (January), 8–10. *Moods* (1926).

2. 'Fulfilment', *Holland's Magazine*, XLIII (February), 7–9, 31. *Chains*.

3. 'Jealousy', *Harper's Bazar*, LIX (August), 84–85, 92, 94, 96. *Chains* (as 'The Shadow').

4. 'The Irish Section Foreman Who Taught Me How to Live', *Hearst's International*, XLVI (August), 20–21, 118–21.

5. 'The Mercy of God', *American Mercury*, II (August), 457–64. *Chains*.

6. 'Five Poems', New York *Post Literary Review*, 20 December, p. 8. *Moods* (1926).

1925

A:

1. *An American Tragedy:* Boni and Liveright.

2. 'The Great Blossom', in *Leonardo, Annual Magazine of the Leonardo da Vinci Art School, 1924/25*, p. 54. *Moods* (1926).

3. 'H. L. Mencken and Myself', in *The Man Mencken*, by Isaac Goldberg, pp. 378–81: Simon and Schuster.

4. Contribution to *Thomas Hardy: Notes on His Life and Work*, p. 15: Harper.

B:

1. 'Glory Be! McGlathery', *Pictorial Review*, XXVI (January), 5–7, 51–52, 54, 71. *Chains* (as 'St. Columba and the River').

2. 'The Most Successful Ball-Player of Them All', *Hearst's International*, XLVII (February), 82–83, 102–6. [Ty Cobb.]

3. 'America and the Artist', *Nation*, CXX (15 April), 423–25.

4. 'Chauncey M. Depew', *Hearst's International-Cosmopolitan*, LXXIX (July), 86–87, 183–85.

5. "Convention', *American Mercury*, VI (December), 398–408. *Chains*.

6. '"The Cliff Dwellers"—A Note on the Painting by George Bellows', *Vanity Fair*, XXV (December), 55, 118.

1926

A:

1. Introduction to *Lilith, A Dramatic Poem*, by George Sterling, pp. vii–xii: Macmillan.

2. *Moods, Cadenced and Declaimed:* Boni and Liveright.

B:

1. 'My Favorite Fiction Character', *Bookman*, LXIII (April), 175.

2. 'This Florida Scene', *Vanity Fair*, XXVI (May), 51, 100, 110.

3. 'Music', *Vanity Fair*, XXVI (June), 68. *Moods* (1926).

4. 'This Florida Scene', *Vanity Fair*, XXVI (June), 43, 98, 100.

5. 'This Florida Scene', *Vanity Fair*, XXVI (July), 63, 94, 96.

6. 'Recent Poems of Life and Labour', *Vanity Fair*, XXVI (August), 61. *Moods* (1926).

7. 'Recent Poems of Love and Sorrow', *Vanity Fair*, XXVII (September), 54. *Moods* (1926).

8. 'The Wages of Sin', *Hearst's International-Cosmopolitan*, LXXXI (October), 42–45, 175–81. *Chains* (as 'Typhoon').

9. 'Recent Poems of Youth and Age', *Vanity Fair*, XXVII (October), 70. *Moods* (1926).

10. 'Paris—1926', *Vanity Fair*, XXVII (December), 64, 136, 147–50.

1927

A:

1. *Chains:* Boni and Liveright.

2. *The Financier:* Boni and Liveright. A revision of the 1912 edition.

3. *The Hand of the Potter:* Boni and Liveright. A revision of the 1918 edition.

4. Foreword to *Poorhouse Sweeney: Life in a County Poorhouse*, by Ed Sweeney, pp. v–xi: Boni and Liveright.

5. Introduction to Volume I of the *Sandgate Edition of H. G. Wells,* pp. v–xi: Duffield.

6. Introduction to *The Songs of Paul Dresser,* pp. v–x: Boni and Liveright.[27]

B:

1. 'The Victim Speaks', *Vanity Fair,* XXVII (February), 40. *Moods* (1928).

2. 'Is America's Restlessness a Symbol of Hidden Power?', New York *American,* 10 April, Section E, p. 3.[28]

3. 'Victory', *Jewish Forward,* 24 April (English Section), pp. 12–13, 23. *Chains.*

4. 'Can a Criminal Come Back to Society? No', *Smoker's Companion,* I (May), 19, 82.

5. 'Are We in America Leading the Way to a Golden Age in the World?', New York *American,* 22 May, Section E, p. 3.

6. 'Fools of Success', New York *American,* 31 July, Section E, p. 4.

7. 'Fools for Love', New York *American,* 28 August, Section E, p. 4.

8. 'Portrait of a Woman', *Bookman,* LXVI (September), 2–14. *GW* (as 'Ernestine').

9. 'The Romance of Power', *Vanity Fair,* XXIX (September), 49, 94, 96, 98.

1928

A:

1. Foreword to *A Bibliography of the Writings of Theodore Dreiser,* by Edward D. McDonald, pp. 11–12: Centaur Book Shop (Philadelphia).

2. Introduction to Volume VIII (*McTeague*) in the *Collected Edition of Frank Norris,* pp. vii–xi: Doubleday, Doran (Garden City, N.Y.).

3. Introduction to *The Crime of Dr. Garine,* by Boris Sokoloff, pp. vii–xii: Covici, Friede.

4. *Dreiser Looks at Russia:* Liveright.

5. *Moods, Cadenced and Declaimed:* Boni and Liveright.[29]

[27]Contains as well 'On the Banks of the Wabash', for which Dreiser wrote a preliminary version of the first verse and the chorus.

[28]The first of six articles syndicated in various newspapers throughout the country under differing titles but on the same days from 10 April 1927 to 11 March 1928.

[29]Adds 26 poems to the 1926 edition.

6. Introduction to *The Road to Buenos Ayres*, by Albert Londres, pp. v–xviii: Constable (London).

B:

1. 'Dreiser Analyzes the Rebellion of Women', New York *American*, 5 February, Section E, p. 3.

2. 'Theodore Dreiser Finds Both Hope and Failure in Russian Soviet Drama', Chicago *Daily News*, 6 February, pp. 1–2.[30]

3. 'Dreiser on Matrimonial Hoboes', New York *American*, 11 March, Section E. p. 4.

4. 'Mr. Dreiser Excepts', New York *Times*, 15 March, p. 24. Letter to the Editor.

5. 'Soviet Plan to Spread to U.S., Dreiser Thinks', New York *World*, 18 March, pp. 1, 8.[31]

6. 'Dreiser Looks at Russia', New York *World*, 19 March, p. 13.

7. 'Dreiser Looks at Russia', New York *World*, 20 March, p. 15.

8. 'Dreiser Looks at Russia', New York *World*, 21 March, p. 15.

9. 'Dreiser Looks at Russia', New York *World*, 22 March, p. 15.

10. 'Dreiser Looks at Russia', New York *World*, 23 March, p. 15.

11. 'Dreiser Looks at Russia', New York *World*, 24 March, p. 17.

12. 'Dreiser Looks at Russia', New York *World*, 25 March, p. 6.

13. 'Dreiser Looks at Russia', New York *World*, 26 March, p. 15.

14. 'Dreiser Looks at Russia', New York *World*, 27 March, p. 15.

15. 'Dreiser Looks at Russia', New York *World*, 28 March, p. 17.

16. 'Rella', *Hearst's International-Cosmopolitan*, LXXXIV (April), 36–39, 199–204. *GW*.

17. 'Russian Vignettes', *Saturday Evening Post*, CC (28 April), 18–19, 80–82. *Dreiser Looks at Russia*.

18. 'Olive Brand', *Hearst's International-Cosmopolitan*, LXXXIV (May), 47–49, 130–34. *GW*.

19. 'The Rights of a Columnist', *Nation*, CXXVI (30 May), 608.

20. 'Russia, The Great Experiment', *Vanity Fair*, XXX (June), 47–48, 102.

21. 'Regina C——', *Hearst's International-Cosmopolitan*, LXXXIV (June), 56–58, 144–49. *GW*.

22. 'American Tragedies', New York *Herald-Tribune Books*, 10

---

[30] Datelined Odessa, 13 January.

[31] The first of Dreiser's articles on Russia syndicated by the North American Newspaper Alliance. Although these articles often contain material similar to that in *Dreiser Looks at Russia*, they are not portions of the book.

June, pp. 1–2. Review of *The New Criminology* by Max Schlapp and Edward H. Smith.

23. 'Woods Hole and the Marine Biological Laboratory', *Collecting Net*, III (21 July), 1–2.

24. 'Best Motion Picture Interview Ever Written', *Photoplay*, XXXIV (August), 32–35, 124–31. [Mack Sennett.]

25. 'Statement of Belief', *Bookman*, LXVIII (September), 25.

26. 'Citizens of Moscow', *Vanity Fair*, XXXI (October), 55–56, 102, 104.

27. 'Theodore Dreiser on the Elections', *New Masses*, IV (November), 17.

28. 'My City', New York *Herald-Tribune*, 23 December, Section III, p. 1. *My City*.

1929

A:

1. *The Aspirant:* Random House. A poem published as a Random House Poetry Quarto.

2. *The Carnegie Works at Pittsburg:* Privately printed (Chelsea, N.Y.).

3. Foreword to *Catalogue of an Exhibition of Paintings by Jerome Blum . . . Jan. 28–Feb. 9*, pp. [2–3].

4. *Epitaph: A Poem:* Heron Press. *Moods* (1935).

5. *A Gallery of Women:* Liveright.

6. *My City:* Liveright.

B:

1. 'Dreiser on Hollywood', *New Masses*, IV (January), 17–18.

2. 'This Madness—An Honest Novel About Love', *Hearst's International-Cosmopolitan*, LXXXVI (February), 22–27, 192–203. 'Aglaia'.[32]

3. 'Comments on Film Arts Guild', *West 8th St. Film Guild Cinema*, 1 February, pp. 6, 9.

4. 'The Muffled Oar', *Nation*, CXXVIII (27 February), 258. *Moods* (1935).

5. 'Another American Tragedy', *Forum*, LXXXI (March), xlviii–li. Letter to the Editor.

6. 'This Madness . . .', *Hearst's International-Cosmopolitan*, LXXXVI (March), 44–47, 160–66. 'Aglaia'.

7. 'This Madness . . .', *Hearst's International-Cosmopolitan*, LXXXVI (April), 81–85, 117–20. 'Elizabeth'.

---

[32] The first in a series of portraits similar to those in *GW*.

8. 'Portrait of an Artist', *Vanity Fair,* XXXII (April), 70, 108, 110. [Jerome Blum.]

9. 'This Madness . . . ', *Hearst's International-Cosmopolitan,* LXXXVI (May), 80–83, 146–54. 'Elizabeth'.

10. 'The Meddlesome Decade', *Theatre Guild Magazine,* VI (May), 11–13, 61–62.

11. 'This Madness . . . ', *Hearst's International-Cosmopolitan,* LXXXVI (June), 83–87, 156–68. 'Sidonie'.

12. 'Theodore Dreiser Says', *Film Guild Cinema . . . Fifteenth Program, June 29–July 5,* p. 3.

13. 'This Madness . . . ', *Hearst's International-Cosmopolitan,* LXXXVII (July), 86–87, 179–86. 'Sidonie'.

14. 'Deutschland von "Drüben" Gesehen', *Deutsche Allgemeine Zeitung* (August) (America-Germany Supplement), n.p.

15. 'Dreiser Discusses Dewey Plan', New York *Telegram,* 28 September, p. 4. Letter to the Editor.

16. 'Anatole France: A Post-Mortem Five Years Later', *Tambour* (Paris), No. 5 (November), 25–26.

17. 'What I Believe', *Forum,* LXXXII (November), 279–81, 317–20. *Living Philosophies,* 1931 : Simon and Schuster.

18. 'Fine Furniture', *Household Magazine,* XXIX (December), 5, 29–32. *Fine Furniture.*

1930

A:

1. *Fine Furniture:* Random House. A short story published as a Random House Prose Quarto.

2. *John Reed Club Answer.* A broadside, datelined Portland, Oregon, 10 June 1930.

3. 'Modern Marriage Is a Farce', *Divorce as I See It,* pp. 43–50: Noel Douglas (London).

4. Foreword to *The Symbolic Drawings of Hubert Davies for "An American Tragedy",* pp. vii–x: Liveright.

B:

1. 'Divorce as I See It', London *Daily Express,* 23 January, p. 8. *Divorce as I See It.*

2. 'Group Here Scores Anti-Soviet Drive', New York *Times,* 16 March, p. 7. Contains a Dreiser letter.

3. 'Whom God Hath Joined Together', *Plain Talk,* VI (April), 401–4.

4. 'The First Reader', New York *World,* 9 May, p. 11. Contains a Dreiser telegram.

5. 'The New Humanism', *Thinker,* II (July), 8–12.

6. 'Mooney and America', *Hesperian,* I (Winter), [2–4].

1931

A:

1. *Dawn:* Liveright.

2. *How the Great Corporations Rule the United States.* Haldeman-Julius Little Blue Book No. 1590 (Girard, Kansas), pp. 5–12.

3. *Tragic America:* Liveright.

B:

1. 'The Early Adventures of Sister Carrie', *Colophon,* Part 5 (January), pp. 1–4. Preface, *Sister Carrie,* 1931: Modern Library Edition.

2. 'Prosperity for Only One Percent of the People', *Daily Worker,* 28 January, p. 1.

3. 'Intellectual Unemployment', *New Freeman,* II (11 March), 616–17. Letter to the Editor.

4. 'The American Press and Political Prisoners', *Daily Worker,* 9 May, p. 6.

5. 'Where Is Labor's Share?', New York *Times,* 13 May, p. 24. Letter to the Editor.

6. 'Silencing of Press by Gag Laws Flayed by Dreiser', *Progressive* (Madison), 23 May, p. 1.

7. 'Dreiser on Scottsboro', *Labor Defender,* VI (June), 108.

8. 'Tempted, I Stole', *Hearst's International-Cosmopolitan,* XC (June), 48–49, 196. *Dawn.*

9. 'Why I Believe the Daily Worker Should Live', *Daily Worker,* 24 June, p. 4.

10. 'Miners in Strike Zones Live Like Slaves, Theodore Dreiser Writes After a Visit', New York *World-Telegram,* 26 June, pp. 1, 10.

11. 'Remarks', *Psychoanalytic Review,* XVIII (July), 250.

12. 'Dreiser Warns Films on "American Tragedy"', New York *Times,* 8 July, p. 20. Contains a Dreiser letter.

13. 'Humanitarianism in the Scottsboro Case', *Contempo,* I (mid-July), 1.

14. 'Theodore Dreiser Denounces Campaign Against Communists', *Progressive* (Madison), 5 September, pp. 1–2.

15. 'America and Her Communists', *Time and Tide,* XII (31 October), 1247–48.

16. 'Take a Look at Our Railroads', *Liberty*, VIII (7 November), 24–27.

17. '"Law" in Capitalists' Hands in Labor War, Says Dreiser', Knoxville *News-Sentinel*, 9 November, p. 11.

18. 'I Go to Harlan', *Labor Defender*, VII (December), 233.

19. 'Dreiser Charges Tyranny in Musicians' Union', New York *World-Telegram*, 15 December, p. 23.

1932

A:

1. Introduction to *Harlan Miners Speak*, pp. 3–16: Harcourt, Brace.[33]

B:

1. 'A Statement by Theodore Dreiser', *Experimental Cinema*, No. 4 (n.d.), p. [v].

2. 'Individualism and the Jungle', *New Masses*, VII (January), 1–2. *Crawford's Weekly*, 2 January, p. 6. Introduction to *Harlan Miners Speak*.

3. 'Theodore Dreiser Picks the Six Worst Pictures of the Year', *New Movie Magazine*, V (January), 25–27, 98.

4. 'Mr. Dreiser Replies', New York *Herald-Tribune Books*, 14 February, p. 18. Letter to the Editor.

5. 'A Symposium of American Writers and Scholars on Goethe', *Monatshefte für Deutschen Unterricht*, XXIV (March–April), 78–79.

6. 'The Seventh Commandment', *Liberty*, IX (2 April), 7–11.

7. 'The Seventh Commandment', *Liberty*, IX (9 April), 34–38.

8. 'A New Group Would Like to Know', New York *Times*, 10 April, p. 3. Contains a Dreiser letter.

9. 'At Boulder Dam', New York *Times*, 11 April, p. 14. Letter to the Editor.

10. 'War and America', *International Literature*, Nos. 2–3 (n.d.), pp. 110–11.

11. 'The Real Sins of Hollywood', *Liberty*, IX (11 June), 6–11.

12. 'America—And War', *Labor Defender*, VIII (August), 143, 157.

13. 'America—And War', *Labor Defender*, VIII (September), 169, 175.

14. 'The Days of Surfeit', *American Spectator*, I (November), 2–3.

15. 'The Great American Novel', *American Spectator*, I (December), 1–2. *The American Spectator Yearbook*, ed. George Jean Nathan, 1934.

[33]Dreiser also appears in much of the testimony published in the book.

1933

A:

1. Introduction to *Forced Labor in the United States*, by Walter Wilson, pp. 7–8: International Publishers.

2. Introduction to *Tom Mooney, Story in Pictures*, by Anton Refregier, p. [2]: International Labor Defense.

3. *Tom Mooney*. A five-page pamphlet, part of the Souvenir Program of the Free Tom Mooney Cabaret Ball, San Francisco, 26 April 1933.

B:

1. 'Cattails – November', *American Spectator*, I (January), 3. *Moods* (1935).

2. *International Literature*, No. 1 (January), 126. Contains a Dreiser letter.

3. 'Appearance and Reality', *American Spectator*, I (February), 4. *American Spectator Yearbook*, ed. George Jean Nathan, 1934.

4. 'A Writer Looks at the Railroads', *American Spectator*, I (March), 4.

5. 'A Letter to the Outlander', *Outlander*, I (Spring), 50.

6. 'The Child and the School', *American Spectator*, I (April), 2.

7. 'Townsend', *American Spectator*, I (June), 2. Story.

8. 'A Tribute', *Greenwich Villager*, I (June), 1. [Hubert Davis.]

9. 'The Martyr', *American Spectator*, I (July), 4. *Moods* (1935).

10. 'Flies and Locusts', New York *Daily Mirror*, 1 August, pp. 19, 31. *Common Sense*, II (December 1933), 20–22 (as 'The Profit-Makers Are Thieves').

11. 'Editorial Conference', *American Spectator*, I (September), 1.[34]

12. *International Literature*, No. 4 (October), 123. Contains a Dreiser letter.

13. 'Query', *American Spectator*, II (November), 2.

14. 'Challenge to the Creative Man', *Common Sense*, II (November), 6–8. *Artists' and Writers' Chapbook*, 15 December 1933, pp. 9–11, 45–46.

15. 'Solution', *Woman's Home Companion*, LX (November), 18–20, 132–35. Story.

16. 'Birth Control', *American Spectator*, II (December), 1.

17. 'Winterton', *American Spectator*, II (December), 3–4. Sketch.

18. 'Tabloid Tragedy', *Hearst's International-Cosmopolitan*, XCV (December), 22–25, 115–16, 119–21. Story.

---

[34]With George Jean Nathan, James Branch Cabell, Eugene O'Neill and Ernest Boyd.

The AMERICAN SPECTATOR

A LITERARY NEWSPAPER

EDITED BY

GEORGE JEAN NATHAN · ERNEST BOYD · THEODORE DREISER · JAMES BRANCH CABELL · EUGENE O'NEILL

PUBLISHED BY

THE AMERICAN SPECTATOR, INC.
RICHARD R. SMITH, PRESIDENT
12 EAST 41st STREET, NEW YORK CITY

(Iroki, RFD #3)
(Mt.Kisco,N.Y.)
Oct. 4, 1932.

Diego Rivera,
Detroit Institute of Art,
Detroit, Michigan.

Dear *Rivera*

This slip, and the enclosed publisher's announcement,
will explain a little something about a new monthly
literary newspaper, the editorial welfare of which
has been taken over by George Jean Nathan, Ernest Boyd,
James Branch Cabell, Eugene O'Neill and myself.

While the publisher's slip emphasizes, as usual, what
is important to him -- names, the editors are eager
for the type of critical reaction which ignores the
conventionalist, the moralist, the religionist, and
favors the unaccepted and the misunderstood as opposed
to the accepted and the understood.

At first, The Spectator will be a monthly, and the
rate of payment for material one cent a word. No
article, unless there is some very exceptional reason,
can be more than 1500 words, nor less than 500, the
preferred length being 1000. No single editor can
accept anything. The editors do so. Any of the five
editors, however, can do what I am doing -- indicating to
the preferred mind or temperament his desire for some
reaction of the preferred one to his or her favorite
mental preoccupation. If such a document reaches me
and convinces me, depend on it I will do my best
to convince the other four, and so make this invitation
unanimous.

*I recall our chief visit in 1928 with
so much genuine pleasure*

Theodore Dreiser

Cable: Richsmith, New York

PLATE 3

1934

A:

   1. Preface to *Mr. President: Free the Scottsboro Boys!*, pp. 3–4: International Labor Defense.

B:

   1. 'Editorial Note', *American Spectator*, II (February), 1.

   2. 'Three Poems', *American Spectator*, II (February), 4. *Moods* (1935).

   3. 'The Myth of Individuality', *American Mercury*, XXXI (March), 337–42.

   4. 'Keep Moving or Starve', *Today*, I (March 3), 6–7, 22–23.

   5. ' "They Shall Not Die" Indicts North as Well as the South', New York *Post*, 24 March, p. 8.

   6. 'Rally Round the Flag', *Common Sense*, III (May), 23.

   7. 'Mathewson', *Esquire*, I (May), 20–21, 125. Sketch.

   8. 'Mathewson', *Esquire*, I (June), 24–25, 114.

   9. 'Temperaments, Artistic and Otherwise', *Golden Book*, XIX (June), 650–54.

   10. 'Why Capitalists Praise Democracy', *Common Sense*, III (July), 19–20.

   11. 'Where We Stand', *International Literature*, No. 3 (July), 80–82.

   12. 'What Has the Great War Taught Me?', *New Masses*, XII (7 August), 15.

   13. 'Mr. Dreiser Denies Report', New York *Times*, 15 August, p. 16. Letter to the Editor.

   14. 'An Address to Caliban', *Esquire*, II (September), 20–21, 158D. *1935 Essay Annual*, ed. Erich A. Walter, 1935.

   15. 'Will Fascism Come to America?', *Modern Monthly*, VIII (September), 459–61.

   16. 'A Start in Life', *Scribner's*, XCVI (October), 211–17.

   17. 'Theodore Dreiser Describes "American Tragedy"', New York *Post*, 2 October, pp. 1, 6.[35]

   18. 'Theodore Dreiser Describes "American Tragedy"', New York *Post*, 3 October, p. 3.

   19. 'Theodore Dreiser Describes "American Tragedy"', New York *Post*, 4 October, p. 23.

   20. 'Theodore Dreiser Describes "American Tragedy" ', New York *Post*, 5 October, p. 12.

[35]The first in a series of newspaper articles by Dreiser on a contemporary murder trial.

21. 'Theodore Dreiser Describes "American Tragedy"', New York *Post*, 6 October, p. 3.

22. 'You, the Phantom', *Esquire*, II (November), 25–26. *The Bedside Esquire*, ed. Arnold Gingrich, 1940.

23. 'The Epic Sinclair', *Esquire*, II (December), 32–33, 178B–79. [Upton Sinclair.]

1935

A:

1. Introduction to *Magnificent Hadrian*, by Sulamith Ish-Kishor, pp. 1–5: Minton, Balch.

2. *Moods: Philosophical and Emotional (Cadenced and Declaimed)*: Simon and Schuster.[36]

3. 'Theodore Dreiser's American Tragedy Cocktail', *So Red the Nose*, ed. Sterling North and Carl Kroch, p. 30: Farrar and Rinehart.

4. Introduction to *Waiting for Nothing*, by Tom Kromer, pp. xi–xix: Constable (London).

B:

1. Kismet', *Esquire*, III (January), 29, 175–76.

2. 'I Find the Real American Tragedy', *Mystery Magazine*, XI (February), 9–11, 88–90.

3. 'Five Moods in a Minor Key', *Esquire*, II (March), 25. *Moods* (1935).

4. 'I Find the Real American Tragedy', *Mystery Magazine*, XI (March), 22–23, 77–79.

5. 'I Find the Real American Tragedy', *Mystery Magazine*, XI (April), 24–26, 90–92.

6. 'Is Dreiser Anti-Semitic?', by Hutchins Hapgood, *Nation*, CXL (17 April), 436–38. Contains Dreiser letters of 10 October and 28 December 1933. *Letters*, II, 649–53, 658–64.

7. 'Dreiser Denies He Is Anti-Semitic', *New Masses*, XV (30 April), 10–11. Contains a Dreiser letter.

8. 'I Find the Real American Tragedy', *Mystery Magazine*, XI (May), 22–24, 83–86.

9. 'I Find the Real American Tragedy', *Mystery Magazine*, XI (June), 20–21, 68–73.

10. 'Crime Analyzed by Dreiser', Los Angeles *Examiner*, 23 July, pp. 1–2.

11. 'Overland Journey', *Esquire*, IV (September), 24, 97.

[36]Revised and enlarged version of the 1928 edition.

12. 'Mark Twain: Three Contacts', *Esquire*, IV (October), 22, 162, 162A, 162B.

13. 'Mark the Double Twain', *English Journal*, XXIV (October), 615–27.

1936

A:

1. Introduction to *The Way of All Flesh*, by Samuel Butler, pp. v–xxx: Limited Edition Club.

B:

1. 'Four Cases of Clyde Griffiths', New York *Times*, 8 March, Section 9, pp. 1–2.

2. 'Theodore Dreiser Defends His Brother's Memory', New York *Post*, 27 March, p. 14. Letter to the Editor.

3. 'What Is Americanism?', *Partisan Review and Anvil*, III (April), 3–4.

4. 'An American Tragedy', *National Epic*, I (June), 9.

5. 'Tribute to Gorky', *Soviet Russia Today*, V (July), 7.

6. 'Book Marks', by Carolyn Marx, New York *World-Telegram*, 25 September, p. 23. Contains a letter by Dreiser to Mike Gold, 7 August 1928. *Letters*, II, 472.

7. 'Like the Good Deed', *New Masses*, XXI (15 December), 9.

1937

A:

1. Foreword to *Paintings and Drawings by Biala . . . Feb. 23–March 13, Gallery of Georgette Passedoit*, p. 2.

2. 'Theodore Dreiser Writes', in *Hubert Davis: Lithographs*, an exhibition 13–27 March, pp. [2–3].

B:

1. 'Is Leon Trotsky Guilty?', *Modern Monthly*, X (March), 5.

2. 'Legalizing Games of Chance', New York *Times*, 4 May, p. 24. Letter to the Editor.

3. 'I Am Grateful to Soviet Russia', *Soviet Russia Today*, VI (November), 11. *International Literature*, No. 12 (December), 107–8.

4. 'Foreword', *Direction*, I (December), 2.

5. 'If Man Is Free, So Is All Matter', *Forum*, XCVIII (December), 301–4.

1938

A:

1. *Conférence Extraordinaire Tenue à Paris le 25 Juillet 1938* (Collec-

tion de L'Association Internale des Éscrivains pour la Defense de la Culture), pp. 13–19: Denoel (Paris). A speech by Dreiser, in French.

2. Foreword to *Hubert Davis: Lithographs-Drawings*, an exhibition 16 May–4 June, p. [2].

3. Introduction to *Of Human Bondage*, by Somerset Maugham, pp. iii–xiv: Limited Edition Club.

4. *Writers Take Sides: Letters About the War in Spain*, pp. 20–21: League of American Writers.

B:

1. 'A Conversation', *Direction*, I (January), 2–4, 28. Between Dreiser and John Dos Passos.

2. 'Lessons I Learned from an Old Man', *Your Life*, II (January), 6–10.

3. 'Is College Worth While? No!', *Your Life*, II (March), 8–12.

4. 'The Tithe of the Lord', *Esquire*, X (July), 36–37, 150, 155–58. Story. *The Armchair Esquire*, ed. Arnold Gingrich, 1958.

5. 'Good and Evil', *North American Review*, CCXLVI (Autumn), 67–86.

6. 'Dreiser Gives Vivid Picture of Conditions in Spain', Philadelphia *Bulletin*, 10 September, p. 7.

7. 'Dreiser Recounts Loyalist Tension', New York *Times*, 11 September, p. 30.

8. 'Barcelona's Modernity Shines Through Battle Damage', Philadelphia *Bulletin*, 12 September, p. 9.

9. 'Equity Between Nations', *Direction*, I (September–October), 5–6, 11.

10. 'Barcelona in August', *Direction*, I (November–December), 4.

1939

A:

1. *The Dawn Is in the East.* Undated broadside.

2. *I Believe: The Personal Philosophies of Certain Eminent Men and Women of Our Time*, ed. Clifton Fadiman, pp. 355–62: Simon and Schuster.

3. 'Presenting Thoreau', *The Living Thoughts of Thoreau*, pp. 1–32: Longmans, Green.

4. *We Hold These Truths . . .* , pp. 45–47: League of American Writers. Statements on anti-Semitism by 54 American writers.

B:

1. 'Answer to French Labor', *Direction*, II (January–February), 19.

2. 'Message to Congress', *Direction*, II (May–June), 2.

3. 'Life at Sixty-Seven', *Rotarian*, LV (August), 8–10.

4. 'Women Are the Realists', *You*, II (Fall), 5, 48–49.

5. 'The Dawn Is in the East', *International Literature*, No. 11 (November), pp. 109–11. *Common Sense*, VIII (December), 6–7. *The Dawn Is in the East.*

6. 'Daily News Ears Batted Down by Dreiser', Los Angeles *Daily News*, 27 November, p. 6.

1940

A:

1. *Concerning Dives and Lazarus.* Broadside, in reply to a telegram by Jessica Smith dated 15 March.

2. *Editor and Publisher.* Broadside, containing a Dreiser letter dated 18 September in reply to a letter from the editor of *Editor and Publisher.*

3. *A Request and an Answer.* Broadside, containing a letter dated 10 July in reply to a letter from Boys Brotherhood Republic.

4. *Shall It Be War for America?*, pp. [1–2]. A four-page pamphlet. Contains a speech by Dreiser on 29 October 1940, in support of Earl Browder for President.

5. *U.S. Must Not Be Bled for Imperial Britain.* Broadside, based on an address given over CBS on 9 November 1940.

6. *War.* Broadside, undated.

B:

1. 'Theodore Dreiser Snubs Hoover', *People's World*, 12 January, pp. 1, 6. Contains a Dreiser letter to Fred Smith, dated 9 January 1940.

2. 'The Soviet-Finnish Treaty and World Peace', *Soviet Russia Today*, VIII (April), 8–9.

3. 'Lenin', *International Literature*, Nos. 4–5 (April–May), p. 82. *People's World*, 20 April, p. 5 (as 'Tribute to Lenin').

4. 'Theodore Dreiser Condemns War', *People's World*, 6 April, p. 7. *War.*

5. 'Upton Sinclair', *Clipper*, I (September), 3–4.

6. 'Theodore Dreiser and the Free Press', *People's World*, 2 October, p. 5. *Editor and Publisher.*

7. 'The Story of Harry Bridges', *Friday*, I (4 October), 1–8, 28.

8. 'The Story of Harry Bridges', *Friday*, I (11 October), 14–17.

9. 'The Meaning of the USSR in the World Today', *Soviet Russia Today*, IX (November), 23, 47. *Current History*, LII (10 December), 28–30.

10. 'U.S. Must Not Be Bled for Imperial Britain', *People's World*,

12 November, p. 6. *U.S. Must Not Be Bled for Imperial Britain.*

11. 'What Is Democracy?', *Clipper*, I (December), 3–7. *America Is Worth Saving.*

1941

A:

1. *America Is Worth Saving:* Modern Age.

2. *Concerning Our Helping England Again.* Undated four-page pamphlet.

3. Introduction to *More Dangerous Thoughts*, by Mike Quin, pp. 7–8: People's World (San Francisco).

4. *Mrs. Franklin Delano Roosevelt.* Broadside dated 25 April 1941.

5. 'Russia's Cause Is True Democracy's Cause', in *In Defense of Civilization Against Fascist Barbarism*, p. 89: USSR Society for Cultural Relations with Foreign Countries (Moscow).

6. *To the Writers' League of America.* Four-page pamphlet, dated 13 May 1941.

B:

1. 'This Is Churchill's "Democracy"', *New Masses*, XXXVIII (18 February), 35–36. *Concerning Our Helping England Again.*

2. 'Sherwood Anderson', *Clipper*, II (May), 5. *Story*, XIX (September–October), 4.

3. 'Nothing So Important to American People Now as Aiding USSR — Dreiser', *People's World*, 2 July, p. 1. Contains a Dreiser telegram.

4. 'Freedom of the Press', *In Fact*, III (29 September), p. 1.

5. 'Writers Declare: "We Have a War to Win"', *Daily Worker*, 21 December, Section 2, p. 6.

1942

A:

1. *Editors.* Four-page pamphlet, dated 6 October 1942, on Dreiser's Toronto difficulties.

B: None.

1943

A:

1. Preface to *The Truth About 'Reader's Digest'*, by Sender Garlin: Forum Publishers. *Letters*, III, 986–87.[37]

[37]The fourth printing of this pamphlet uses Dreiser's letter to Martha Millet, dated 28 April 1943, as a preface.

B:

    1. 'Myself and the Movies', *Esquire*, XX (July), 50, 159.

1944

A: None.

B:

    1. 'The Russian Advance', *Soviet Russia Today*, XIII (July), 9.

    2. 'Black Sheep Number One: Johnny', *Esquire*, XXII (October), 39, 156–60.[38]

    3. *The Magazine of Sigma Chi*, LXIII (October–November), 39–40. [George Ade.]

    4. 'Black Sheep Number Two: Otie', *Esquire*, XXII (November), 65.

1945

A: None.

B:

    1. 'Black Sheep Number Five: Clarence', *Esquire*, XXIII (February), 49, 129–30.

    2. 'Black Sheep Number Six: Harrison Barr', *Esquire*, XXIII (March), 49, 131.

    3. 'What To Do', *Free World*, IX (March), 10. Poem.

    4. *Daily Worker*, 30 July, p. 5. 'Dreiser and the Communists', *Masses and Mainstream*, VIII (December 1955), 23–25. A Dreiser letter to William Z. Foster, dated 20 July 1945.

    5. 'Interdependence', *Free World*, IX (September), 69–70.

Posthumous[39]

A:

    1. *The Bulwark:* Doubleday, 1946.

    2. *The Stoic:* Doubleday, 1947.

B:

    1. 'Harlot Press', *In Fact*, XII (14 January 1946), 1.

    2. 'Women Can Take It', New York *Journal-American* (Saturday Home Magazine), 13 April 1946, p. 10.

[38]The first of a series of six articles in *Esquire*. Although all the sketches are signed by Dreiser, it is clear from correspondence in the Dreiser Collection that at least two of the sketches were written by friends: 'Number Three' by Sylvia Bradshaw and 'Number Four' by Louise Campbell.

[39]I omit material from Dreiser's unpublished letters and manuscripts which has appeared in scholarly articles and books.

3. 'Women Can Take It', New York *Journal-American* (Saturday Home Magazine), 20 April 1946, p. 10.

4. 'Women Can Take It', New York *Journal-American* (Saturday Home Magazine), 27 April 1946, p. 17.

5. 'What My Mother Meant To Me', *True Confessions*, XLVI (May 1946), 25, 54, 56.

6. 'Dreiser Discusses *Sister Carrie*', *Masses and Mainstream*, VIII (December 1955), 20–22. Contains two letters by Dreiser.

7. 'Background for "An American Tragedy"', *Esquire*, L (October 1958), 155–57.

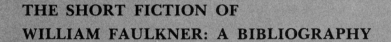

THE SHORT FICTION OF
WILLIAM FAULKNER: A BIBLIOGRAPHY

JAMES B. MERIWETHER

WILLIAM FAULKNER WAS PRIMARILY A NOVELIST, AND MOST STUDIES OF his work have, then, quite properly concentrated upon his achievement in that field. But Faulkner was also one of the great masters of the short story, and although his accomplishment in this field has been widely recognized, it has been little studied. A few of the most-taught, most-anthologized stories have received considerable, if often superficial, attention. But on the whole it seems fair to say that the most neglected area in Faulkner studies is his short fiction. There are other gaps: the poetry has received very little attention, and the late novels have not yet been examined with the care that has been accorded those of the first half of Faulkner's career. But at present the area of greatest challenge, and potentially of greatest reward, to the Faulkner critic is the fiction he wrote of less than full-scale novel size. Many of his stories are very fine, and a few are small-scale masterpieces; but even his lesser works in this form throw light upon Faulkner's development as an artist, and all of them deserve careful study in order to understand their relationship to each other and to the novels.

This bibliography, then, is offered as an aid to the further study of Faulkner's short fiction. It lists all textually significant forms known to me of all his works of fiction shorter than full-length novels. Locations are given for manuscript, typescript, and proof versions. In order to establish their relationships, all published versions listed here have been collated; it was not always possible to collate the manuscripts and typescripts completely, but they were spot-collated in sufficient detail to establish their probable order of composition. The annotations provide discussion, where it seems necessary, of problems of dates, titles, and relationships.

The bibliography is divided into three major sections, with an introduction and a title index. Section I, Stories, is further subdivided into A. Published, B. Unpublished, and C. Lost Stories. Section II lists Excerpts from Novels. Section III, The Collections, provides essential information concerning Faulkner's own collections of stories. A rationale for these divisions and subdivisions and definitions of my terms are provided in the Introduction.

For permission to examine manuscript and typescript material and for assistance in its use, I am grateful to the staffs of the Alderman Library of the University of Virginia, the Princeton University Library, the Humanities Research Center of the University of Texas, and the Beinecke Library of Yale University. I am particularly indebted to the late Harold Ober, Faulkner's literary agent, who first permitted me to examine the records of his agency, and to Ivan von Auw, who has continued to provide me with information from the records of Harold Ober Associates. Data from the Random House records were provided by two of Faulkner's editors, Albert Erskine and the late Saxe Commins.

Much of the research for this bibliography was done while I held a Guggenheim Fellowship, and I wish to acknowledge my debt to the John Simon Guggenheim Memorial Foundation, and to its president, Dr. Gordon N. Ray.

I am grateful to Mrs. Jill Faulkner Summers for permission to use and quote from unpublished material.

INTRODUCTION

Faulkner's fiction, in every form, has always resisted clear-cut definitions. Yet it is more than the exercise of an irrelevant pedantry to attempt to distinguish between two categories of his short fiction: stories, and excerpts from novels. Faulkner wrote a large number of short stories which are clearly just that. He also wrote a number of stories which he later rewrote and incorporated into novels; just as clearly, they continue to belong, in their original form, in any list of Faulkner's short stories. On the other hand, he wrote several novels from which he extracted episodes which he could sell to magazines before they appeared in their parent novels. To determine the difference between these two categories is not only useful, it may be essential to the understanding both of Faulkner's novels and of his stories.

The final episode of *The Town*, for example, which was separately published, under the title 'The Waifs', in a magazine, a few days before the publication of the novel, clearly belongs in the category of an excerpt from a novel, not a short story. The text was taken from the galley proofs of the novel without modification by the author; the title was supplied by an editor; it was clearly identified in the magazine as an excerpt from the forthcoming book. To include it in a list of Faulkner's short stories, on the grounds that it was separately published, and is sufficiently self-contained to stand alone as an independent work of fiction, is not an argument that can be accepted unless one is also prepared to include as short stories all those other episodes in Faulkner's novels—and there must be hundreds—which could, even now, be editorially excerpted and critically defended.

The basic distinction made in this bibliography, then, is one based on identity. 'The Waifs' is not included in the primary list of Faulkner's stories because it is identical to the ending of *The Town*. On the other hand, Faulkner several times took an excerpt from a completed novel and reworked it sufficiently to give it a clear and demonstrable identity of its own. 'The Bear' is an example of such a story; although to a considerable extent it follows very closely the text of the completed chapter of *Go Down, Moses* from which Faulkner took it, there was enough revision to provide ample justification for calling it a separate work.

Admittedly the 'identity' test is not infallible; the less such an excerpt as 'The Bear' has been revised for separate publication, the more subjective the test becomes. Just how much revision is enough? But it seems the most satisfactory way of making a distinction which clearly should be made, and in most cases can be made.

Although a few of the novel-excerpts ('The Bear', *Notes on a Horsethief*, and 'Hell Creek Crossing' are the most obvious examples) caused problems, I tried to be neither inflexible nor ungenerous in compiling the list of Faulkner's identifiable stories in Section I. If I erred, it was in the direction of inclusiveness, and a purist might object to the inclusion of such an anomaly as 'Hell Creek Crossing', for which Faulkner merely wrote two and one-half pages of summary and introduction to go with twenty pages from the finished novel. But those two and one-half pages suffice to give the excerpt an identity separate from the text of the novel; and the quality of the two and one-half pages, the neatness with which they were cobbled to the main body of the episode, the independence of the episode as a whole, the question whether author or an editor was responsible for the title, and, finally, the $3,000 which was paid for it, are all factors which are irrelevant to the category in which the piece belongs.

If the dividing line between these two basic categories of Faulkner's short fiction, stories and novel-excerpts, is not always easy to draw, further problems arise in determining which excerpts from Faulkner's novels are to be listed, and which should be omitted from the bibliography entirely. Obviously the making of anthologies is a never-ending process, and presumably the inclusion of new excerpts from Faulkner's novels in them will continue for a long time. When, after the publication of one of his novels, an editor secured permission from Faulkner's publisher to use a chunk of it in an anthology, Faulkner was, during his lifetime, sometimes consulted and sometimes not. But his approval or non-approval of such projects is usually impossible to prove and is in any case irrelevant. I have excluded from this listing all such excerpts made after the original publication of Faulkner's novels; they belong in precisely the same category as do the numberless reprintings of his short stories in freshman textbooks. A few such excerpts have been so often reprinted that some readers may be confused by their absence; I have referred to them briefly in the headnote to Section II, but excluded them from the listing.

ABBREVIATIONS

CtY	Yale University
NjP	Princeton University
Ober	Harold Ober Associates
TxU	University of Texas (Austin)
ViU	University of Virginia

Literary Career   James B. Meriwether. *The Literary Career of William Faulkner: A Bibliographical Study* (Princeton: Princeton University Library, 1961; Columbia: University of South Carolina Press, 1971).

New Orleans Sketches   *William Faulkner: New Orleans Sketches*, ed. Carvel Collins (New York: Random House, 1968).

I. STORIES

A. Published Stories

For each story, the first publication in English (magazine or book) is given. Except for early, out-of-copyright work, the only textually significant reprintings of any of Faulkner's short stories are those he included in his own books. These are listed here by short title and date only; full details are given in Section III below. There have been several reprintings of most of the out-of-copyright pieces, but only the more reliable texts are listed here.

Where collation has revealed no authorial revision in later published versions of these stories, the term 'reprinted' has been used, but in all such texts, compositorial and editorial changes are to be expected. Where more than one manuscript or typescript version exists, they are listed in order of composition, and in all cases, later versions are to be assumed revised from earlier ones.

Publication dates for books are taken from the records of the publisher involved, or from *Publishers' Weekly*.

AD ASTRA   *American Caravan IV*, eds. Alfred Kreymborg, Lewis Mumford, and Paul Rosenfeld (New York: Macaulay, 1931), pp. 164–81. (Publication date, 27 March 1931.) Revised for *These 13*, 1931; that version reprinted in *Collected Stories*, 1950. MS., 11 pp., ViU.

AFTERNOON OF A COW   *Furioso*, II (Summer 1947), 5–17. First published in a French translation by Maurice Edgar Coindreau, 'L'Après-midi d'une Vache', *Fontaine*, 27–28 (June–July 1943), 66–81. Carbon TS., 17 pp., NjP.

ALL THE DEAD PILOTS   *These 13*, 1931. Reprinted in *Collected Stories*, 1950. MS., 10 pp., ViU.

AMBUSCADE   *Saturday Evening Post*, CCVII (29 September 1934), 12–13, 80, 81. Revised for *The Unvanquished*, 1938.

APPENDIX: COMPSON, 1699 – – – 1945   *The Portable Faulkner*, ed. Malcolm Cowley (New York: Viking, 1946), pp. 737–56. (Publication date, 29 April 1946.) A slightly different version appears as Foreword to *The Sound and the Fury & As I Lay Dying* (New York: Modern Library, 1946), 3–22. (Publication date, 20 December 1946.) The precise relationship between these two versions is difficult to determine; both have been heavily edited. Carbon TS. (incomplete), 12 pp.; carbon TS., 22 pp., ViU.

Note: On the typescripts listed above, Faulkner entitled this piece 'APPENDIX | COMPSON | 1699 – – – 1945'; and it was written specifically for inclusion in the *Portable Faulkner*, as an appendix to that volume, and to an excerpt from *The Sound and the Fury* which appeared there. Even where it appears separately from the *Portable Faulkner*, however, it seems best to retain the word 'Appendix' in the title, with the implication that it is an Appendix to *The Sound and the Fury*, or to the story of the Compsons generally. There is no excuse for retaining the description of it as a Foreword (from the 1946 Modern Library double volume), but to refer to it as the Compson Appendix (without quotes or italics) may be a useful compromise.

ARTIST AT HOME   *Story*, III (August 1933), 27–41. Reprinted in *Collected Stories*, 1950. MS., entitled 'An Artist at Home', 13 pp., ViU.

BARN BURNING   *Harper's*, CLXXIX (June 1939), 86–96. Reprinted in *Collected Stories*, 1950. MS., 17 pp.; TS., 32 pp.; carbon TS. (of the preceding), 32 pp., ViU.

Note: 'Barn Burning' was originally written as the opening chapter of *The Hamlet*, 1940. See *Literary Career*, p. 70.

THE BEAR   *Saturday Evening Post*, CCXIV (9 May 1942), 30–31, 74, 76, 77. The records of his agent, Harold Ober, reveal that Faulkner extracted this episode from the fifth chapter of his completed but unpublished book, *Go Down, Moses* (publication date, 11 May 1942), and revised it sufficiently to enable Ober to sell it to the

Post as a short story in November 1941. (See also under 'Lion'.) Carbon TS. (not typed by author), 21 pp., Ober.

A BEAR HUNT   *Saturday Evening Post*, CCVI (10 February 1934), 8–9, 74, 76. Reprinted in *Collected Stories*, 1950. Revised for *Big Woods*, 1955.

BEYOND   *Harper's*, CLXVII (September 1933), 394–403. Reprinted in *Doctor Martino*, 1934; that version reprinted in *Collected Stories*, 1950. TS., entitled 'Beyond the Gate', 27 pp.; MS., entitled 'Beyond', 9 pp., ViU.

BLACK MUSIC   *Doctor Martino*, 1934. Reprinted in *Collected Stories*, 1950. MS., 11 pp., ViU. TS., 29 pp., TxU.

THE BROOCH   *Scribner's*, XCIX (January 1936), 7–12. Reprinted in *Collected Stories*, 1950. MS., 5 pp.; carbon TS., 15 pp.; carbon TS., 29 pp., ViU.

BY THE PEOPLE   *Mademoiselle*, XLI (October 1955), 86–89, 130, 131, 132, 133, 134, 135, 136, 137, 138, 139. Incorporated in *The Mansion*, 1959 (chapter 13). TS., 26 pp.; carbon TS. (not typed by author), 25 pp., NjP.

CARCASSONNE   *These 13*, 1931. Reprinted in *Collected Stories*, 1950. TS., 7 pp.; revised TS., 7 pp., ViU.

CENTAUR IN BRASS   *American Mercury*, XXV (February 1932), 200–210. Reprinted in *Collected Stories*, 1950. Incorporated in *The Town*, 1957 (chapter 1).

CHANCE   New Orleans *Times-Picayune* Sunday magazine section, 17 May 1925, p. 7. Reprinted in *New Orleans Sketches*.

CHEEST   New Orleans *Times-Picayune* Sunday magazine section, 5 April 1925, p. 4. Reprinted in *New Orleans Sketches*.

THE COBBLER   New Orleans *Times-Picayune* Sunday magazine section, 10 May 1925, p. 7. Reprinted in *New Orleans Sketches*.

[COMPSON APPENDIX   SEE APPENDIX: COMPSON, 1699 --- 1945]

COUNTRY MICE   New Orleans *Times-Picayune* Sunday magazine section, 20 September 1925, p. 7. Reprinted in *New Orleans Sketches*.

A COURTSHIP   *Sewanee Review*, LVI (Autumn 1948), 634–53. Reprinted in *Collected Stories*, 1950. Carbon TS., 22 pp., ViU.

CREVASSE   *These 13*, 1931. Reprinted in *Collected Stories*, 1950. (See under 'Victory' for TSS.)

DAMON AND PYTHIAS UNLIMITED   New Orleans *Times-Picayune* Sunday magazine section, 15 February 1925, p. 7. Reprinted in *New Orleans Sketches*.

DEATH-DRAG   *Scribner's*, XCI (January 1932), 34–42. Reprinted, entitled 'Death Drag', in *Doctor Martino*, 1934; that version reprinted in *Collected Stories*, 1950. MS., 11 pp.; carbon TS., entitled 'A Death-Drag', 27 pp., ViU.

DELTA AUTUMN   *Story*, XX (May–June 1942), 46–55. Revised for *Go Down, Moses*, 1942; part of that version revised for ending of *Big Woods*, 1955. TS., 18 pp., ViU.

DIVORCE IN NAPLES   *These 13*, 1931. Reprinted in *Collected Stories*, 1950. MS., 6 pp. (also bears canceled title, 'Equinox'); carbon TS., 17 pp., ViU.

DOCTOR MARTINO   *Harper's*, CLXIII (November 1931), 733–43. Reprinted in *Doctor Martino*, 1934; that version reprinted in *Collected Stories*, 1950. MS., 14 pp.; revised MS., 10 pp.; TS., 5 pp. (incomplete), ViU.

DRY SEPTEMBER   *Scribner's*, LXXXIX (January 1931), 49–56. Revised for *These 13*, 1931; that version reprinted in *Collected Stories*, 1950. MS., entitled 'Drouth', 8 pp.; carbon TS., 19 pp., ViU.

ELLY   *Story*, IV (February 1934), pp. 3–15. Reprinted in *Doctor Martino*, 1934; that version reprinted in *Collected Stories*, 1950. MS., entitled 'Selvage', 6 pp.; TS., entitled 'Selvage', 14 pp.; MS., entitled 'Elly', 11 pp., ViU.

EPISODE   New Orleans *Times-Picayune* Sunday magazine section, 16 August 1925, p. 2. Reprinted in *New Orleans Sketches*.

AN ERROR IN CHEMISTRY *Ellery Queen's Mystery Magazine*, VII (June 1946), 4–19. Reprinted in *Knight's Gambit*, 1949. Carbon TS., 22 pp., ViU.

THE FIRE ON THE HEARTH *Go Down, Moses*, 1942; untitled (and revised from the TS. versions below), the story is the third and last section of chapter 2 of the book, 'The Fire and the Hearth'. TS., entitled 'An Absolution' (an alternate title, 'Apotheosis', apparently added later by the author, in pencil), 17 pp. (incomplete); TS., entitled 'The Fire and the Hearth', 20 pp.; TS., 26 pp. (from several versions, none complete), ViU.

FOOL ABOUT A HORSE *Scribner's*, C (August 1936), 80–86. Incorporated in *The Hamlet*, 1940 (Book One, chapter 2). MS., 10 pp.; TS., 21 pp. (incomplete); carbon TS., 33 pp., ViU.

FOX HUNT *Harper's*, CLXIII (September 1931), 393–402. Reprinted in *Doctor Martino*, 1934; that version reprinted in *Collected Stories*, 1950. MS., entitled 'A Fox-Hunt', 11 pp.; TS., entitled 'Foxhunt', 26 pp., ViU.

GO DOWN, MOSES *Collier's*, CVII (25 January 1941), 19–20, 45, 46. Revised for *Go Down, Moses*, 1942. TS., 14 pp.; TS., 1 p. (first page only, apparently later than preceding); carbon TS., 17 pp., ViU.

   Note: Russell Roth, 'The Brennan Papers: Faulkner in Manuscript', *Perspective*, II (Summer 1949), 219–24, describes and briefly quotes from 15 TS. pages of an early version – or versions – of this story, and of 'Was'. It is not clear there how many of the pages belong to each story.

GOLDEN LAND *American Mercury*, XXXV (May 1935), 1–14. Reprinted in *Collected Stories*, 1950.

GOLD IS NOT ALWAYS *Atlantic*, CLXVI (November 1940), 563–70. Revised for *Go Down, Moses*, 1942, where it appears, untitled, as the second section of chapter 2 of the book, 'The Fire and the Hearth'. TS., 5 pp. (from one or more incomplete versions); TS., 19 pp., ViU. TS., 21 pp.; *Atlantic* galley proof, corrected, 7 sheets, CtY.

HAIR *American Mercury*, XXIII (May 1931), 53–61. Revised for *These 13*, 1931; that version reprinted in *Collected Stories*, 1950.

HAND UPON THE WATERS *Saturday Evening Post*, CCXII (4 November 1939), 14–15, 75, 76, 78, 79. Reprinted in *Knight's Gambit*, 1949. TS., 2 pp. (incomplete); TS., 30 pp.; TS., 30 pp. (incomplete), ViU.

HELL CREEK CROSSING *Saturday Evening Post*, CCXXXV (31 March 1962). Reprinted in *The Reivers* (publication date, 4 June 1962), where it appears, untitled, in chapter 4. TS., 3 pp. (incomplete); carbon TS., 24 pp. (not typed by author), Ober.
Note: The records of his agent, Harold Ober, reveal that Faulkner wrote a two and one-half page introduction to go with twenty pages of the typescript of the novel. It was received by the agency on 6 December 1961.

THE HILL *The Mississippian*, 10 March 1922, pp. 1, 2. Reprinted in *William Faulkner: Early Prose and Poetry*, ed. Carvel Collins (Boston: Little, Brown, 1962).

HOME New Orleans *Times-Picayune* Sunday magazine section, 22 February 1925, p. 3. Reprinted in *New Orleans Sketches*.

HONOR *American Mercury*, XX (July 1930), 268–74. Reprinted in *Doctor Martino*, 1934; that version reprinted in *Collected Stories*, 1950. (See *Literary Career*, pp. 173, 174, for possibility that an earlier title was 'Point of Honor'.)

THE HOUND *Harper's*, CLXIII (August 1931), 266–74. Reprinted in *Doctor Martino*, 1934. Incorporated in *The Hamlet*, 1940 (Book Three, chapter 2).

IDYLL IN THE DESERT New York: Random House, 1931, 17 pp. (limited, signed edition, only 400 copies). MS., 4 pp.; TS., 19 pp., ViU.

JEALOUSY New Orleans *Times-Picayune* Sunday magazine section, 1 March 1925, p. 2. Reprinted in *New Orleans Sketches*.

A JUSTICE *These 13*, 1931. Reprinted in *Collected Stories*, 1950; a part revised for prelude to 'A Bear Hunt' in *Big Woods*, 1955. MS., 10 pp., ViU.

Note: See also Section I-B for an untitled, unpublished TS. related to this sketch (and to 'Frankie and Johnny', in 'New Orleans', *Double-Dealer*, VII [January–February 1925]).

THE KID LEARNS   New Orleans *Times-Picayune* Sunday magazine section, 31 May 1925, p. 2. Reprinted in *New Orleans Sketches.*

THE KINGDOM OF GOD   New Orleans *Times-Picayune* Sunday magazine section, 26 April 1925, p. 4. Reprinted in *New Orleans Sketches.*

KNIGHT'S GAMBIT   *Knight's Gambit,* 1949; as the title story of the 1949 collection, 'Knight's Gambit' is a short novel, greatly expanded from, and incorporating, the typescript short story version below. The Ober records reveal that the story was written by January 1942. TS., 23 pp.; TS. and carbon TS., 50 pp. (miscellaneous pages from versions, none complete, of both story and short novel), ViU.

LANDING IN LUCK   *The Mississippian*, 26 November 1919, pp. 2, 7. Reprinted in *William Faulkner: Early Prose and Poetry*, ed. Carvel Collins (Boston: Little, Brown, 1962).

LEG   *Doctor Martino*, 1934. Reprinted, entitled 'The Leg', in *Collected Stories*, 1950. MS., entitled 'The Leg', 10 pp., ViU. TS., 26 pp., TxU. Carbon TS. (of the preceding), 26 pp., ViU.

THE LIAR   New Orleans *Times-Picayune* Sunday magazine section, 26 July 1925, pp. 3, 6. Reprinted in *New Orleans Sketches.*

LION   *Harper's*, CLXXII (December 1935), 67–77. Greatly revised and expanded for chapter 5, 'The Bear', in *Go Down, Moses*, 1942. (See also under 'The Bear' for a short story made from the new material.) Four of the five parts (part four omitted) of the *Go Down, Moses* version included in *Big Woods*, 1955.

LIZARDS IN JAMSHYD'S COURTYARD   *Saturday Evening Post*, CCIV (27 February 1932), 12–13, 52, 57. Incorporated in *The Hamlet*, 1940 (Book One, chapter 3, and Book Four, chapter 2).

LO! *Story*, V (November 1934), 5–21. Reprinted in *Collected Stories*, 1950.

MIRRORS OF CHARTRES STREET New Orleans *Time-Picayune* Sunday magazine section, 8 February 1925, pp. 1, 6. Reprinted in *New Orleans Sketches*.

MISSISSIPPI *Holiday*, XV (April 1954), 33–47. A part was revised for the prelude to 'Race at Morning' in *Big Woods*, 1955. The text of the whole piece in *Essays, Speeches & Public Letters by William Faulkner*, ed. James B. Meriwether (New York: Random House, 1966), is based on the author's original typescript. TS., 40 pp.; carbon TS. (not typed by author), 38 pp., NjP.

Note: Although this piece was commissioned and published as an essay, and the author made use of a considerable amount of historical and autobiographical fact in it, the technique is fictional — its affinities with the narrative prologues of *Requiem for a Nun* (1951) are obvious — and there may be as much reason for including it among Faulkner's short fiction as among his nonfiction prose.

MISS ZILPHIA GANT Dallas: Book Club of Texas, 1932, 29 pp. (limited edition, only 300 copies). MS., 9 pp.; TS., 18 pp., ViU. TS., 23 pp., TxU. Carbon TS. (of the preceding), 23 pp., ViU.

MISTRAL *These 13*, 1931; reprinted in *Collected Stories*, 1950. MS., 17 pp.; carbon TS., 46 pp., ViU.

MONK *Scribner's*, CI (May 1937), 16–24. Reprinted in *Knight's Gambit*, 1949.

A MOUNTAIN VICTORY *Saturday Evening Post*, CCV (3 December 1932), 6–7, 39, 42, 44, 45, 46. Revised, entitled 'Mountain Victory', in *Doctor Martino*, 1934; that version reprinted in *Collected Stories*, 1950. MS., 18 pp.; carbon TS., 42 pp., ViU. TS., 46 pp., TxU.

MR. ACARIUS *Saturday Evening Post*, CCXXXVIII (9 October 1965), 26–27, 28, 29, 30, 31. Carbon TS., entitled 'Weekend Revisited', 19 pp., ViU. Carbon TS., entitled 'Weekend Revisited', 22 pp. (not typed by author; two copies), NjP.

Note: The files of the Ober Agency reveal that Faulkner gave them the typescript of 19 pp. on 19 February 1953. It was retyped, in four copies, the following month; presumably the carbons at NjP are of this retyped version; they are in the Saxe Commins papers and, according to the Ober records, copies of the story were sent to Commins on 9 June 1953, and 15 November 1954. According to Michel Gresset, 'Weekend, Lost and Revisited', *Mississippi Quarterly*, XXI (Summer 1968), p. 173*n.*, Rust Hills, the former fiction editor of the *Saturday Evening Post*, has a typescript of the story, entitled 'Mr. Acarius'.

MULE IN THE YARD   *Scribner's*, XCVI (August 1934), 65–70. Reprinted in *Collected Stories*, 1950. Incorporated in *The Town*, 1957 (chapter 16). MS., 10 pp.; TS., 10 pp. (incomplete), ViU.

MY GRANDMOTHER MILLARD AND GENERAL BEDFORD FORREST AND THE BATTLE OF HARRYKIN CREEK   *Story*, XXII (March–April 1943), 68–86. Reprinted in *Collected Stories*, 1950. TS., 2 pp. (incomplete); carbon (of the preceding) TS., 2 pp., ViU. TS., 42 pp., NjP. Carbon (of the preceding) TS., 42 pp., ViU.

A NAME FOR THE CITY   *Harper's*, CCI (October 1950), 200–214. Revised, entitled 'The Courthouse (A Name for the City)', as the narrative prologue to Act I of *Requiem for a Nun*, 1951.

   Note: Faulkner wrote his agent, Harold Ober, when sending him this story, 'The enclosed is a by-product of my play.' (The Ober records reveal that the letter, and a 24-page TS., arrived at the agency 5 July 1950.)

NEW ORLEANS   *Double-Dealer*, VII (January–February 1925), 102–7. Eleven brief sketches make up this piece: 'Wealthy Jew', 'The Priest', 'Frankie and Johnny', 'The Sailor', 'The Cobbler', 'The Longshoreman', 'The Cop', 'The Beggar', 'The Artist', 'Magdalen', and 'The Tourist'. The text in *New Orleans Sketches* incorporates corrections made by Faulkner in the original published text, and further corrections made in accordance with the original typescript (see the editor's preface, p. vi).

   Note: See also Section I-B for an untitled, unpublished TS. related to one of these sketches, 'Frankie and Johnny' (and to the sketch 'The Kid Learns', New Orleans *Times-Picayune*, 31 May 1925).

NOTES ON A HORSETHIEF   Greenville, Mississippi: Levee Press, 1951, 71 pp. (limited, signed edition, only 975 copies). Revised for *A Fable*, 1954, where it appears (untitled) pp. 151–89. (Publication date, 2 August 1954.) Entitled 'Notes on a Horsethief', pp. 151–204 of the novel were published in *Vogue*, CXXIV (July 1954), 46–51, 101, 102, 103, 104, 105, 106.

AN ODOR OF VERBENA   *The Unvanquished*, 1938. MS., 23 pp.; TS., 54 pp., ViU.

Note: Correspondence now in ViU, between Faulkner and his agent, Morton Goldman, reveals that attempts were made to sell 'An Odor of Verbena' as a short story before it was finally published as the seventh and last chapter of *The Unvanquished*.

THE OLD PEOPLE   *Harper's*, CLXXXI (September 1940), 418–25. Revised for *Go Down, Moses*, 1942; that version reprinted in *Big Woods*, 1955. TS., 17 pp., ViU.

"ONCE ABOARD THE LUGGER —— " *Contempo*, I (1 February 1932), pp. 1, 4.

Note: A TS., 12 pp., of this story was sold at auction by Parke-Bernet, 14 January 1964. Through the courtesy of Mr. Robert Metzdorf I was permitted to examine it prior to the sale. The title of the typescript is the same as that given at the head of the continuation of the story on p. 4 of the published version; that is, it has the title in quotation marks, with a long dash at the end. The title at the beginning of the published version is in quotation marks, but lacks the dash.

OUT OF NAZARETH   New Orleans *Times-Picayune* Sunday magazine section, 12 April 1925, p. 4. Reprinted in *New Orleans Sketches*.

PANTALOON IN BLACK   *Harper's*, CLXXXI (October 1940), 503–13. Revised for *Go Down, Moses*, 1942. Carbon TS., 24 pp., ViU.

PENNSYLVANIA STATION   *American Mercury*, XXXI (February 1934), 166–74. Reprinted in *Collected Stories*, 1950. MS., 8 pp.; MS., 1 p. (incomplete); TS., 2 pp. (incomplete); TS., 4 pp. (incomplete); TS., 20 pp., ViU.

Note: A 2-page MS., incomplete, of an early version of this story is in TxU. It is entitled 'Bench for Two'. The sending schedule of his stories which Faulkner kept in the early 1930s notes that he sent a story to two magazines in September 1930 which he refers to as '2 Bench' and 'Two on Bench'. See *Literary Career*, pp. 175, 178, 179.

A POINT OF LAW *Collier's*, CV (22 June 1940), 20–21, 30, 32. Revised for *Go Down, Moses*, 1942, where it appears, untitled, as the first section of chapter 2 of the book, 'The Fire and the Hearth'. TS., 21 pp., ViU.

RACE AT MORNING *Saturday Evening Post*, CCXXVII (5 March 1955), 26–27, 103, 104, 106. Revised for *Big Woods*, 1955. TS., 20 pp., NjP. Galley proof of *Post* version, 8 sheets, ViU.

RAID *Saturday Evening Post*, CCVII (3 November 1934), 18–19, 72, 73, 75, 77, 78. Revised for *The Unvanquished*, 1938.

RED LEAVES *Saturday Evening Post*, CCIII (25 October 1930), 6–7, 54, 56, 58, 60, 62, 64. Revised for *These 13*, 1931; that version reprinted in *Collected Stories*, 1950; a part revised for prelude of 'The Old People' in *Big Woods*, 1955. MS., 12 pp.; carbon TS., 36 pp., ViU.

RETREAT *Saturday Evening Post*, CCVII (13 October 1934), 16–17, 82, 84, 85, 87, 89. Revised for *The Unvanquished*, 1938.

RIPOSTE IN TERTIO *Saturday Evening Post*, CCIX (14 November 1936), 12–13, 121, 122, 124, 126, 128, 130, entitled 'The Unvanquished'. Revised and entitled 'Riposte in Tertio' for *The Unvanquished*, 1938.

THE ROSARY New Orleans *Times-Picayune* Sunday magazine section, 3 May 1925, p. 2. Reprinted in *New Orleans Sketches*.

A ROSE FOR EMILY *Forum*, LXXXIII (April 1930), 233–38. Slightly revised for *These 13*, 1931; that version reprinted in *Collected Stories*, 1950. MS., 6 pp. (incomplete); carbon TS., 17 pp., ViU.

SEPULTURE SOUTH: GASLIGHT *Harper's Bazaar*, LXXXVIII (December 1954), 84–85, 140, 141. TS. and MS., entitled 'Sepulchure South: in Gaslight', 8 pp. (title, last part of p. 4, and pp. 5 and 6

in MS.); TS., 1 p. (incomplete); TS., 5 pp. (incomplete); TS., entitled 'Sepulchure South: Gaslight', 3 pp. (incomplete), NjP.
Note: Although this piece was commissioned and published as an article, it is actually a short story. See James B. Meriwether, 'Two Unknown Faulkner Short Stories', in *Recherches anglaises et américaines* (Strasbourg), IV (1971).

SHALL NOT PERISH *Story,* XXIII (July–August 1943), 40–47. Reprinted in *Collected Stories,* 1950. Carbon TS., 16 pp.; TS., 4 pp. (incomplete); carbon TS., 11 pp. (miscellaneous pp. from several versions, none complete), ViU.

SHINGLES FOR THE LORD *Saturday Evening Post,* CCXV (13 February 1943), 14–15, 68, 70, 71. Reprinted in *Collected Stories,* 1950. Carbon TS., 21 pp., ViU.

SKIRMISH AT SARTORIS *Scribner's,* XCVII (April 1935), 193–200. Revised for *The Unvanquished,* 1938.

SMOKE *Harper's,* CLXIV (April 1932), 562–78. Reprinted in *Doctor Martino,* 1934; that version reprinted in *Knight's Gambit,* 1949. MS., 12 pp.; TS., 1 p. (typed from *Doctor Martino* version for *Knight's Gambit*), ViU.

SPOTTED HORSES *Scribner's,* LXXXIX (June 1931), 585–97. Incorporated in *The Hamlet,* 1940 (Book Four, chapter 1).
Note: It is possible that an alternate title for this story was 'Peasants' (see *Literary Career,* p. 174).

SUNSET New Orleans *Times-Picayune* Sunday magazine section, 24 May 1925, 4, 7. Reprinted in *New Orleans Sketches.*

THE TALL MEN *Saturday Evening Post,* CCXIII (31 May 1941), 14–15, 95, 96, 98, 99. Reprinted in *Collected Stories,* 1950. Carbon TS., 18 pp., ViU.

THAT EVENING SUN GO DOWN *American Mercury,* XXII (March 1931), 257–67. Revised and entitled 'That Evening Sun' in *These 13,* 1931; that version reprinted in *Collected Stories,* 1950. MS., entitled 'Never Done No Weeping When You Wanted to Laugh',

6 pp. (incomplete), CtY. Carbon TS., entitled '—That Evening Sun Go Down', 26 pp., ViU.

THAT WILL BE FINE   *American Mercury*, XXXV (July 1935), 264–76. Reprinted in *Collected Stories*, 1950.

THERE WAS A QUEEN   *Scribner's*, XCIII (January 1933), 10–16. Reprinted in *Doctor Martino*, 1934; that version reprinted in *Collected Stories*, 1950. MS., untitled, 5 pp. (incomplete); MS., entitled 'An Empress Passed', and with canceled title 'Through the Window', 8 pp.; TS., 25 pp.; carbon TS. (of the preceding), 25 pp., ViU.

THRIFT   *Saturday Evening Post*, CCIII (6 September 1930), 16–17, 76, 82. MS., 5 pp. (incomplete); TS., 18 pp. (incomplete), ViU.

TOMORROW   *Saturday Evening Post*, CCXIII (23 November 1940), 22–23, 32, 35, 37, 38, 39. Reprinted in *Knight's Gambit*, 1949. TS., untitled, 20 pp., ViU.

TURN ABOUT   *Saturday Evening Post*, CCIV (5 March 1932), 6–7, 75, 76, 81, 83. Revised for *Doctor Martino*, 1934; that version, entitled 'Turnabout', reprinted in *Collected Stories*, 1950. MS., 16 pp., ViU.

TWO DOLLAR WIFE   *College Life*, XVIII (January 1936), 8–10, 85, 86, 88, 90.
   Note: See also under 'Christmas Tree' in Section II.

TWO SOLDIERS   *Saturday Evening Post*, CCXIV (28 March 1942), 9–11, 35, 36, 38, 40. Reprinted in *Collected Stories*, 1950.

UNCLE WILLY   *American Mercury*, XXXVI (October 1935), 156–68. Reprinted in *Collected Stories*, 1950.

[THE UNVANQUISHED   SEE RIPOSTE IN TERTIO]

VENDÉE   *Saturday Evening Post*, CCIX (5 December 1936), 16–17, 86, 87, 90, 92, 93, 94. Revised for *The Unvanquished*, 1938.

VICTORY *These 13*, 1931. Reprinted in *Collected Stories*, 1950. MS., 9 pp. (incomplete); TS., 56 pp. (incomplete); TS., 49 pp. (incomplete), ViU.

Note: The two typescripts listed above contain, as an episode, the story 'Crevasse', published separately in *These 13*.

WAS *Go Down, Moses*, 1942. TS., untitled, 22 pp., ViU.

Note: Russell Roth, 'The Brennan Papers: Faulkner in Manuscript', *Perspective*, II (Summer 1949), 219–24, describes and briefly quotes from 15 TS. pages of an earlier version—or versions—of this story, then entitled 'Almost', and of 'Go Down, Moses'. It is not clear how many of the pages belong to each story. The Ober records reveal that a 22-page TS. of the story, entitled 'Almost', was received from the *Saturday Evening Post* on 1 July 1940. (Faulkner apparently had sent it direct to the magazine, which rejected it.) The 15 pages were given by Faulkner to Dan Brennan on 19 July 1940.

WASH *Harper's*, CLXVIII (February 1934), 258–66. Reprinted in *Doctor Martino*, 1934. Incorporated in *Absalom, Absalom!*, 1936, where it appears (untitled) in chapter 7. The *Doctor Martino* version is reprinted in *Collected Stories*, 1950.

[WEEKEND REVISITED see MR. ACARIUS]

THE WISHING TREE *Saturday Evening Post*, CCXXXV (8 April 1967), 48–49, 50, 51, 52, 53, 57, 58, 60, 61, 62, 63. Reprinted, New York: Random House, 1967, 81 pp. (Publication date, 10 April 1967). TS., entitled 'The Wishing-Tree', 47 pp.; TS., entitled 'The Wishing-Tree', 43 pp.; carbon TS. (of the preceding), entitled 'The Wishing-Tree', 42 pp. (incomplete), ViU. Carbon TS., entitled 'The Wishing-Tree', 44 pp. (incomplete), TxU.

Note: Several other typescripts of this story exist in private collections. One of them is that from which the published version was made; a 'Publisher's Note' in the volume gives as the source of its text a typescript which Faulkner dated 5 February 1927. It is dedicated to '*Victoria on her eighth birthday*'—that is, to Victoria Franklin, who became his stepdaughter when Faulkner married Estelle Oldham Franklin in 1929. He also gave, in 1927, a copy to Margaret Brown, daughter of Mrs. Calvin Brown, which Mrs. Brown showed to me in Oxford, Mississippi, in July

1956. In 1948, according to Mrs. Brown, Faulkner borrowed her copy in order to type one for his godson, Philip Stone (see *Literary Career*, p. 35).

YO HO AND TWO BOTTLES OF RUM   New Orleans *Times-Picayune* Sunday magazine section, 27 September 1925, pp. 1, 2. Reprinted in *New Orleans Sketches*.

B. Unpublished Stories

Listed here are the Faulkner short stories known to me which are unpublished, but which survive in complete, or virtually complete, manuscript or typescript versions.

The relationships of these stories with each other and with a number of Faulkner's published stories and novels are complex, and the brief notes provided here are intended only to identify the stories and to suggest the most obvious of these relationships. But it is to be hoped that ultimately we will have more thorough and comprehensive studies of Faulkner's shorter fiction that will date these stories (as well as many of the published ones) more accurately than has heretofore proved possible, and will clarify their relationships with his other work. Such studies could provide an extraordinarily illuminating view of Faulkner as literary craftsman, as the few brief attempts made along such lines have indicated. Michael Millgate, for example, has pointed out that Faulkner took an entire episode in *Absalom, Absalom!* from 'The Big Shot'.[1] The same story contains a character who is recognizably the Popeye of *Sanctuary*. But was Faulkner drawing upon the unpublished short story when he wrote the novel, or, as would appear more probable, was he drawing upon the unpublished original version of the novel when he wrote the story?[2]

[1] *The Achievement of William Faulkner* (New York: Random House, 1966), pp. 159–61. Cited hereafter as *Achievement*.

[2] The first version of *Sanctuary* was written between January and May 1929, according to Faulkner's own contemporary notes (*Literary Career*, p. 66). The date of the writing of 'The Big Shot' is not known, but it existed by January 1930, and he ceased submitting it after sending it to the *Saturday Evening Post* in April 1930 (*Literary Career*, p. 170). After initially rejecting it, Faulkner's publisher undertook the book, and composition began in May 1930. (See Linton Massey, 'Notes on the Unrevised Galleys of Faulkner's *Sanctuary*', *Studies in Bibliography*, VIII [1956], 197.) Did Faulkner cease sending out 'The Big Shot' when he learned that *Sanctuary* was to be published?

'Rose of Lebanon' is by no means the poorest of the stories Faulkner wrote in the early 1930s, but he ceased sending it to magazines late in July 1931 after only three submissions—and these, uncharacteristically, were several months apart. Do the gaps between submissions indicate the author's dissatisfaction with it, and that he was either revising it or considering that possibility? He apparently ceased sending the story shortly before beginning the writing of *Light in August* in August 1931; and, in fact, that novel draws upon the story for a few details.[3] Did Faulkner consider that the novel had, to use Fitzgerald's word for it, 'stripped' the story? There is evidence that Faulkner was still trying to sell a version of it, under a different title, several years later. If a copy of this version turns up, will it prove to omit the material Faulkner used in *Light in August?*

Faulkner published what surely must be the worst story he ever wrote, 'Two Dollar Wife', in 1936. When he wrote it is not known, but it sounds more as if it belonged to the 1920s than to the 1930s, and it uses characters and draws upon material in 'The Devil Beats His Wife' and 'Christmas Tree', the first of which dates from no later than the late 1920s. But the relationship between the two early pieces is obscure, and it is not certain which, if either, Faulkner was drawing upon in 'Two Dollar Wife'.

Not only are there characters and episodes, but also there are less readily identifiable borrowings from these stories scattered elsewhere in Faulkner's work. Verbal echoes, brief incidents, and bits of description appear, or seem to, in other stories and in novels written approximately at the same time, or later. Ultimately we shall need a study of Faulkner's reuse of material which will point out these borrowings, along with those others confined to his published work which have already received a certain amount of attention. Used with discretion, such evidence can provide important clues to Faulkner's artistry and craftsmanship, as well as helping to date some of the fiction, including fragments, to which we can now assign only an approximate date.

Faulkner deposited his own collection of his papers in NjP in March 1957, and entrusted me with the task of sorting and organizing them. On 12 March 1958, when he was visiting in Princeton, I interviewed him at the library and asked him a number of questions about the papers, including the dates of the unpublished stories. Faulkner's memory for dates was not, generally speaking, very good,

[3] *Literary Career*, pp. 175, 67; *Achievement*, p. 130.

and after he had volunteered at least one that was clearly wrong, I encouraged him to try to date them by relating them to events in his life and to other writings of a known date, like his trip abroad in 1925 or the writing of various novels. He was cordial, cooperative, and remarkably exact in his memory of the works themselves (as opposed to their dates). I tried not to take up an undue amount of his time, in the interview. But I wish now that I had known enough then to ask him some more questions.

ADOLESCENCE   Written 'in the early 1920s', according to Faulkner (interview, 12 March 1958), this story has a few elements in common with *Soldiers' Pay* and *As I Lay Dying*, as Millgate has pointed out (*Achievement*, p. 11). Characters include Juliet Bunden, her father, Joe Bunden, and her stepmother and grandmother. TS., 26 pp., ViU.

THE BIG SHOT   According to Faulkner's sending schedule of short stories, this existed before 23 January 1930 (*Literary Career*, p. 170). Characters include Don Reeves (relating the story to 'Mistral', and perhaps to 'Snow'), Popeye (*Sanctuary*), and Dal Martin, whose story, as Millgate has pointed out, furnished Faulkner with material for *Absalom, Absalom!* (*Achievement*, pp. 159–61). Other elements in the story were apparently drawn upon in *Light in August* and *The Town* (*Achievement*, p. 161). TS., 37 pp., ViU.

CHRISTMAS TREE   This story is a version, and apparently a later one, of 'The Devil Beats His Wife', a three-page manuscript which Faulkner kept in his papers. A private collector has permitted me to examine a three-page manuscript and a five-page typescript or carbon typescript of 'Christmas Tree'. (The manuscript also bears the canceled title 'Whoopee'.)

Faulkner (interview, 12 March 1958) recalled the title 'The Devil Beats His Wife' as one which he 'started to use for something', perhaps around the time of *Sartoris*. When reminded that his friend and, at one time, literary agent Ben Wasson had used the title for a novel published late in 1929, Faulkner said that he 'discarded it and Wasson took it', but he was not entirely clear whether it was a novel or a story that he had planned to use the title for. My notes on the interview are sketchy at this point for Faulkner digressed into personal matters, and I did not take notes, at the time, on what he said. But since he drew upon the material for a short story, it is possible that he conceived or began 'The Devil Beats His Wife' as a novel, and in 1958 he was recollecting both novel and later story. On the other hand, 'The Devil Beats His Wife' could be a more-or-less completed draft of a story rather than a novel fragment. Wasson (interview, July 1957), who knew Faulkner well at the time and worked with him closely on the publication of both *Sartoris* and *The Sound and the Fury* in 1928 and 1929, recalled that it was a novel which Faulkner began and abandoned in favor of *Sartoris* (then entitled *Flags in the Dust*), which would place it as early as 1926. (See also James B. Meriwether, 'Two Unknown Faulkner Short Stories', *Recherches anglaises et américaines* [Strasbourg], IV [1971].)

Characters in 'The Devil Beats His Wife' include Hubert Semmes, his wife Doris, and their servant, Della. Millgate considers Della to be 'a first sketch for Dilsey in *The Sound and the Fury*' (*Achievement*, p. 23). Hubert and Doris reappear in 'Christmas Tree', but Della is renamed Ruby. In the story 'Two Dollar Wife', not published till 1936 but perhaps written earlier, several characters are the same but the plot differs. Faulkner presumably drew upon the earlier story for Doris and her mother, Mrs. Houston, and Doris's friend Lucille. A few other elements of the two stories are in common, but 'Two Dollar Wife' differs sufficiently to be called a separate work. 'The Devil Beats His Wife', MS., 3 pp., ViU. 'Christmas Tree', MS., 3 pp.; TS. or carbon TS., 5 pp., private collection.

[THE DEVIL BEATS HIS WIFE see CHRISTMAS TREE]

[ELMER see A PORTRAIT OF ELMER]

HOG PAWN The records of Faulkner's agent, Harold Ober, reveal that he received the typescript of this story 10 January 1955. It was retyped and submitted unsuccessfully to several magazines before being returned to the author on 13 March 1958. A copy of the retyped text, 28 pp., survives in the Ober files; it is an early version of the Meadowfill episode of *The Mansion* (1959), chapter 14.

[KNIGHT'S GAMBIT see Section I-A]

LOVE According to Faulkner (interview, 12 March 1958), this obviously early story was written 'around 1921', and such a date is probably not too far off. Characters include Beth Gordon, and Bob Jeyfus; Millgate briefly summarizes the plot (*Achievement*, p. 11).

MAYDAY The plot of this work has been briefly summarized by Carvel Collins in the introduction to *New Orleans Sketches*, p. xxx. Dating it 1926 and referring to it as an 'unpublished forty-eight-page novelette', Collins also discusses 'Mayday' on pp. 236n., 237n., and 238n. of 'The Interior Monologues of *The Sound and the Fury*', Irving Malin, ed. *Psychoanalysis and American Fiction* (New York, 1965). Millgate has pointed out its affinities with 'The Wishing-Tree' (*Achievement*, p. 11). Private collection.

MOONLIGHT According to Faulkner (interview, 12 March 1958), this was 'about the first story I ever wrote', and dates from 'around 1919, 1920, or 1921.' Characters include George and Cecily, and a scene between them anticipates elements of *Soldiers' Pay*, as Millgate has pointed out (*Achievement*, p. 11). Carbon TS., 16 pp. (incomplete), ViU.

A PORTRAIT OF ELMER This story is based upon, or drawn from, the unpublished novel 'Elmer' which Faulkner (interview, 12 March 1958) recalled as having been written 'in Paris in 1924.' A question elicited the reply that this was during the trip abroad he took after being in New Orleans. (I did not remind him that the date of the trip was 1925.) It was to have been his second novel, he said, but he did not finish it because it was funny, 'but not funny enough.' He had at one time another title for it, not 'Elmer', but just what he did not recall. Among his papers Faulkner kept 4 pp. of manuscript and 130 pp. of typescript from or relating to this novel. The basic title was clearly 'Elmer', but various drafts of the beginning are entitled 'Elmer and Myrtle', 'Growing Pains', and 'Portrait of Elmer Hodge' (*Literary Career*, p. 81).

At the time I discussed the work with Faulkner, I was unaware of the existence of the short story 'A Portrait of Elmer', a typescript of which has been recently acquired by ViU. Clearly of later date, it draws upon the novel for much of its material and the characterization of Elmer, and some of the MS. and TS. pages I have listed under the novel 'Elmer' may belong to drafts of the story, which is discussed by Millgate (*Achievement*, pp. 21–22) under the title 'Portrait of Elmer Hodge'. TS., 57 pp., ViU.

ROSE OF LEBANON   According to his short story sending schedule, Faulkner submitted this story to a magazine 7 November 1930, and there is no reason to think it was written much earlier (*Literary Career*, p. 175). The characters include Gavin Blount, Randolph Gordon, and Gordon's mother, Lewis Randolph. Millgate discusses the story (*Achievement*, pp. 130, 131), and points out some relationships with *Light in August*. (See under Lost Stories, 'A Return', for a later story obviously based upon this one.) MS., 9 pp. (incomplete?), ViU.

SNOW   According to the records of his agent, Harold Ober, he received this story from Faulkner on 17 February 1942. It was apparently 21 pp. in length at that time. A revised version, apparently 16 pp. long, was received 22 July 1942. Faulkner retained among his papers a carbon copy 18 pp. long which is likely to be this revised version; the ending of the story is on p. 16, but it includes two extra pages (13a and 13b). Characters include Don (relating the story to 'Mistral', with which it has other elements in common, and to 'The Big Shot'), and a German general, von Ploeckner. TS., 3 pp. (incomplete), ViU. TS., 18 pp., Random House files. Carbon TS. (of the preceding), 18 pp., ViU.

[Untitled]   This obviously early story combines two sketches which Faulkner published in 1925: 'Frankie and Johnny', which is one of the brief pieces in 'New Orleans', *Double-Dealer*, VII (January–February 1925); and 'The Kid Learns', New Orleans *Times-Picayune*, 31 May (see Section I-A). Faulkner may well have divided and recast this unpublished TS. for these two pieces, but it is possible that the TS. represents a later attempt to combine them. TS., 23 pp., ViU.

WITH CAUTION AND DISPATCH   According to Faulkner (interview, 12 March 1958), this story dates from about 1932 to 1933, 'about the time of "Turn About"'. The *Saturday Evening Post* was interested in it, he added. ('Turn About' was written late in December 1931 or early January 1932 and sent to his agent on 9 January 1932. It was published in the *Post* 5 March 1932. See *Literary Career*, p. 175, and *Achievement*, pp. 32–33.) This is another World War I flying story, involving one of the Sartoris twins of *Sartoris*, 'Ad Astra', and 'All the Dead Pilots'. The records of Faulkner's agent, Harold Ober, reveal that this story, in two parts (no total number of the pages is given) was received by him on 14 February 1940, and sent to Random House 25 February 1948. The versos of 9 pp. of the final typescript of *The Hamlet*, which was published 1 April 1940 (pp. 530–36, and the extra pp. 535–36; see *Literary Career*, pp. 87–88), bear pages from various other versions. Since Faulkner's memory of it being done around the time of 'Turn About' is not likely to have been at fault, the typescript sent to Ober, and the drafts on the typescript of *The Hamlet*, are presumably a later revision made when the original failed to sell. TS., 2 pp. (incomplete); TS., 47 pp. (incomplete), ViU. TS. in two parts, 17 pp. and 21 pp., Random House files.

C. Lost Stories

Listed here are nine Faulkner short stories that are known to have existed once, but for which no text, published or unpublished, now appears to survive. Seven of them appear on the sending schedule of his stories that Faulkner kept for about two years in the early 1930s; they are listed here, with the date of the earliest entry that occurs in the schedule, with a reference to the appendix of *Literary Career* in which additional data on the schedule can be found.

Though it is likely that some of these stories have been destroyed, others may turn up. Some, however, are likely to be ghosts, works that had a separate existence in title only, and survive in other forms. 'Dull Tale', for example, was sent to the *Saturday Evening Post* on 14 November 1930, but there is no record that he submitted it to any other magazine. It is highly unlikely that Faulkner simply abandoned a story that he considered good enough to try on the *Post*. When it was rejected, did he revise it under a different name? It is quite likely that if further evidence concerning them turns up, several of the stories included here will prove to be alternate titles for stories which exist in other versions, published or unpublished. Another possibility is that some of these stories may have been incorporated into novels, and survive only in unidentifiable form as episodes in

As I Lay Dying, Sanctuary, or *Light in August,* for example. We know from the sending schedule that Faulkner tried twice to place 'Evangeline' in July 1931. What happened to it thereafter? In *Light in August,* which apparently was begun in August 1931 (*Literary Career,* p. 67), when Calvin Burden sees the woman his son is to marry, he says, 'Evangeline!' Apparently this was the name of his own dead wife; and the broader significance of the title would certainly be appropriate to the story of Joanna Burden's family, which is told in chapter 11. Did Faulkner stop sending out the story when he decided to use it in the novel?

On the other hand, I have omitted here any mention of a few stories which actually may have existed, but for which the evidence is less tangible or reliable. Faulkner made the statement as early as 1937 that he had begun *The Sound and the Fury* as a short story. Does the beginning of the manuscript of *The Sound and the Fury,* which Faulkner preserved among his papers, represent that story? And does the title 'Twilight' which appears at the beginning of the manuscript, represent the title of the story? (*Achievement,* pp. 86, 90.) But we cannot be certain that the story ever existed in any form much more concrete than the author's imagination.

ARIA CON AMORE   Sending schedule, 2 February 1931 (*Literary Career,* pp. 169–70).

BUILT A FENCE   Sending schedule, 29 November 1930; also referred to as 'Built Fence' (*Literary Career,* p. 171).

A DANGEROUS MAN   Sending schedule, 6 February 1930 (*Literary Career,* p. 171).

DULL TALE   Sending schedule, 14 November 1930 (*Literary Career,* p. 172).

EVANGELINE   Sending schedule, 17 July 1931 (*Literary Career,* p. 172).

FIRE AND CLOCK   Sending schedule, 23 January 1930; listed as 'Fire & Clock' (*Literary Career,* p. 172).

PER ARDUA   Sending schedule, 5 February 1930 (*Literary Career,* p. 174).

THIS KIND OF COURAGE   In a letter (ViU) to his agent Morton Goldman, probably written in late October 1934, Faulkner refers to a story by this name as one which he wishes to recall, since he is making it into a novel. The novel obviously is *Pylon*, which he completed in the late fall or early winter of 1934, and which was published in March 1935.

A RETURN   The records of Faulkner's agent Harold Ober reveal that Faulkner sent in a fifty-three–page story by this title, which was received 13 October 1938. From the brief plot summary made by Ober, it appears that the story used material from the unpublished story 'Rose of Lebanon', and might even simply be a revision of that story.

II. EXCERPTS FROM NOVELS

Included here are only those excerpts from Faulkner's novels which he published, or tried to publish, before the publication of the novels themselves, and in which he made no textual revision. Thus 'Hell Creek Crossing' is excluded; Faulkner revised it sufficiently to give it a separate identity, and it is listed in Section I-A. Also excluded, of course, are the numerous novel excerpts which have been made later, and by other hands. Malcolm Cowley, for example, in the Viking *Portable Faulkner* (New York, 1946), included excerpts from several of Faulkner's novels, and other editors have often imitated him. Cowley had taken from *The Wild Palms* its subplot, 'Old Man'; from *Go Down, Moses* its fifth chapter, 'The Bear'; and from *The Hamlet* chapter 1 of Book 4, to which he gave the title 'Spotted Horses' (after an earlier short story version of the episode). All three excerpts were also included in *The Faulkner Reader*, which Faulkner's own publishers brought out in 1954, and there have been almost numberless other reprintings of them, including a separate paperback of 'Old Man' which was retitled *The Old Man*. With such anomalies this bibliography is not concerned.

ABSALOM, ABSALOM!   *American Mercury*, XXXVIII (August 1936), 466–74. Published as a part of Faulkner's forthcoming novel of that title. Appears as chapter 1 of *Absalom, Absalom!* (publication date, 26 October 1936). There are a number of minor differences between the two texts, perhaps some of them authorial, though most appear to be editorial in origin. It is likely that proofs of the book furnished printer's copy for the excerpt.

THE EDUCATION OF LUCIUS PRIEST *Esquire*, LVII (May 1962), 109–16. Published as part of Faulkner's forthcoming novel, *The Reivers* (publication date, 4 June 1962), in which it appears in chapters 5, 6, and 7. The records of Faulkner's agent, Harold Ober Associates, reveal that they received copies (presumably photocopies) of pp. 111–35 and 182–93 of the original typescript of the novel on 6 December 1961 and sold the piece on 4 January 1962.

INTRUDER IN THE DUST The records of Faulkner's agent, Harold Ober, reveal that galleys of the novel *Intruder in the Dust* (publication date, 27 September 1948) were received on 7 July 1948, and two attempts were made to place the excerpt, under this title, with magazines later that month. The records do not reveal which, or how many, galleys were involved, nor is it possible to tell now in which part of the published book the excerpt appears.

THE JAIL *Partisan Review*, XVIII (September–October 1951), 496–515, 598–608. Published as a part of Faulkner's forthcoming novel, *Requiem for a Nun* (publication date, 27 September 1951), in which it appears as the narrative prologue to Act III. The records of Faulkner's agent, Harold Ober, show that the piece was sold 27 June 1951, and that the text consisted of proofs of the book.

LUCAS BEAUCHAMP The records of Faulkner's agent, Harold Ober, reveal that a copy of this excerpt from *Intruder in the Dust* (publication date, 27 September 1948) was received from the publisher on 12 May 1948. Presumably this copy consisted of pages from the typescript of the novel, for the piece was re-typed and the original returned to Random House 14 May. (The Random House records reveal that the composition order for the printer was 28 May 1948.) A twenty-six–page carbon TS., not typed by the author, survives in the Ober files; it constitutes, with minor differences, the first two chapters of the novel.

MINK SNOPES *Esquire*, LII (December 1959), 226–27, 228, 229, 230, 247, 248, 249, 250, 252–64. Published as a part of Faulkner's forthcoming novel, *The Mansion* (publication date, 13 November 1959), in which it appears as chapter 1. According to the records of Faulkner's agent, Harold Ober Associates, copy for the excerpt consisted of the first seventeen galleys of the novel, and it was sold on 30 July 1959.

THE WAIFS *Saturday Evening Post*, CCXXIX (4 May 1957), 26, 116, 118, 120. Published as an excerpt from Faulkner's forthcoming novel, *The Town* (1 May 1957), in which it appears as the concluding episode, in chapter 14. The records of Faulkner's agent, Harold Ober, reveal that copy for the excerpt consisted of the last five galleys of the book, and it was sold 22 January 1957.

Note: Faulkner's editor, the late Saxe Commins, told me sometime during the spring of 1957 that Faulkner's title for the excerpt was 'Them Indians' (see *The Town*, p. 369).

[Untitled excerpt from THE REIVERS] *Faulkner at West Point*, eds. Joseph L. Fant and Robert Ashley (New York: Random House, 1964), pp. 8–46. This account of the race between Acheron and Lightning, which is spread over parts of four chapters in *The Reivers* (publication date, 4 June 1962), was read, from a pre-publication copy of the book, by Faulkner to an audience at the United States Military Academy on 19 April 1962. The lecture was tape-recorded, and the transcription published here shows a number of minor changes which Faulkner made from the printed text in his reading.

III. THE COLLECTIONS

Faulkner published three miscellaneous collections of his short fiction: *These 13* in 1931, *Doctor Martino and Other Stories* in 1934, and *Collected Stories* in 1950. In addition, he published two short collections which are built upon a central character or theme, *Knight's Gambit* in 1949 and *Big Woods* in 1955, both of which may be by-products of the thinking about his short fiction that the 1950 collection forced upon him.

Other Faulkner works, which are more properly considered novels, like *The Unvanquished* in 1938 and *Go Down, Moses* in 1942, are built up from revised versions of a number of his stories, and several of his other novels incorporate still other stories. They are listed here in chronological order of the original publication of the book.

These 13. (Stories.) New York: Cape and Smith, [21 September] 1931.

321

Contains: 'Victory', 'All the Dead Pilots', 'Crevasse', 'A Justice', 'Mistral', 'Divorce in Naples', and 'Carcassonne', all printed for the first time; 'Ad Astra' (revised from *American Caravan IV*, 1931), 'Red Leaves' (revised from *Saturday Evening Post*, 25 October 1930), 'A Rose for Emily' (slightly revised from *Forum*, April 1930), 'Hair' (revised from *American Mercury*, May 1931), 'That Evening Sun' (revised from 'That Evening Sun Go Down', *American Mercury*, March 1931), and 'Dry September' (revised from *Scribner's*, January 1931).

All thirteen stories are reprinted in *Collected Stories of William Faulkner*.

Doctor Martino and Other Stories. (Stories.) New York: Smith and Haas, [16 April] 1934.

Contains: 'Black Music' and 'Leg', both printed for the first time; 'Doctor Martino' (reprinted from *Harper's*, November 1931), 'Fox Hunt' (reprinted from *Harper's*, September 1931), 'The Hound' (reprinted from *Harper's*, August 1931), 'Death Drag' (reprinted, with minor changes, from 'Death-Drag', *Scribner's*, January 1932), 'There Was a Queen' (reprinted from *Scribner's*, January 1933), 'Smoke' (reprinted, with minor changes, from *Harper's*, April 1932), 'Turn About' (revised from *Saturday Evening Post*, 5 March 1932), 'Beyond' (reprinted from *Harper's*, September 1933), 'Wash' (reprinted from *Harper's*, February 1934), 'Elly' (reprinted from *Story*, February 1934), 'Mountain Victory' (revised from 'A Mountain Victory', *Saturday Evening Post*, 3 December 1932), and 'Honor' (reprinted from *American Mercury*, July 1930).

'The Hound' was incorporated, extensively revised, in *The Hamlet;* 'Smoke' was reprinted in *Knight's Gambit*. The other twelve stories were reprinted in *Collected Stories*, 'Leg' under the title 'The Leg' and 'Turn About' under the title 'Turnabout'. ('Wash', although reprinted in *Collected Stories*, had been incorporated, extensively revised, in *Absalom, Absalom!*)

Absalom, Absalom! (Novel.) New York: Random House, [26 October] 1936.

Pp. 278–92 of chapter 7 incorporate, extensively revised, the short story 'Wash' (from *Doctor Martino;* reprinted in *Collected Stories*). Chapter 1 (pp. 7–30) had appeared, entitled 'Absalom,

Absalom!' and with a number of minor changes, in *American Mercury*, August 1936.

The Unvanquished. (Novel.) New York: Random House, [15 February] 1938.

The first six chapters had been previously published as short stories and were revised for the book. The first five had appeared in *Saturday Evening Post:* 'Ambuscade' (29 September 1934), 'Retreat' (13 October 1934), 'Raid' (3 November 1934), 'Riposte in Tertio' (entitled 'The Unvanquished', 14 November 1936), and 'Vendée' (5 December 1936). Chapter 6, 'Skirmish at Sartoris', is revised from *Scribner's*, April 1935. The final chapter, 'An Odor of Verbena', is here printed for the first time.

The Hamlet. (Novel.) New York: Random House, [1 April] 1940.

Incorporates extensively revised versions of 'Fool about a Horse' (pp. 33–53; from *Scribner's*, August 1936), 'The Hound' (pp. 250–96; from *Doctor Martino*), 'Spotted Horses' (pp. 309–79; from *Scribner's*, June 1931), and 'Lizards in Jamshyd's Courtyard' (pp. 383–421; from *Saturday Evening Post*, 27 February 1932). Part of the story of 'Barn Burning' (*Harper's*, June 1939) is told here (pp. 15–21) but it is not taken over as a whole. A source for the episode on pp. 197–99 is in the short story 'Afternoon of a Cow' (first printed in 1943, but the NjP TS. is dated 1937).

Go Down, Moses. (Novel.) New York: Random House, [11 May] 1942.

Contains: 'Was' (printed for the first time); 'The Fire and the Hearth' (incorporates 'Gold Is Not Always', *Atlantic*, November 1940, and 'A Point of Law', *Collier's*, 22 June 1940); 'Pantaloon in Black' (revised from *Harper's*, October 1940); 'The Old People' (revised from *Harper's*, September 1940); 'The Bear' (incorporates, extensively revised, 'Lion', *Harper's*, December 1935, and 'The Bear', *Saturday Evening Post*, 9 May 1942); 'Delta Autumn' (revised from *Story*, May–June 1942); and 'Go Down, Moses' (revised from *Collier's*, 25 January 1941).

'The Old People' and all but the fourth section of 'The Bear' were reprinted in *Big Woods*, and part of 'Delta Autumn' was used, revised, for its epilogue.

Knight's Gambit. (Stories.) New York: Random House, [7 November] 1949.

Contains: 'Smoke' (reprinted from *Doctor Martino*), 'Monk' (reprinted from *Scribner's*, May 1937), 'Hand upon the Waters' (reprinted from *Saturday Evening Post*, 4 November 1939), 'Tomorrow' (reprinted from *Saturday Evening Post*, 23 November 1940), 'An Error in Chemistry' (reprinted from *Ellery Queen's Mystery Magazine*, June 1946), and 'Knight's Gambit' (printed for the first time). The title story is long enough (about 33,000 words) to be considered a short novel rather than a short story.

Collected Stories of William Faulkner. (Stories.) New York: Random House, [21 August] 1950.

All forty-two stories in this collection were reprinted from their sources without revision. They are listed here alphabetically: 'Ad Astra' (*These 13*), 'All the Dead Pilots' (*These 13*), 'Artist at Home' (*Story*, August 1933), 'Barn Burning' (*Harper's*, June 1939), 'A Bear Hunt' (*Saturday Evening Post*, 10 February 1934), 'Beyond' (*Doctor Martino*), 'Black Music' (*Doctor Martino*), 'The Brooch' (*Scribner's*, January 1936), 'Carcassonne' (*These 13*), 'Centaur in Brass' (*American Mercury*, February 1932), 'A Courtship' (*Sewanee Review*, Autumn 1948), 'Crevasse' (*These 13*), 'Death Drag' (*Doctor Martino*), 'Divorce in Naples' (*These 13*), 'Doctor Martino' (*Doctor Martino*), 'Dry September' (*These 13*), 'Elly' (*Doctor Martino*), 'Fox Hunt' (*Doctor Martino*), 'Golden Land' (*American Mercury*, May 1935), 'Hair' (*These 13*), 'Honor' (*Doctor Martino*), 'A Justice' (*These 13*), 'The Leg' (*Doctor Martino*, entitled 'Leg'), 'Lo!' (*Story*, November 1934), 'Mistral' (*These 13*), 'Mountain Victory' (*Doctor Martino*), 'Mule in the Yard' (*Scribner's*, August 1934), 'My Grandmother Millard and General Bedford Forrest and the Battle of Harrykin Creek' (*Story*, March–April 1943), 'Pennsylvania Station' (*American Mercury*, February 1934), 'Red Leaves' (*These 13*), 'A Rose for Emily' (*These 13*), 'Shall Not Perish' (*Story*, July–August 1943), 'Shingles for the Lord' (*Saturday Evening Post*, 13 February 1943), 'The Tall Men' (*Saturday Evening Post*, 31 May 1941), 'That Evening Sun' (*These 13*), 'That Will Be Fine' (*American Mercury*, July 1935), 'There Was a Queen' (*Doctor Martino*), 'Turnabout' (*Doctor Martino*, entitled 'Turn About'), 'Two Soldiers' (*Saturday Evening Post*, 28 March 1942), 'Uncle Willy' (*American Mercury*, October 1935), 'Victory' (*These 13*), and 'Wash' (*Doctor Martino*).

'A Bear Hunt' was included, revised, in *Big Woods*. 'Centaur in Brass' and 'Mule in the Yard' were incorporated, extensively revised, in *The Town*.

Part of 'Red Leaves' was used — revised — as the prelude of 'The Old People', and part of 'A Justice' was used — revised — as the prelude of 'A Bear Hunt', *Big Woods* (1955).

Requiem for a Nun. (Novel.) New York: Random House, [27 September] 1951.

Each of the three acts has a title and includes a narrative prologue: Act I, 'The Courthouse (A Name for the City)'; Act II, 'The Golden Dome (Beginning Was the Word)'; Act III, 'The Jail (Nor Even Yet Quite Relinquish)'. The narrative prologue to Act I is revised from 'A Name for the City', *Harper's*, October 1950; the narrative prologue to Act III appeared as 'The Jail', *Partisan Review*, September–October 1951.

Pp. 101–5 were reprinted as the prelude of 'The Bear', *Big Woods*.

A Fable. (Novel.) New York: Random House, [2 August] 1954.

Pp. 151–89 contain, revised, the episode published separately as *Notes on a Horsethief;* pp. 151–204 appeared, under the same title, in *Vogue*, July 1954.

Big Woods. (Stories.) New York: Random House, [14 October] 1955.

Contains four hunting stories, each introduced by a prelude, with a final epilogue: 'The Bear' (sections one, two, three, and five reprinted from 'The Bear', *Go Down, Moses;* prelude reprinted from pp. 101–5 of *Requiem for a Nun*); 'The Old People' (reprinted from *Go Down, Moses;* prelude revised from part of 'Red Leaves', from *Collected Stories*); 'A Bear Hunt' (revised from *Collected Stories;* prelude revised from part of 'A Justice', from *Collected Stories*); and 'Race at Morning' (revised from *Saturday Evening Post*, 5 March 1955; prelude revised from part of 'Mississippi', *Holiday*, April 1954); epilogue (revised from part of 'Delta Autumn', *Go Down, Moses*).

The Town. (Novel.) New York: Random House, [1 May] 1957.

Incorporated here are extensively revised versions of 'Centaur in Brass' (in chapter 1) and 'Mule in the Yard' (in chapter 16;

both in *Collected Stories*). Pp. 359–71 appeared in *Saturday Evening Post*, 4 May 1957, entitled 'The Waifs'.

The Mansion. (Novel.) New York: Random House, [13 November] 1959.

A revised version of 'By the People' (from *Mademoiselle*, October 1955) appears in chapter 13. Chapter 1, entitled 'Mink Snopes', appeared in *Esquire*, December 1959. A revised version of 'Hog Pawn' (see Section I-B) appears in chapter 14.

The Reivers. (Novel.) New York: Random House, [4 June] 1962.

Portions of chapters 5 and 7, entitled 'The Education of Lucius Priest', appeared in *Esquire*, May 1962. An excerpt from chapter 4, entitled 'Hell Creek Crossing', and with an introduction revised by Faulkner from the preceding part of the novel, appeared in *Saturday Evening Post*, 31 March 1962. Excerpts from the account of the race between Acheron and Lightning (pp. 236–303) were read, from an advance copy of the novel, by Faulkner to an audience at the United States Military Academy on 19 April 1962. In his reading Faulkner made a number of minor changes in the printed text, and a transcription of the text as he delivered it appears in *Faulkner at West Point*, eds. Joseph L. Fant and Robert Ashley (New York: Random House, 1964), pp. 8–46.

Index of Titles

Listed here are all the titles of Faulkner's short fiction which appear elsewhere in this bibliography, including the introductions to the different parts. However, slightly differing titles for the same work which would not affect alphabetization (for example, LEG/THE LEG) are omitted, though the page references for them are of course included. Titles of Faulkner's collections of stories and of his novels are omitted; where a novel title appears (for example, ABSALOM, ABSALOM!), it refers to the excerpt from that novel, published under that title.

DUMMY: *THE "GENIUS"*, BY THEODORE DREISER

JOSEPH KATZ

ELEVEN YEARS AFTER THE BEDEVILED PUBLICATION OF *Sister Carrie*, Theodore Dreiser began the novel that was to cause him even more trouble. *The "Genius"* was motivated by a frankly autobiographical impulse to resolve in fiction the manifold complications arising from his attempt to manage serious work and equally serious womanizing while maintaining a bad marriage in turn-of-the-century America. Art and life compounded explosively. A few months after the book appeared in 1915, *The "Genius"* was banned in Boston, and the rifts, rages, suits, and countersuits that followed polarized the country around the issues of sex, censorship, and literature. Dreiser's position as a twisted man, or as a creative hero, depending upon who was speaking, became solidified. *The "Genius"* was crucial in his career.

Its history before suppression is cloudy. According to Robert H. Elias, Dreiser began relatively simply in 1911 with the story of Eugene Witla, newspaperman; but soon he found an outside correlative for his concerns with the role of the artist in the painter Everitt Shinn, and modified Witla's story accordingly.[1] Although the novel was complete by August 1911, 'lying on ice, all neatly typewritten, awaiting its turn' for publication in October,[2] it could not find a home immediately. Between that time and publication four years later, events intervened to complicate its story: Dreiser drafted a number of his friends to read and make comments on the book; he had typescripts prepared of it; those scripts were lost; he rewrote the book in 1914; he encouraged the advice of several more informal readers; he prepared a serialization that seems never to have been published (although a later serial version made by his friend Lengel was); and a host of people—including friends, lovers, and various members of John Lane's staff—took a hand in editing the copy that eventually was printed.

There is a further complication yet unnoticed. At some point after July 1914 when John Lane contracted for *The "Genius"*, probably in the few months before September 1915 when they published it in America, the company produced a dummy for their travelers to use in selling the book. There has not yet been an intensive study of publishers' dummies, but one would suppose that during this time, as after, publishers would have seized upon using existing type pages as the most economical way of creating the few samples their men would need in the field. That is not true in this case. The dummy of *The "Genius"* is radically different from the first printing, and all subsequent printings, of the book published only a few months later.

I

From the outside, the dummy of *The "Genius"* looks like the first American edition, except that it is noticeably slimmer. It is in the same gold-stamped red T cloth casing, but it has only 304 pages instead of the 736 pages in the book. There are nineteen gatherings in eights in the dummy, but only the first gathering is printed—the re-

[1] *Theodore Dreiser, Apostle of Nature* (New York: Alfred A. Knopf, 1948), p. 155.

[2] W. A. Swanberg, *Dreiser* (New York: Charles Scribner's Sons, 1965), p. 146. Dreiser to William C. Lengel, 15 October 1911; in Robert H. Elias, *Letters of Theodore Dreiser* (Philadelphia: University of Pennsylvania Press, 1959), I, 122.

maining eighteen gatherings are blanks. To reduce waste in supplying a number of blanks in the dummy equal to the number of printed pages in the book, the manufacturer used wove paper .007+ inches thick in place of wove paper .005 inches, slackening the margin around the spine stamping to take up the slack. The casual examiner of externals may find the only clue to the dummy's character the rubber-stamped 'SAMPLE' on the top edge.

When he opens the dummy, however, he finds a far different situation. One difference is in preliminary pagination. The book's text begins on page 9. Preceding it are: half title, [1]; 'BY THEODORE DREISER', [2]; title, [3]; copyright page, [4]; ' "Eugene Witla, wilt thou have this woman . . ." ', [5]; blank, [6]; 'BOOK I | [rule] | YOUTH', [7]; blank, [8]. The dummy, however, has two fewer pages of preliminaries, and its text begins on page 7; it omits the extract from the marriage ceremony and the blank which backs it and replaces the section half title with an additional book half title. These changes bring the dummy to the text quickly and economically, as well as checking the impression that the novel is large and multi-sectioned. They seem not to have other significance.

There seems to be significance in the variation of the dummy's title page from that of the book, however. The dummy omits the Toronto imprint of S. B. Gundy, present in the book. This suggests that the arrangement for Canadian publication was made relatively late in 1915, after the dummy was printed.

The most striking divergences between the dummy and the book, though, are in the texts themselves. There are only two chapters of text in the dummy. But these are not the first two chapters of the book, even though they are numbered 1 and 2. Instead, they are a stringent condensation of the events in the book's first seven chapters. Chapters 1 and 2 in the dummy outline Eugene's background, early life, first job on the Alexandria *Appeal*, and meeting with Angela Blue; but they include no mention of his early affair with Stella, awakening commitment to art, departure for Chicago, work there, later affair with Margaret, enrollment in the Chicago Art Institute, or return to Alexandria. That is a simpler story than the one read by purchasers of the book, and it is a story that is much closer to Dreiser's original conception. With no reference to Eugene's early experiments with sex, livelihood, or career, this is a faster paced beginning that leads directly to his life with Angela. The correspondence between the structure of the dummy and that of the book roughly is as follows:

DUMMY	BOOK
chapter 1	chapter 1: 1.1–13.3; chapter 2: 22.1–23.32
chapter 2	chapter 2: 23.33–26.15; chapter 7: 60.39–63.24

But if condensation were the only feature of the dummy, it would be easy to suggest its origin in a facile editor's having been assigned by the publisher to move the story along so that it could catch large orders from buyers for big bookstores. There are, however, at least four striking instances in which the dummy text is more expansive than the text of the book—not less. The first two concern Eugene's introduction to the newspaper on which he began his working career, the Alexandria *Appeal.* His meeting with publisher Benjamin C. Burgess is described in *greater* detail in the dummy than in the book:

Dummy (p. 10)	Book (p. 23)
So it was that he stopped in at the office of the *Appeal,* on the ground floor of the three-story *Appeal* building, in the public square, one sunny April afternoon, and saw Mr. Burgess. The latter looked at him quizzically when he stated his business. He was a fat man, slightly bald, with a round head, smooth shaven, and a short nose surmounted by a pair of steel-rimmed spectacles. What little hair he had was grey.	He stopped in one sunny April afternoon at Mr. Burgess' office. It was on the ground floor of the three-story *Appeal* building in the public square. Mr. Burgess, a fat man, slightly bald, looked at him quizzically over his steel rimmed spectacles. What little hair he had was gray.

Later, he sees the *Appeal* office. Although the dummy's description is shorter than the book's, it does contain particulars not in the published edition.

Dummy (p. 11)	Book (p. 23)
The office of the *Appeal* was not different from that of any other country newspaper. The ground floor was given over to	The office of the *Appeal* was not different from that of any other country newspaper office within the confines of our two

the business and cash office, with the flat-bed press and the three hand and foot job printing presses lined up in a large and fairly well lighted room in the rear. On the second floor was the composing room, with its rows of type cases on their high racks and the one dingy office of the so-called editor, or managing editor, or city editor, for all three meant the same person, Mr. Caleb Williams.

hemispheres. On the ground floor in front was the business office, and in the rear the one large flat bed press and the job presses. On the second floor was the composing room with its rows of type cases on their high racks—for this newspapers was, like most other country newspapers, still set by hand; and in front was the one dingy office of the so-called editor, or managing editor, or city editor—for all three were the same person, a Mr. Caleb Williams whom Burgress had picked up in times past from heaven knows where.

The other two instances in which the dummy provides information not in the book concern Eugene's meeting with Angela. In the first, Bangs introduces them amidst some social teasing:

Dummy (pp. 13–14)

"Did you make that?" asked Eugene.
"Of course I did."
"Well, that's really pretty," said Bangs, moving away and looking at her.
"Mr. Bangs is such a flatterer," she smiled at Eugene. "He doesn't mean anything he says. He just tells me one thing after another."
"He's right," said Eugene. "I agree as to the dress, and somehow it fits the hair."
"She wears it for that reason," added Bangs. "Look at that brown ribbon down there."

Book (p. 62)

"Did you make that?" asked Eugene.
"Of course I did."
Bangs moved away a little, looking at her as if critically. "Well, that's really pretty," he pronounced.
"Mr. Bangs is such a flatterer," she smiled at Eugene. "He doesn't mean any thing he says. He just tells me one thing after another."
"He's right," said Eugene. "I agree as to the dress, and it fits the hair wonderfully."
"You see, he's lost, too," laughed Bangs. "That's the way they all do. Well, I'm going to

He talked familiarly in the general small town way.

"Now you hush," she pleaded. "You mustn't say I'm vain. I don't want to be."

"You're not," encouraged Eugene.

"You see, he's lost too," laughed Bangs. "That's the way they all do. I'm going to leave you two. I've got to get back. I left your sister in the hands of a rival of mine."

leave you two. I've got to get back. I left your sister in the hands of a rival of mine."

In the second, there is exposition of Angela's background leading the scene to a close:

Dummy (p. 14)	Book (pp. 62–63)
For some reason, and in spite of the moving interest of the scene, they fell into each other's histories. She was from Blackwood, only eighty-five miles from Chicago, and had lived there all her life. There were eight brothers and sisters. Her father was evidently a farmer and politician and what not, for Eugene gathered from scraps of her conversation that they must be well thought of, though poor. One brother-in-law was spoken of as a banker; another as the owner of a grain elevator. She, herself, was a school teacher — had been for several years.	They fell to telling each other their histories. She was from Blackwood, only eighty-five miles from Chicago, and had lived there all her life. There were several brothers and sisters. Her father was evidently a farmer and politican and what not, and Eugene gleaned from stray remarks that they must be well thought of, though poor. One brother-in-law was spoken of as a banker; another as the owner of a grain elevator; she herself was a school teacher at Blackwood — had been for several years.

II

The "Genius" dummy is an important key to the textual history of the novel. In the Theodore Dreiser Collection of the Charles Patterson Van Pelt Library at the University of Pennsylvania, there is a typescript identified by Dreiser as 'Original Copy'.[3] Without the dummy, the significance of that typescript is obscure. A transcription of the manuscript in the Theodore Dreiser Collection, the typescript has been heavily edited in pencil. It seems to be true editing, not the result of authorial revision: one would be hard pressed to identify from the slashes deleting material just who made them, but the insertions and substitutions do not appear to be Dreiser's. Once the dummy is known, however, it is clear that the typescript was its ultimate source. But because the typescript shows no signs of having passed through the hands of a compositor it probably was not setting copy. That likely was a fair copy, now missing. The same fair copy, though, could not have served also for setting the first edition, because it would have recorded the editing that distinguishes the dummy's text from that of the first edition. Obviously, separate printer's copy was needed for each. Just as obviously, the surviving typescript indicates that the missing first-edition printer's copy was descended from the unedited text of the typescript, and then went through independent editing of its own.

Too much is missing for the textual history of The "Genius" to be anything but a matter of speculation, but with the dummy as a key it is possible to develop an hypothesis. If Dreiser was not simply stalling Mencken, 'two complete typewritten copies' of the novel had been lost and were slowly being replaced in June 1914, when they were 'nearly recopied.'[4] Early that November he had the first sixty-one chapters, 'rather badly pencil-marked because (for serial purposes), certain things were marked to be left out. I am promised 62 to 104 this Saturday—marked in the same way. Now I could wait until I get all of this stuff in hand and having turned it over to Lane for safe-keeping send you the unmarked copy they have, but Jones rather objects to that. If you think you could wade through the marked copy I can send you what I have now and the balance when I get it. Nothing is out—only portions marked out[.]'[5] Although Mencken eagerly agreed to read the marked-up copy, Dreiser decided not to send it to him. At the end of November, Dreiser wrote

[3]For extraordinary cooperation in giving me access to photocopies of the draft materials in the Van Pelt Library, and for information about their physical appearance, I am most grateful to Mrs. Neda Westlake, curator of the Rare Book Collection. I also acknowledge the kind permission of The Trustees of the University of Pennsylvania to reproduce those portions that appear here.

[4]Letters, I, 169.

[5]Letters, I, 181–82.

him that 'By Adams express, today, prepaid I sent you chapters 1 to 66 (I believe) of the typewritten ms. — of *"The Genius"*, 2nd carbon, unrevised.'[6]

In all likelihood, the marked-up script Mencken did not get to see is the one surviving in the Van Pelt Library. The date of it is right: Dreiser's address on its cover is 3609 Broadway, the apartment he shared with his wife from July 1911 until their breakup in October 1913 — and his mailing address until April 1914.[7] If so, the probability is that one of the unmarked copies of that script was what Lane's editors used in their preparation of the first-edition text. And this means that at some point the publisher had both the script they were editing and the one that already had been edited for serial purposes. One led to the first edition, the other to the dummy. In that case, the ancestral relationship between the two texts would have been something like this:

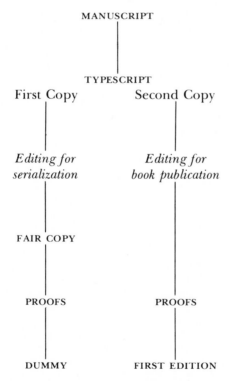

MANUSCRIPT

TYPESCRIPT

First Copy   Second Copy

*Editing for   Editing for
serialization   book publication*

FAIR COPY

PROOFS   PROOFS

DUMMY   FIRST EDITION

[6] *Letters*, I, 183. The words '2nd carbon' raise a small question. Had Dreiser indeed meant that there were a ribbon copy and two carbon copies of it; or

Why this would have been done is another question, the answer to which would shed some light on one aspect of book publishing and marketing during the period 1910–20. One likely possibility is that Lane's editors had to do such a large job of editing that they had to proceed without the distraction of participating in the preparation of the travelers' dummy. Another is that the dummy had to have been prepared before the editing of the book was launched, and that the marked-up script therefore was the handiest way of launching it. A third is that Lane decided that the condensation provided a more attractive text as a sample for marketing purposes. And the inevitable fourth is that the publisher really preferred to publish the serial version in book form, but was dissuaded from doing so until after the dummy was put into production.

Whatever the reasons for its existence, the text of the dummy has clear implications for that of the novel. One is that the surviving typescript, its serial editing ignored, should serve as copy-text for a critical edition. Another, more interesting, is that the dummy supplies the editor with a rare tool, a standard for determining to some degree the publisher's editing of the first edition. For if dummy and first edition both were descended from the same ancestral script, but each was edited independently, and the intermediate script for one survives, it is relatively easy to triangulate onto the kinds of things done to either one.

It seems clear that the study of publishers' dummies should not be neglected.

*

had he slipped, intending to say '2nd copy' — meaning one carbon? If there had been three copies — one held by the publisher, one sent out for serial editing, and one other — the wonder is why Dreiser made such a fuss about Mencken having to read the marked copy rather than immediately offering to send the unedited third copy. After all, he should have preferred to hold onto the copy on which so much work had been expended, instead of thinking to trust its being away from him after two previous scripts had been lost.

[7]Swanberg, *Dreiser,* pp. 145, 169, 175.

Genius

The Genius

Chapter I — 31 Pages

This story has its origin in the town of Alexandria,
Illinois, between 1884 and 1889, at the time
when that place had a population of about seven to
ten thousand. There was about it just enough of the air of a city
to take away the sense of rural life which much smaller places suffer
from. It had one street car line running from
its environs on the west to its environs on the East
It was connected with car lines from other towns and cities
There was a theatre or rather an opera house, so called — (why no

PLATE 1

one might say (for *mafia* was our *informed* there)
~~several~~ Two railroads, with two stations,
a business heart comprising four brisk sides
of a *public* square, the centre of which was
occupied by the ~~the~~ county court house and
several ~~news~~ newspapers, ~~two~~ morning and two
evening which made the population fairly alive
~~the~~ to the fact that life was full of issues
local and national and that there were very
many interesting and ~~too~~ varied things to do *entail*
the little *river* of *making* a *living* in *this* place.
One of its most *pleasing* *aspects* was the *presence* of *several* *lakes*
in the *wood* and that one *might* be *fairly*
and a pretty *stream*, all on the edge of the town *which grew*
to it an *atmosphere*, not *unlike* to *that* of a *moderately* *priced*
if and *doing* *to succeed*. *It was brisk*,
summer *resort*. Architecturally *the town was neat*
new, mostly built of wood, as all American

PLATE 2

The Genius.   36

Chapter I.

This story has its origin in the town of Alexandria, Illinois,
between 1884 and 1889, at the time when the place had a population of
about ten thousand. There was about it just enough of the air of a city
to take away from it the sense of rural life, ~~which such smaller places
suffer from. It had one street car line running from its environs on the
east to its environs on the east, later connected~~ with car lines from
other towns and cities. There was a theatre, or rather an opera house,
so called -(why no one might say, for no opera was ever performed there,
two railroads, with two stations, a business heart, composed of four
brisksides to a public square, the center of which was occupied by the
county court house and severalnewspapers, two morning and two evening,
which made the population fairly alive to the fact that ~~there were very~~
life was full of issues,local and national, and that there were very
many interesting and varied things to do or see. One of its most pleasing aspects was the presence of several lakes, and a pretty stream, all
on the edge of the town, which gave it an atmosphere not unakin to a
moderate priced summer resort. Architecturally the town was not new, mostly built of wood, as all American towns were at this time, but laid
out prettily in some sections, with houses that sat back in great yards,
far from the streets, and where flower beds,brick walks, and green trees
were concomitants of a comfortable ~~and life. It was, all told, as
clean as it was ambitious and energetic.~~ Alexandria was a city of young

PLATE 3

Americans. Its spirit was young. ~~Before~~ ~~everybody~~
~~financially~~

In one part of this city there lived at this time a family of
five people, father, mother, two daughters and a son, which in its
character and composition might well have been considered typically American, and middle western ~~~~. It was not by any means
poor - or, at least,-did not consider itself so; it was in no sense
rich. Thomas Jefferson Witla, the father, was a sewing machine agent
with the complete control of sale in that county ~~~~ one of the best
known and best selling machines made ~~~~. ~~county. He had the right to appoint agents under him and no one~~
could interfere with him nor take his trade away. From each twenty,
thirty-five or sixty dollar machine which he sold, he took a profit o
of thirty-five percent. The sale of machines was not great , but it
was enough to yield him nearly two thousand dollars a year, and on
that he had managed to buy a house and lot, to furnish it comfortably, to send his children to school and to maintain a local store
on the public square where the latest styles of machines were dis-
played. He also took old machines of other makes in exchange for his
new ones, allowing ten to fifteen dollars each against the purchase
price of a new machine. He also repaired machines, and with that peculiar energy of the American mind, tried to do a little insurance
business on the side. His first idea was that his son, Eugene o'Tennyson Witla, might take charge of this latter property once he became
old enough, and the insurance trade had developed sufficiently.
~~He did not know this now then might come to be, but it was~~
~~well in there ~~~~.~~ He was a quick , wiry,
active man of no great stature, sandy-haired, with blue eyes with
noticeable eye-brows, an eagle nose , and a rather radiant and in-

THE "GENIUS"

BY THEODORE DREISER

SISTER CARRIE

JENNIE GERHARDT

A TRAVELER AT FORTY

. . . .

A TRILOGY OF DESIRE
1. THE FINANCIER
2. THE TITAN
3. ********

PLATE 6

THE
"GENIUS"

BY
THEODORE DREISER

NEW YORK: JOHN LANE COMPANY
LONDON: JOHN LANE, THE BODLEY HEAD
MCMXV

Press of
J. J. Little & Ives Company
New York, U. S. A.

PLATE 8

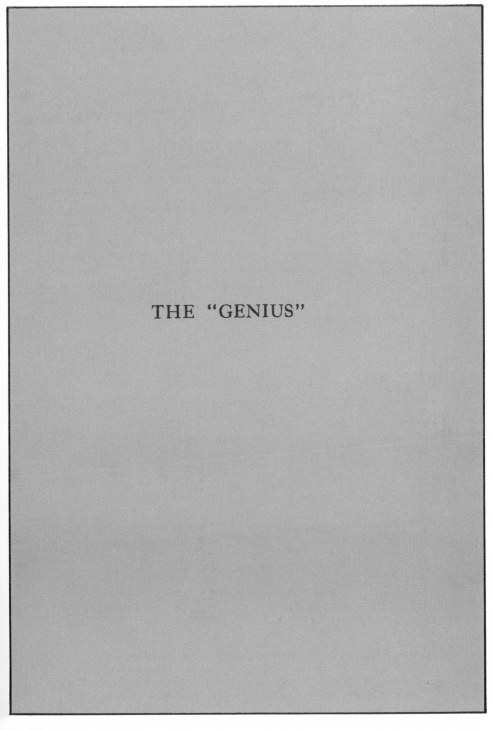

THE "GENIUS"

PLATE 9

PLATE 10

THE "GENIUS"

CHAPTER I

THIS story has its origin in the town of Alexandria, Illinois, between the years 1884 and 1889, at the time when the place had a population of around ten thousand. There was about it just enough of the air of a city to take away from it the sense of rural life, Alexandria was a city of young Americans. Its spirit was young.

In one part of this city there lived, at that time, a family of five people—father, mother, two daughters and a son—which in its character and composition, might well have been considered typically American and Middle Western. This family was by no means poor, or at least did not consider itself so; it was in no sense rich, however. Thomas Jefferson Witla, the father, was a sewing-machine agent, with the complete control of sale in that territory for one of the best-known and best-selling machines made. He was a quick, wiry, active man, of no great stature, sandy-haired, with blue eyes and noticeable eyebrows, an eagle nose and a rather radiant and ingratiating smile. He knew how to approach people pleasantly. His wife thought too pleasantly. Still, he was honest, hardworking and thrifty. They had been waiting a long time for the day when they could say they owned their own home and had a little something laid away for a rainy day, but they were in that position now, and it was not half bad.

Miriam Witla was well preserved, good-looking, poetic under a marked outward reserve. It was she who had insisted upon naming her only son Eugene Tennyson, a tribute at once to a brother named Eugene, and to the celebrated romanticist of verse, because she had been so impressed with his "Idylls of the King." Eugene Tennyson seemed rather strong to Witla pere, as the first name of a Middle Western Ameri-

7

can boy, but he loved his wife, and gave her her way in most things. He rather liked the names of Sylvia and Myrtle, which she had christened the two girls. All three of the children were good-looking; Sylvia, a girl of twenty-one, having black hair, blackish-brown eyes, a smooth dark skin with a touch of red in her cheeks and red lips. She was full-blown, like a rose—healthy, active, smiling. Myrtle was of a less vigorous constitution, small, pale, shy, but intensely sweet, like the flower she was named after, her mother said.

Eugene Witla was the apple of his family's eye, younger than either of his two sisters by two years, and, like them, dark. He had straight, smooth, black hair, which, even at the age of sixteen, he parted in the middle. He had dark, almond-shaped eyes, a straight nose, a shapely but not aggressive chin. His teeth were even and white, showing with a curious delicacy when he smiled, as if he were proud of them. He was not very strong, to begin with; moody, and to a notable extent, artistic. Because of a belief in a weak stomach and a semi-anæmic condition of his blood, he did not really appear as strong as he was, though later in life he became intensely virile. He had emotion, fire, divine longings in a way, but they were concealed at this time behind a wall of reserve. He was shy, proud, sensitive and very uncertain of himself. When at home he lounged about the house, reading Dickens, Thackeray, Scott and Poe. He browsed idly through one book after another, wondering about life. The great cities appealed to him. He thought of travel as a wonderful thing. In school he read Taine and Gibbon between recitation hours, wondering at the luxury and beauty of the great courts of the world. He cared nothing for grammar, nothing for mathematics, nothing for botany or physics, except odd bits here and there. Curious facts would strike him; the composition of clouds, the composition of water, the chemical elements of the earth. He liked to lie in the hammock at home, Spring, Summer or Fall, and look at the blue sky showing through the trees. A soaring buzzard poised in its speculative flight held his attention fixedly. The wonder of a snowy cloud piled high like wool and drifting as an island, was like a song to him. He had wit, a keen sense of humor, a sense of pathos. Sometimes he thought he would draw; sometimes write. He had a little talent for both, he felt, but he did practically nothing

8

PLATE 12

with either. He would sketch now and then, in a feeling, impressive sort of way, but only fragments: a small roof-top, with smoke curling from a chimney and birds flying; a bit of water with a willow bending over it and perhaps a boat anchored; a mill pond with ducks afloat and a boy or woman on the bank. He really had no vast talent for interpretation at this time, but he did have an intense sense of beauty.

When he had passed the twelve-year mark, his father began to see that Eugene was not much for business, and when he was sixteen he had well convinced him of it. Myrtle, his sister, who was two classes ahead of him, but sometimes in the same room, reported that he dreamed too much. He was always looking out of the window.

"I think we ought to get Eugene into newspaper work, or something like that," Witla senior suggested to his wife.

"It looks as though that's all he would be good for, at least now," replied Mrs. Witla, who was satisfied that her boy had not yet found himself. "I think he'll do something better later on. His health isn't very good, you know."

Witla half suspected that his boy was naturally lazy, but he wasn't sure. Eugene's addiction to lying in the hammock was great. He suggested that Benjamin C. Burgess, the prospective father-in-law of Sylvia, and the editor of the *Morning Appeal*, might give Eugene a place as a reporter or typesetter, in order that he might learn the business from the ground up. The *Appeal* carried few employees, but Mr. Burgess might have no objections to starting Eugene as a reporter if he could write, or as a student of typesetting, or both. He appealed to Burgess one day on the street and that personage told him to have Eugene call and see him.

Mr. Witla went home and told Eugene and his wife of this rather interesting opportunity, but Eugene was not at all enthusiastic.

"Burgess says he might give you a position as a typesetter or a reporter on the *Appeal*, if you'd come in some day," explained Witla, looking over to where his son was reading by the lamplight.

"Does he?" replied Eugene calmly. "Well, I can't write. I might set type. Did you ask him?"

"Yes," said Witla. "You'd better go to him some day."

Eugene bit his lip. He realized that this was a commentary

9

PLATE 13

on his loafing propensities. He wasn't doing very well; that was certain. Still, typesetting was no bright field for a person of his temperament. "I will," he concluded, "when school is over."

"Better speak before school ends. Some of the other fellows might ask for it around that time. It wouldn't hurt you to try your hand at it."

"I will," replied his son obediently.

So it was that he stopped in at the office of the *Appeal,* on the ground floor of the three-story *Appeal* building, in the public square, one sunny April afternoon, and saw Mr. Burgess. The latter looked at him quizzically when he stated his business. He was a fat man, slightly bald, with a round head, smooth shaven, and a short nose surmounted by a pair of steel-rimmed spectacles. What little hair he had was grey.

"So you think you would like to go into the newspaper business, do you?" queried Burgess.

"I'd like to try my hand at it," replied the boy. "I'd like to see whether I like it."

"I can tell you right now that there's very little in it. Your father says you like to write."

"I'd like to, well enough, but I don't think I can. I wouldn't mind learning typesetting. If I ever could write, I'd be perfectly willing to."

"When do you think you'd like to start?"

"At the end of school, if it's all the same to you."

"It doesn't make much difference. I'm not really in need of anybody, but I could use you. Would you be satisfied with five a week?"

"Yes, sir."

"Well, come in when you're ready. I'll see what I can do."

He waved the prospective typesetter away with a movement of his fat hand, and turned to his black walnut desk, dingy, covered with newspapers and lit by a green-shaded electric light. Eugene went out, the smell of fresh printing ink in his nose, and the equally interesting smell of damp newspapers. It was going to be an interesting experience, he thought, but perhaps a waste of time. He did not think so much of Alexandria. Sometime he was going to get out of it.

10

PLATE 14

CHAPTER II

THE office of the *Appeal* was not different from that of any other country newspaper. The ground floor was given over to the business and cash office, with the flat-bed press and the three hand and foot job printing presses lined up in a large and fairly well lighted room in the rear. On the second floor was the composing room, with its rows of type cases on their high racks and the one dingy office of the so-called editor, or managing editor, or city editor, for all three meant the same person, Mr. Caleb Williams. The office was run very quietly and efficiently, and in most ways, pleasantly. It was a sunny place in which to work.

Eugene, who came here at the end of his eleventh school year, and when he had just turned seventeen, was impressed with the personality of Mr. Williams. He liked him. He came to like a Jonas Lyle, who worked at what might be called the head desk of the composing room. It was Lyle who taught Eugene the art of typesetting. He demonstrated on the first day the theory of the squares or pockets in a case; how some letters were placed more conveniently to the hand than others; why some letters were well represented as to quantity; why capitals were used in certain offices for certain purposes, in others not. "Now, on the *Chicago Tribune,* we used to italicize the names of churches, boats, books, hotels, and things of that sort. That's the only paper I ever knew to do that," he, for example, sagely remarked. He wanted his knowledge taken seriously, and Eugene, because of his innate respect for learning of any and all kinds, was very glad to give Lyle his serious attention. He did not know what he wanted to do, but he knew quite well that he wanted to see everything.

This shop was interesting to him for some little time, for this reason, for though he soon found that he did not want to be a typesetter or a reporter, or indeed anything in connection with a country newspaper, he was learning about life. He worked at his desk cheerfully, smiling out upon the world

11

PLATE 15

which indicated its presence to him through an open window, read the curious bits of news or opinion or local advertisements as he composed them, and dreamed of what the world might have in store for him. He thought mostly that he would like to be an artist. He was not vastly ambitious as yet, but hopeful, and yet, withal, a little melancholy. He could see boys and girls idling in the streets or on the corner squares. There were thoughts in his mind of fishing, boating, lolling somewhere with some pretty girl, but alas, girls did not take to him so very readily, apparently. He was too shy. If he were only rich, what a life he would lead, how happy he would be! Almost up to the time that Eugene was called to take his place in the world, his experience with girls had not been very wide. There were those very minor things that occur in early youth—girls whom we furtively kiss, or who equally furtively kiss us. The latter had been the way in Eugene's case, but he had no notable interest in any one girl.

He was twenty years of age when Myrtle announced one evening after he had reached home from the office that he was to go with her and Mr. Bangs to a party. There were going to be games and refreshments. After supper, Mr. Bangs called, and with him and Myrtle Eugene attended a typical small town affair. There were some twenty-two young men and women all crowded into three fair-sized rooms and on a porch, the windows and doors leading to which were open. Outside were grass and some Autumn flowers. Early crickets were chirping and there were late fireflies. It was warm and pleasant.

As usual, the opening efforts to be sociable were a trifle stiff. There were introductions all around, much smart badinage among town dandies, for most of them were there. Although there were games and jests, it was almost impossible for Eugene to break through the opening sense of reserve which clogged his actions at everything in the way of social diversion. He was a little nervous because he was afraid of criticism. That was his vanity and deep egotism. He stood about, trying to get into the swing of the thing, with a bright remark or two. Just as he was beginning to bubble, a girl came in from one of the other rooms. Eugene had not met her. She was with his prospective brother-in-law, Bangs, and

12

PLATE 16

was laughing in a sweet, joyous way which arrested his attention. She was dressed in white, he noticed, with a band of copper-colored ribbon pulled through the loops above the flounces which characterized the bottom of her dress. Her hair was of a wonderful ashen yellow—a great mass of it—and laid in big, thick braids above her forehead and ears. Her nose was straight, her lips, thin and red, her cheekbones faintly but curiously noticeable. Somehow, there was a sense of distinction to her, a faint aroma of personality, which Eugene did not understand. It appealed to him. Bangs brought her over. He was a tight, smiling youth, as sound as oak, as clear as good water.

"Here's Miss Blue, Eugene. She's from up in Wisconsin. I told her you ought to know her."

"Say, that's good luck, isn't it?" smiled Eugene. "I'm sure I'm glad to know you. What part of Wisconsin do you come from?"

"Blackwood," she laughed, her greenish-blue eyes dancing.

"Her hair is yellow, her eyes are blue, and she comes from Blackwood," commented Bangs. "How's that?" His big mouth, with its even teeth, was wide with a smile.

"Fine, only you left out the blue name and the white dress. She ought to wear white all the time."

"Oh, it does harmonize with my name, doesn't it?" she cried. "At home I do wear white mostly. You see, I'm just a simple country girl, and I make most of my things."

"Did you make that?" asked Eugene.

"Of course I did."

"Well, that's really pretty," said Bangs, moving away and looking at her.

"Mr. Bangs is such a flatterer," she smiled at Eugene. "He doesn't mean anything he says. He just tells me one thing after another."

"He's right," said Eugene. "I agree as to the dress, and somehow it fits the hair."

"She wears it for that reason," added Bangs. "Look at that brown ribbon down there."

He talked familiarly in the general small town way.

"Now you hush," she pleaded. "You mustn't say I'm vain. I don't want to be."

13

PLATE 17

"You're not," encouraged Eugene.

"You see, he's lost too," laughed Bangs. "That's the way they all do. I'm going to leave you two. I've got to get back. I left your sister in the hands of a rival of mine."

Eugene turned to the girl, who was clinging, subtle, emotional and passionate, but not ultimately big, and laughed his reserved laugh. "I was just thinking what was going to become of me."

"I'm worse yet. I've been here two weeks and I scarcely know anyone. Mrs. King takes me around everywhere, but it's all so new I can't get hold of it. I think Alexandria is lovely."

"It is nice. I suppose you have been out on the lakes?"

"Oh, yes, we've fished, and rowed and camped. I've had a lovely time, but I must go back to-morrow."

"Do you?" said Eugene. "That's too bad."

For some reason, and in spite of the moving interest of the scene, they fell into each other's histories. She was from Blackwood, only eighty-five miles from Chicago, and had lived there all her life. There were eight brothers and sisters. Her father was evidently a farmer and politician and what not, for Eugene gathered from scraps of her conversation that they must be well thought of, though poor. One brother-in-law was spoken of as a banker; another as the owner of a grain elevator. She, herself, was a school teacher—had been for several years.

Eugene did not realize it, but she was all of five years older than he was, with the tact and the superior advantage which so much difference in years brings. She was sick of school teaching, though he did not know that; sick of caring for the babies of married sisters; sick of being left to work and stay at home when the ideal marrying age was rapidly passing. She was interested in able people and silly village boys did not appeal to her. There was one who was begging her to marry him at that time, but he was a slow soul up in Blackwood, and not actually worthy of her capacity nor able to support her nicely. She was hopefully, sadly, vaguely, madly longing sometimes for something better, and as yet, nothing had ever eventuated. This meeting with Eugene was nothing which promised anything of a way out. (She was not seeking in any such urgent way—did not give introductions that sort of a

14

PLATE 18

twist in her consciousness exactly.) But this young man had an appeal for her beyond anyone who had been introduced to her recently. They were in sympathetic accord, apparently. She liked his clear, big eyes, his dark hair, his rather waxy complexion. He seemed at once, something better than she had known, and she hoped that he would be nice to her.

PLATE 19

THE CENTENARY HAWTHORNE EIGHT YEARS LATER: A Review Article

O M BRACK, JR.

ALMOST EVERYONE RECOGNIZES *The Centenary Edition of the Works of Nathaniel Hawthorne*, published by The Ohio State University Press, as the pioneering modern editorial project in American literary scholarship. A history of its immediate results begins in 1962, with the appearance of *The Scarlet Letter* as Volume I, at a time when most academics recommended bibliographical and textual work only as a refuge for the intellectually sterile. Times have changed, and the historian of literary studies must use the publication record of the Centenary Hawthorne for some of the most prominent landmarks in the story of that change: Volume II, *The Blithedale Romance* and *Fanshawe*, 1964; III, *The House of the Seven Gables*, 1965; IV, *The Marble Faun*, 1968; and—most recently—V, *Our Old Home*, 1970. In the years intervening between the publication of the first and fifth volumes, the CEAA was founded (1963) and given some funding, it created a seal (1967) with which it guaranteed a text's adherence to certain minimal standards, and it provided an umbrella under which

358

individual projects could gather to the advance of their own work and to the benefit of the profession. It is with some amazement, then, that one realizes that the Centenary Hawthorne itself is only eight years old: so much has been done in so little time. Because that is the case, it is especially instructive to give the entire project a backwards glance from the perspective of the latest volume.

The editorial performance in *Our Old Home* is of the same high quality that has distinguished the Centenary Hawthorne from the beginning, and it has resulted in appurtenances that will not seem strange to those familiar with preceding volumes of the project. In addition to all forms of the texts produced in Hawthorne's lifetime, the editors have collated as usual all resettings of the text through the 1900 Autograph Edition. Appendixes record the findings and the specific decisions based on them: alterations in the manuscripts, editorial emendations, rejected first-edition substantive variants, and word-divisions. As is true of all the volumes, *Our Old Home* also contains special appendixes dictated by the nature of this text. Particularly useful here is 'Cross-references with *The English Notebooks*', the edition produced in 1941 by Randall Stewart. The other ways in which the *Notebooks* are used, however, raise some questions about the gradual modification of textual practices in the Centenary Hawthorne.

As Claude M. Simpson explains in the historical 'Introduction to *Our Old Home*', while Hawthorne was serving as American consul in Liverpool he kept a voluminous journal with a view to using these notes in future publications. His first use of them was shortly after his return from Italy in 1860, when he wrote 'Some of the Haunts of Burns' for the October issue of the *Atlantic Monthly*, apparently at the urging of its publisher, William D. Ticknor. Thus began a series based on the *Notebooks* material, which eventually would become the volume *Our Old Home*. The final essay in the series, 'Civil Banquets', appeared in the *Atlantic* for August 1863. During the years between, all of the essays included in the volume appeared first in the *Atlantic*, with the exception of 'Consular Experiences' (which was reserved for the book) and 'Lichfield and Uttoxeter', (a new essay made from the earlier 'Uttoxeter', which had been published first in *The Keepsake* [London, 1857] and then reprinted in *Harper's New Monthly Magazine* for April 1857).

The relative complexity of this history presents some difficult textual problems, a number of which probably never will be resolved with any real certainty. Manuscripts of the twelve sketches have been located for all except 'Some of the Haunts of Burns' and 'Outside Glimpses of English Poverty', although the manuscript of 'About Warwick' is seriously incomplete. Since apparently no proof survives, the most common textual problem in *Our Old Home* is the need to determine the author's hand in a series in which the preserved manuscript was printer's copy for the magazine appearance and an authorially corrected copy of that text was used as setting copy for the book publication.

The decision here was to follow the basic practice of earlier volumes of the Centenary Hawthorne, using the preserved manuscripts as copy-texts and the major authority for accidentals. For the two sketches not represented in manuscript, copy-texts are the *Atlantic Monthly* appearances. So much is orthodox. The debatable procedure is emendation of accidentals for these two sketches on authority of the *Notebooks* when the textual editor believes they 'preserve Hawthorne's usual characteristics more faithfully than the print and may be presumed to represent what would have stood in the lost manuscripts' (p. cxv). Since, as Professor Bowers explains earlier in the textual introduction, 'Some of the Haunts of Burns' relies heavily on the *Notebooks* while 'Outside Glimpses of English Poverty' does not, the attempt at induction is of dubious value. It is not increased when he also draws on the *Notebooks* for evidence concerning accidentals in the missing portions of the 'About Warwick' manuscripts, which he says fall somewhere in between these two extremes of reliance on the earlier notes.

This procedure seems to blur a basic distinction in evaluating the textual authority of manuscripts. It is one thing to accept them for the texture of accidentals when they clearly were prepared for use by a printer for publication. Then they may be presumed to represent something at least close to the author's final intentions. It is, however, quite another thing to choose accidentals from pre-publication forms of the text—especially when, as in the case of *Our Old Home*, Hawthorne plainly did not intend to publish the *Notebooks* in that form when he wrote in them. In blurring this distinction the editor has obscured the interesting fact that as Hawthorne gained experience in working his journal entries into publishable essays he patently moved away from the informal style he used in his notebooks. Even such early sketches as 'Near Oxford' and 'Pilgrimage to Old Boston'—which transcribe or paraphrase the *Notebooks*—show a movement towards a more formal style. And, of course, although there are in- stances where his usages are extremely consistent between the *Note- books* and the publications, there are others in which he seems to have been inconsistent, indifferent. The probability is that Haw- thorne's usages would have been more consistent in a fair copy he consciously was preparing for publication than they would be in a journal he was keeping for his eyes only. In support of that prob- ability is his attempt to adopt English spellings for certain words in *The Marble Faun* manuscript because he knew that that book would be set in England.

This being the case, it would seem particularly dangerous to mine the private *Notebooks* in order to predict Hawthorne's public style in any specific instance. For example, the Centenary *Our Old Home* adopts the *Notebooks'* 'ale-house' rather than the *Atlantic's* 'alehouse' (199.33), but retains the *Atlantic's* 'farm-yard', 'donkey-stables', and 'pig-sties' (201.13, 16, 17) in preference to the *Notebooks'* 'farm yard', 'donkey stables', and 'pigsties'.[1] There appears to have been no moti- vating principle to the editor's choice. More important, there evi- dently was none when Hawthorne wrote in his journals. Evidence for his indifference is in the very next sentence in the *Notebooks*, where he wrote 'farm-yard'. What evidently has happened here editorially is that Professor Bowers had moved quietly away from positions he had taken once.

Bowers's basic editorial position, of course, essentially is that which W. W. Greg presented in 'The Rationale of Copy-Text' to the English Institute in 1949 and which Bowers published the next year in *Studies in Bibliography*. That same year Bowers himself began restating and refining those principles, elaborating them as time passed. Because Greg was concerned primarily with books for which there is extant no pre-publication form, one of Bowers's major contributions to textual theory has been to back up a step and argue that 'when an author's manuscript is preserved, this has paramount authority.'[2] Of course he did not maintain that *any* preserved manu- script automatically becomes copy-text. In every instance where some

---

[1] Nathaniel Hawthorne, *The English Notebooks*, ed. Randall Stewart (New York: Modern Language Association of America, 1941), p. 504. The page and line numbers given in parentheses throughout my essay are to the volumes of the Centenary Hawthorne.

[2] 'Some Principles for Scholarly Editions of Nineteenth-Century American Authors', *Studies in Bibliography*, XVII (1964), 226.

manuscript exists for a printed work, that manuscript's relationship to the first printing must be determined. Since, as Bowers said, the goal of critical editions is to 'approximate as nearly as possible an inferential authorial fair copy', if an author worked in such a way that the earliest printing of a text comes nearer to that fair copy than any preserved manuscript, that first printing should be copy-text.[3]

The question did not come up in *The Scarlet Letter*, since no known manuscript survives. For Volume I of the Centenary Hawthorne, therefore, the editorial task was uncomplicated.[4] Once it was established that Hawthorne rarely revised his work after it was in print, and then just to make corrections of obvious errors, later editions generally could be ignored textually and need have been reported only for historical reasons. In the case of *The Scarlet Letter*, none of the seventy variants between the first and second editions have to be attributed to Hawthorne. The few readings adopted from the second edition in the Centenary text are necessary corrections made by the Centenary editor—'adopted' here being a rough equivalent of 'historically sanctioned by', not 'authorized by'. In such an editorial situation, as Bowers says elsewhere, 'the editor attempts to approximate

---

[3]'Textual Criticism', in *The Aims and Methods of Scholarship in Modern Languages and Literatures*, ed. James Thorpe (New York: Modern Language Association of America, 1963), p. 26.

[4]In textual terms lack of complications does not insure perfection. The second printing of the Centenary *Scarlet Letter* does not acknowledge revisions from the first printing, but in it the text has been changed in two places—silently—and 'Editorial Emendations in the Copy-Text' has been emended—also silently—to include the following:

63.26   mid-day] E; midday 1850[1]—III
109.21   hall-window] IV; ~.~ 1850[1]—III, E

In the first Centenary printing the text records readings to the right of the brackets. In addition, one entry has been added to 'Word-Division: 1. End-of-the-Line Hyphenation in the Centenary Edition' to report belatedly an occurrence in the text:

52.11   town-beadle

I am grateful to Professor David J. Nordloh, Indiana University, for this information.

Obviously its importance is not that human beings can err—unless one claims that they do not. Its significance here is that the second impression of the Centenary *Scarlet Letter* has been revised without notice. One hopes that notice of revision will be added as soon as possible to copies not yet distributed.

the correctness of the manuscript, within the limitations of the evidence of the first edition, the only authoritative document.'[5]

The situation of *Fanshawe* would seem to be the same as that of *The Scarlet Letter:* no manuscript; only the first printed appearance has any authority. But, by the time Volume II of the Centenary Hawthorne was ready two years later, the editorial approach had modified. Bowers argued that one key to this kind of situation was the consistency of accidentals in the printed text: 'all internally consistent features of a first-edition copy-text must be retained in default of the evidence of the lost manuscript' (pp. 327–28). In *Fanshawe*, he goes on to say, accidentals in the copy-text are inconsistent because they depended on the individual usages of the five compositors who set the book. Presumably these people followed the difficult manuscript characteristics in different ways, and sometimes one, two, three, or — occasionally — four, agree in reproducing a known Hawthorne usage.

Under these circumstances no one can defend the proposition that every such variable in the first edition of *Fanshawe* has other than technical authority. It follows that when variation is present, and when some one form can be established from manuscript (even though later) as representing Hawthorne's known characteristic, without ever forsaking documentary authority in the print an editor can go a long way by emendation of non-characteristic variants toward reconstructing with confidence some authentic feature of the lost manuscript. . . . In this manner the edited text can actually be more authoritative in a number of details than the variable first edition, but never without reference to some authoritative reading within that edition. On the other hand, when all compositors are uniform, no authority exists within the print to justify emendation of the texture of the accidentals; and the first edition, the only documentary authority there is, has been faithfully followed without regard for its agreement or non-agreement with ascertained Hawthorne usage [p. 329].

This ingenious argument is unconvincing here. One reason is the casual way in which 'authority' is supplemented by the term 'technical authority'. Certainly no one would wish to argue that the accidentals in the first edition of *Fanshawe* have other than 'technical' authority. But by the same token no one could argue that the accidentals in *The Scarlet Letter* have other than 'technical' authority.

[5]'Textual Criticism', in Thorpe, *Aims and Methods*, p. 26 n. 9.

'Authority' is a technical term; and here it means that in the absence of a manuscript the first-edition accidentals ought to be accepted in lieu of more accurate information. The editor's duty in rejecting those accidentals in any instance is to argue successfully for their replacements — to convey conviction about his having more accurate information. I simply am not convinced that this was true for *Fanshawe*. There seem to be too many variables and not enough certainties.

Weak is the assumption that the lost *Fanshawe* manuscript was relatively consistent within itself. Certainly as Hawthorne developed his career as a novelist he tended towards consistency, but *Fanshawe* was his first novel. In the light of Hawthorne's subsequent attitude towards his first novel, it would seem dangerous to make many assertions about its manuscript on the basis of his later practices. When the editor assumes that Hawthorne's characteristics in 1828 were much like those in 1851–52, and tries to induce the *Fanshawe* manuscript from those of *The House of the Seven Gables* and *The Blithedale Romance* two decades later, he is on shaky grounds.

Another weakness is in the way the editor decided on places in which emendation was needed. He obtained his information from a compositorial analysis of the first edition; but ultimately this analysis must be judged highly conjectural. In the first place, thirty-two pages — about one-fourth — of the text could not be assigned with any certainty to any one of the compositors. In the second place, none of the takes that the editor felt confident in identifying provide a reasonably large sampling of material for analysis. Compositors A and D were considered to have set 30 and 33 pages respectively; but C is assigned 9 pages, B 17 pages, and E 18 pages (p. 317). Bowers later admitted that the two systems for assigning compositorial stints were not fully understood when *Fanshawe* was edited.[6] In the light of all this, the appropriate editorial course with *Fanshawe* would have been to treat it like *The Scarlet Letter* — accepting the first-edition accidentals, emending only clear errors, and acknowledging that the resulting text preserves an unassignable mixture of usages.

With the text of the remaining novels — *The House of the Seven Gables, The Blithedale Romance*, and *The Marble Faun* — the ground is both more treacherous and more solid. The printer's copy manuscripts for all three books have been preserved, and they serve as copy-texts for the Centenary Hawthorne. Editorially, the problem

[6] See the chart, p. 327.

364

here is deciding which of the many variants between manuscripts and first editions came from Hawthorne. In *The Blithedale Romance*, the differences in accidentals alone total close to 2,000; in *The House of the Seven Gables*, they are almost 3,000. The complicating factor, of course, is that the proof sheets for these novels are lost too. In their absence, the editor has to undertake the formidable task of determining what Hawthorne might have done in correcting them.

The difficulty in recovering Hawthorne's corrections is compounded by the obscurity of his handwriting, his recognition of the trouble it would cause a compositor, and his attitude towards proof. On 15 January 1850 he wrote James T. Fields that 'The proof-sheets will need to be revised by the author. I write such an infernal hand that this is absolutely indispensable.' And to Fields again, on 27 January 1851: 'I intend to put the House of the Seven Gables into the express-man's hands to-day. . . . I deem it indispensable that the proof-sheets should be sent me for correction. . . . My autography is sometimes villainously blind; and it is odd enough that whenever the printers do mistake a word, it is just the very jewel of a word, worth all the rest of the dictionary' (I, lxi). Although Hawthorne insisted upon seeing proof, the available evidence suggests that he considered proofreading a necessary chore to insure that what he had written was set correctly — not as a welcomed opportunity to make literary revisions — and that his major concern was for substantives, not for accidentals.[7]

Without the proof sheets, Hawthorne's precise corrections can never be known, only surmised. But for *The Blithedale Romance* and *The House of the Seven Gables* several classes of variants could be eliminated with some safety from consideration as Hawthorne's. In most cases the compositors' takes are marked on the manuscripts, so it was possible to isolate the work of a given compositor in order to learn the kinds of things he customarily did in setting Hawthorne's copy. This avoided the weaknesses of the *Fanshawe* compositorial analysis. Because both *The House of the Seven Gables* and *The Blithedale Romance* were set in the same shop — and by some of the same compositors — within a year of one another, the sampling was larger and the results more substantial than they would have been if there were different printers or a greater time differential. Since the pat-

---

[7] Information concerning Hawthorne's proofreading practices appear in the textual introductions to all of the volumes. See also Bowers's 'Hawthorne's Text', in *Hawthorne Centenary Essays*, ed. Roy Harvey Pearce (Columbus: The Ohio State University Press, 1964), pp. 401–25.

tern of accidentals generally is the same for both novels, the editor could logically assume it unlikely that Hawthorne would have abandoned his manuscript usage when correcting proof for *The House of the Seven Gables* only to return to it again in writing the manuscript of *The Blithedale Romance* a short time later (II, xxxviii).

The Centenary Hawthorne certainly is the best Hawthorne now available, but it raises some questions that ought to be considered. They are important questions both because they are at the heart of professional editorial practices and because modern editors converting the heathen have made much of them in public. We base much of what we do on our detailed knowledge of publishing and printing practices, but what were the practices in specific shops at specific times? Was the manuscript returned to the author with the proof? Did he see revised proof? When did it become the custom for the publisher—rather than the printer—to style the author's manuscript?[8] We talk a lot about 'house styling'. The implication is of some system of accidentals uniformly imposed on work that passes through the hands of a publisher or printer. What was that system for any particular publisher or printer? Did Ticknor and Fields or Hobart and Robbins have a house style? If so, what was it? There probably can be no quickly determined answer to any of these questions, but every modern edition must at least consider them if knowledge is to be moved forward in the way the apparatus of the Centenary Hawthorne moves towards the answers of other questions. Until these answers have been found, however, the handling of accidentals will remain the most tentative part of any edition.

At our best we still can produce better editions than those now available for most American writings. As Bowers states in his concluding paragraph to the textual introduction of *The Scarlet Letter*, the history of that text 'is a particularly sorry one'. He meant that readers of an edition after the first grew increasingly more distant from Hawthorne the later the text they used. Modern editors insist on two complementary dicta: (1) the shining treasure of a nation is its literary heritage, and (2) that heritage is counterfeit when the

[8]These and other questions are raised by Bowers in 'Old Wine in New Bottles: Problems of Machine Printing', in *Editing Nineteenth Century Texts*, ed. John M. Robson (Toronto, 1967), pp. 9–36. In many cases the question also arises whether the author has approved the accidentals of the printed book or has merely accepted them perforce.

general public can read only corrupt texts. Unfortunately, the publication of the Centenary *Scarlet Letter* has not managed to arrest this situation completely. Of the several republications of the Centenary text for the popular market, I have collated chapters 16, 21, and 23 of four. These are the presumed first printings of the Viking Press's *Portable Hawthorne,* Harper and Row's Perennial Classic edition, Bobbs-Merrill's The Library of Literature edition, and the Charles E. Merrill Publishing Company's Standard Edition.

The results were shocking. In his textual introduction to the Centenary text, Bowers notes as 'significant' the corruption of 'concentred' into 'concentrated' (57.2) in the second edition of *The Scarlet Letter.* The *Portable Hawthorne* is tainted by that very error at 255.28—and also by 'as' for 'at' ('he bowed his head forward on the cushions of the pulpit, at the close of his Election Sermon') at 250.3; and by 'tinge.' for 'tinge,' at 230.10. The Bobbs-Merrill reprint is also flawed by 'upon' for 'along' ('a gleam of flickering sunshine might now and then be seen at its solitary play along the path') at 183.16. On the basis of this limited survey, the worst reprint is the one published by Harper and Row. (Ironically, it quotes Bowers's statement on the 'particularly sorry' history of the text on its back wrapper!) This text omits 'to' in 'the childlike loyalty which the age awarded to its rulers' (250.19), and omits the second 'the' in 'that mighty swell of many voices, blended into one great voice by the universal impulse which makes likewise one vast heart out of the many' (250.31). Still more: it prints 'eyes' for 'eye' (231.3), 'coats' for 'cloaks' (233.22), and 'pause,' for 'pause;' (251.34). These three collated chapters account for roughly ten percent of the novel. If this sampling of errors is representative, the Harper and Row text would have approximately fifty unauthorized departures from the Centenary Hawthorne text it purports to reprint. That is a particularly disheartening thought: the Riverside edition of 1883—long the standard edition—was found by the Centenary editors to be the most corrupt edition it collated—but it had only sixty-two departures from the first edition. The only bright light shining through the bleak landscape of reprints of the Centenary *Scarlet Letter* is the Charles E. Merrill Standard Edition. A facsimile of the Centenary text, it is therefore a faithful reproduction. The others are not. Despite the elaborate procedures set up by the Center for Editions of American Authors to safeguard the approved texts from corruption by reprint publishers to which they are made available, three out of the four reprints managed to slip by in deplorable condition.

THE SERIF SERIES: BIBLIOGRAPHIES AND CHECKLISTS—A Review Article

WILLIAM R. CAGLE

A BOOKSELLER OF THE LAST GENERATION, A SPECIALIST IN MODERN first editions of English and American literature, remarked late in his career to a younger colleague that bibliographies had spoiled the trade. 'Time was', he said, 'when all you needed for a first edition was a right date on the title page'. Time has changed all that and today's collector is not so easily satisfied. Time was, also, when a 'bibliography' needed be only a list of titles, with place and date of publication, but that too has changed. Bibliography has developed into a highly refined technology, with clearly established processes and a precise technical language.

One product of this refinement is the distinction between analytical bibliography and enumerative bibliography. Some understanding of these categories is necessary to a reasoned assessment of the works published in The Serif Series: Bibliographies and Checklists.[1] In an analytical bibliography one should expect (1) full descriptions, in-

[1]The Serif Series: Bibliographies and Checklists, William White, general editor (Kent, Ohio: The Kent State University Press). In this essay I review

cluding quasi-facsimile transcription or photographic reproduction at least of title pages as well as collational formulas showing the makeup of each work treated; (2) a history of the transmission of text from the author's manuscript to its first appearance in print and then from edition to edition; (3) as complete and detailed as possible a publishing history of the works treated, showing the relation of editions, printings, issues and states and presenting a record of each book's popularity, in translation as well as its original language, and of its commercial success. A sound analytical bibliography is a source of information for the book collector, the textual editor, and the literary historian.

On the other hand, the enumerative bibliography, or, as it is frequently called, the 'checklist', is less a history and more a road map. Primarily, it is an ordered presentation of a designated group of works, usually built around an author or a subject, complete within clearly stated limits and more restricted in both scope and detail than the bibliography. It does not require elaborate descriptions and may ignore textual and, to a large extent, publishing history. Nor are the content and format of the checklist as clearly defined as they are for the bibliography. As might be expected, in the absence of generally accepted standards or an established format, enumerative bibliographies today run the full gamut from naïve to sophisticated. Those published in The Serif Series are no exception.

To date, all the titles published in the series are enumerative rather than analytical. They are checklists varying in scope, descriptive detail, annotations, and form of entry. The editorial hand has been loosely applied and there is apparently no guide to assist compilers to achieve anything like uniformity with other volumes in the series. Complete uniformity may be neither possible nor desirable, but such

the following seven volumes:

John Updike: A Bibliography. By C. Clarke Taylor. [1968.] vii, 82 pp. $4.25.

Raymond Chandler: A Checklist. By Matthew J. Bruccoli. [1968.] x, 35 pp. $3.25.

Erle Stanley Gardner: A Checklist. By E. H. Mundell. [1969.] xii, 91 pp. $5.50.

Bernard Malamud: An Annotated Checklist. By Rita Nathalie Kosofsky. [1969.] xiv, 63 pp. $4.25.

Samuel Beckett: A Checklist of Criticism. By James T. F. Tanner and J. Don Vann. [1969.] vi, 85 pp. $4.50.

Tolkien Criticism: An Annotated Checklist. Compiled by Richard C. West. [1970.] xvi, 73 pp. $4.25.

Thomas Wolfe: A Checklist. By Elmer D. Johnson. [1970.] xiii, 278 pp. $5.00.

a basic matter as a standard form of entry would greatly facilitate use of the checklists. Why should we be less demanding of precision here than we are for footnotes in a scholarly article? In the course of reading and preparing many checklists for publication, The Serif Series editors must have observed approaches and forms which are more successful than others. If so, there is no evidence they are communicating this information to their authors. Hopefully, as the series continues, they will begin to do so.

Two works in the series treating detective fiction writers, Matthew J. Bruccoli's *Raymond Chandler* and E. H. Mundell's *Erle Stanley Gardner*, illustrate widely varied approaches to compiling a checklist. Bruccoli's work was formulated as a reduction of an analytical bibliography, beginning with the larger idea and paring it down to the bare essentials while retaining the sound basic structure which underlies the original concept. It thus continues to serve the three primary audiences of a full-dress analytical bibliography: the literary historian, the textual editor, and the book collector. Basic information is provided from which to identify first editions; relations between editions, printings, and issues are indicated; notable reprints are recorded. All this is done very concisely and, as Bruccoli points out in his introduction (p. vii), does not take the place of the more detailed bibliography:

At best this Raymond Chandler checklist can claim to suggest a rationale for *descriptive*—or even, and this is looking for trouble, *bibliographical*—checklists. Although this descriptive checklist should be useful to collectors and critics, and although it should permit anyone except possibly a few librarians to identify a Chandler item in hand, it fails to provide the detailed descriptive and analytical information about paper, type, binding, printing, and text—especially text— that a true bibliography, no matter how degressive, must provide.

Mundell's *Erle Stanley Gardner*, on the other hand, is a scissors-and-paste job. It is compiled from other lists with, apparently, only occasional examination of the books themselves. No descriptive details are given; the term 'edition' is incorrectly applied—without making the required distinction between 'edition' and 'printing'. We are told that all books were first published by William Morrow in New York, but no information is given about later American publishers, the British publishers, or the publishers of the translations. Furthermore, the form of entry is frustratingly vague. The following is the first entry under book fiction:

1933

The Case Of The Velvet Claws
New York (4) editions, London (3), Paris, Milan.

As there are no further entries for this title under later dates, we must assume the four New York 'editions' include everything from 1933 on. Was Gardner's first book an immediate success, going through three of four printings in the year of original publication — or did it fall flat only to be revived with the popularity of his later work — or what? Do the four New York 'editions' include paperbacks or are they all full-price clothbound copies? Was the first English edition published in 1933, or when and by whom? And when were the translations made?

The section headed 'Short Fiction', in which magazine appearances are recorded, is more helpful, but even here there is evidence of a much too casual approach to the task at hand. For example, an entry appears under 1924 which reads: '(?) *Smart Set   The Cave* by Green' (i.e., Charles M. Green, a Gardner pseudonym). Certainly it is no great matter to check *Smart Set* for 1924 to see if the story does or does not appear.

The amateurishness which is characteristic of this book from its introduction to its curious indexes which read from left to right rather than in columns — a distinction which must be unique and, hopefully, will remain so — does no credit to The Serif Series. Indeed, it raises the question whether or not there was, in this case, any bibliographical supervision by the series editors. It is noted that it is one of the few books in the series not designed by Merald E. Wrolstad.

The Bruccoli and Mundell volumes represent extremes in the series, the one providing more than we normally expect in a check-list, the other falling short of the basic requirements. Yet, while it may be ideal to begin, as Bruccoli did, with much of the information necessary to a full-dress bibliography and then to compress this into a shortened form retaining the relationships between editions and printings as well as the essential descriptive points, it is not practical to expect every compiler of a checklist to be so extensive in his researches any more than it is to expect experienced bibliographers to spend much of their time compiling checklists. A middle ground, something less demanding, must be used as a general model.

Two other volumes in The Serif Series, Rita Nathalie Kosofsky's *Bernard Malamud* and C. Clarke Taylor's *John Updike,* come somewhat closer to what we are seeking in an 'enumerative checklist'. It should be stated immediately that both works are aimed at the student of literature; they serve the collector only incidentally and the textual editor not at all. But they are not to be faulted for this as neither makes any pretense of providing analytical or descriptive data. Taken, then, as student guides to their respective authors, both are eminently useful books, sound in arrangement and sufficiently precise in form of entry.

Each would have been improved immeasurably by the addition of an index. The reader looking for the magazine publication of Updike's poem 'Parable' must seek it among 237 chronologically arranged titles. Malamud is less of a problem because he has published fewer separate works, but an index still would be useful for, among other things, locating reviews of his work published in a particular periodical or criticism by a specific critic. A reference work without an index is rather like a hand without a thumb — useable, but considerably impaired in its effectiveness.

Miss Kosofsky has been able to be more expansive in her treatment of anthology reprints of Malamud's short stories than Taylor has been for Updike. The amount of material to be covered is the reason: in Section A listing the author's works, there are 41 entries for Malamud and 390 for Updike. Also, in the section treating the author's books, Miss Kosofsky has included both first English and American publication, a plus we hope other compilers will imitate.

But these differences are few compared with the overall similarity of scope and arrangement in the two checklists. In the treatment of the author's works, each employs the conventional arrangement, first listing books and then contributions to periodicals. Form of entry in each case is not greatly dissimilar from that described in the *MLA Style Sheet,* though additional information is occasionally included — the contents of a volume of short stories in the book section or a note indicating in which volume a magazine contribution was later collected. Similarly, both compilers have added synopses or evaluations to criticism and review entries.

Two further volumes in The Serif Series which are designed specifically as guides for scholarly study of the subject authors are James T. F. Tanner's and J. Don Vann's *Samuel Beckett: A Checklist of Criticism* and Richard C. West's *Tolkien Criticism: An Annotated Checklist.* Both titles affirm that the volumes are checklists of certain criticism. Neither pretends to be a bibliography and, indeed, information about the authors' own works is secondary — in the case of Beckett almost incidental — to the compilers' main task. Tanner and Vann state in their introduction that their 'intention has been simply to provide a checklist of criticism *about* Samuel Beckett. We have not interested ourselves in Beckett's primary works, except that at the close of this introduction we list, for the convenience of the researcher, Beckett's major books in chronological order.' While we concede the compilers' right to set their own limits, we cannot but regret that they did not include, for the researcher's even greater convenience, a list of Beckett's contributions to periodicals. West has provided a section for Tolkien's writings and, as the body of work to be recorded is small, has sensibly combined periodical appearances and book publication in a single chronology. However, the greater part of the book, as the title proclaims, is a checklist of criticism.

In both the Beckett and Tolkien volumes, the compilers have chosen an alphabetical listing within the sections treating criticism. This is less satisfactory than the chronological arrangement employed by Kosofsky and Taylor in the Malamud and Updike checklists. The latter allows the reader to approach the criticism historically, to see its development or fluctuation as the author's reputation grows, and, when combined with an author/title index, also gives the reader access to all the criticism by a specific writer. The alphabetical arrangement provides the specific-writer approach but sacrifices the historical, which cannot be satisfactorily retrieved through indexes.

Less successful than the four 'enumerative checklists' above, is Elmer D. Johnson's attempt at a 'descriptive checklist' of the writings of Thomas Wolfe. The most ambitious work yet published in The Serif Series, it stumbles badly on the ground of numerous inaccuracies. It also violates rules worked out and presented by Fredson Bowers in his *Principles of Bibliographical Description* (Princeton: Princeton University Press, 1949). To ignore these principles and revert to a system of transcription reminiscent of the 1920s is an unfortunate choice. Johnson's transcriptions fail to distinguish between upper- and lower-case letters as well as between italic and roman type. Furthermore, they are liberally strewn with error and inconsistency. The presence of printer's rules and type ornaments is indicated in some transcriptions and ignored in others; in some instances line endings are indicated where they do not exist (A39: 'to / the' should be '*to the*') and omitted where they should appear (A11: 'by Maxwell' should be 'BY / MAXWELL'); presence of publisher's devices is inconsistently indicated (A39: noted as present; A2: ignored); false punctuation is introduced (A151: '1919.' should be '1919'; A152, 'New York, 1939' should be 'New York 1939'). Oc-

II. *Of Time and the River*

A39 First Edition:

Of Time and the River / A Legend of Man's Hunger /
in his Youth / by / Thomas Wolfe

"Who knoweth the spirit of man that goeth upward, /
and the spirit of the beast that goeth downward to /
the Earth?" * /

(Publisher's device) / Charles Scribner's Sons /
New York / 1935.

7 l., 3-912 p., 2 l. 21.5 by 15 cm. Published March 8, 1935.

*The quotation is *Ecclesiastes* 3:21.

OTATR is divided into eight books: I. Orestes: Flight
before Fury; II. Young Faustus; III. Telemachus;
IV. Proteus: The City; V. Jason's Voyage; VI. Antaeus:
Earth Again; VII. Kronos and Rhea: The Dream of Time;
VIII. Faust and Helen.

A40 English Edition:

Same as above except for publisher's device and imprint:
William Heinemann Ltd.; London / 1935.

Published August 19, 1935. Reprint edition issued in 1937.

A41 Grosset and Dunlap Reprint Edition:

Identical with first edition except for imprint, and a
slightly larger format: 23 by 15 cm. Published in 1939.

A42 Sun Dial Press Reprint Edition:

Identical with first edition except for imprint and a
smaller format: 21 by 14 cm. Published in 1944
and issued simultaneously in Toronto by the
Blue Ribbon Press.

10

PLATE 1

OF TIME AND THE RIVER

A LEGEND OF MAN'S HUNGER

IN HIS YOUTH

By

Thomas Wolfe

*"Who knoweth the spirit of man that goeth upward, and
the spirit of the beast that goeth downward to the earth?"*

CHARLES SCRIBNER'S SONS

NEW YORK

1935

casionally the author shifts from quasi-facsimile transcription to short entry form without warning the reader (A155 and A156). The examples noted above are but a few among many, many more. It is painfully obvious that none of these transcriptions was read in proof — perhaps not in copy — against the books by either the author or the editor.

Yet an enormous amount of industry has gone into this Wolfe checklist. The scope is grand in design and the amount of material Johnson has gathered is impressive; but, like Wolfe's own massive manuscripts, it badly needs an editor. Section C, titled 'Parts of Books by Wolfe' is a hodgepodge, including everything from anthology reprints to the titled sections of Wolfe's novels; the continual use of a long list of abbreviations keeps the reader repeatedly flipping to the front of the book to see what the entry says (West's Tolkien checklist suffers from this also); the alphabetical listing of critical works, as noted in our discussion of the Tolkien and Beckett volumes, sacrifices the historical perspective and is even less defensible here as there is an author index to provide the alphabetical approach. All these are faults the series editor should have pointed out to the compiler. Johnson's truly impressive assemblage of material by and about Wolfe deserved more careful editorial attention than The Serif Series, apparently, was prepared to give it.

As this brief survey of a few volumes in The Serif Series: Bibliographies and Checklists shows, there is little consistency and less uniformity among the works published to date. Credit for the good work which the series has produced rests with those separate authors who have produced it, while we must take the editors to task for not seeing that the other volumes are of an equally high standard. Bibliographical as well as copy editing is required if The Serif Series is to realize its potential and provide the great service it should to literary scholarship.

THE REGISTER OF
CURRENT PUBLICATIONS: 1971

ARTEM LOZYNSKY

THE REGISTER IS A SELECTIVE RECORD OF IN-PRINT SEPARATE PUB-
lications judged to be of interest to the field of American bibliographical and textual studies. It includes only books that were
submitted by publishers to *Proof* for examination by the compiler.
Entries are descriptive, not evaluative. Books entered in the Register
may be reviewed at length in *Proof*.

Entries in the Register are arranged in thirteen areas, with each
book listed only in its *major* area of interest. Since many books are
useful in more than one area, users of the Register are urged to scan
related areas when searching for a particular kind of work.

Each of the following subject areas into which the Register is subdivided includes facsimile reprints of significant works, except for
the first group—Edited Primary Works—which are original editions
prepared according to a textual theory.

1. Edited Primary Works
2. Reprinted Primary Works

377

3. Author Bibliographies and Checklists
4. Subject Bibliographies and Checklists
5. National Bibliographies and Checklists
6. Writing and Autographs
7. Printing, Binding, Publishing, and Bookselling
8. Copyright and Intellectual Property
9. Libraries and Book Collecting
10. Bibliographical and Textual Theory and Practice
11. Concordances
12. Dictionaries, Rhetorics, and Guides to Language
13. Miscellaneous

1. EDITED PRIMARY WORKS

ANDERSON, SHERWOOD

Sherwood Anderson's Memoirs: A Critical Edition. Edited by Ray Lewis White. Chapel Hill: The University of North Carolina Press, [1969]. xl, 579 pp. (plus frontispiece and 16 pp. of illustrations). $15.00. LC 73-80019. '. . . every word of the present book is taken from manuscripts and typescripts, never from published material' (p. xxxiv). Contents: Acknowledgments; Introduction; Preface; A Dedication and an Explanation; Foreword; I, Childhood and Young Manhood; II, Work and War; III, Business; IV, Chicago; V, The Twenties; VI, The Thirties; A Selected Bibliography; Index.

BROWN, CHARLES BROCKDEN

Three Early American Novels. Edited by William S. Kable. Columbus: Charles E. Merrill Publishing Company, [1970]. vi, 391 pp. $3.95. SBN 675-09406-2. LC 72-95305. 'This volume contains the only available reprints of the authoritative texts of *Charlotte,* "Carwin," and *Wieland* and for the first time makes available . . . many hundreds of readings present only in the first printings. The unique London, 1971, edition of *Charlotte* is reprinted accurately here for the first time. The original periodical appearance of "Carwin"

378

(1803–05) and the first edition of *Wieland* (New York, 1798) are followed with precision. Any changes whatsoever in the original texts are listed in the "Notes on the Texts of this Volume"' (p. ii). Contents: Introduction; Select Bibliography; Notes on the Text of this Volume; Susanna Haswell Rowson, *Charlotte: A Tale of Truth;* Charles Brockden Brown, 'Memoirs of Carwin the Biloquist'; [Brown], *Wieland; or The Transformation.* Charles E. Merrill Literary Texts.

CALHOUN, JOHN C.

The Papers of John C. Calhoun. Volume III, 1818–1819. Edited by W. Edwin Hemphill. Columbia: University of South Carolina Press, 1967. xxxiv, 774 pp. $10.00. LC 59-10351. Contents: Preface; Introduction; *The Papers of John C. Calhoun,* August 1818–March 1819; Symbols; Bibliography; Index.

The Papers of John C. Calhoun. Volume IV, 1819–1820. Edited by W. Edwin Hemphill. Columbia: University of South Carolina Press, 1969. xx, 802 pp. (plus frontispiece). $15.00. SBN 87249-150-1. LC 59-10351. Contents: Preface; Introduction; *The Papers of John C. Calhoun,* April 1819–March 1820; Symbols; Bibliography; Index.

CRANE, STEPHEN

Bowery Tales: Maggie, George's Mother. Edited by Fredson Bowers; Introduction by James B. Colvert. Charlottesville: University Press of Virginia, [1969]. xcviii, 184 pp. (plus frontispiece and 2 pp. of illustrations). $10.00. SBN 8139-0258-4. LC 68-8536. The University of Virginia Edition of *The Works of Stephen Crane,* Vol. I. A CEAA approved text. The copy-texts for both *Maggie* and *George's Mother* are the first editions. Contents: Foreword; The Text of the Virginia Edition; Introduction to *Maggie;* Textual Introduction to *Maggie;* Publisher's Note; An Appreciation by William Dean Howells; *Maggie;* Textual Apparatus; Introduction to *George's Mother;* Textual Introduction to *George's Mother; George's Mother;* Textual Apparatus.

Stephen Crane in the West and Mexico. Edited by Joseph Katz. Kent: The Kent State University Press, 1970. xxv, 110 pp. $6.75. ISBN 0-87338-094-0. LC 73-106970. Copy-texts vary for these seventeen syndicated travel pieces. Contents: Introduction; Travel Sketches; Mexican Tales; Texual Afterword.

Tales of Adventure. Edited by Fredson Bowers; Introduction by J. C. Levenson. Charlottesville: University Press of Virginia, [1970]. cxcvi, 242 pp. (plus frontispiece and 8 pp. of illustrations). $15.00. SBN 8139-0302-5. LC 68-8536. The University of Virginia Edition of *The Works of Stephen Crane,* Vol. V. A CEAA approved text. The copy-texts vary. Contents: Foreword; Introduction; Textual Introduction; The Pace of Youth; One Dash — Horses; The Wise Men: A Detail of American Life in Mexico; The Five White Mice; A Man and Some Others; The Open Boat; Flanagan and His Short Filibustering Adventure; The Bride Comes to Yellow Sky; Death and the Child; The Blue Hotel; Twelve O'Clock; Moonlight on the Snow; A Poker Game; Textual Apparatus.

Tales of War: The Little Regiment, "An Episode of War", Wounds in the Rain, "Spitzbergen Tales". Edited by Fredson Bowers; Introduction by James B. Colvert. Charlottesville: University Press of Virginia, [1970]. cxcii, 401 pp. (plus frontispiece and 8 pp. of illustrations). $22.50. SBN 8139-0294-0. LC 69-8536. The University of Virginia Edition of *The Works of Stephen Crane,* Vol. VI. A CEAA approved text. The copy-texts vary. Contents: Foreword; Introduction; Textual Introduction; *The Little Regiment;* An Episode of War; *Wounds in the Rain;* Spitzbergen Tales; Textual Apparatus.

Tales of Whilomville: "The Monster", "His New Mittens", Whilomville Stories. Edited by Fredson Bowers; Introduction by J. C. Levenson. Charlottesville: University Press of Virginia, [1969]. lx, 277 pp. (plus frontispiece and 5 pp. of illustrations). $10.00. SBN 8139-0259-2. LC 68-8536. The University of Virginia Edition of *The Works of Stephen Crane,* Vol. VII. A CEAA approved text. The copy-texts vary. Contents: Foreword; Introduction; Textual Introduction to "The Monster"; "The Monster"; Textual Apparatus; Textual

Introduction to "His New Mittens"; "His New Mittens"; Textual Apparatus; Textual Introduction to *Whilomville Stories; Whilomville Stories;* Textual Apparatus.

DREISER, THEODORE

Selected Poems (from 'Moods') by *Theodore Dreiser.* Edited by Robert Palmer Saalbach. New York: Exposition Press, 1964. 254 pp. $7.50. LC 68-27311. Contents: Preface; Introduction; Text; Notes. *Note:* Accompanied by a one-page errata slip.

EMERSON, RALPH WALDO

The Early Lectures of Ralph Waldo Emerson. Vol. I: 1833–1836. Edited by Stephen E. Whicher and Robert E. Spiller. Cambridge: The Belknap Press of Harvard University Press, 1966. xxx, 545 pp. (plus 8 pp. of illustrations). $12.50. LC 59-5160. Contents: Introduction; I, Science; II, Italy; III, Biography; IV, English Literature; Bibliography of Principal Sources; Textual Notes and Variant Passages; Index.

The Journals and Miscellaneous Notebooks of Ralph Waldo Emerson. Vol. I: 1819–1822. Edited by William H. Gilman, Alfred R. Ferguson, George P. Clark, and Merrell R. Davis. Cambridge: The Belknap Press of Harvard University Press, [1960]. 1, 430 pp. (plus 12 pp. of illustrations). $10.95. LC 60-11554. Contents: Introduction; Foreword to Volume I; Part One: The Texts of the Journals; Part Two: The Texts of the Miscellaneous Notebooks; Textual Apparatus; Index.

The Journals and Miscellaneous Notebooks of Ralph Waldo Emerson. Vol. II: 1822–1826. Edited by William H. Gilman, Alfred R. Ferguson, and Merrell R. Davis. Cambridge: The Belknap Press of Harvard University Press, 1961. xvi, 438 pp. (plus 4 pp. of illustrations). $10.00. LC 60-11554. Contents: Foreword to Volume II; Part One: The Texts of the Journals; Part Two: The Texts of the Miscellaneous Notebooks; Textual Notes; Index.

HAWTHORNE, NATHANIEL

The Blithedale Romance and Fanshawe. Edited by Fredson Bowers; Introductions by Roy Harvey Pearce. Columbus: The Ohio State University Press, [1964]. lviii, 502 pp. (plus 2 pp. of illustrations). $8.50. *The Centenary Edition of the Works of Nathaniel Hawthorne*, Vol. III. The manuscript in the Morgan Library is copy-text for *The Blithedale Romance;* the copy-text for *Fanshawe* is the first edition. Contents: Introduction to *The Blithedale Romance;* Textual Introduction: *The Blithedale Romance; The Blithedale Romance;* Textual Apparatus; Introduction to *Fanshawe;* Textual Introduction: *Fanshawe; Fanshawe;* Textual Apparatus; The Centenary Texts: Editorial Principles.

The House of the Seven Gables. Edited by Fredson Bowers; Introductions by William Charvat. Columbus: The Ohio State University Press, [1965]. lxvi, 418 pp. (plus 2 pp. of illustrations). $9.50. *The Centenary Edition of the Works of Nathaniel Hawthorne*, Vol. II. Copy-text is the manuscript at the Houghton Library. Contents: Introduction to *The House of the Seven Gables;* Textual Introduction: *The House of the Seven Gables;* Note on the Typesetting; *The House of the Seven Gables;* Textual Apparatus; The Centenary Texts: Editorial Principles.

The Scarlet Letter. Edited by Fredson Bowers; Introduction by William Charvat. Columbus: The Ohio State University Press, [1962]. lxviii, 290 pp. (plus 3 pp. of illustrations). $6.75. *The Centenary Edition of the Works of Nathaniel Hawthorne*, Vol. I. Copy-text is the first edition. Contents: Introduction to *The Scarlet Letter;* A Preface to the Text; Textual Introduction: *The Scarlet Letter;* Preface to the Second Edition; *The Scarlet Letter;* Textual Apparatus.

The Marble Faun. Edited by Fredson Bowers; Introduction by Claude M. Simpson. Columbus: The Ohio State University Press, [1968]. cxl, 611 pp. (plus 2 pp. of illustrations). $10.00. *The Centenary Edition of the Works of Nathaniel Hawthorne*, Vol. IV. A CEAA approved text. Copy-text is the manuscript in the British Museum. Contents: Introduction to *The Marble Faun;* Textual Introduction: *The Marble Faun; The Marble Faun;* Textual Apparatus; The Centenary Texts: Editorial Principles.

Our Old Home. Edited by Fredson Bowers; Introduction by Claude M. Simpson. Columbus: The Ohio State Univesity Press, [1970]. cxvi, 497 pp. (plus 1 p. of illustrations). $12.50. *The Centenary Edition of the Works of Nathaniel Hawthorne,* Vol IV. A CEAA approved text. Copy-texts of the pieces vary. Contents: Introduction to *Our Old Home;* Textual Introduction: *Our Old Home; Our Old Home;* Textual Apparatus.

HOWELLS, WILLIAM DEAN

The Altrurian Romances. Introduction and Notes to the Text by Clara and Rudolf Kirk; Text Established by Scott Bennett. Bloomington and London: Indiana University Press, 1968. xxxiv, 494 pp. (plus 1 p. of illustrations). $15.00 (cloth), $3.95 (paper). LC 68-29522. *A Selected Edition of W. D. Howells,* Vol. 20. A CEAA approved text. For *A Traveller from Altruria* the *Cosmopolitan* appearance is the copy-text; 'the *Cosmopolitan* is copy-text for the first part of *Through the Eye of the Needle;* for the "Introduction" and the second part of this book, published for the first and only time in 1907, the book is of course copy-text. For the "Bibliographical" introduction written for the projected but never-published Library Edition of *A Traveller from Altruria* and *Through the Eye of the Needle,* the page proofs, which are the only surviving text, are copy-text' (p. 464). Contents: Introduction; 'Bibliographical'; *A Traveller from Altruria; Letters of an Altrurian Traveller* I–V; *Through the Eye of the Needle;* Textual Apparatus.

Literary Friends and Acquaintance. Edited by David F. Hiatt and Edwin H. Cady. Bloomington and London: Indiana University Press, 1968. xxxv, 399 pp. (plus 11 pp. of illustrations). $12.50. LC 68-29523. *A Selected Edition of W. D. Howells,* Vol. 32. A CEAA approved text. The copy-text of each of the eleven sections of the book varies. Contents:

Introduction; *Literary Friends and Acquaintance;* Textual Apparatus; Index.

The Shadow of A Dream and *An Imperative Duty.* Introduction and Notes to the Text by Martha Banta; Text Established by Martha Banta, Ronald Gottesman, and David J. Nordloh. Bloomington and London: Indiana University Press, 1970. xxii, 124, xii, 114 pp. (plus 1 p. of illustrations). $10.00. SBN 253-35190-1. LC 71-79475. *A Selected Edition of W. D. Howells,* Vol. 17. A CEAA approved text. Copy-texts are the *Harper's Monthly* appearances for both works. Contents: Introduction; *The Shadow of a Dream;* Textual Apparatus; Introduction; *An Imperative Duty;* Textual Apparatus.

The Son of Royal Langbrith. Introduction and Notes to the Text by David Burrows; Text Established by David Burrows, Ronald Gottesman, and David J. Nordloh. Bloomington and London: Indiana University Press, 1969. xxiv, 320 pp. (plus 2 pp. of illustrations). $10.50. SBN 253-35393-9. LC 75-79476. *A Selected Edition of W. D. Howells,* Vol. 26. A CEAA approved text. The novel survives in six substantive documents ending with the 1904 book publication by Harper and Brothers; the five earlier documents are copy-texts for various portions of the novel. Contents: Introduction; *The Son of Royal Langbrith;* Textual Apparatus.

Their Wedding Journey. Edited by John Reeves. Bloomington and London: Indiana University Press, 1968. xxxiv, 242 pp. (plus 3 pp. of illustrations). $10.00. LC 68-14604. *A Selected Edition of W. D. Howells,* Vol. 5. A CEAA approved text. Copy-text is the *Atlantic* appearance. Contents: Introduction; *Their Wedding Journey;* Textual Apparatus.

LAURENS, HENRY

The Papers of Henry Laurens. Volume One: Sept. 11, 1746–Oct. 31, 1755. Edited by Philip M. Hamer, George C. Rogers, Jr., and Maude E. Lyles. Columbia: University of South Carolina Press, [1968]. xl, 408 pp. (plus frontispiece). $15.00. SBN 87249-128-5. LC 67-29381. Contents: Introduction; The Family of John Laurens; Principal Dates of Henry

Laurens' Life; *The Papers of Henry Laurens*, 11 September 1746–31 October 1755; Appendix, Inventory of John Laurens' Estate; Index.

The Papers of Henry Laurens. Volume Two: Nov. 1, 1755–Dec. 31, 1758. Edited by Philip M. Hamer, George C. Rogers, Jr., and Peggy J. Wehage. Columbia: University of South Carolina Press, [1970]. xxvi, 581 pp. (plus frontispiece). $15.00. ISBN 0-87249-141-2. LC 67-29381. Contents: Introduction; List of Abbreviations; Principal Dates of Henry Laurens' Life; *The Papers of Henry Laurens*, 1 November 1755–15 December 1758; Index.

MELVILLE, HERMAN

Mardi: and A Voyage Thither. Edited by Harrison Hayford, Hershel Parker, and G. Thomas Tanselle; Historical Note by Elizabeth S. Foster. Evanston and Chicago: Northwestern University Press and The Newberry Library, 1970. xviii, 731 pp. (inc. 2 pp. of illustrations). $15.00 (cloth), SBN 8101-0015-0; $3.95 (paper), SBN 8101-0014-2. LC 67-21602. The Northwestern-Newberry Edition of *The Writings of Herman Melville*, Vol. 3. A CEAA approved text. The first impression of the first American edition is the copy-text. Contents: Preface; *Mardi;* Editorial Appendix.

Omoo: A Narrative of Adventures in the South Seas. Edited by Harrison Hayford, Hershel Parker, and G. Thomas Tanselle; Richard Colles Johnson, Bibliographical Associate; Historical Note by Gordon Roper. Evanston and Chicago: Northwestern University Press and The Newberry Library, 1968. xvi, 381 pp. (inc. 2 pp. of illustrations). $10.00 (cloth), $2.95 (paper). LC 67-11991. The Northwestern-Newberry Edition of *The Writings of Herman Melville*, Vol. 2. A CEAA approved text. The first impression of the first American edition is the copy-text. Contents: Preface; Introduction; *Omoo;* Editorial Appendix.

Redburn: His First Voyage. Edited by Harrison Hayford, Hershel Parker, and G. Thomas Tanselle; Historical Note by Hershel Parker; Merlin Bowen, Contributing Scholar. Evanston

and Chicago: Northwestern University Press and The Newberry Library, 1969. xii, 385 pp. $10.00 (cloth), SBN 8101-
0013-4; $2.95 (paper), SBN 8101-0016-9. LC 67-21601. The
Northwestern-Newberry Edition of *The Writings of Herman
Melville,* Vol. 4. A CEAA approved text. The first impression
of the first American edition is the copy-text. Contents:
Redburn; Editorial Appendix.

Typee: A Peep at Polynesian Life. Edited by Harrison Hayford,
Hershel Parker, and G. Thomas Tanselle; Richard Colles
Johnson, Bibliographical Associate; Historical Note by Leon
Howard. Evanston and Chicago: Northwestern University
Press and The Newberry Library, 1968. xiv, 375 pp. (inc.
3 pp. of illustrations). $10.00 (cloth), $2.95 (paper). LC
67-11990. The Northwestern-Newberry Edition of *The
Writings of Herman Melville,* Vol. 1. A CEAA approved text.
The first impression of the first English edition is the copy-
text. Contents: Preface; *Typee;* Editorial Appendix.

White-Jacket: or The World in a Man-of-War. Edited by Harrison
Hayford, Hershel Parker, and G. Thomas Tanselle; Historical Note by Willard Thorp. Evanston and Chicago: Northwestern University Press and The Newberry Library, 1970.
xiv, 501 pp. (inc. 2 pp. of illustrations). $12.50 (cloth),
SBN 8101-0257-9; $3.50 (paper), SBN 8101-0258-7. LC
67-21603. The Northwestern-Newberry Edition of *The
Writings of Herman Melville,* Vol. 5. A CEAA approved text.
The first impression of the first American edition is the copy-
text. Contents: *White-Jacket;* Editorial Appendix.

ROWSON, SUSANNA HASWELL

Charlotte: A Tale of Truth. See Brown, Charles Brockden, *Three
Early American Novels,* ed. William S. Kable.

SIMMS, WILLIAM GILMORE

The Letters of William Gilmore Simms. Volume I, 1830–1844. Edited
by Mary C. Simms Oliphant, Alfred Taylor Odell, and T. C.
Duncan Eaves; Introduction by Donald Davidson; Bio-

graphical Sketch by Alexander S. Salley. Columbia: University of South Carolina, 1952. clii, 456 pp. (plus frontispiece and 8 pp. of illustrations). $10.00. Contents: Preface; Depositories or Owners of Manuscripts; List of Letters; Introduction; Biographical Sketch of Simms; Simms' Circle; The Family Circle; The Negroes at Woodlands; *The Letters of William Gilmore Simms*, 1830–1844; Index.

The Letters of William Gilmore Simms. Volume II, 1845–1849. Edited by Mary C. Simms Oliphant, Alfred Taylor Odell, and T. C. Duncan Eaves. Columbia: University of South Carolina Press, 1953. xxx, 610 pp. (plus frontispiece and 8 pp. of illustrations). $10.00. Contents: Preface; Depositories or Owners of Manuscripts; List of Letters; *The Letters of William Gilmore Simms*, 1845–1849; Index.

The Letters of William Gilmore Simms. Volume III, 1850–1857. Edited by Mary C. Simms Oliphant, Alfred Taylor Odell, and T. C. Duncan Eaves. Columbia: University of South Carolina Press, 1954. xxvi, 564 pp. (plus frontispiece and 8 pp. of illustrations). $10.00. Contents: Preface; Depositories or Owners of Manuscripts; List of Letters; *The Letters of William Gilmore Simms*, 1850–1857; Index.

The Letters of William Gilmore Simms. Volume IV, 1858–1866. Edited by Mary C. Simms Oliphant, Alfred Taylor Odell, and T. C. Duncan Eaves. Columbia: University of South Carolina, 1955. xxvi, 643 pp. (plus frontispiece and 8 pp. of illustrations). $10.00. Contents: Preface; Depositories or Owners of Manuscripts; List of Letters; *The Letters of William Gilmore Simms*, 1858–1866; Index.

The Letters of William Gilmore Simms. Volume V, 1867–1870. Edited by Mary C. Simms Oliphant, Alfred Taylor Odell, and T. C. Duncan Eaves. Columbia: University of South Carolina, 1956. xxiv, 571 pp. (plus frontispiece and 8 pp. of illustrations). $10.00. Contents: Preface; Depositories or Owners of Manuscripts; List of Letters; *The Letters of William Gilmore Simms*, 1867–1870; Appendix I, Letters of Uncertain Date; Appendix II, Supplementary Letters of Certain or Probable Date; Appendix III, Errata and Addenda, Volumes I–IV; Index, Volumes I–V.

Voltmeier, or The Mountain Men. Introduction and Explanatory Notes by Donald Davidson and Mary C. Simms Oliphant; Text established by James B. Meriwether. Columbia: University of South Carolina Press, [1969]. xxxii, 446 pp. (plus 2 pp. of illustrations). $15.00. SBN 87249-140-4. LC 68-9190. The Centennial Edition of *The Writings of William Gilmore Simms*, Vol. I. A CEAA approved text. The copy-text is the only surviving document, installments in the *Illuminated Western World.* Contents: General Preface to the Centennial Edition; Introduction to Volume I; *Voltmeier, or The Mountain Men;* Explanatory Notes; Textual Apparatus.

TWAIN, MARK

Correspondence with Henry Huttleston Rogers, 1893–1909. Edited with an Introduction by Lewis Leary. Berkeley and Los Angeles: University of California Press, 1969. xviii, 768 pp. (plus frontispiece). $15.00. LC 68-23900. *The Mark Twain Papers.* A CEAA approved text. 'This book contains the complete texts of all known correspondence between Clemens and Rogers, as well as relevant letters to and from their wives and secretaries. The texts have been transcribed from the letters the authors originally sent whenever these were available' (p. vi). Contents: Editor's Preface, Abbreviations; I, 'Fussing with Business'; II, 'As Long as the Promise Must be Made'; III, 'Our Unspeakable Disaster'; IV, 'You and I Are a Team'; V, 'This Everlasting Exile'; VI, 'This Odious Swindle'; VII, 'Nothing Agrees with Me'; VIII, 'I Wish Henry Rogers Would Come Here'; Afterword, Appendixes, A Calendar of Letters; Biographical Directory; Genealogical Charts; Index.

Hannibal, Huck & Tom. Edited with an Introduction by Walter Blair. Berkeley and Los Angeles: University of California Press, 1969. xii, 500 pp. (plus frontispiece). $12.50. LC 69-10575. *The Mark Twain Papers.* A CEAA approved text. Except for 'Huck Finn and Tom Sawyer among the Indians' and 'Tom Sawyer: A Play', the copy-texts are various manuscripts. For the former the Paige typesetter galley proof is copy-text; for the latter, the typescript is copy-text.

Contents: Introduction; Hannibal: 'Villagers of 1840–3'; 'Jane Lampton Clemens'; 'Tupperville-Dobbsville'; 'Clairvoyant'; 'A Human Bloodhound'; Huck & Tom: 'Huck Finn and Tom Sawyer among the Indians'; 'Doughface'; 'Tom Sawyer's Gang plans a Naval Battle'; 'Tom Sawyer's Conspiracy'; 'Tom Sawyer: A Play'; Explanatory Notes; Appendixes; Textual Apparatus.

Mysterious Stranger Manuscripts. Edited with an Introduction by William M. Gibson. Berkeley and Los Angeles: University of California Press, 1969. x, 606 pp. (plus frontispiece). $12.50. LC 69-10576. *The Mark Twain Papers.* A CEAA approved text. The manuscripts are copy-text. Contents: Abbreviations; Introduction; 'The Chronicle of Young Satan'; 'Schoolhouse Hill'; 'No. 44, The Mysterious Stranger'; Appendixes; Explanatory Notes; Textual Apparatus.

Satires & Burlesques. Edited with an Introduction by Franklin R. Rogers. Berkeley and Los Angeles: University of California Press, 1967. x, 485 pp. (plus frontispiece). $10.00. LC 64-24886. *The Mark Twain Papers.* 'The aim of the editor has been to present a readable text which represents as closely as possible Twain's intention as that intention is reflected in his last revision of the various manuscripts' (p. v). Contents: Editor's Preface; Introduction; Burlesque *Il Trovatore;* A Novel: *Who Was He?;* The Story of Mamie Grant, the Child-Missionary; L'Homme Qui Rit; Burlesque *Hamlet;* 1,002^d Arabian Night; The Hellfire Hotchkiss Sequence; The Simon Wheeler Sequence; Appendixes.

Which Was the Dream? and Other Symbolic Writings of the Later Years. Edited with an Introduction by John S. Tuckey. Berkeley and Los Angeles: University of California Press, 1967. xii, 588 pp. (plus frontispiece). $10.00. LC 66-19100. *The Mark Twain Papers.* A CEAA approved text. The copy-texts are the various surviving manuscripts. Contents: Introduction; 'Which Was the Dream?'; 'The Enchanted Sea-Wilderness'; 'An Adventure in Remote Seas'; 'The Great Dark'; 'Indiantown'; 'Which Was It?'; 'Three Thousand Years Among the Microbes'; Appendix ('The Passenger's Story', 'The Mad Passenger', 'Dying Deposition', and 'Trial of the Squire').

2. REPRINTED PRIMARY WORKS

CRANE, STEPHEN

The Red Badge of Courage. Introduced by Joseph Katz. Columbus:
Charles E. Merrill Publishing Company, [1969]. xiv, ii,
233 pp. $6.95 (cloth); $.85 (paper). LC 69-13318. 'This text
of *The Red Badge of Courage* is a facsimile of the first impression, first edition, published by D. Appleton & Company,
1895. From a copy in the collection of Joseph Katz' (p. iv).
Contents: Introduction; *The Red Badge of Courage.* Charles E.
Merrill Standard Editions.

DE FOREST, JOHN WILLIAM

Miss Ravenel's Conversion from Secession to Loyalty. Introduced by
Arlin Turner. Columbus: Charles E. Merrill Publishing
Company, [1969]. xx, iv, [7]–521. $6.95 (cloth), SBN 675-
09391-0; $.95 (paper), SBN 675-09390-2. LC 75-100633.
'This text of *Miss Ravenel's Conversion from Secession to
Loyalty* is a facsimile of the first impression, first edition
published by Harper & Brothers, 1867 — from a copy in the
Kent State University Library' (p. iv). Contents: Introduc-
tion; *Miss Ravenel's Conversion from Secession to Loyalty.* Charles
E. Merrill Standard Editions.

DREISER, THEODORE

Sister Carrie. Introduced by Louis Auchincloss. Columbus:
Charles E. Merrill Publishing Company, [1969]. xii, iv,
557 pp. $6.95 (cloth); $1.15 (paper). LC 69-13798. 'The
text of Sister Carrie is a facsimile of the first impression,
first edition, published by Doubleday, 1900. From a copy in
the collection of Hugh C. Atkinson' (p. iv). Contents: Introduction; *Sister Carrie.* Charles E. Merrill Standard Editions.

EMERSON, RALPH WALDO

Essays and *Essays: Second Series.* Introduced by Morse Peckham.
Columbus; Charles E. Merrill Publishing Company, [1969].

xvi, vi, 303, iv, 313 pp. $6.95 (cloth), SBN 675-09389-9; $1.35 (paper), SBN 675-09388-0. LC 79-100634. 'These texts of Emerson's *Essays* and *Essays: Second Series* are facsimiles of the first printings in the McKissick Library, University of South Carolina' (p. iv). Contents: Introduction; *Essays; Essays: Second Series.* Two volumes in one. Charles E. Merrill Standard Editions.

GARLAND, HAMLIN

Main-Travelled Roads. Introduced by Donald Pizer. Columbus: Charles E. Merrill Publishing Company, [1970]. xviii, 260 pp. $6.95 (cloth), SBN 675-09375-9; $1.35 (paper), SBN 675-09374-0. LC 79-103888. 'This text of *Main-Travelled Roads* is a facsimile of the first printing of the first edition published by the Arena Company, 1891. The book was sold bound in cloth or in paper wrappers. The copy from which this facsimile was made was in wrappers. It has been presented to the McKissick Library, University of South Carolina' (p. iv). Contents: Introduction; A Note on the Text; *Main-Travelled Roads.* Charles E. Merrill Standard Editions.

HAWTHORNE, NATHANIEL

The House of the Seven Gables. Introduced by Harry Levin. Columbus: Charles E. Merrill Publishing Company, [1969]. xviii, 319 pp. $6.95 (cloth), SBN 675-09471-2; $1.25 (paper), SBN 675-09470-4. LC 71-83153. 'The text of *The House of the Seven Gables* is that of the Centenary Edition of the Works of Nathaniel Hawthorne, a publication of the Ohio State University Center for Textual Studies and the Ohio State University Press' (p. xviii). Contents: Introduction; *The House of the Seven Gables.* Charles E. Merrill Standard Editions.

The Scarlet Letter. Introduced by Edwin H. Cady. Columbus: Charles E. Merrill Publishing Company, [1969]. xiv, iv, 264 pp. $6.95 (cloth); $.95 (paper). LC 69-13317. 'The Text of *The Scarlet Letter* is that of the Centenary Edition of the Works of Nathaniel Hawthorne, a publication of the Ohio State University Center for Textual Studies and the Ohio

State University Press' (p. iv). Contents: Introduction; Preface to the Second Edition; The Custom-House — Introductory; *The Scarlet Letter*. Charles E. Merrill Standard Editions.

JAMES, HENRY

The Wings of the Dove. Introduced by Reynolds Price. Columbus: Charles E. Merrill Publishing Company, [1970]. xx, iv, 576 pp. $6.95 (cloth), SBN 675-09335-X; $1.25 (paper), SBN 675-09334-1. LC 75-113743. 'This text of *The Wings of the Dove* is a facsimile of the first English edition (London: Constable, 1902) — from a copy in the McKissick Library, University of South Carolina (813.4/J27/W71)' (p. iv). Contents: Introduction; *The Wings of the Dove*. Charles E. Merrill Standard Editions.

LINCOLN, ABRAHAM

The Literary Works of Abraham Lincoln. Edited, with an introduction by David D. Anderson. Columbus: Charles E. Merrill Publishing Company, [1970]. xiv, 274 pp. $3.95. ISBN 0-675-09316-3. LC 70-120766. Copy-text is *The Collected Works of Abraham Lincoln*, edited by Roy P. Basler and assisted by Marian Delores Pratt and Lloyd A. Dunlap (Rutgers, New Jersey: Rutgers University Press, 1953). Contents: Introduction; I, The Early Years; II, Political and Legal Success; III, The Slavery Crisis; IV, The Presidency. Charles E. Merrill Standard Editions.

NORRIS, FRANK

The Pit. Introduced by James D. Hart. Columbus: Charles E. Merrill Publishing Company, [1970]. xvi, viii, 421 pp. $6.95 (cloth), SBN 675-09367-8; $1.25 (paper), SBN 675-09368-6. LC 75-105109. 'This text of *The Pit* is a facsimile of the first state, first impression, first edition, published by Doubleday, Page & Co. in 1903. From a copy presented by the publishers to Mr. Charles B. Greene, in the collection of

Joseph Katz' (p. iv). Contents: Introduction; A Note on the Text; *The Pit.* Charles E. Merrill Standard Editions.

POE, EDGAR ALLAN

Tales and The Raven and Other Poems. Introduced by Jay B. Hubbell. Columbus: Charles E. Merrill Publishing Company, [1969]. xxvi, vi, 228, viii, 91 pp. $6.95 (cloth), SBN 675-09529-9; $1.35 (paper), SBN 675-09530-1. LC 69-13800. LC 69-13800. 'This text of *Tales* is a facsimile of the first impression, first edition published by Wiley & Putnam, 1845 — from a copy in the Alderman Library, The University of Virginia (*PS2612.Al. 434628). The text of The Raven And Other Poems is a facsimile of the first impression, first edition published by Wiley & Putnam, 1845 — from a copy in the Alderman Library, The University of Virginia (*PS 2609.Al. 433521). This is an unretouched facsimile of the original copies: — the foxing in this edition is in the originals' (p. iv). Contents: Introduction; *Tales; The Raven and Other Poems.* Two volumes in one. Charles E. Merrill Standard Editions.

STOWE, HARRIET BEECHER

Uncle Tom's Cabin. Introduced by Howard Mumford Jones. Columbus: Charles E. Merrill Publishing Company, [1969]. xviii, x, 646 pp. $6.95 (cloth); $1.15 (paper). 'This text of *Uncle Tom's Cabin* is a facsimile of the Ohio State University Libraries copy of the first printing (PS 2954/U5/1852a)'. Two volumes in one. Charles E. Merrill Standard Editions.

THOREAU, HENRY DAVID

Walden. Introduced by Willard Thorp. Columbus: Charles E. Merrill Publishing Company, [1969]. xx, 357 pp. $6.95 (cloth), SBN 675-09469-0; $.85 (paper), SBN 675-09468-2. LC 78-80832. 'This text of *Walden* is a facsimile of the first impression, first edition published by Tichnor [*sic*] and Fields, 1854 — from a copy in The Ohio State University

Libraries (PS 3048/A1)' (p. iv). Contents: Introduction; A Note on the Text; *Walden.* Charles E. Merrill Standard Editions.

3. AUTHOR BIBLIOGRAPHIES AND CHECKLISTS

ANDERSON, MAXWELL

Avery, Laurence G. *A Catalogue of the Maxwell Anderson Collection at the University of Texas.* Austin: The Humanities Research Center, The University of Texas, [1968]. vi, 175 pp. (plus 16 pp. of illustrations). $7.50. LC 67-64544. Tower Bibliographical Studies. 'The catalogue . . . attempts to provide a bibliography of Maxwell Anderson's published work and to describe or list all available Anderson papers' (p. 1). Contents: Introduction; A, Published Works; B, Contributions to Books; C, Contributions to Periodicals; D, Unpublished Works; E, Letters by Anderson; F, Diaries; G, Letters to Anderson; Index.

ANDERSON, SHERWOOD

White, Ray Lewis, compiler. *The Merrill Checklist of Sherwood Anderson.* Columbus: Charles E. Merrill Publishing Company, [1969]. iv, 36 pp. $.75. SBN 675-09410-0. LC 79-93673. Charles E. Merrill Checklists.

CHANDLER, RAYMOND

Bruccoli, Matthew J. *Raymond Chandler: A Checklist.* Kent: The Kent State University Press, [1968]. x, 35 pp. $3.25. SBN 87338-015-0. LC 68-16892. The Serif Series, No. 2. 'At best this Raymond Chandler checklist can claim to suggest a rationale for *descriptive*—or even, and this is looking for trouble, *bibliographical*—checklists' (p. vii). Contents: Introduction; A Checklist; First Book Appearances; Stories; Articles; Reviews; Columns; Letters; Poems; Blurbs; Interview; Statement; References.

CRANE, HART

Schwartz, Joseph. *Hart Crane: An Annotated Critical Bibliography.* New York: David Lewis, 1970. xi, 276 pp. $15.00. LC 72-141996. SBN 912012-11-0. An enumerative bibliography. Contents: Preface; Hart Crane Chronology; Published Writings of Hart Crane; Bibliography; Biography and Criticism; Addendum; Appendix.

CRANE, STEPHEN

Katz, Joseph, compiler. *The Merrill Checklist of Stephen Crane.* Columbus: Charles E. Merrill Publishing Company, [1969]. iv, 41 pp. $.75. SBN 675-09461-5. LC 78-91215. Charles E. Merrill Checklists.

DEWEY, JOHN

Boydston, Jo Ann, ed. *Guide to the Works of John Dewey.* Carbondale and Edwardsville: Southern Illinois University Press, 1970. xvii, 396 pp. $15.00. Contents: (1) Herbert W. Schneider, 'Dewey's Psychology'; (2) Lewis E. Hahn, 'Dewey's Philosophy and Philosophical Method'; (3) Gail Kennedy, 'Dewey's Logic and Theory of Knowledge'; (4) Herbert W. Schneider (Part I) and Darnell Rucker (Part II), 'Dewey's Ethics'; (5) Wayne A. R. Leys, 'Dewey's Social, Political, and Legal Philosophy'; (6) Bertram Morris, 'Dewey's Theory of Art'; (7) S. Morris Eames, 'Dewey's Theory of Valuation'; (8) Horace L. Friess, 'Dewey's Philosophy of Religion'; (9) William W. Brickman, 'Dewey's Social and Political Commentary'; (10) George E. Axtelle and Joe R. Burnett, 'Dewey on Education and Schooling'; (11) Max H. Fisch, 'Dewey's Critical and Historical Studies'; (12) Ou Tsuin-Chen, 'Dewey's Lectures and Influence in China'; Checklist of Miscellaneous Works; Checklist of Collections; Index.

DICKINSON, EMILY

Clendenning, Sheila T. *Emily Dickinson, A Bibliography: 1850–1966.* Kent: The Kent State University Press, [1968]. xxx,

145 pp. $5.00. SBN 87338-016-9. LC 67-65585. The Serif Series, No. 3. Contents: Preface; Introduction: Emily Dickinson's Editors, Biographers, and Critics; Abbreviations of Periodicals; I, Bibliographies; II, Works by Emily Dickinson (A, Editions of Poems and Letters; B, Poems and Letters Published in Journals and Anthologies; C, Translations); III, Books about Emily Dickinson; IV, Chapters and Parts of Chapters on Emily Dickinson; V, Articles and Parts of Articles on Emily Dickinson; VI, Doctoral Dissertations; Index of Poetry Explications; Index of Authors.

DREISER, THEODORE

Atkinson, Hugh C., compiler. *The Merrill Checklist of Theodore Dreiser.* Columbus: Charles E. Merrill Publishing Company, [1969]. iv, 43 pp. $.75. SBN 675-09542-5. LC 69-13797. Charles E. Merrill Checklists.

ELIOT, THOMAS STEARNS

Gunter, Bradley, *The Merrill Checklist of T. S. Eliot.* Columbus: Charles E. Merrill Publishing Company, [1970]. iv, 43 pp. $.75. SBN 675-09383-X. LC 75-102410. Charles E. Merrill Checklists.

EMERSON, RALPH WALDO

Cooke, George Willis, ed. *A Bibliography of Ralph Waldo Emerson.* New York: Kraus Reprint Corporation, 1968. x, 340 pp. (inc. frontispiece). $15.00. Facsimile – Boston: Houghton, Mifflin and Company, 1908. Contents: Preface; List of Emerson's Works; Bibliographies of Emerson; Alphabetical List of Single Titles; Chronological List of Separate Works and Editions; Works edited by Emerson or to which he contributed Introductions; Collected Works; Selections and Compilations; Biographies, Letters, and Reminiscences; Notices and Criticisms; Poems addressed to and about Emerson; Index (of Newspapers and Periodicals).

Ferguson, Alfred R., compiler. *The Merrill Checklist of Ralph Waldo Emerson.* Columbus: Charles E. Merrill Publishing Company, [1970]. iv, 44 pp. $.75. SBN 675-09466-6. LC 75-101586. Charles E. Merrill Checklists.

FAULKNER, WILLIAM

Meriwether, James B. *The Literary Career of William Faulkner: A Bibliographical Study.* Authorized Reissue. Columbia: University of South Carolina Press, [1971]. xii, 192 pp. $14.95. ISBN O-87249-213-3. LC 79-149488. Contents: Preface to the University of South Carolina Reissue; Foreword; I, The Exhibition (Introduction, Catalogue); II, The Manuscripts (Introduction, Handlist); III, The English Editions (Introduction, Bibliography); IV, The Translations (Introduction, Check List); V, Motion Pictures and Television (Introduction, Check List); Appendix, Short Story Lending Schedule; Index; Errata.

————, compiler. *The Merrill Checklist of William Faulkner.* Columbus: Charles E. Merrill Publishing Company, [1970]. ii, 37 pp. $.75. SBN 675-09382-1. LC 70-102409. Charles E. Merrill Checklists.

FREDERIC, HAROLD

O'Donnell, Thomas F., compiler. *The Merrill Checklist of Harold Frederic.* Columbus: Charles E. Merrill Publishing Company, [1969]. iv, 34 pp. $.75. SBN 675-09465-8. LC 72-92598. Charles E. Merrill Checklists.

FROST, ROBERT

Greiner, Donald J., compiler. *The Merrill Checklist of Robert Frost.* Columbus: Charles E. Merrill Publishing Company, [1969]. iv, 42 pp. $.75. SBN 675-09551-4. LC 69-13799. Charles E. Merrill Checklists.

GARDNER, ERLE STANLEY

Mundell, E. H. *Erle Stanley Gardner: A Checklist.* Kent: The Kent State University Press, [1968]. xii, 91 pp. $5.50. SBN 87338-034-7. LC 70-97619. The Serif Series, No. 6. Contents: Introduction; Short Fiction; Book Fiction; Short Non-Fiction; Book Non-Fiction; Miscellanea; Indexes.

HAMMETT, DASHIELL

Mundell, E. H. *A List of the Original Appearances of Dashiell Hammett's Magazine Work.* Kent: The Kent State University Press, [1970]. x, 52 pp. $5.00. SBN 87338-033-9. LC 75-97620. The Serif Series, No. 13. A reprint of Mundell's 1968 private publication.

HAWTHORNE, NATHANIEL

Browne, Nina E., ed. *A Bibliography of Nathaniel Hawthorne.* New York: Johnson Reprint Corporation, 1968. x, 215 pp. (inc. frontispiece). $7.50. Facsimile — Boston and New York: Houghton, Mifflin and Company, 1905. Contents: Preface; Explanations; Chronological List of Hawthorne's Works; Pseudonyms used by Hawthorne; Collected Works; Separate Works; Translations; Dramatizations; Biography and Criticism (Lives, Diaries, and Letters; Biographical and Critical Sketches; Miscellaneous; Poems); Alphabetical List of Hawthorne's Works; Index to Authors and Magazines cited.

Clark, C. E. Frazer, Jr., compiler. *The Merrill Checklist of Nathaniel Hawthorne.* Columbus: Charles E. Merrill Publishing Company, [1970]. ii, 45 pp. $.75. SBN 675-09467-4. LC 78-103049. Charles E. Merrill Checklists.

HELLMAN, LILLIAN

Triesch, Manfred. *The Lillian Hellman Collection at the University of Texas.* Austin: The Humanities Research Center, The University of Texas, [1968]. 168 pp. $7.50. LC 67-64819.

The University of Texas Bibliographical Series. 'A descriptive catalogue such as this must be a compromise between mere cataloguing and the attempt to follow the development of each work. The various typescript versions of each play are arranged in chronological sequence according to internal evidence so the reader can follow the development of each play' (p. 9). Contents: Introduction; A, Autograph Manuscripts and Typescripts; B, Contributions; C, Letters; D, Secondary Sources; E, Appendix; F, Index.

HEMINGWAY, ERNEST

White, William, compiler. *The Merrill Checklist of Ernest Hemingway.* Columbus: Charles E. Merrill Publishing Company, [1970]. ii, 45 pp. $.75. SBN 675-09370-8. LC 70-104079. Charles E. Merrill Checklists.

Young, Philip, and Charles W. Mann. *The Hemingway Manuscripts: An Inventory.* University Park, Pennsylvania and London: The Pennsylvania State University Press, 1969. xiv, 138 pp. (plus 6 pp. of illustrations). $5.95. SBN 271-0080-5. LC 68-8189. 'The great bulk of the surviving manuscripts of Ernest Hemingway are in the possession of Mrs. Hemingway, sole executrix of his estate, until such time as they may be suitably deposited and arranged for examination by scholars in years to come. This inventory of her husband's literary estate was originally prepared for her. . . . It should be made clear, first off, that this publication pretends to be no more than what it says: an "inventory" . . . and not the much more elaborate catalogue . . . that should be made when the papers have reached their permanent repository' (p. vii). Contents: Preface; Acknowledgments; Books; Short Fiction; Journalism and Other Non-Fiction; Poetry; Fragments; Letters; Miscellaneous; Copies of Books and Magazines; Index.

INGERSOLL, ROBERT G.

Stein, Gordon. *Robert G. Ingersoll: A Checklist.* Kent: The Kent State University Press, [1969]. xxx, 128 pp. $5.00. SBN

87338-047-9. LC 78-626234. The Serif Series, No. 9. 'Because Ingersoll's lectures were published with different titles and varying contents, a great number of difficulties arise in the classification and even identification of the contents of the lectures. Hence the presence of a complete title index in this checklist' (p. xiv). Contents: Introduction; How to Use This Checklist; Ingersoll Chronology; Abbreviations; Location Symbols; I, Separately Published Titles by Ingersoll; II, Works with Contributions by Ingersoll; III, Ingersoll's Contributions to Periodicals; IV, Collected Essays and Works by Ingersoll; V, Translations of Works by Ingersoll; VI, Works About Ingersoll (A, Biographies; B, Periodical Articles; C, Non-Biographical Books and Pamphlets); Appendix; Index.

IVES, CHARLES

De Laerma, Dominique-Rene. *Charles Ives, 1874–1954: A Bibliography of His Music.* Kent: The Kent State University Press, [1970]. xii, 212 pp. $7.50. ISBN 0-87338-057-6. LC 72-99083. Contents: Preface; Introduction; Bibliography; Publication Index; Medium Index; Chronological Index; Index of Arrangers, Poets and Librettists; Phonorecord Index; Performer Index.

JEFFERS, ROBINSON

Nolte, William H., compiler. *The Merrill Checklist of Robinson Jeffers.* Columbus: Charles E. Merrill Publishing Company, [1970]. iv, 25 pp. $.75. ISBN 0-675-09355-4. LC 70-116043. Charles E. Merrill Checklists.

LEWIS, SINCLAIR

Lundquist, James, compiler. *The Merrill Checklist of Sinclair Lewis.* Columbus: Charles E. Merrill Publishing Company, [1970]. iv, 36 pp. $.75. ISBN 0-675-09306-6. LC 71-124551. Charles E. Merrill Checklists.

MALAMUD, BERNARD

Kosofsky, Rita Nathalie. *Bernard Malamud: An Annotated Checklist.* Kent: The Kent State University Press, [1969]. xiv, 63 pp. $4.25. SBN 87338-037-1. LC 75-626236. The Serif Series, No. 7. Contents: Preface; Author's Note; Works of Bernard Malamud (Books, Stories); Secondary Sources (Criticism in Books, Criticism in Periodicals, Book Reviews).

MELVILLE, HERMAN

Vincent, Howard, compiler. *The Merrill Checklist of Herman Melville.* Columbus: Charles E. Merrill Publishing Company, [1969]. iv, 44 pp. $.75. SBN 675-09462-3. LC 79-89952. Charles E. Merrill Checklists.

MENCKEN, H. L.

Nolte, William H., compiler. *The Merrill Checklist of H. L. Mencken.* Columbus: Charles E. Merrill Publishing Company, [1969]. iv, 30 pp. $.75. SBN 675-09412-7. LC 76-92548. Charles E. Merrill Checklists.

NORRIS, FRANK

Hill, John S., compiler. *The Merrill Checklist of Frank Norris.* Columbus: Charles E. Merrill Publishing Company, [1970]. iv, 32 pp. $.75. ISBN 0-675-09305-8. LC 70-125347. Charles E. Merrill Checklists.

POE, EDGAR ALLAN

Robbins, J. Albert, compiler. *The Merrill Checklist of Edgar Allan Poe.* Columbus: Charles E. Merrill Publishing Company, [1969]. iv, 44 pp. $.75. SBN 675-09463-1. LC 72-90037. Charles E. Merrill Checklists.

POUND, EZRA

Hénault, Marie, compiler. *The Merrill Checklist of Ezra Pound.*

Columbus: Charles E. Merrill Publishing Company, [1970]. iv, 44 pp. $.75. SBN 675-09373-2. LC 75-103887. Charles E. Merrill Checklists.

STEVENS, WALLACE

Huguelet, Theodore L., compiler. *The Merrill Checklist of Wallace Stevens.* Columbus: Charles E. Merrill Publishing Company, [1970]. iv, 35 pp. $.75. SBN 675-09384-8. LC 71-101585. Charles E. Merrill Checklists.

TATE, ALLEN

Fallwell, Marshall, Jr. *Allen Tate: A Bibliography.* New York: David Lewis, 1969. vii, 112 pp. $10.00. LC 75-7563. Fugitive Bibliographies. An enumerative bibliography. Contents: Introduction; Poems; Essays; Periodical Book Reviews; Book Reviews for the Nashville *Tennessean;* Miscellanea; Bibliographical and Critical Material.

THOREAU, HENRY DAVID

Allen, Francis H., ed. *A Bibliography of Henry David Thoreau.* [New York]: Johnson Reprint Corporation, 1967. xviii, 201 pp. (inc. frontispiece, plus tipped-in facsimile). $8.50. Facsimile — Boston and New York: Houghton Mifflin Company, 1908. Contents: Preface; Note on the Frontispiece and Other Portraits of Thoreau; Thoreau's Books (Single Publications, Collected Works); Selections from Thoreau's Writings (Books entirely devoted to Thoreau, Other Books containing selections from Thoreau); Articles and Poems by Thoreau; Biographies and other Books relating exclusively to Thoreau; Books containing Critical and Biographical Matter; Newspaper and Periodical Articles concerning Thoreau and his Works; Auction Prices; Appendix (A, A List of the Poems and Bits of Verse contained in Thoreau's Prose Works exclusive of the Journal; B, Addenda; C, Erratum); Index.

WARREN, ROBERT PENN

Huff, Mary Nance. *Robert Penn Warren: A Bibliography.* New York: David Lewis, 1968. xii, 171 pp. $10.00. LC 68-28007. Fugitive Bibliographies. An annotated enumerative bibliography. Contents: Introduction; Books; Translations of Warren's Books; Short Stories; Poems; Essays and Articles; Book Reviews; Miscellanea; Biographical and Critical Material.

WHITMAN, WALT

Tanner, James T. F. *Walt Whitman: A Supplementary Bibliography, 1961–1967.* Kent: The Kent State University Press, [1968]. vi, 59 pp. $3.75. SBN 87338-019-3. LC 67-65586. The Serif Series, No. 5. 'My intention . . . is simply to bring up to date . . . a bibliography of works *about* Walt Whitman' (p. v). Contents: Introduction; A, Bibliographies; B, Criticism, Biography, and Reviews.

WILBUR, RICHARD

Field, John P. *Richard Wilbur: A Bibliographical Checklist.* Kent: The Kent State University Press, [1971]. x, 85 pp. $4.50. ISBN 0-87338-035-5. LC 79-626237. The Serif Series, No. 16. Contents: A Note by Richard Wilbur; Introductory Note; I, Works by Richard Wilbur (A, Books; B, Individual poems [including translations]; C, Articles, stories [including translations], and short editorial work; D, Book reviews; E. Interviews; F, Manuscripts; G, Other [drawings, statements, letters, records, tapes, films]); II, Works about Richard Wilbur (A, Books; B, Critical articles and commentary in books; C, Book reviews; D, Biography).

WILLIAMS, WILLIAM CARLOS

Engels, John, compiler. *The Merrill Checklist of William Carlos Williams.* Columbus: Charles E. Merrill Publishing Company, [1969]. iv, 39 pp. $.75. SBN 675-09404-6. LC 74-98475. Charles E. Merrill Checklists.

WOLFE, THOMAS

Reeves, Paschal, compiler. *The Merrill Checklist of Thomas Wolfe.*
Columbus: Charles E. Merrill Publishing Company, [1969].
iv, 43 pp. $.75. SBN 675-09403-8. LC 71-98477. Charles E.
Merrill Checklists.

4. SUBJECT BIBLIOGRAPHIES AND CHECKLISTS

BLACK LITERATURE

Deodene, Frank, and William P. French. *Black American Fiction
Since 1952; A Preliminary Checklist.* Chatham, N. J.: The
Chatham Bookseller, 1970. iv, 25 pp. $2.50. LC 78-96384.
'In this list the compilers have tried to include all first editions of books of fiction by black authors born or living in
the United States, published from 1953 to mid-1969, excluding translations (except of works unpublished in
English), juveniles and anthologies' (p. iii). Contents: Preface; Checklist.

DETECTIVE FICTION

Hagen, Ordean A. *Who Done It?: A Guide to Detective, Mystery and
Suspense Fiction.* New York: R. R. Bowker, 1969. SBN 8352-
0234-8. LC 69-19209. xx, 834 pp. $18.95. Contents: Part I,
A Comprehensive Bibliography of Mystery Fiction, 1841–
1967; Part II, A Bibliographic Guide to Mystery Fiction;
Appendix; Title Index to the Comprehensive Bibliography.

DRAMA

Wegelin, Oscar. *Early American Plays 1714–1830: A Compilation
of the titles of Plays and Dramatic Poems written by authors born
in or residing in North America previous to 1830.* Second Revised Edition. [New York]: Johnson Reprint Corporation,
1968. x, 11–94 pp. (plus 3 pp. of illustrations). $6.00. Fac-
simile — New York: The Literary Collector Press, 1905.

Contents: Preface; Compilation; Plays in Manuscript; Index to Titles of Published Plays.

JOURNALISM

Cannon, Carl L. *Journalism: A Bibliography.* Detroit: Gale Research Company, 1967. viii, 360 pp. $13.00. LC 66-25646. Facsimile—New York: The New York Public Library, 1924. Contents: Bibliography; Periodicals; General Works; Amateur Journalism; Army and Navy Newspapers; Associated Press; Associations and Clubs; Biography, American; Biography, British; Country Press; Diction; Directories; Editorials: Editors and Editing; Ethics; Foreign Language Press; Headlines; History; Individual Papers; Influence; Interviewing; Journalism as a Career; Jurisprudence; Liberty of the Press; Manuals; Military Censorship; The Morgue; The Negro Press; Newspapers as Historical Sources; Paragraphing; Reference Books; Relation to Literature; Religious Journalism; Reporting; Sensational Journalism; Study and Teaching; War Correspondence; Women in Journalism; Index.

WAR

Genthe, Charles V. *American War Narratives 1917–1918: A Study and Bibliography.* New York: David Lewis, [1969]. xii, 195 pp. $10.00. LC 75-96422. Contents: Introduction; 1917; 1918; Conclusion; Notes; An Annotated Bibliography of Personal War Narratives Published in America 1914–1918; Index.

THE WEST

Adams, Ramon F. *Six-Guns and Saddle Leather: A Bibliography of Books and Pamphlets on Western Outlaws and Gunmen.* New Edition, Revised and Greatly Enlarged. Norman: University of Oklahoma Press, [1969]. xxvi, 810 pp. $19.95. SBN 8061-0849-5. LC 69-16729. The first edition was published in 1954. The dust jacket notes that this new edition 'contains 2,491 entries—more than twice as many as the first'. Contents: Acknowledgments for the Revised Edition; Acknowledgments for the First Edition; Introduction to the First Edition; Table of Abbreviations; A Bibliography of Books and Pamphlets on Western Outlaws and Gunmen; Addenda; Index.

5. NATIONAL BIBLIOGRAPHIES AND CHECKLISTS

Bryer, Jackson R., ed. *Fifteen Modern American Authors: A Survey of Research and Criticism.* Durham, N.C.: Duke University Press, 1969. xviii, 493 pp. $10.00. ISBN 0-8223-0208-X. LC 78-83720. Contents: Preface; Acknowledgments; Key to Abbreviations; Walter B. Rideout, 'Sherwood Anderson'; Bernice Slote, 'Willa Cather'; Brom Weber, 'Hart Crane'; Robert H. Elias, 'Theodore Dreiser'; Richard M. Ludwig, 'T. S. Eliot'; James B. Meriwether, 'William Faulkner'; Jackson R. Bryer, 'F. Scott Fitzgerald'; Reginald L. Cook, 'Robert Frost'; Frederick J. Hoffman, 'Ernest Hemingway'; John Henry Raleigh, 'Eugene O'Neill'; John Espey, 'Ezra Pound'; Ellsworth Barnard, 'Edwin Arlington Robinson'; Warren French, 'John Steinbeck'; Joseph N. Riddel, 'Wallace Stevens'; C. Hugh Holman, 'Thomas Wolfe'; Notes on Contributors; Index by Joseph M. Flora.

Van Patten, Nathan. *An Index to Bibliographies and Bibliographical Contributions Relating to the Works of American and British Authors, 1923–1932.* New York: Johnson Reprint Corporation, 1969. viii, 324 pp. $15.00. Facsimile—Stanford University, Calif.: Stanford University Press, 1934. Contents: An Index to Bibliographies and Bibliographical Contributions . . . ; Supplement; Appendix; Index.

6. WRITING AND AUTOGRAPHS

Benjamin, Mary A. *Autographs: A Key to Collecting.* Second Printing of Corrected and Revised Edition. New York: Walter R. Benjamin Autographs, 1966. xxii, 313 pp. (plus 35 pp. of illustrations). $5.95. LC 63-10776. Contents of Part One: Preface to Reissue; Foreword; Introduction by Julian P. Boyd; I, A Historical Summary; II, The A.B.C.'s of Terminology; III, Evaluation; IV, What to Collect; V, Where to Buy; VI, The Forger and his Work; VII, Facsimiles, Reproductions and Manuscript Copies; VIII, Detection; IX, The Hidden Signature; X, The Strange Case of Button Gwinnet; XI, Confused Identities; XII, The Importance of the Collector. Contents of Part Two: XIII, Care and Preservation; XIV, How to Arrange; Tables (Approximate Dates Relating to Paper, Ink, and Printing; French Revolutionary Calendar; Titles of Napoleon's Marshals; Titles of Napoleon's Family); A Select List of Reference Works; Index.

7. PRINTING, BINDING, PUBLISHING, AND BOOKSELLING

Devinne, Theodore L. *The Invention of Printing: A Collection of Facts and Opinions Descriptive of Early Prints and Playing Cards, the Block-Books of the Fifteenth Century, the Legend of Lourens Janszoon Coster, of Haarlem, and the Work of John Gutenberg and his Associates. Illustrated with Fac-similes of Early Types and Woodcuts.* Detroit: Gale Research Company, 1969. ii, 556 pp. (inc. 33 pp. of illustrations). $14.50. Facsimile – New York: Francis Hart & Co., 1876. Contents: I, The Different Methods of Printing; II, Antique Methods of Impression and their Failure; III, The Key to the Invention of Typography; IV, The Image Prints of the Fifteenth Century; V, Printed and Stenciled Playing Cards; VI, The Chinese Method of Printing; VII, The Early Printing of Italy; VIII, The Introduction of Paper in Europe; IX, The Bookmakers of the Middle Ages; X, The Preparation for Printing; XI, Block-Books of Images without Text; XII, Block-Books of Images with Text; XIII, The Donatus, or Boy's Latin Grammar; XIV, The Speculum Salutis, or Mirror of Salvation; XV, The Works and Workmanship of an Unknown Printer; XVI, The Period in Which the Speculum was Printed; XVII, The Legend of Lourens Janszoon Coster; XVII, The Growth of the Legend; XIX, The Downfall of the Legend; XX, John Gutenberg at Strasburg; XXI, Gutenberg and his Earlier Work at Mentz; XXII, The Later Work of Gutenberg; XXIII, The Work of Peter Schoeffer and John Fust; XXIV, Alleged Inventors of Printing; XXV, The Spread of Printing. XXVI, The Tools and Usage of the First Printers; Authorities Consulted; Index.

Gilmer, Walker. *Horace Liveright: Publisher to the Twenties.* New York: David Lewis, [1970]. xiv, 287 pp. (plus frontispiece). $8.95. SBN

912012-02-1. LC 75-125880. 'This book is intended to be an account of the publishing career of Horace Brisbin Liveright. It was the professional Liveright who first attracted my attention, and it is his public career that I have attempted to delineate' (p. vii). Contents: Preface; Acknowledgments; Boni & Liveright; The Radical Writers; Theodore Dreiser; John Sumner's Vice Society; The B & L Offices; New Writers and New Ventures; Sherwood Anderson; Hemingway, Faulkner, Jeffers, and Crane; *An American Tragedy;* Two Censorship Trials; Eugene O'Neill; Horace Liveright, Inc.; 1929–1930; Epilogue; Notes; Index. *Note:* A facsimile of the eight-page Boni & Liveright list, 'GOOD BOOKS | *FALL 1925*', is tucked into copies of the book. This is nowhere marked as a facsimile.

Greist, Guinevere L. *Mudie's Circulating Library and the Victorian Novel.* Bloomington and London: Indiana University Press, 1970. xii, 272 pp. $8.95. ISBN 253-15480-4. LC 76-126210. 'Drawing upon previously untapped sources in personal letters and nineteenth-century periodicals, Miss Greist presents a well-documented study of the economics of the book trade and the mechanics of book distribution during the period, which will provide a fresh angle of vision for viewing the masterpieces of Victorian fiction' (dust jacket). Contents: Preface; (1) The Age of Mudie: Background; (2) Mudie's The Leviathan; (3) Mudie's and the Three-Decker; (4) Publishers, Profits, and the Public; (5) Novelists, Novels, and the Establishment; (6) Readers, Reactions, and Restriction; (7) The Collapse; (8) The Vanishing Three-Decker; (9) The End of an Era; Select Bibliography; Notes; Index.

Hildeburn, Charles R. *Sketches of Printers and Printing in Colonial New York.* Detroit: Gale Research Company, 1969. xvi, 189 pp. (plus 2 portraits). $8.50. LC 68-17975. Facsimile—New York: Dodd, Mead & Co., 1895. 'The author has included three etched portraits and twenty-eight facsimiles of title pages as well as a chronological list of thirty-three printers with the dates when each was in business in New York' (publisher's release). Contents: I, William Bradford, the Founder of the Press in the Middle Colonies; II, The Zengers (more especially John Peter Zenger), and the Liberty of the Press; III, The Parkers, and their Numerous Establishments; IV, Henry De Foreest, and the Minor Presses of the Middle of the Century: Samuel Brown, William

Weyman, Samuel Farley, Benjamin Mecom, and Samuel Campbell; V, Hugh Gaine, the Irish Printer, and his Journalistic Straddle; VI, Whigs and Tories, or the Holts and the Robertsons; VII, James Rivington, "the only London Bookseller in America"; VIII, James Rivington, and his "Lying Gazette"; IX, A group of Small Fry prior to the Revolution: Inslee & Car, Hodge & Shober, John Anderson, and Samuel Loudon; X, The Loyalist Printers of the Revolution: Macdonald & Cameron, Mills & Hicks, William Lewis, Morton & Horner, and Christopher Sower, 3d.

Jacobi, Charles Thomas. *The Printers' Vocabulary*. Detroit: Gale Research Company, 1969. viii, 164 pp. $6.50. LC 68-30613. Facsimile—London: The Chiswick Press, 1888. 'This collection of over 2,500 printers' terms is a lexicographic history of the art from the time of Caxton. The dictionary includes not only terms frequently used in the nineteenth century but also those that have become obsolete or superseded' (publisher's release). Contents: Introduction; *The Printers' Vocabulary of Technical Terms, Phrases, Abbreviations, and Other Expressions;* Appendixes: Marks and signs used by Printers' readers in correcting proofs.

Jaspert, W. Pincus, W. Turner Berry, and A. F. Johnson. *The Encyclopedia of Type Faces*. Fourth Edition. New York: Barnes & Noble, 1970. [xvi], 420 pp. $18.50. SBN 389-04043-6. Contents: Preface; Introduction; Typeface Nomenclature; Classification; Romans; Lineales; Scripts; Some Literature on Type & Type Founding; Typefounder's Addresses; Index to Designers; Index to Type Faces.

Kingsford, R. J. L. *The Publishers Association 1896–1946*. Cambridge: Cambridge University Press, 1970. x, 228 pp. $10.00 SBN 521-07756-7. LC 74-101445. Contents: Preface; Introduction: the 1852 verdict; (1) 1895–1900: the founding of the Association and the Net Book Agreement; (2) 1901–1908: through the Book War; (3) 1908–1914: copyright and novel prices; (4) 1914–1919: World War I; (5) 1919–1927: reconstruction and strikes; (6) 1924–1930: new aims and opportunities; (7) 1931–1939 (a): the Great Depression, markets and rights; (8) 1931–1939 (b): book clubs, Book Tokens, book weeks; (9) 1939–1946 (a) World War II: the book front; (10) 1939–1946 (b): World War II: the export markets, trade relations at home; Epilogue: the 1962 verdict; Appendixes: (1, The first Rules of the Association; 2, The members in 1896 and the first Council; 3, The Officers and Secretaries of the Association, 1896–1962); Bibliography; Index.

Longman, W. *Tokens of the Eighteenth Century, Connected with Book-sellers and Bookmakers (Authors, Printers, Publishers, Engravers and Paper Makers)*. Detroit: Gale Research Company, 1970. 90 pp. (inc. frontispiece, plus 10 pp. of illustrations). $7.50. LC 70-78192. Facsimile – London: Longmans, Green & Co., 1916. Contents: Introduction; I, Tokens issued by Authors, Book-sellers, Circulating Librarians, Engravers, Newspaper Proprie-tors, Paper Manufacturers, Printers and Publishers; II, Tokens struck by People unconnected with any Branch of the Book Trade, but which refer to, and in most cases portray an Author; III, Miscellaneous Tokens of Interest to the Bookselling and Allied Trades; Index.

McClary, Ben Harris, ed. *Washington Irving and the House of Murray*. Knoxville: The University of Tennessee Press, 1969. xlvi, 242 pp. (inc. 5 pp. of illustrations, plus 2 portraits). SBN 87049-094-X. LC 73-77843. Professor McClary has presented 'within the framework of sixty-eight Irving letters to the Murrays – of which fifty-eight are previously unpublished . . . the neglected story of the most consequential author-publisher relationship of the nineteenth century' (dust jacket). Contents: Preface; Acknowledgments; Introduction (Washington Irving to 1817, The House of Murray to 1817); I, Introduction to the Drawing-Room Circle; II, Murray's Most Valued Author; III, The Re-turn of a Prodigal; IV, The Absentee; V, Back after a Five-Year Absence; VI, Estrangement and Reconciliation; VII, The Last Years. Appendixes (I, Lost Letters: Washington Irving to the John Murrays; II, The John Murrays to Washington Irving: A Survey of Epistolary Remains; III, Official Documents at 50 Albemarle Street Concerning Washington Irving's Writings; IV, Washington Irving's Notes Used in the Preparation of Letter 64; V, Official Copyright Registry Dates of Irving Titles Pub-lished by John Murray II); Bibliography; Index.

McKay, George L. *American Book Auction Catalogues, 1713–1934: A Union List*. Supplements 1946 and 1948. The New York Public

Library, 1937. xxxii, 560 pp. (including frontispiece, plus 3 pp. of illustrations). Facsimile by Gale Research Company, Detroit. $13.75. LC 66-27840. The publisher's release notes: 'This is a Union List of catalogues prepared for 10,000 American auctions of books, pamphlets, broadsides, newspapers, manuscripts, autographs, and bookplates.' Contents: List of Illustrations; Preface; Principal Works Consulted; List of American Book Auction Houses; History of Book Auctions in America, by Clarence S. Brigham; Symbols used in the List; The List of Catalogues; American Book Auctions before 1801 the Authorities for which do not Mention Catalogues; Anglo-American Auctions; Additions and Corrections; Index of Owners; Supplements.

Moore, John Weeks, compiler. *Moore's Historical, Biographical, and Miscellaneous Gatherings, in the Form of Disconnected Notes Relative to Printers, Printing, Publishing, and Editing of Books, Newspapers, Magazines, and Other Literary Productions, Such as the Early Publications of New England, the United States, and the World, from the Discovery of the Art, or from 1420 to 1886: With Many Brief Notices of Authors, Publishers, Editors, Printers, and Inventors.* Detroit: Gale Research Company, 1969. $24.50. 604 pp. LC 68-17977. Facsimile — Concord, N.H.: Republican Press Association, 1886. Contents: Proemial Note; Part I, [Miscellaneous]; Part II, First Printing in North and South America; Part III, Manchester: Her Newspapers and Publications; Part IV, New England Editors, Publishers, Papers, and Printers; Notice; Index.

Pasko, Wesley Washington. *American Dictionary of Printing and Bookmaking, Containing A History of These Arts in Europe and America, with Definitions of Technical Terms and Biographical Sketches.* Detroit: Gale Research Company, 1967. [1–6], iv, 592 pp. (inc. frontispiece). $19.00. LC 66-27215. Facsimile — New York: Howard Lockwood & Co., 1894. 'Lockwood's *American Dictionary of Printing and Bookmaking*' with a new introduction by Robert E. Runser.

Rau, Jack. *The Codex as a Book Form.* New York: The Pre-Columbian Press, 1970. [16 pp.] plus 2 pp. of illustrations. $5.00. 500 copies, numbered and signed.

Steiner-Prag, Eleanor F. *American Book Trade Directory.* 19th Edition. New York and London: R. R. Bowker Company, 1969. x, 699 pp. $25.00. SBN 8352-0243-7. LC 15-23627. Contents: Foreword; Section I: Book Trade Information (Auctioneers of Literary Property, Book Clubs, Book Trade Periodicals & Reference Books, Dealers in Foreign Books, Cross Reference Index by Languages, Export Representatives, Exporters-Importers, Greeting Card Publishers, Private Book Clubs, Rental Library Chains); Section II: Publishers in the U.S. (Directory of Book Publishers in the U.S., Publishers' Imprints, Affiliated Companies, Subsidiaries & Special Distribution Arrangements, Former Publishing Companies); Section III: Directory of Booksellers & Antiquarians (In the United States, In Regions administered by the United States); Section IV: Directory of Wholesalers in the U.S. & Canada (National Distributors of Paperbacks, Wholesale Remainder Dealers, Wholesalers in the U.S. & Canada); Section V: Index to Booksellers & Wholesalers; Section VI: Book Trade in Great Britain, the Republic of Ireland & Canada (Publishers in Great Britain, American Representatives of British Publishers, British Representatives of American Publishers, Publishers in the Republic of Ireland, Publishers in Canada, Booksellers in Great Britain, Booksellers in the Republic of Ireland, Booksellers in Canada).

Towner, Wesley. *The Elegant Auctioneers.* Completed by Stephen Varble. New York: Hill & Wang, [1970]. viii, 632 pp. (inc. 7 pp. of illustrations). $10.00. ISBN 0-8090-4171-5. LC 70-116871. Contents: Publisher's Note; (1) The Hammer and the Heart's Desire; (2) Madison Square; (3) Two Windows and the Bloom of the Peach; (4) The Titans in the Market Place; (5) Art and the High Life; (6) Bibliomania; (7) The Pale Horseman and the Million-Dollar Voice; (8) Enter Mr. Bishop; (9) In the Wing Glow of the Angel; (10) Ponder on These Things; (11) Drifting Toward Eternity; (12) The Venus on Madison Avenue; Index.

Woodberry, George E. *A History of Wood Engraving.* Detroit: Gale Research Company, 1969. 221 pp. (inc. 10 pp. of illus.). $10.00 LC 69-17490. Facsimile — New York: Harper & Brothers, 1883. Contents: Preface; I, The Origin of the Art; II, The Block-Books; III, Early Printed Books in the North; IV, Early Italian Wood-Engraving; V, Albert Dürer and His Successors; VI, Hans

Holbein; VII, The Decline and Extinction of the Art; VIII, Modern Wood-Engraving; A List of the Principal Works upon Wood-Engraving Useful to Students; Index.

8. COPYRIGHT AND INTELLECTUAL PROPERTY

No entry.

9. LIBRARIES AND BOOK COLLECTING

Barrett, C. Waller, introducer. *The American Writer in England: An Exhibition Arranged in Honor of the Sesquicentennial of the University of Virginia.* Foreword by Gordon N. Ray. Charlottesville: The University Press of Virginia, [1969]. xxxvi, 137 pp. (inc. frontispiece and 28 pp. of illustrations). $10.00. SBN 8139-0288-6. LC 70-93030. The purpose of this exhibition was 'to show the extent to which early American writing was an outgrowth of the English literature of the period, the way the American writer developed when directly exposed to British life and culture, and the evolution in the end of an independent American literature' (p. ix). Contents: Foreword; Preface; Introduction: The American Writer in England; Catalogue of the Exhibit; Index of Authors.

Grieder, Theodore, ed. *New York University Libraries Fales Library Checklist.* New York: AMS Press, Inc., [1970]. 2 vols. Vol. I, xii: 1-575 pp; Vol. II: vi, 576-1104 pp. $82.50. ISBN 0-404-07947-4 (Vol. I); 0-404-07948-3 (Vol. II); 0-404-07946-6 (Complete Set). LC 71-122494. Contents of Vol. I (A–K): Introduction; Abbreviations; Codes; *Fales Library Checklist.* Contents of Vol. II (L–Z): Abbreviations; Codes; *Fales Library Checklist.*

10. BIBLIOGRAPHICAL AND TEXTUAL THEORY AND PRACTICE

Allen, Michael. *Poe and the British Magazine Tradition.* New York: Oxford University Press, 1969. x, 255 pp. $6.50. LC 69-12350. 'Poe consciously tried to solve the "quality-popularity dilemma" by adapting certain British journalistic conventions to his own

ends and audience. . . .' (dust jacket). Contents: Preliminary:
The Writer and His Audience; I, Introduction: Poe's Reading
of the British Magazines; II, The Blackwoods's Pattern and
Poe's Journalism; III, Personalities and Critical Controversy;
IV, Literary Personality; V, Learning and Journalism; VI,
Journalism as Art; VII, Poe's Inconsistencies; VIII, Poe and the
American Reality; IX, Poe's Popularity; X, Poe's Elitism and
the 'Stylus'; XI, Conclusion: Poe and the British Magazine Tra-
dition; Notes; Index.

Gottesman, Ronald, and Scott Bennett, compilers and eds. *Art and
Error: Modern Textual Editing.* Bloomington and London: Indiana
University Press, [1970]. xiv, 306 pp. (inc. 4 pp. of illustrations).
$10.95. SBN 253-30165-2. LC 70-103927. 'This compilation . . .
draws special attention to textual problems presented by post-
Renaissance literature and to the rich variety of solutions de-
veloped to overcome these problems' (p. ix). Contents: Preface;
Acknowledgments; A. E. Housman, 'The Application of Thought
to Textual Criticism'; W. W. Greg, 'The Rationale of Copy-Text';
R. C. Bald, 'Editorial Problems—A Preliminary Survey'; Fredson
Bowers, 'Some Principles for Scholarly Editions of Nineteenth-
Century American Authors'; James Thorpe, 'The Aesthetics
of Textual Criticism'; David M. Veith, 'A Textual Paradox:
Rochester's "To a Lady in a Letter"'; Robert Halsband, 'Editing
the Letters of Letter-Writers'; Thomas H. Johnson, 'Establishing
a Text: The Emily Dickinson Papers'; John Butt, 'Editing a
Nineteenth-Century Novelist'; Dennis Welland, 'Samuel Clemens
and his English Publishers: Biographical and Editorial Problems';
Russell K. Alspach, 'Some Textual Problems in Yeats'; Harry
M. Geduld, *'Back to Methusela:* Textual Problems in Shaw'; James
B. Meriwether, 'Notes on the Textual History of *The Sound and
the Fury';* Vinton A Dearing, 'Computor Aids to Editing the Text
of Dryden'; William M. Gibson and George R. Petty, Jr., 'The
Ordered Computor Collation of Unprepared Literary Text';
Further Readings.

Horne, Thomas Hartwell. *An Introduction to the Study of Bibliography,
to Which is Affixed a Memoir on the Public Libraries of the Antients.*
Detroit: Gale Research Company, [1967]. 2 vols. Vol. I: xvi,
xxv, [26]–402 pp.; Vol. II: iv, [403]–[760], [i]–clvi pp. (plus
9 pp. of illustrations). $37.50. LC 66-28260. Facsimile—London:

T. Cadell and W. Davies, 1814. Contents: Preface; Introductory Memoir on the Public Libraries of the Antients; Introduction to the Study of Bibliography; *Part I* (I, On the different substances employed for Manuscripts and printed Books; II, On Manuscripts in general, including the origin of Writing; III, Origin and Progress of Printing, Mechanism of the Art, etc.); *Part II* (On Books—I, General Remarks on the Denominations, Sizes, etc. of Books; II, Of the knowledge of books, their relative value and scarcity, Prices of books, etc.; III, Essay towards an improved System of Classification for a Library); *Part III* (A Notice of the Principal Works Extant on Literary History in General, and on Bibliography in Particular—I, Literary History; II, Writing; III, Works on Printing; IV, Books; V, Bibliographical Systems, Catalogues, etc.); Appendix.

11. CONCORDANCES

Graham, Philip, and Joseph Jones. *A Concordance to the Poems of Sidney Lanier.* [New York]: Johnson Reprint Corporation, 1969. vi, 447 pp. $25.00. Facsimile—Austin: The University of Texas Press, 1939. 'We have endeavored to list in alphabetical order every word occurring in the poems, and, with the exceptions noted under "List of Words Partially Treated" (p. iv), to supply the text of the line in which the word occurs, the page number, the title, and the line number for each occurrence' (p. iii). Contents: Preface; List of Words Partially Treated; List of Abbreviations; *Concordance.*

12. DICTIONARIES, RHETORICS, AND GUIDES TO LANGUAGE

Hyamson, Albert M. *A Dictionary of English Phrases; Phraseological Allusion, Catchwords, Stereotyped Modes of Speech and Metaphors, Nicknames, Sobriquets, Derivations from Personal Names, etc. With Explanations and Thousands of Exact References to Their Sources or Early Usage.* Detroit: Gale Research Company, 1970. xvi, 365 pp. LC 66-22673. $12.00. Facsimile—New York: E. P. Dutton & Co., 1922. Contents: Preface; A Few of the Principal Reference Works Consulted; Abbreviations; *Dictionary of Phrases.*

415

Vizetelly, Frank H., and Leander J. de Bekker. *A Desk-Book of Idioms and Idiomatic Phrases in English Speech and Literature.* Detroit: Gale Research Company, 1970. viii, 498 pp. $14.50. LC 73-121208. 'This is a facsimile reprint of the 1923 edition published in New York by Funk & Wagnalls Company' (p. iv). Contents: Introduction; *A Desk-Book of Idioms and Idiomatic Phrases.*

Webster, Noah. *An American Dictionary of the English Language.* Introduced by Mario A. Pei. New York and London: Johnson Reprint Corporation, 1970. 2 vols. Vol. I: vi, [1005] pp.; Vol. II: vi, [934] pp. $90.00. LC 77-117409. Facsimile — New York: S. Converse, 1828. Contents of Vol. I: *An American Dictionary of the English Language* (Preface, Introduction, A Philosophical and Practical Grammar of the English Language, Directions for the Pronunciation of Words, *Dictionary:* A–I). Contents of Vol. II: *Dictionary:* J–Z; Additions; Corrections; Advertisement.

13. MISCELLANEOUS

No entry.

INDEX

The largest part of three articles and the whole of a fourth are excluded from this Index. 'The Library of Stephen and Cora Crane' (James E. Kibler, Jr.), pages 199–246, is a catalog of the Cranes' books arranged alphabetically by author. 'The Publications of Theodore Dreiser: A Checklist' (Donald Pizer), pages 247–92, is an enumerative bibliography of Dreiser with the items arranged chronologically. 'The Short Fiction of William Faulkner: A Bibliography' (James B. Meriwether), pages 293–329, lists all textually significant forms of Faulkner's short fiction, an index of the titles being supplied on pages 326–29. 'The Register of Current Publications: 1971' (Artem Lozynsky), pages 377–416, records in-print publications pertinent to American bibliographical and textual studies, arranging them in thirteen distinct categories and alphabetizing them according to author, subject, editor, or compiler.

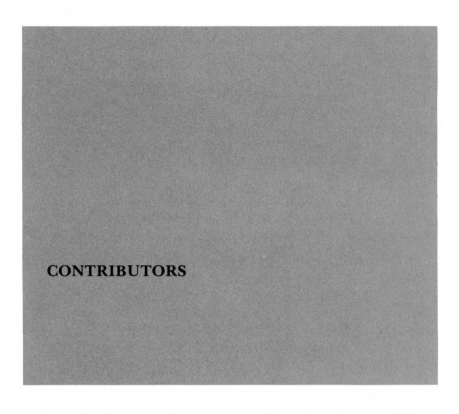

CONTRIBUTORS

O M BRACK, JR., is Associate Professor of English at the University of Iowa. He currently is Chairman of the Eighteenth-Century Short-Title Catalogue Committee and an editor of The Smollett Edition.

WILLIAM R. CAGLE is Assistant Librarian of the Lilly Library, Indiana University. He is on the editorial board of the Pittsburgh Series in Bibliography and is at work on the Soho Bibliography of Joseph Conrad.

C. E. FRAZER CLARK, JR., is President of Paramarketing of Detroit. A distinguished Hawthorne collector with strong academic ties, he has compiled *The Merrill Checklist of Nathaniel Hawthorne,* is editor of *The Nathaniel Hawthorne Journal,* and is at work on *The Literary Manuscripts of Nathaniel Hawthorne* for Calendars of American Literary Manuscripts (CALM).

LILLIAN B. GILKES of Tryon, North Carolina, once was a ghost writer's ghost writer. In propria persona she is the biographer of Cora Crane, and is now completing a biography of Park Benjamin.

HARRISON HAYFORD is Professor of English at Northwestern University. A member of the Executive Board of the Center for Editions of American Authors, he is General Editor of the North-western-Newberry Edition of *The Writings of Herman Melville*.

WILLIAM S. KABLE is Associate Professor of English at the University of South Carolina. Most recently he has published a mono-graph, *Spellings in the Pavier Quartos*, and editions of *The Power of Sympathy* and *Three Early American Novels*.

JOSEPH KATZ is Professor of English at the University of South Carolina. He continues his explorations of the relationship of bibliographical and textual studies to general scholarship and criticism.

JAMES E. KIBLER, JR., is Assistant Professor of English at the University of Georgia. His articles have appeared in *The Mississippi Quarterly*.

ARTEM LOZYNSKY is a graduate student in English at the University of South Carolina.

JAMES B. MERIWETHER is McClintock Professor of Southern Letters at the University of South Carolina. Returning from a Ful-bright-Hays Professorship in France, he continues as a member of the Executive Board of the Center for Editions of American Authors and the Textual Editor of The Centennial Edition of *The Writings of William Gilmore Simms*.

HERSHEL PARKER is Professor of English at the University of Southern California. The Associate General Editor of the North-western-Newberry Edition of *The Writings of Herman Melville*, he has just completed an anthology of Hawthorne and Melville for the Charles E. Merrill Literary Texts Series.

MORSE PECKHAM is Distinguished Professor of English and Comparative Literature at the University of South Carolina. He is one of the editors of the Ohio edition of *The Complete Works of Robert Browning*, and recently has published *The Triumph of Romanticism* (collected essays) and editions of Swinburne's *Poems and Ballads* and *Atalanta in Calydon*.

DONALD PIZER is Professor of English at Newcomb College,

Tulane University. The author and editor of books on Hamlin Garland, Frank Norris, and American realism, he currently is engaged in studies of Theodore Dreiser.

G. THOMAS TANSELLE is Professor of English at the University of Wisconsin. He is Bibliographical Editor of the Northwestern-Newberry Edition of *The Writings of Herman Melville.*

PROOF: THE YEARBOOK OF AMERICAN BIBLIO-
GRAPHICAL AND TEXTUAL STUDIES is composed
principally in Linofilm Baskerville, with Caslon Old Style
being used only on the title page. PROOF has been printed
by offset lithography on Warren's University Text, an acid-
free bookpaper noted for its longevity, which has been especially watermarked with the University of South Carolina
Press colophon. The binding, manufactured in a special
finish for PROOF, is Holliston's Sturdite. Composition,
photoengraving, printing, and binding have been performed by Kingsport Press, Inc. PROOF was designed by
Robert L. Nance.

The frontispiece is reproduced in full-color only in the
first printing. In any subsequent impressions, the four
plates will be printed in black and white.

PROOF 1 (1971) was published in an edition of 1,500
copies on 27 December 1971, preceded by a dummy—
limited to 500 copies with a special statement on salesmen's
dummies by Joseph Katz—for the friends of PROOF. (The
dummy includes the color frontispiece and the first thirty-
two pages from the sheets of the first printing.)

DATE DUE

APR 0			